D0427139

GLOBAL HUMAN RESOURCE MANAGEMENT

To my mother, wife, brother and daughters
Willy McCourt

To Janet, Jillian and Sarah
Derek Eldridge

GLOBAL HUMAN RESOURCE MANAGEMENT

Managing people in developing and transitional countries

Willy McCourt

Senior Lecturer in Human Resource Management, Institute for Development Policy and Management, University of Manchester, UK

Derek Eldridge

Capacity Building Director, Centre on Regulation and Competition, Institute for Development Policy and Management, University of Manchester, UK

Edward Elgar
Cheltenham, UK • Northampton, MA, USA

Published by
Edward Elgar Publishing Limited
Glensanda House
Montpellier Parade
Cheltenham
Glos GL50 1UA
UK

Edward Elgar Publishing, Inc.
136 West Street
Suite 202
Northampton
Massachusetts 01060
USA

A catalogue record for this book
is available from the British Library

Library of Congress Cataloguing in Publication Data
McCourt, Willy.
    Global human resource management : managing people in developing and
transitional countries / Willy McCourt, Derek Eldridge.
      p. cm.
    Includes bibliographical references and index.
    1. Personnel management—Developing countries. 2. International business
enterprises—Developing countries—Personnel management. I. Eldridge, Derek,
1942– II. Title.

    HF5549.2.D48M33 2004
    658.3'009172'4—dc21

                                           2003049213

ISBN 1 84064 529 6

Typeset by Manton Typesetters, Louth, Lincolnshire, UK.
Printed and bound in Great Britain by MPG Books Ltd, Bodmin, Cornwall.

Contents

Figures

Tables

Boxes

About the Authors

Willy McCourt, originally from Belfast in Northern Ireland, started his career as an assistant lecturer in the national university of Nepal. In the UK he worked for a British development NGO, and in adult education and local government, before joining the Institute for Development Policy and Management (IDPM) in 1994. He has an undergraduate degree in English from Cambridge, and Master's degrees from the universities of Lancaster and London in Management Learning and Organizational Behaviour, respectively. He traqaed as a teacher at the University of Manchester, and completed his PhD, also at Manchester, in 2001. Willy has carried out recent consultancy and research assignments in Bangladesh, Cambodia, Malaysia, Mauritius, Morocco, Nepal, South Africa, Sri Lanka, Swaziland, Tanzania and Uganda. He has acted as an adviser to the British Council and the Department for International Development in the UK, and the United Nations Research Institute for Social Development and the World Bank. He has published on the human resource management topics of recruitment and selection, training and development and employment reform in developing and transitional countries, and also more generally on public management in developing countries. He is married and has two daughters.

Derek Eldridge joined the Institute for Development Policy and Management in 1978 after working for ten years in various public sector organizations, which included roles in urban and corporate planning. His current responsibilities include teaching aspects of human resource planning and development and directorship of the postgraduate Workplace Transformation Programme. He is also Capacity Building Director in the Centre on Regulation and Competition at the University of Manchester. Formerly, he was Director of the MSc in Human Resource Development. His research and consultancy interests in recent years have centred on institutional development and human resource issues in a range of east and southern African countries, and in China, Malaysia and the Philippines. In 2000 he also led a major evaluation study of the UK's Higher Education Links Scheme which brings together, in over 400 links, academics in developing countries and their colleagues in UK universities to promote research and institution building.

1 Global Human Resource Management: a 'Crossvergent' Approach*

Willy McCourt

What this chapter is about

Our opening chapter sets out the scope of human resource management (HRM), which deals with the way that organizations manage their staff and help them to develop, and we explain why we view these issues mostly from a management perspective. After presenting the activities of HRM, we discuss the feature of our book which distinguishes it from other HRM textbooks: our insistence on the need to study HRM *in context*, taking account of the contrast between what textbooks say should happen (prescription) and what actually does happen (description), but also taking account of the particular organizations and countries in which HRM 'good practice' is used. We explain why we believe that each and every HRM practice, whether in the area of managing pay or learning and training or anywhere else, must be assessed critically in the particular setting in which we want to use it, and then adopted, rejected or adapted accordingly. That process of critical adaptation of international models of 'good practice' is what we mean by 'global HRM'.

What you will learn

At the end of this chapter you should be able to:

* We would like to thank Professor Henry Bernstein of the School of Oriental and African Studies at the University of London for the invaluable help and guidance he gave us with the original drafting of our book.

1

- explain why HRM is based on a management perspective;
- outline the principal HRM activities;
- explain how 'good practice' interacts with features of organizational and national contexts;
- explain how a HRM practitioner makes the choice between adopting, rejecting and adapting a given 'good practice' method.

1   Introduction

Is managing people the same everywhere? The idea that there is 'one best way' that will work in any organization and in any country has been with us since the start of the modern management era (Kanigel, 1997), and it is still vigorous: its most distinguished current advocate is the American Jeffrey Pfeffer (1998), who claims that there are some HRM practices which have a universal validity. But we have written our book in the belief that the HRM practitioner always operates in an environment with particular features that affect the choice of management methods; and we want to show how a practitioner might make that choice. While what we have said applies everywhere, our book concentrates on organizations in developing and transitional countries. Their environments are sufficiently distinctive, but also sufficiently similar, to justify that concentration. There are also few HRM books that concentrate on them. Working with students who mostly come from those countries, in a university department (the Institute for Development Policy and Management at the University of Manchester in the UK) which exists to promote their development, we have felt the need for a book that focuses on the way organizations manage people in those countries, where the vast majority of the world's population lives and where the vast majority of the world's organizations operate.

2   The activities of human resource management in sequence

2.1   A definition

We define HRM as *The way an organization manages its staff and helps them to develop*. Notice the focus on the organization. HRM is particularly interested in how people behave in formal work settings: it has little to say about people when they are not working, or about people who work in informal settings. Subsistence agriculture remains the most important economic activity in many developing countries, but HRM is not concerned with subsistence farmers. The contribution that women make to the economy through their domestic work is important, but it is not the province of HRM. Nor is HRM concerned with people who work for themselves in the 'informal economy', whether they are selling vegetables in a market, repairing bicycles on a pavement or cooking snacks for travellers on a railway station platform. We respect their contribution to the economy, but none of them, for better or worse, is an employee or a manager. As soon, though, as one of them decides that she can afford to employ someone to help them, she enters HRM's domain. For HRM, like the study of management generally, concerns itself only with people who contribute to the economy as workers in formal organizations – any and every formal organization, large or small, private or public. Thus the companies that arrange for complex menus of fresh food to be delivered to workers at their workplaces at lunchtime in some Indian cities, an activity that requires precise organization and timing, are very much within the scope of our book. While such organizations are to be found everywhere, in industrialized and developing countries, in Africa, America, Asia and Europe alike, our book focuses on countries that are not fully industrialized. However, we will from time to time draw on the experience of industrialized countries as a source of examples.

2.2   The activities of HRM

In Chapter 2 we give you a framework for studying HRM in the form of a 'strategic' model of HRM, one that should help you to see how HRM fits into the overall management of an organization. After Chapter 2, the remainder of the book is taken up with the day-to-day HRM activities which are the 'bread and butter' of HRM work. Virtually all writers assume that there is a set of core activities, and that there is a body of good practice associated with each of them. Let us now review them briefly.

Human resource planning (Chapter 3)
Human resource planning refers to the group of techniques which enables managers to plan the staffing of an organization. Organizations, especially large ones, need to forecast their staffing needs. If, for instance, a government has made a commitment to provide universal primary education, as in Uganda in the late 1990s, it must estimate how many teachers to recruit in order to realize that commitment. To do so it will need information on such matters as how many teachers are being trained each year by the teachers' colleges, and how many leave the service each year as a result of retirement and so on. Using that information, the Ministry of Education can then forecast its recruitment needs some distance into the future.

The planner often begins by working out the human resource implications of a new policy or objective by the organization, as in the example above. But even where policies are stable, there may be a need for continual estimates of staffing needs as circumstances change. For example, there may be an increase in the number of staff resigning voluntarily, possibly because a company's salaries have fallen behind what other companies are paying. The organization needs to gather data on the scale of the increase so that it can respond appropriately.

Human resource planning is carried out at the level of the organization as a whole or, sometimes, at the level of an individual company within a large corporate group (in the private sector) or at the level of an individual ministry or public enterprise (in the public sector).

Job analysis (Chapter 4)

Job analysis is complementary to human resource planning, being carried out at the level of the individual job or 'family' of jobs. It refers to the group of techniques which is used to determine the content of jobs (job descriptions) and the knowledge, skills and abilities that jobholders require to carry them out (person specifications).

Managing pay (Chapter 5)

Deciding how much and in what way staff should be paid is a major part of HRM. Pay decisions are usually based on some sense of the content of the jobs that staff occupy. (You will sometimes find managing pay referred to as 'rewards management' in textbooks.)

Recruitment and selection (Chapter 6)

Armed with a job description and person specification, and with a salary to offer to candidates, the organization can proceed to recruit staff to fill the jobs that it has identified. At the recruitment stage the organization attracts candidates to apply for its jobs; at the selection stage it selects the best person for the job from among the candidates it has attracted. Recruitment and selection, therefore, refers to the group of techniques which is used to recruit and select staff to carry out the jobs which the organization has identified.

Performance management and appraisal (Chapter 7)

Once the best person has been identified and has started work, organizations may wish to monitor their performance and to help them to develop. In the first instance that will be through the normal processes of day-to-day work, where staff develop themselves with the support of their managers. However, many organizations take a systematic approach, and use a formal annual review of performance, conducted jointly by the employee and his or her manager: this is what is called 'performance appraisal'. It serves the same function as an older approach still practised in many developing country governments called the 'annual confidential report'. Some organizations have gone one step further, applying the principles of annual appraisal to day-to-day management of staff throughout the year, and doing so in the context of the overall strategy of the organization: this is 'performance management'.

Learning and training (Chapter 8)
Although staff develop their skills through day-to-day work, organizations often provide additional formal learning opportunities. They may be off-the-job training courses, or they may be work-based development programmes. In either case they are a recognition that staff need to develop new skills, both for their own development and to meet the organization's needs.

Job reduction (Chapter 9)
It is a fact of life that organizations contract as well as grow. It happens to private companies in an economy that is in recession, but it also happens in economies that are growing, as part of the 'creative destruction' that the economist Schumpeter (1947) famously saw as inherent in capitalism. Public agencies might appear to be insulated from such turbulence, but in recent years the almost continuous growth in public employment in most developing countries following independence has come to an end, usually because of budgetary difficulties, and often in the specific context of a World Bank or International Monetary Fund structural adjustment programme. In the transitional countries of Central and Eastern Europe, reduction in the size of the public sector has been an aspect of the movement away from Communism.

All of this has resulted in a need for private and public organizations alike to reduce the number of jobs, which in turn has sometimes entailed retrenching employees. Clearly there is a role for the HRM specialist here, even though almost all HRM textbooks choose to ignore this unpleasant aspect of the HRM specialist's duties. Although experience of job reduction is still recent, some evidence of what might constitute good practice is starting to appear.

Employee relations (Chapter 10)
Employee relations deals with the management of the relationship between the organization and the staff as a whole. In many countries and organizations staff are represented by a trade union or unions. However, we shall argue that employee relations is a concern of the manager even if his or her organization is not 'unionized': he or she must still decide, among other things, how the organization is going

to communicate with its staff, and the extent to which staff will participate in the management of the organization.

Diversity

There is one major issue which we cannot consider as an activity, but which permeates the book as a whole: the issue of 'diversity', which concerns how organizations deal with differences in their workforce, between women and men, members of different ethnic groups, disabled and able-bodied people and so on. We want to encourage readers to think about how they can capitalize on the different abilities of their staff, and also how they can avoid disadvantaging employees because of some personal characteristic – whether their race, their gender or anything else – which has nothing to do with their ability to do the job. Diversity is an important part of Chapters 5 and 6, where we look at the issues of unfair discrimination in recruitment and selection and of equal pay.

Study task 1: defining HRM activities

We will refer to these HRM activities again and again in subsequent chapters, so it is important that you are familiar with them from the very start. Use Table 1.1 to write your definitions of the eight key activities before we move on.

Table 1.1   Definitions of HRM activities

Activity	Definition
Human resource planning	
Job analysis	
Managing pay	
Recruitment and selection	
Performance management and appraisal	
Learning and training	
Job reduction	
Employee relations	

2.3   The HRM sequence

The order of topics in our book, following our presentation of the Strategic Human Resource Management model in Chapter 2, is based on the idea of a *sequence*, shown in Figure 1.1. The sequence is *logical* rather than *chronological*: while we can think about the HRM activities

Figure 1.1   The HRM sequence

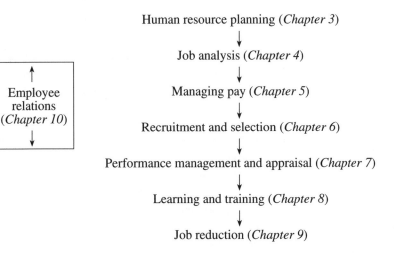

as arising in this logical order, in practice organizations, unless they are brand new, are doing all the activities at the same time.

Let us briefly recapitulate on the activities to see how the sequence works. It starts with *human resource planning*, which enables the organization to take an overall view of its staffing needs: how many jobs, in which areas, and so on. Moving from the level of the organization to the level of the individual job, or family of jobs, brings us to *job analysis*, which enables us to specify the content of individual jobs. Once we know this, we can decide how much to pay people to do them (*managing pay*) and go on to recruit the people who will actually do them: this is *recruitment and selection*.

Once the people we have recruited have started work, *performance management and appraisal* provides a way of managing their performance. Carrying it out will probably throw up development needs, and we meet them through *learning and training*. Finally, *job reduction* deals with the way organizations take steps to reduce the number of jobs when it is necessary to do so.

The last of our activities, *employee relations*, is strictly outside the sequence (which is why we show it to one side in Figure 1.1). There may be an employee relations issue in relation to any of the other activities. For example, a trade union representing staff may negotiate with management about the design of the organization's performance management system. In practice, however, the most acute employee relations problems concern pay: when unions call their members out on strike, that is usually the reason.

2.4   A management perspective

Our concentration on HRM issues in organizations, rather than in the economy as a whole, or in society outside the work setting, is the first assumption on which our book is based. The second assumption is that we are looking at those issues mostly from the perspective of the organization, and that means looking at them from *a management perspective*. We will be interested in how the organization *manages* its staff: how it plans, organizes and controls their work. This is by no means the only perspective we might adopt. There is a long tradition of sociological and anthropological research that treats organizations as if they were societies, and simply tries to understand how they operate in reality. A famous example is the experiments at the Hawthorne factory in the United States which, among other things, showed how workers set their own production norms, and operated a system of informal, but powerful, sanctions against workers who were either too productive or not productive enough, despite the best efforts of their managers to control them (Roethlisberger and Dickson, 1964).

A management perspective is one that looks at staff management from the vantage point of the organization's need to deploy its staff to best advantage. It is not necessarily the same as the perspective of individual managers. They will naturally tend to identify their personal interests with the interests of the organization as a whole, and will tend to view any challenge to their authority as illegitimate and to try to suppress it. The English writer on employee relations, Alan Fox (1974), has labelled this the 'unitarist' view. He contrasts it with what he calls the 'pluralist' view, one that holds that an organization has more than one legitimate source of authority, notably the trade unions which represent staff interests in many organizations. We will discuss both the unitarist and the pluralist views at length in Chapter 10 when we discuss employee relations. Throughout the book we will take care to distinguish between a management perspective and the perspective of the particular managers who manage the organization. We will also try to understand the employee's point of view. Managers, after all, will not be able to manage staff successfully if they do not understand them. But in the end HRM is one of the subdivisions of management in organizations, and when we look at the way employees go about their jobs, we look from a management perspective.

3 Practising HRM in context

3.1 Two aspects of context

The world is full of HRM textbooks. The distinctive feature of this one is its insistence on the need for an approach to HRM that takes account both of 'good practice' models of HRM and of the particular environments – the context, in other words – in which they are applied. Practising HRM in context has two aspects:

- the contrast between what textbooks say should happen in an ideal world (*prescription*) and what actually happens in the real world (*description*);
- the contrast between the view that organizations in different countries are essentially similar, or at least that they are getting more and more alike (*convergence*), and the view that organizations in different countries are very different from each other, or perhaps are getting even more different as time passes (*divergence*).

3.2 Prescription and description

Textbooks, including this one, are written to tell practitioners what to do and what to avoid: they are *prescriptive*. On the other hand there are books and articles that try to describe how organizations actually do HRM: they are to that extent *descriptive*. Prescription and description are frequently confused. So, for example, in learning and training there is a widely quoted model of 'levels of maturity' (Burgoyne, 1988) in the approaches that organizations take to the development of their managers. These levels range from a bottom level where there is no sign that the organization is doing anything at all, to a top level where, not only is the organization taking active steps to develop its managers, but feedback from management development activities actually informs the organization's overall strategy.

But readers will misunderstand Burgoyne's model if they do not realize that it is a *prescriptive* model, and that Burgoyne is being deliberately utopian. His model is not a stick to beat organizations with for failing to develop their managers strategically; nor should practitioners dismiss Burgoyne as an 'ivory tower' academic out of touch with reality. He freely admits in his article that few if any organizations are operating at the top level of his model. He wants to suggest that perhaps they could aspire to do so in future, even if they do not at present.

The discrepancy between prescription (what ought to happen) and description (what actually does happen) is sometimes referred to as the 'reality gap', especially in the context of recruitment and selection (Chapter 6), where the discrepancy is particularly glaring. Thus the well-established finding that the interview as traditionally practised is a very poor method of selection seems hardly to have affected its persistence as the bedrock of most organizations' selection procedures.

Where there is a discrepancy, should prescriptive textbook writers like ourselves move closer to what actually happens in the real world, or should practitioners make more of an effort to apply the prescriptions of the textbook writers? It depends on the particular case. Certainly, where management development is concerned, it will be in organizations' interests to listen to writers like Burgoyne and do more to help their managers to develop. But it could also be that the writers have missed something important about the real world. If organizations persist in using interviews for recruitment and selection, is it possible that they know something that specialists do not know? That is essentially what Peter Herriot (1993), a specialist in recruitment, suggests, and indeed there is recent research evidence to support his view.

The point we want to make here is that we always have to look at the 'good practice' models that the prescriptive writers advocate in a real context, to see if they are going to work in a particular country or a particular organization. They might work in theory, but do they work in practice? Conversely, we certainly need to take a fresh look at what our organizations do. An organization may have been taking one approach to recruitment and selection for many years, but is there a better way?

3.3   Convergence, divergence and 'crossvergence'

To ask whether a particular model works in practice is to ask about the application of 'good practice' models in particular contexts. Can they be applied in non-western countries, or in the public or NGO (non-governmental organization) sector rather than the private sector? The answer depends largely on the extent of the similarity between organizations in industrialized countries on one hand and in developing and transitional countries on the other. It seems likely that a model originating in industrialized countries will be relevant elsewhere to the extent that organizational conditions are sufficiently similar.

Let us recognize first of all that there is indeed a level at which all organizations everywhere are the same. It is an inherent feature of formal work organizations that they split their work up into person-sized chunks, which we call jobs, or occasionally into group-sized chunks, which we call team tasks: no one believes that it makes sense in any but the very smallest organizations to operate on the basis that 'everybody does a bit of everything'. To that extent, modern organizations remain as 'bureaucratic' as they were when the German sociologist Max Weber (1947) identified this characteristic over a century ago. The HRM activities that we will outline in a moment follow logically from that inherent feature: it is helpful to be able to say what those jobs or team tasks consist of (job analysis); the people who do them may need to develop new skills (learning and training at work); the organization may find that a certain job has outlived its usefulness

---

Box 1.1   The interaction between 'good practice' and organizational contexts: deciding whether to use occupational tests

Suppose that line managers in your organization have been complaining to you about the quality of the latest batch of new staff that the HRM department has appointed, and you have been asked to suggest a better way of recruiting and selecting staff. In exploring the different options, you come across evidence that 'objective' occupational tests are particularly effective in helping organizations identify 'the best person for the job'.

On further inquiry, however, you find out that the commercially produced tests that you have heard about are not available in your country, for the simple reason that no test publishing company has thought it worth its while to market them. You find out that you can buy them from an overseas country – let us say the United States. But even supposing that you can afford to buy them (and tests can be expensive), a glance at the test publisher's website raises the worry that the publisher's tests will not work in your country, because they were developed in a different cultural setting and there is no sign that the test publisher has tried to adapt them to a country like yours.

You go on to wonder if you could develop your own tests. However, when you ask a test specialist for advice, she proposes a process of test construction and validation that, while excellent from a professional point of view, is *very* time-consuming. You are left with a choice between spending a lot of time and money to produce a 'state of the art' test, or producing a 'quick and dirty' test that does not meet the highest professional standards, or giving up the idea of using occupational tests altogether – and the last option would, of course, leave you exactly where you started.

(job reduction); and so on. Thus it seems reasonable to say that the basic activities are indeed universal. But the way in which organizations carry them out – even, in an extreme case like job reduction, whether they carry them out at all – will be conditioned by the character of the organization, and of the country in which it operates.

To what extent, then, are organizations in different countries essentially like or unlike each other? Some argue that it is simply impossible to generalize: every organization and every country is unique, and trying to compare them is fruitless. Certainly, in the end, you will make your own unique choice about what approach is appropriate in your organization. But your choice need not be arbitrary. Consciously or unconsciously, it will be shaped by your knowledge of different approaches, and your view of what will be appropriate, given the conditions that prevail in your organization and in your country. Please see Box 1.1, which illustrates this point.

We should reassure you that in Chapter 6 you will see that there are plenty of things that organizations can do to improve the quality of their appointments, even if they can not afford to use published tests. But the point of Box 1.1 is to illustrate the inevitable interaction between 'good practice' models on the one hand and particular organizational contexts on the other that takes place as soon as we think about what we can do to improve the way our organizations manage their staff.

Clearly the question of interaction between 'good practice' and particular contexts depends on the deeper question of how similar or different organizations and countries really are. The *convergence* argument (Negandhi and Prasad, 1979) is that differences between countries are the product of technological, economic, legal and social conditions, and that, as those conditions are converging rapidly, they can be discounted as an influence on the way that organizations behave: everywhere is like everywhere else – or, if not, then everywhere is *getting like* everywhere else. The argument has gained strength in recent years as people have begun to talk about the 'globalization' of the world economy. It would follow that all we have to do is identify the current 'good practice' model in a given area of HRM – say recruitment and selection – and go right ahead and apply it.

The *divergence* argument, on the other hand, is that the differences between countries and between organizations are profound, and are more likely to increase than to disappear. Those differences, it is suggested, can take different forms. One example is the difference between the legal frameworks in different countries. As Malcolm Warner points out in a study that we discuss in Chapter 2, although Hong

Kong is now part of China, its legal framework for managing staff is based on British law, a hangover from the period when Hong Kong was a British colony. So even though Hong Kong and China have the same Chinese culture, there is at least one important difference in the way that staff are managed. (This is what the Chinese government meant when it talked about 'one country, two systems' in the period leading up to the British departure.)

3.4   Convergence and divergence in the public sector

The convergence/divergence model applies not only to differences between countries, but also to differences between the three major sectors of the economy (private/public/NGO). In the public sector, the convergence argument is that the introduction of the 'new public management' (Dunleavy and Hood, 1994), with its emphasis on general management skills at the expense of the professional priorities of teachers, doctors and so on, and the introduction of structural models deriving from the private sector, has blurred the distinction between private and public management (Colling, 1997). One such structural model is the 'agency' model, where management functions are devolved from government ministries or departments to semi-autonomous agencies. This can be seen in an area like managing pay. In the late 1990s the government of Ghana decentralized the payment of its health staff, giving greater responsibility for pay decisions to local managers as part of the reorganization of its health services, and bringing it into line with the practice of many private companies.

On the other hand, the divergence argument is that the fundamentally different character of the public sector means that the 'political logic' of government will override the 'agency logic' of the new public management, and that political control will be reasserted over devolved management units, restoring the distinctiveness of public management (Ferner, 1994).

3.5   Adaptation: the 'crossvergence' option

You may be able to see that the 'good practice' models, to the extent that organizations adopt them, are a force for convergence, since they represent a common pool that is available to everyone. Conversely, organizational contexts are a force for divergence, to the extent that they affect the way organizations manage their staff. But do we have to choose between the alternatives of convergence and divergence, emphasizing the 'good practice' models or our particular environ-

Figure 1.2   'Crossvergence': the interaction between 'good practice' and particular contexts

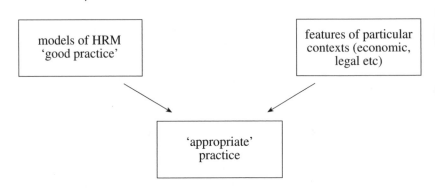

ment as the case may be? It is now time to give you our own view, which is summed up in Figure 1.2.

We reject the extreme view that prescriptive 'good practice' models, usually developed in western countries, and particularly the English-speaking countries,[1] have nothing to offer to other countries, and that organizations there should invent their own models from scratch. But we also reject the opposite view that there are universal models of good practice that we can take off the shelf and apply essentially unaltered in every country and every kind of organization. Against both those views, we insist that good practice models do have the potential to improve the performance of organizations, but we insist equally strongly that they can never be taken at face value, but must be assessed critically in the light of the conditions in particular organizations, and only then adopted or rejected – or adapted if necessary. Thus it is not so much a question of 'good practice', but of 'appropriate practice'. The 'state of the art' model of staff management may not be the best one, just as the most expensive and up-to-date technology may not be the most suitable.

Performance management and appraisal is a good example of what we mean. As you will see in Chapter 7, we can trace the evolution of practice from a confidential report written by a line manager without discussion with the member of its staff who is its subject, through an 'open' annual appraisal meeting between the manager and the member of staff, to a system of performance management where discussion between the two parties takes place throughout the year, not just once every 12 months. Now you may well say that, other things being equal, the performance management approach is superior to the confidential report and the annual appraisal – and we would agree with you if you did. But other things rarely are equal. It is quite possible, for example, for trust between managers and staff in a particular organization to be so low that introducing an open system would actually do more harm than good. It would merely bring latent hostility between managers and staff out into the open; it is even possible that it would lead to violence. Introducing fully open appraisal in such an atmosphere would fail or, to put it another way, it would not be *sustainable*. And introducing an approach that failed might make it impossible to try again for years to come. The government of Mauritius made an abortive attempt to get performance appraisal off the ground in 1987. By 2003 it had still not succeeded in introducing an alternative.

Box 1.2   Adopt, reject or adapt?

ADOPT: In Box 1.1 we gave the example of a HRM specialist who has been asked to suggest ways of improving the quality of recruitment and selection in his organization. As you will see in Chapter 6, recent research has suggested that the 'traditional' panel interview, with which most of us are familiar but which many of us have criticized, can still be an effective selection method. In particular, research indicates that an interview that has a systematic structure which is the same for every candidate can be effective, whereas an interview that is unstructured, so that the actual questions which each candidate gets asked are quite different, is not effective. We suggest that this is an example of good practice that is actually universal, in that we can apply it in any organization in any country, in the private, public and NGO sectors alike.

REJECT: Outdoor learning is a widely practised method of employee development. We define it as 'any type of development activity that takes place outside the traditional training environment of a classroom, usually in nature's surroundings'. It is a powerful way of helping employees to develop their personal and team skills. But it is possible that a particular organization might still reject it. This might be because the organization cannot identify trainers who are skilled in outdoor learning, or because it cannot identify a suitable outdoor location – or simply because the organization is already using other approaches which it believes achieve the same objectives in a different way.

ADAPT: In Chapter 2 we present the strategic management model, which essentially tries to define what an organization is trying to achieve, and then uses management methods to help it achieve it. You will learn that there are several versions of the model, and that some of them are very elaborate. In Chapter 2 we look at the model in the context of small firms in Mexico. We will see that such firms find it difficult to adopt the model in its full-blown version, but that some of them have adapted it to give them a basic strategic awareness of their financial and market position, without necessarily having an elaborate written strategy.

The process that we depicted in Figure 1.1, of an interaction between 'good practice' and the circumstances of a particular organization or country, especially where the 'appropriate' practice is an adaptation of the 'good practice' model, is very similar to what Ralston *et al.* (1997: 183) have called 'crossvergence', which occurs 'when an individual incorporates both national culture influences and economic ideology influences synergistically to form a unique value system that is different from the value set supported by either national culture or economic ideology.' Note the authors' use of the word 'synergistically': Ralston and his colleagues are implying that the result of the interaction will be creative and beneficial, and we agree. Let us look at three simple examples to see how this creative crossvergence can operate.

Study task 2 will help you to consolidate your understanding of this process of crossvergence by looking at how the process might work in the example we gave of improving recruitment and selection methods in Box 1.1.

Study task 2: using occupational tests: adopt, reject or adapt?

1 *Suppose that the HRM specialist in Box 1.1 works in the local subsidiary of a large multinational firm which is based in the USA. You know that the firm is already using occupational tests produced by a US publisher in its US headquarters, but is not using tests in any of its overseas operations. Should the HRM specialist adopt, reject or adapt the tests that his firm is using in the USA? Write down what you think, and why.*

2 *Now suppose that the HRM specialist works in the Public Service Commission in a large country (the Public Service Commission is the government agency responsible for recruitment and selection of civil servants in many Commonwealth countries in Africa, Asia and the Caribbean). Again, should the HRM specialist adopt, reject or adapt tests that can be bought from abroad, but which are not available locally? Once again, write down what you think, and why. You can compare your answers with the suggested answers at the back of the book. ✍*

What we have covered in this section is effectively summarized in Figure 1.2. In a word, because of the gap between prescription and description, and between different countries and different sectors of the economy, we always need to consider 'good practice' models in particular contexts to see if they apply there. We also need to see what adaptations we should make to them, if any, so that we can use them to improve the way our organizations manage their staff. What we have called 'crossvergence' is the outcome of this process of consideration and adaptation.

You may have been wondering why we did not include a fourth alternative in Figure 1.2: *invent*. After all, cannot organizations invent models of their own, which will be uniquely suited to their own circumstances? We do not want to play down the importance of creativity. On the contrary, we hope that this book will help you to produce creative and imaginative solutions to problems in your organization or in organizations where you will work in the future. But nor do we want to encourage you to 'reinvent the wheel', as the saying goes. In reality, creativity in organizations does not usually mean inventing from scratch, but choosing from a range of alternatives, whether available locally or overseas, and adapting them creatively where necessary to suit the circumstances of a particular organization.

Thus what we mean by 'global human resource management', the phrase that appears in the title of our book, is not a single 'one size fits all' model conquering all before it, but instead a *process* where organizations take account of international 'good practice' models by applying, rejecting or adapting them in the light of their own individual and national circumstances.[2]

For those developing countries or transitional countries still recovering psychologically from the imperial domination of a western power like France or the United Kingdom, or of the Soviet Union in Eastern Europe and central Asia, what we have outlined is arguably part of the process of attaining full independence. The novelist and student of Indian religion Christopher Isherwood (1965: 154), observed in relation to Britain's conquest of India in the nineteenth century:

> One of the many evils of foreign conquest is the tendency of the conquered to ape their conquerors. This kind of imitation is evil because it is uncritical; it does not choose certain aspects of the alien culture and reject others, but accepts everything slavishly, with a superstitious belief that if you ape your conquerors you will acquire their superior power.

We hope that our 'crossvergent' model of HRM, and its application throughout the book, will help readers to make critical and independent choices, and so contribute to burying the psychological legacy of imperialism once and for all.

4   The style of the book

There is no getting round the fact that reading textbooks is a chore. We have tried to sweeten the pill by writing clearly and accessibly. In particular, we have provided a summary at the start of each chapter ('what this chapter is about') and also at the end to recap on the main points. We have also provided learning objectives for each chapter ('what you will learn'), which you can use to check that you have grasped what each chapter covers. A third feature of our book is that most chapters include one or more *study tasks*. Often they take the form of questions directing you to key points. Sometimes they help you to reflect on the application of good practice to your own country or your own organization.

In some cases, *specimen answers* are given at the back of the book. They enable you to assess your own progress in mastering the material you are studying. When a study task has a specimen answer, you will see this sign: ✍ Try to resist the temptation to go straight to the answer rather than carry out the study task. The purpose of the study tasks is not so much to find the 'right answer' (very often there isn't a single right answer anyway) as to engage in a process of critical thinking about a concept, or a process of creative application of particular HRM techniques. Such critical thinking and creative application are vital for success in HRM, and especially in senior roles.

5   Summary and conclusion

In this opening chapter we have introduced the subject matter of our book. We have set out what we believe to be the scope of HRM, which deals with the way that organizations manage their staff and help them to develop, and we explain why we view these issues mostly from a management perspective. After presenting the activities of HRM, we discuss the feature of our book which distinguishes it from other HRM textbooks, namely our insistence on the need to study HRM *in context*, taking account of the contrast between what textbooks say should happen (prescription) and what actually does happen (description), but also taking account of the particular organizations and countries in which HRM 'good practice' is used. While we have recognized that there are those who believe that good practice is universal, in the end we believe that any and every HRM practice, whether in the area of managing pay or learning and training or anywhere else, must always be assessed critically in the particular setting in which we are proposing to use it, and then adopted, rejected or adapted accordingly, in a process that we called 'crossvergence'. That is what we mean by 'global human resource management'.

Having set the scene for the book as a whole, we move on in Chapter 2 to present the Strategic Human Resource Management (SHRM) model, a powerful framework for organizing how you think about HRM.

Notes

1   Not all developments have come from western countries. Significant developments have come from Japan and elsewhere, notably total quality management. In Chapter 10, for example, we look at developing countries' experiments with employee participation in management.
2   Our argument, that the spread of international models of good practice will result in diversity rather than homogeneity in HRM practice, is close to John Gray's (1998) argument that the collapse of communism has led to the growth of several varieties of capitalism, from the family- and clan-oriented variety increasingly practised in China and the Chinese diaspora to the individualist variety prevalent in the United States.

2 Strategic Human Resource Management

Willy McCourt

What this chapter is about

This chapter presents the Strategic Human Resource Management (SHRM) model. We begin by looking at its origins in personnel management, before moving on to the model itself, with its key concept of strategic integration, in both its vertical and horizontal aspects, and the other items on the 'new HRM agenda' of commitment, flexibility, quality and line manager ownership. We look briefly at one alternative to SHRM in the form of the 'good practice' approach. We then assess the evidence that 'good' HRM leads to organizational success. Lastly, we look at the SHRM model in an international context, with studies from the Asia/Pacific region and China, and a comparison between the desirability of line manager ownership in Mauritius and Nepal.

What you will learn

At the end of this chapter you should be able to:

- outline relevant features of the personnel management model, and of the context in which it emerged;
- specify the link between the strategic management model and the strategic human resource management (SHRM) model;
- give a critical account of the SHRM model, including Guest's 'new agenda';
- explain how vertical and horizontal integration work;
- assess the evidence that good HRM practice leads to organizational success;

- assess to what extent the SHRM model is applicable in particular organizations and countries, including your own.

1 From personnel management to strategic human resource management: the old personnel management model

1.1 Introduction

We now move on to the SHRM model which is the organizing framework for the book as a whole. Although in logical terms the SHRM model can be seen as the application of the strategic management model to staff management, in *chronological* terms it has grown out of the approach to managing people at work that we are going to call personnel management. We will discuss it, and the context in which it emerged, before moving on to the SHRM model itself.

We have to be careful, when we talk about personnel management, not to imply that it is dead and buried, or that it was bad and the 'new' SHRM necessarily good. Throughout this book we take a contingency view. Every organization, and every country, has its own characteristics, in the light of which it should choose an appropriate model. Moreover, management approaches are somewhat 'path-dependent': once an organization has decided to go down a particular 'path', as it were, it will not switch lightly to a different one.

1.2 The personnel management model in context

Three approaches to managing staff
In the mid-1980s Tyson and Fell (1986) identified three broad approaches to managing staff in UK organizations. Comparing them to three roles in a building construction project, they called them the clerk of works, contracts negotiator and architect roles. The *clerk of works* is a routine administrative role, one that consists mainly of ensuring that employees' files are up-to-date, that they are paid on time and so on. The *contracts negotiator* is a role which concentrates on negotiations between the employer and a trade union or unions which represent staff. It is important to note that these two roles correspond to what we are calling the personnel management model; indeed, you will find that the older HRM textbooks, especially ones with 'personnel administration' in their titles, are based on one or both of them. The *architect* role corresponds to the SHRM approach which we are

going to outline in this chapter. While the three approaches are analytically distinct, they are not mutually exclusive: we may find elements of all of them in a single organization, even though one usually predominates.

Box 2.1   Three models of HRM

'clerk of works' role	*emphasizes*	routine personnel administration
'contracts negotiator' role	*emphasizes*	negotiation with trade unions
'architect' role	*emphasizes*	SHRM

The context of the personnel management model

In Chapter 1 we argued that the appropriate model of HRM for any organization would be the outcome of the interaction between good practice models and the features of particular contexts. It is therefore instructive to consider the context in which personnel management emerged. What Tyson and Fell call the 'clerk of works' approach grew up in large, labour-intensive industries. We can regard it as the application of the classic bureaucratic model (Weber, 1947) to staff management. The bureaucratic model is one where individuals slot into a system of jobs that is arranged in a hierarchy. People are paid in relation to the particular job that they occupy, rather than as individuals. By and large, the way staff are managed is stable and predictable, and requires administrative efficiency rather than creative management decisions. It can safely be delegated to a fairly low level in the organization, where any competent administrator can carry it out. To cite two typical tasks, no specialist knowledge is needed to ensure that staff receive a pay increment on the due date, and that they leave the organization when they reach the standard retirement age.

The 'contracts negotiator' approach emerged in the particular circumstances of the UK and some other industrialized countries in the period following the end of World War Two in 1945. It was a period when large, labour-intensive industries dominated the economy. Together with government policies that tended to emphasize maintaining full employment, this created what in Chapter 3 we will call a 'tight labour market', one where workers had relatively high bargaining power. The labour that those industries required was largely unskilled or semi-skilled, and so was drawn from the industrial working class. Workers who lived together in large cities, or in towns that might be dominated by a single industry (such as coal mining), had a strong sense of class solidarity, and it was possible for them to organize themselves into trade unions to consolidate their bargaining position with their employers. On the other hand, employers and managers often saw themselves as separate from, and different from, manual workers. This was manifested in numerous trivial ways: separate car parks, separate canteens and different working clothes or uniforms. But, most importantly, it was reflected in a relationship that tended to alternate between paternalism and confrontation. Given the hierarchical, and even social, differences between managers and workers, the relationship between them could be characterized as one of *institutionalized hostility*, with managers and unions facing each other across a room in formal negotiations which had an abrasive and even ritualistic character. It became the job of the personnel manager to manage that relationship, to be what Thomason (1976) called the 'man in the middle' shuttling between managers and workers, though ultimately on the side of the managers.

While the 'clerk of works' and 'contracts negotiator' roles emerged in a particular industrialized country context, it is not confined to those countries. In fact a study of the way governments manage their staff in three African countries – Kenya, Tanzania and Zimbabwe – uses Tyson and Fell's model as an explanatory framework (Taylor, 1992). Taylor equates the way the three governments he studies manage their staff with the 'clerk of works' role. He found that staff responsible for HRM played a restricted and essentially bureaucratic and reactive role, because of the following.

1 The 'cult of the generalist' bequeathed by the United Kingdom, the former colonial power in all three countries, which results in HRM being seen as simply an aspect of general administration, so that staff responsible are not able to give it the attention it deserves.
2 A rather inflexible and centralized approach to staff management, designed to contain the ever-present incidence of favouritism and corruption by strictly limiting the discretion of departments and individual managers.
3 The absence of alternative models of personnel management and of specialist personnel staff, which Taylor attributes to the absence of a professional body like the UK's Institute of Personnel and Development, and of specialist teaching of HRM in colleges and universities in the three countries.[1]

The 'contracts negotiator' role, for its part, is to be found in developing countries where trade unions are strong. South Africa and the countries of the English-speaking Caribbean such as Barbados are examples. (You will read more about relations between employers and workers, and about the role of trade unions, in Chapter 10.)

2   The strategic HRM (SHRM) model

2.1   Strategic HRM and strategic integration

Taylor attributed the absence of an alternative model of personnel management in the three developing countries that he studied in part to the use of an 'amateur pragmatism' in the management of staff, and he suggested that organizations such as those he studied should develop a corporate culture which emphasizes excellence and initiative, and seek to develop a new cadre of staff who would hold 'entrepreneurial' values and would be paid more highly for their performance. As it happens, just as Taylor was writing his article, a new model of managing staff was coming to the fore in western countries, and its influence has subsequently spread more widely. This is the so-called 'Strategic Human Resource Management' (SHRM) model, which corresponds roughly to Tyson and Fell's 'architect' approach. This model provides the main theoretical framework for this book. We have chosen to emphasize it because:

- we believe it has potential for improving the way that organizations manage their staff;
- it is the model that currently dominates professional discussion;
- it provides a partial framework for us to organize the material in this book, and for you to organize your thinking about HRM.

We would like to emphasize the last of those reasons. As writers, we believe that it is useful to have such a model as a structure for the material that we are trying to present. There is also the additional benefit that the model enables you to make sense in a quite fundamental way of the role that HRM can play in an organization. But we make the cautionary point that we do not wish to claim that the model is universally applicable. The question of application is one that we explore later in this chapter and, in a way, throughout the book.

2.2   The basics of strategy: a simple strategic model

As organizations in developing countries become more complex, and as they begin to operate in a less protected and increasingly uncertain, competitive, and often hostile environment characterized by economic restraint and resource scarcity, political and international pressures, sociocultural changes, and technological advances, they are going to need, more than ever before, carefully crafted missions and strategic business plans. For such plans to be implemented meaningfully and to contribute to the development process, they must be backed up by professionally designed strategic human resource management functions that in turn must be translated into practical applications … In this way, the HRM function will have a significant and sustainable impact on the development and utilization of an organization's competence in the performance of its tasks. (Kiggundu, 1989: 158)

The SHRM model, as Kiggundu implies, essentially derives from a broader model of strategic management. We can see strategic management as deriving in turn from the view that work organizations exist to achieve a purpose which they pursue with a single-mindedness that we do not see in other human groupings, such as a crowd waiting for a bus or the people present at a party. Whether the purpose is to make a profit by selling cars, or to reduce infant mortality in the case of a children's health NGO (non-governmental organization), strategic management offers a set of techniques for focusing on and achieving it.

Strategic management is a big subject in its own right. We will give a brief account of it here, bearing in mind that we are merely painting in the background to the SHRM model which is our main concern in this chapter. Armstrong (2000: 30) defines strategy as '*A statement of what the organization wants to become, where it wants to go and, broadly, how it means to get there*'. We can see strategic management as a simple process along the lines shown in Figure 2.1.

Figure 2.1   The strategic process

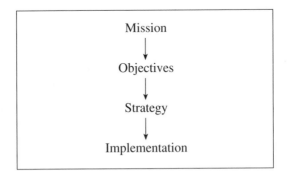

It begins with clarification of the organization's 'mission' (a synonym for 'purpose' in the sense in which we have used that word), very often in the form of a *mission statement*, a short statement of what the organization exists to do. This is operationalized in the form of *strategic objectives*, which are concrete targets that, if reached, will allow the organization to achieve its mission ('increase market share in the small family car market from 15 per cent to 20 per cent' might be an example).

Here are some features of organizational strategies (Johnson and Scholes, 1997):

1 They are distinctive. As of September 2002 the website of IKEA (the Swedish furniture firm which operates in many countries, including Australia, China, Germany, Malaysia and the UK) had a section called 'our vision', which in turn contained a subsection called 'how we're different', where the following statement could be read: *'How is IKEA different from other furnishing stores? They offer a wide range, or good design and function, or low prices, while we offer all of these. That's our business idea.'* It follows that, if different organizations, even within the same industry, have different strategies, they will also need different HRM strategies. There is an important implication here for the design of HRM strategies.
2 Organizations implement their strategies by using their resources and competences. Those resources and competences, crucially, include the human resource – the organization's staff – and the competences or skills that they possess.
3 Strategic decisions demand an *integrated* approach to managing the organization. At the operating end of the organization it is necessary to pull resources, processes and people together into what is sometimes called a *strategic architecture*. This notion of strategic integration is a central feature of the SHRM model.
4 Strategies need the active support of *stakeholders*, that is, of the individuals or agencies that can affect, or are significantly affected by, what the organization does.

2.3 'Blueprint' and 'process' strategies

What does this mean in the real world? While there is evidence that managing strategically in the way we have outlined makes it easier for organizations to succeed, strategies are not always elaborate and systematic – not engraved on tablets of stone, as it were (see Box 2.2).

De Luisa's conclusion does not apply only to small organizations. Many writers on strategic management emphasize that it is the discipline of strategic thinking and working through the strategic process that is the most important component of strategy, rather than the elaborate 'blueprint' models that we sometimes find in the strategic management literature.

> **Box 2.2   Applying strategic management in rural firms in Mexico**
>
> A study of strategic management in small firms in Mexico gives an insight into the application of strategic management in developing countries, and also raises the question of whether it is possible to apply strategic management techniques in small organizations, often family-owned. The starting point was the finding that 'the formal plan-ning methods and book-keeping systems of large-scale business may not be of any operational value for smaller firms'. The study found that, of the 51 surveyed firms, 17 did not manage information in any shape or form, 19 managed information in an elementary way, while the remaining 15 firms managed information adequately. The firms that practised basic strategic management appear to have been doing better than firms that did not. However, even the successful firms were not using very elaborate techniques. De Luisa concludes: 'What seems important is an awareness on the part of entrepreneurs of the financial and market position of the firm, not the degree to which such data are formally documented.' They therefore recommend that it would be helpful to develop an informal, unwritten business planning and ac-counting method appropriate to small firms.

See De Luisa (1996).

2.4   The link between strategic management and SHRM

In the strategic management framework, HRM becomes one of the ways in which organizations realize their strategic objectives. What has come to be known as the 'resource-based view' (Hamel and Prahalad, 1990) is helpful in seeing how this works. It suggests that organizations are differentiated by their resources and the way they manage them. Successful organizations have superior resources and manage them well. Those resources can take various forms: the firm could have a very effective distribution network for its products, for example. But, crucially, the organization's staff can also be seen as one of its resources – hence the phrase 'human resource', which turns out to be something more than meaningless management jargon. Strategic human resource management is thus a way for the organization to realize its strategic objectives through managing its staff effectively. That is the essence of the SHRM model.

We should perhaps dwell for a moment on this view of the contribu-tion of staff to organizational success. One might object that there is nothing new here. Have not organizations always acknowledged this point, in the form of rousing statements like 'Our staff are our greatest asset'? Certainly they have, but arguably they have not reflected it in their actual practice. Traditionally organizations have tended to view their assets in exclusively financial terms: the organization's bank balance and share holdings, of course, and its physical property, its buildings and expensive equipment which are represented in the organization's accounts in elaborate schedules of depreciation. Since it was not considered possible to put a value on intangible assets like staff, or things like a distribution network (our earlier example), and since it *was* possible to quantify the cost of staff in terms of the wages bill, organizations have usually treated staff as a 'liability', in terms of their expenditure on pay, rather than an 'asset' on the balance sheet. So from this point of view the 'human resource' approach, which gives organizations a way of considering their staff as an asset, really does represent a new view of staff management.

2.5   The SHRM model

The argument of seminal texts from the 1980s such as Fombrun *et al.*'s (1984) is that the activities of human resource management should be *strategic*, by which is meant that they should be linked to the organization's overall strategy as that has developed through the strategic management process: this is *strategic integration*. The emphasis is not so much on the content of the HRM activities as with the way they are linked to the overall strategy of the organization (what we will call *vertical integration*), and on the way they are linked to each other (what we will call *horizontal integration*).[2] Invoking research that claims to show that successful companies have a coherent overall philosophy, writers like Fombrun *et al.* suggest that organizations should articulate their human resource strategy in the context of their overall strategy.

The SHRM model: vertical integration

Figure 2.2 shows how *vertical integration* is supposed to work (its visual form makes it clear why this term has come to be used). As you see, the organizational strategy is first 'translated' into a human resource strategy, which is then 'translated' into the different human resource activities which are its practical manifestation (we have listed only four of them, but vertical integration applies in principle to them all).

Vertical integration in practice

Let us see how vertical integration applies to one of the HRM activities, recruitment and selection. Fombrun *et al.* themselves identify three strategic concerns here: designing a selection system that matches

Figure 2.2   Vertical integration in the HRM model

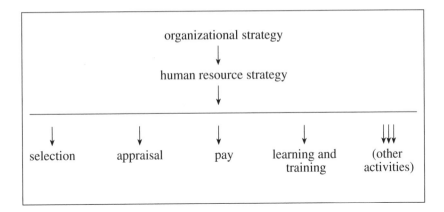

the organization's strategy; monitoring the internal flow of personnel to match emerging business strategies; and matching key executives to business strategies. They illustrate this with examples from American companies. To take the first concern, they show how an oil company's strategy of diversification (moving into new areas of business activity so as to reduce their dependence on oil production and marketing, and so as to capitalize on other opportunities for growth) might create a need to modify its selection of new employees so as to employ more staff who have financial and marketing skills, rather than technical skills specific to the oil industry.

The SHRM model: horizontal integration
The second aspect of strategic integration is horizontal integration, sometimes also called 'horizontal fit' or 'bundling'. While vertical integration refers to links between the HRM activities and the organization's strategy, horizontal integration refers to links between the HRM activities themselves; in other words to the way that the conduct of one HRM task affects the conduct of another. So, for instance, the conduct of selection may affect the conduct of appraisal, and vice versa. Again, the visual form of Figure 2.2 should make it clear why the term 'horizontal integration' or 'fit' is used. Let us look at the way this concept applies to job analysis, a pivotal HRM activity which affects or is affected by most of the other activities and which is the subject of Chapter 4.

Job analysis and human resource planning   Human resource planning identifies broad staffing needs at the level of the organization. Job analysis translates them into the content of individual jobs and the abilities that jobholders will need to do them. So if human resource planning has identified the need for better financial skills, job analysis will identify the content of individual finance jobs, whether the jobs are those of accountants, financial managers or pay clerks.

Job analysis and recruitment and selection   Job content as identified through job analysis is the basis for advertising the job to prospective applicants, attracting those who are eligible and deterring those who are not. The abilities which the jobholder will require, also identified through job analysis, form the basis for decisions about which candidates to invite to the final selection stage, about the design of the final selection stage, and the ultimate decision about which candidate to appoint.

Job analysis and performance management and appraisal   The duties of the job as identified through job analysis are often used to generate objectives for managing performance, and to give the agenda for the annual appraisal interview.

Job analysis and pay management   Judgements about how much to pay an employee are usually made, at least partly, in relation to the level of responsibility which the job requires, as stated in the job content. Job evaluation, one of the most important techniques for making pay decisions, can only operate effectively when it is based on good job analysis data.

Job analysis and learning and training   One way of identifying learning needs is through comparing the abilities which the job requires and the current abilities of the jobholder: the difference between the two is sometimes called the 'performance gap'.

Job analysis and job reduction   A number of developing country governments which have tried to reduce the number of jobs in the public sector have used job analysis data to help them identify where there is scope for reduction. For instance, comparing the content of jobs in two different government ministries may reveal that the same function is being carried out in both, thus offering scope for reduction.

Job analysis and employee relations   To many employers, the most valuable function of job analysis is to provide an objective basis for decisions about pay. This can often lessen damaging conflict which might otherwise occur between trade unions and employers. It is possible to agree on an approach to job analysis whose results will be accepted by both unions and managers.

Study task 1: horizontal integration of HRM activities

Table 2.1 will help you consider how individual HRM activities might be linked together. We have used our example of job analysis to fill in the cells that relate to job analysis; this should illustrate how to go about completing the remaining cells.

From what you have read so far, try to write down some connections between the other HRM activities that we have outlined (try to fill in at least six of the other cells).

Table 2.1   Horizontal integration: linking human resource activities

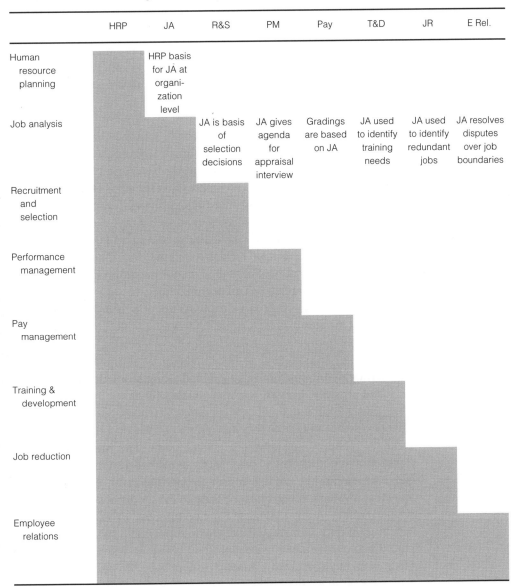

	HRP	JA	R&S	PM	Pay	T&D	JR	E Rel.
Human resource planning		HRP basis for JA at organization level						
Job analysis			JA is basis of selection decisions	JA gives agenda for appraisal interview	Gradings are based on JA	JA used to identify training needs	JA used to identify redundant jobs	JA resolves disputes over job boundaries
Recruitment and selection								
Performance management								
Pay management								
Training & development								
Job reduction								
Employee relations								

2.6   The context of the SHRM model

The new strategic model is every bit as much a product of its context as the personnel management model that it seeks to supplant. This is explicit in Fombrun *et al.*'s presentation, whose urgency derives from the sense of a context that is dramatically different from the context in which the personnel management model emerged. Whereas the latter model grew up in relatively stable and predictable organizations, Fombrun *et al.* paint a picture of organizations reacting to the problem of increasing competition, particularly from Japan, with which the United States in the early 1980s developed a national obsession as Japanese manufactured goods flooded the American market. One form that the reaction took was to focus attention on the way organizations managed their staff in an attempt to increase efficiency. No stone could be left unturned, not least the human resource 'stone' which had lain undisturbed for so long.

It is striking how specific that context is to both the United States and the private sector (invoking the two dimensions of difference that we presented in Chapter 1). Note the three instances of the adjective 'American' in the (fairly representative) first sentence of the chapter in which Fombrun *et al.* outline the SHRM model: 'Discussions of the current state of American industry tend to center on two issues: the declining productivity of the American worker and the declining rate of innovation in American industries' (1984: 33). This immediately raises the question of how useful a model developed in response to one problem is going to be in an organization – say, the civil service of an African country – that faces quite different problems. We take up this important question later in the chapter.

2.7   Strategic integration in practice: linking strategic management and strategic human resource management

The boxes that you probably left empty at the end of Study task 1 serve to make an important practical point. The human resources director of a food company once complained to one of the authors that the lecturers on her HRM training course had given her the impression that strategic integration in the SHRM model was a purely mechanical affair. Vertical integration was supposed to be just a matter of 'reading off' HRM strategy from the organizational strategy, and horizontal integration just a matter of identifying the links between every HRM activity in an almost automatic way. Real life just isn't like that. Some HRM specialists have a rather naïve, 'blueprint' idea of how strategy works. Successful, 'real world' strategies are 'emergent' (to use the term applied by the Canadian writer Henry Mintzberg), and develop over time as organizational conditions change, and as managers learn from the experience of strategy implementation. Strategic planning is useful, but in the long run it is the strategic thinking that goes into the strategy rather than the strategy itself that is of lasting value. Applying that insight to HRM strategy, we can suggest that we should, as it were, hold the strategic steering wheel with a light touch, and – continuing the metaphor – that we should resist the temptation to put the steering mechanism on autopilot. We should be ready to turn the wheel when circumstances change, or even to pull into the side of the road and rethink the journey if we need to.

By all means senior managers and HRM specialists should be aware of the way in which HRM activities are strengthened by linking them together. Certainly, for instance, job analysis data which have been gathered as part of a pay determination exercise should also be used when the agency is recruiting staff into those jobs. They should also be made available to the staff themselves (it is amazing that organizations lavish time and energy on job analysis but do not always think of showing the results to the staff who do the jobs) and also to the managers of those staff for whom they will be a valuable tool. But there is no need to invent spurious links between activities for the sake of completeness. In the specimen answer to Study task 1, we did not show any link between recruitment and selection and employment reform. Now it so happens that organizations have sometimes made a connection: in the former Zaire, government used selection tests designed to select new entrants to the civil service to select employees for redundancy; in the UK, a water company used personality questionnaires, another kind of 'test' also widely used in recruitment and selection, for the same purpose. However, we do not recommend this practice, which distorts the proper purpose for which such tests and questionnaires were developed (and which we discuss in Chapter 6). Again, we think there are relatively few links between human resource planning and the other activities, and we resisted the temptation to invent more in the specimen answer to balance the picture.

The link between strategic management and SHRM

The empty cells in Table 2.1 are not the only way in which real life turns out to be messy. John Purcell (1995), one of the best-known UK writers on HRM, argues that the link between strategic management and SHRM is more problematic than the SHRM literature suggests. The literature assumes that organizations have a single overall strategy with which HRM has to link up. In reality, however, large private companies are increasingly devolving strategic decisions to their business units or subsidiary companies, and the management of the company (or 'group') as a whole interferes very little in the way the unit operates. Its only interest is to ensure that the unit returns a satisfactory profit. Thus vertical integration is impossible, as there is no overall strategy for the HRM strategy to link up with.

Although Purcell confines himself to the private sector, one could argue that the same problem exists in the public sector. In many governments, individual ministries such as the Education and Health ministries manage their affairs virtually autonomously. This makes it hard to have a single strategy, let alone a single HRM strategy, for the whole of government. Moreover, responsibility for different HRM activities may be distributed among different government agencies. Pay management, for example, may be the exclusive responsibility of the Ministry of Finance, and an individual ministry may have little or no control over Finance's decisions.

Purcell's solution to this problem is to suggest that HRM specialists should abandon any hope of linking what they do to an overall strategy which does not exist, and concentrate instead on developing the human resource in a more general way, by selecting better people, by improving their skills through learning and training, and so on. Horizontal integration is possible and desirable, but vertical integration is not. However, we think that we can still retrieve the model by asking the question: 'What is the strategic level in the organization?' Perhaps group headquarters, in the case of a large private company, or the central civil service ministry, in the case of the public sector, does not have an overall strategy. But all that means is that strategies are designed at one level below the top level: at the level of the individual business unit or individual ministry. And it is still perfectly possible to have vertical integration at that level between strategy in general, on the one hand, and HRM strategy or HRM activities on the other.

Another way in which real life may part company with theory is in the role of human resource strategy. In the SHRM model it acts as a kind of transmission belt that 'translates' the organization's overall strategy into the individual HRM activities. While some organizations do have such a strategy, others prefer to skip that stage and make the link between overall strategy and individual HRM activities directly and less formally.

2.8 A new agenda for HRM: David Guest's model

One of the most influential developments of the SHRM model in the 20 years since it appeared has been David Guest's (1989) extension of the model. His starting point is four outcomes that are associated with the new HRM model, and which he claims ultimately lead to distinctive organizational results, including high job performance and high problem solving: these are the 'pay-off' of the HRM model. The first outcome is the notion of strategic integration, already familiar to us. The other three are:

- *commitment*, referring to the acceptance of and belief in the organization's goals and values;
- *flexibility*, referring to the organization's responsiveness to change, and the ability of staff to work in different ways as changing needs dictate;
- *quality*, referring to the quality of the goods and services that the organization produces, but also to the quality of the organization's staff management.

Guest identifies two conceptual difficulties with the application of the new model. The first is the model's 'unitarist' orientation, in other words its assumption that it is exclusively the management side which will dictate the organization's goals. (We referred to the 'unitarist' orientation in Chapter 1, and we shall say more about it in Chapter 10.) The second difficulty is the problematic nature of HRM concepts such as commitment and strategic integration. There are also five conditions which Guest believes must be in place for the model to be implemented successfully: corporate leadership, strategic vision, technological/production feasibility, employee/industrial relations feasibility, and the ability to get HRM policies in place.

Line manager ownership

There is one further element which is implicit in Guest's model: the issue of 'line manager ownership'. Guest (1989: 51) points out that virtually all the American writers on HRM say it must be managed by line managers: 'If HRM is to be taken seriously, personnel managers must give it away.' What Guest and other HRM writers are getting at is that, while some aspects of HRM are best left to HRM specialists, the management of staff needs to be an integral part of any manager's job. For example, it is very desirable that the manager should be involved in the selection of staff to do the jobs for which he or she will be accountable. This is partly because the manager is in a better position than some distant HRM specialist to know what the job requires, and partly because the manager's involvement increases his or her commitment to making the appointment a success (we develop this argument when we look in detail at recruitment and selection in Chapter 6).

This is not some abstract, theoretical concern. In many organizations the manager currently has little real influence in human resource matters that affect the staff that he or she manages: new appointments, judgements about performance, pay decisions and assessments of training needs are all made by the respective central bodies responsible for them without reference to the line manager. As we saw when we discussed Taylor's study, in some countries this may be a deliberate attempt to control favouritism and corruption. While the line between human resource decisions for which line managers and HRM specialists are responsible will be different in different organizations, and rightly so, the principle of line manager ownership of human resource decisions which affect staff remains valid and important.

Study task 2: SHRM in practice

We now have all the theoretical elements of the SHRM model in place. What do they look like in reality? Read the following mini-case study, and answer these questions:

1 *What evidence can you see of SHRM elements in the following description of staff management at British Airways (BA)?*
2 *What constraint(s) is/are there on SHRM at BA?*

Box 2.3   Applying the SHRM model at British Airways

It is instructive to focus on the HRM policies followed by British Airways (BA) in the early 1980s, just before and just after its privatization by the British government. BA had been unprofitable when still in public ownership: in the financial year 1981/2, for instance, it suffered a severe financial loss. While some of the measures taken were drastic and short-term (in particular a reduction in the number of jobs from 60 000 to 38 000 over only a couple of years) others focused on improving staff performance through some of the methods just discussed, including measures aimed at increasing line manager ownership. We shall focus here on its attempts to improve the *quality* of its service.

Following market research showing that the airline's passengers were dissatisfied with its service, in 1982 BA launched an extensive campaign, called 'Putting People First', for all of the 12 000 staff who had direct contact with customers. Up to 150 staff at a time, from baggage handlers to engineers and pilots, took part in customer service events. The campaign was later extended, so that eventually all of BA's staff attended one of the events. 'Customer First' teams were set up to look at ways of improving customer service. Membership of the teams cut across organizational boundaries, with staff from different sections working together. Ten years later, 75 of the teams were still working actively.

By the late 1990s, BA had come to focus on 'key performance indicators' as a principal tool for managing staff. For its managers, there were six such indicators: leadership, managing performance, valuing others, customer focus, business competence and communication. These were the basis for decisions about manager selection, pay and performance management.

Further market research shows that customer satisfaction with the quality of BA's service has increased. Since BA moved from financial loss to spectacular profit over the period when these initiatives took place (in February 1995 it reported record profits of £443 million, with passengers totalling 23.7 million, and by early 2000 it had 65 600 staff), its financial success has been partly attributed to its human resource initiatives. However, it should be noted that some problems lingered – even before the catastrophic effect on BA, in common with all airlines operating the transatlantic route, of the attack on the World Trade Center in September 2001. Despite its HRM initiatives, a staff survey in 1992 showed that staff rated BA poorly as an employer for 'sustaining a working environment that attracts, retains and develops committed employees'. In mid-1997, BA also lost a damaging strike following an attempt to impose a new pay deal on its staff without negotiation. ✐

See Höpfl *et al.* (1992); Lundy and Cowling (1996); Walsh (1997).

2.9   Other models of SHRM: the best practice approach

So far we have seen how the 'old' personnel management emphasized either the routine administration of staffing issues (the 'clerk of works' role) or negotiations with trade unions (the 'contracts negotiator' role); and how, by contrast, the SHRM model emphasizes aligning staff management with the organization's overall strategic objectives (the 'architect' role). We have also seen how Guest adds the three elements of commitment, flexibility and quality. This account simplifies the way in which thinking about HRM has developed over the last 20 years, and there are some influential alternative views. One of them has been labelled the 'best practice approach'. Jeffrey Pfeffer (1998) has suggested that there are seven work practices which reliably improve organizational performance:

- employment security;
- selective recruitment and selection;
- self-managed teams;
- high pay contingent on performance;

- training;
- reduction in status differentials;
- sharing information.

Crucially, Pfeffer argues that these practices are *universal*: they will improve the performance in whatever kind of organization they are applied.

The question that Pfeffer has posed (what *really* works in HRM?) is an important one. HRM, like management in general, is full of gimmicks and short-lived fashions, and there is always room for someone who demands to know where 'the beef' is. The only problem is that the particular set of best practices that Pfeffer proposes is controversial. This is not to say that there is no HRM practice that is universally applicable. We will suggest in Chapter 6, for example, that a structured selection interview is *always and everywhere* better than an unstructured interview. It is just that it is rare to have unambiguous evidence in favour of any HRM practice: recruitment and selection is exceptional in this respect. It seems that the 'holy grail' of universal best practice will not be found for as long as significant differences between countries and sectors of the economy persist. Organizations may still be wise to do what strategy experts advocate, and choose HRM approaches that are distinctive and that match their overall strategies.

However, even though we have privileged the SHRM model, using it to give a partial framework for the book, it is useful that alternatives to it – including the personnel management model – do exist. Nor should we exaggerate the differences between models. In several respects they are complementary. The emergence of SHRM, for instance, does not mean that organizations no longer need to worry about mundane 'old' personnel tasks like ensuring that staff get their annual increment on the right date.

3   Is SHRM happening?

The SHRM model may have theoretical advantages, but are organizations actually using it? Researchers in the UK have carried out a number of surveys of how organizations have been managing their staff in the last 15 years. In Table 2.2 we list selected findings from a survey of employers in the Midlands of England.

These findings are broadly similar to the findings of two other national surveys, which Storey also reports. Taken together, they provide evi-

Table 2.2   Is SHRM happening?

HRM initiative (as listed in survey)	Relevant HRM concept	Initiative employed (%)	Sustained (by those who employed it) (%)	'Considerable contribution' to objectives (%)
Mission statement	strategic management	42	85	67
Devolved management	line manager ownership	65	86	71
Quality circles	quality	35	80	63
Teamworking	commitment	76	87	74
Culture change programme	culture	35	73	65
Increased flexibility between jobs	flexibility	75	89	78

Source: Storey (1995).

dence of an HRM input into strategic business decisions, such as the decision whether to merge with or to acquire another company. There is also further evidence of the use of quality circles and teamworking. Commenting on his own findings, Storey (1995: 19) suggests that these initiatives form a 'set of ideas [that] has now become the new orthodoxy', while in general there is evidence that UK organizations are in fact using many of the elements of the SHRM model.

There are a couple of qualifications to make about these survey findings. First, the evidence comes only from the UK. (We broaden the discussion to take in other countries later in this chapter.) Secondly, while we are entitled to note that many organizations are using SHRM practice, we must in fairness also note that many are not. Moreover, some of the latter, among which are firms which treat their workers pretty brutally, are still successful. They may be a minority among the organizations that researchers have studied, but they demand an explanation. One can speculate that it may not be in the interests of firms that compete exclusively on price at the bottom of a market to invest in the unskilled staff who may be all they need to get the work done, and who in any case have no more commitment to the firm than the firm has to them, so that they will leave at the drop of a hat if someone makes them a better offer.

Despite those qualifications, however, it is arguably more striking that so many organizations have adopted elements of SHRM than that so many have not up to now. We suggested earlier in the chapter that management practice is somewhat 'path-dependent', implying that organizations will be slow to change fundamental working practices. In line with this, we will present evidence later in the chapter of gradual convergence towards a common set of management practices.

4   What difference does SHRM make? HRM and organizational performance

Even if we have evidence of the spread of the SHRM model, why should any particular organization adopt it? Some organizations will manage their staff in this way because they believe it is 'best practice'; they accept, in other words, that this is the most professional approach. But many, if not most, organizations, are more interested still in 'the bottom line': profits in the case of the private sector, providing a good service to citizens in the case of the public sector. Will HRM make any difference to that?

For a long time, the evidence was fragmentary. We had good evidence about the value of good practice in recruitment and selection and, more obliquely, in performance management and appraisal and learning and training. But that evidence dates from the period where HRM activities were treated discretely: no one asked what happened when they were connected to the organization's strategy (vertical integration) or to each other (horizontal integration). Nor did anyone ask about the 'new agenda' proposed by Guest and others. Where all these were concerned, the only honest answer to the question that we posed at the end of the last paragraph was: 'We don't know.' This caused one sardonic writer to characterize HRM as 'big hat, no cattle', alluding to a person whose adoption of the image of a cowboy in the 'Western' movies is confined to buying a big cowboy hat (Skinner, 1987). But the situation changed dramatically in the late 1990s, thanks particularly to Mark Huselid's (1995) research into the relationship between HRM and organizational performance.

To understand Huselid's research, and the other research that it has inspired, you need to know a little about research methodology. Huselid was keen to establish a connection between the way organizations managed their staff and their overall effectiveness. To do this he used a correlational research design, as academics tend to do with this kind of research question. On the one hand, he developed an index of HRM management. He sent a questionnaire to HRM specialists in selected organizations which asked them, among other things, whether employee pay was based on individual performance or merely on the duties of the job that the individual occupied, whether organizations used occupational tests when they were recruiting new employees, and whether they carried out periodic attitude surveys to check the morale of their staff. Questionnaire responses were scored and then summed to give a total score that represented the quality, high or low, of HRM in the organization.

On the other hand, Huselid used measures of organizational performance that are fairly easy to obtain for private companies, being publicly available in annual reports or on the company's website: turnover (typically, the volume of sales of the company's products), productivity (the volume of output produced per worker) and financial performance (profitability or some similar measure).

What Huselid hoped to find was that the organizations that managed their staff 'well' (that is, the firms that got a high score on his index of HRM management) would tend to be successful (that is, their turnover and so on would be high), while the organizations that managed their staff 'badly' would tend to be unsuccessful. He ran a statistical test to calculate the correlation, that is the relationship, between the two factors. And, broadly speaking, he did find a positive correlation: organizations that managed their staff 'well' did tend to be successful; organizations that managed their staff 'badly' did tend to be unsuccessful.

This is an important finding, but it has its own problems. One serious problem is that different researchers who have been inspired by Huselid to do work on this issue use different working definitions of HRM. For example, although Huselid and others include pay in their definition, for Huselid this means pay based on an assessment of the individual's job performance, while for Patterson *et al.* (1997), for example, it means pay that is higher or lower than other firms in the same line of business. This problem is in fact so glaring that one review of the HRM and performance research highlights the discrepancies between the definitions used by different researchers in the table that we reproduce below as Table 2.3.

Having said earlier that the existence of alternative models of HRM has a positive aspect, here we have a negative one, in the form of the somewhat irritating contradictions between different models. Certainly you will have difficulty relating some of the items in Table 2.3 to the SHRM model as we have presented it in this chapter.

Table 2.3   High performance work practices, by authors

Practice	Kochan & Osterman	MacDuffie	Huselid	Cutcher-Gershenfeld	Arthur
Self-directed work teams	Yes	Yes		Yes	Yes
Job rotation	Yes	Yes			
Problem-solving groups/ quality circles	Yes	Yes		Yes	Yes
TQM	Yes	Yes			
Suggestions received or implemented		Yes			
Hiring criteria, current job v. learning		Yes			
Contingent pay		Yes	Yes		Yes
Status barriers		Yes			
Initial no. of weeks training for employees		Yes			
Hours per year after initial training		Yes			Yes
Information sharing (e.g. Newsletter)			Yes		
Job analysis			Yes		
Hiring (non-entry) from within v. outside			Yes		
Attitude surveys			Yes		
Grievance procedure			Yes		
Employment tests			Yes		
Formal performance appraisal			Yes		
Promotion rules (merit, seniority, combination)			Yes		
Selection ratio			Yes		
Feedback on production goals			Yes	Yes	Yes
Conflict resolution (speed, steps, how formal)				Yes	Yes
Job design (narrow or broad)					Yes
Percentage of skilled workers in facility					Yes
Supervisor span of control					Yes
Social events					
Average total labour cost					
Benefits/total labour cost					

Source: Becker and Gerhart (1996: 785).

When we take the above problem and also some other problems that there are with the research in this area (notably, in our context, that most of the research has been done in the private sector in the United States and the United Kingdom), we are left with the encouraging finding that 'something' in the broad area of HRM correlates with organizational success. However, as Guest (1997: 188) concludes in a review of the literature on this topic, 'This is a skeletal finding and we need to put a lot of flesh on the bones.'

As we complete our discussion of the evidence about the SHRM model's impact on organizational performance, we should keep in mind that this is not necessarily the only reason why HRM matters. There is a long tradition of writers who have argued that HRM is intrinsically important, as it represents a commitment by the organization to managing its staff *decently*: that is, fairly, and showing respect for their intrinsic worth as people.

Let us now turn our attention to the application of the model in particular countries and sectors of the economy. As we saw, research on the relationship between HRM and organizational success has so far mostly been confined to western, and particularly Anglo-Saxon, countries, so we need to spend some time thinking through the issues of application to countries elsewhere.

5   Convergence and divergence in HRM

5.1   Convergence and divergence between countries

Having discussed the issue of convergence and divergence in a general way in Chapter 1, let us apply it specifically to the SHRM model. Malcolm Warner (2000) used a summary of the articles in a symposium on HRM in the Asia–Pacific region as the basis for a discussion about whether HRM is converging or diverging, either within the region or between the region as a whole and western countries as a whole. Warner did not find that countries overall are moving either together or apart at a dramatic speed, but he did find numerous instances of individual practices converging. Examples included flexibility in Chinese firms, performance appraisal in Japan, use of temporary employees in Singapore and occupational sex segmentation.

Where divergence is concerned, the evidence of the symposium is that countries are not so much diverging as continuing to differ in some important ways. An important difference between Hong Kong and the rest of China, for example, is that they have different labour laws, a difference which has continued even after Hong Kong's reversion to Chinese rule, and despite the essential cultural identity between the two. Warner suggests that the legacy of Confucian thought, in areas such as respect for elders, remains an important difference between the region as a whole and western countries as a whole. Both differences appear to be instances of countries or regions continuing to differ, rather than diverging further.

Thus with some practices converging while other practices merely maintain past differences, Warner's evidence points towards gradual convergence, even while we recognize that important differences persist. Does this mean that we can expect to see ever-greater similarities between HRM practices across the region? That is a hard question to answer. However, we can safely say that such convergence as is taking place is gradual rather than rapid, and that there will be significant differences between countries for some considerable time to come.

Warner's discussion of the Asia–Pacific region as a whole is complemented by a study that he carried out of HRM in China alone (Warner, 1993). In it he asks whether HRM elements like strategic integration will work in China or not. His findings are summarized in Table 2.4.

Table 2.4   Application of the HRM model in China

HRM element	Condition(s) conducive to application of element	Condition(s) not conducive to application
Strategic integration	Centralization of management decision making	
Commitment	Workplace is central focus of workers' lives; Widespread participation	
Flexibility/adaptability	Increasing flexibility, especially in private companies and joint ventures	Persisting effects of former labour allocation system
Quality	Quality is an 'official goal'	
Line manager ownership		Management decision making is strongly centralized

Warner's account shows that there are some aspects of organizational life in China that are conducive to the application of the SHRM model. However, it is also clear that important differences remain which mean that it is likely that, at best, the model will have to be adapted in order to be implemented successfully. Warner's final judgement is that the 'conditions conducive to application' represent only 'limited family resemblances', and that 'HRM has not yet taken root in Chinese enterprises'.

Let us now look in a little more detail at the applicability of one element of Guest's new HRM agenda in different contexts.

5.2   A contingency perspective on line manager ownership

The SHRM model prescribes delegating staff management to line managers. A contingency perspective, however, shows how this is not always appropriate. In 1995, the Public Service Commission (PSC) of Nepal, the national body responsible for recruiting and promoting civil servants, considered the suggestion of an international donor agency to promote line manager ownership by devolving its responsibility to the ministries, along the lines of similar reforms in the UK civil service. A study (McCourt, 2001a: 337–8), however, reached the following conclusion:

> On the face of it, delegation, with its emphasis on the primacy of the internal customer/line manager, is very relevant to the PSC. Current public management doctrine suggests that the introduction of a quasi-market discipline would have a beneficial effect on recruitment, in the way that has been argued for public recruitment in the UK. But we were forced to yield to the weight of opinion among our informants in the Nepali government. We had been unprepared for the ferocity with which they rejected the suggested devolution. For our informants, especially those in the public enterprises, the effect of previous World Bank-sponsored reforms which had delegated recruitment from the PSC to the public enterprises was painfully evident. Far from unleashing entrepreneurial zeal by removing the dead hand of government, control by unresponsive but impartial central bureaucrats was merely replaced by control by politicians who were neither responsive nor impartial.

In Nepal, every management innovation must be judged in terms of its potential to increase or reduce favouritism. Organizations in other countries may be able to assume that managers will appoint 'the best person for the job', but not in Nepal. Nepali managers do not always apply the 'relatively general and practically significant reaction of disapproval' without which, Weber emphasized, administration based on merit does not exist. We have seen in this chapter that the interest in 'line manager ownership' as part of the SHRM model grew up in a context of intense business competition where maximizing performance was vital. But, in Nepal, fighting against favouritism is an even bigger priority (McCourt, 2001a).

Does it follow that line manager ownership is unsuitable in developing countries? Not necessarily: we must judge each case on its merits. Mauritius provides an instructive contrast to Nepal (McCourt and Ramgutty-Wong, 2003). As in Nepal, a key factor in staff management in the government is nepotism: one observer (Minogue, 1992: 646) even claims that 'Mauritian politics [is] ... overwhelmingly the politics of ethnic competition' between the Indian, Creole and other ethnic groups. Accordingly, staff management is every bit as centralized as it is in Nepal. However, unlike the situation in Nepal, officials stress the disadvantages as well as the advantages of this arrangement: 'The actual centralized system favours "passing the buck",' said one very senior official. From a department head's point of view, 'You want people to behave as managers, but you're not giving them the opportunity ... I have to bear with people like (x), (y), (z) and others. They are chosen *elsewhere* ... People are even removed from my organization without my knowledge!' Managers were very well aware of the advantages of line manager ownership: 'Once you determine pay levels, it should be left to the department to recruit. If I do the selection decision myself, I know that I will be stuck with a bad decision for life,' as another department head pointed out. Thus staff management may be centralized, but the argument for devolution to line managers was a powerful one.

How can we explain the contrast between managers' views in the two governments, whose structure is so similar? In Mauritius, nepotism is in decline: the growth of an industrial economy means that appointments are increasingly made on merit. Moreover, while in Nepal the centre is fair while the individual departments are not, in Mauritius, you are as likely to find nepotism in the centre as in the departments. Finally, Mauritius, a dynamic and successful island economy, is increasingly subject to the same competitive pressures that, as we saw, were the context for the formulation of the SHRM model in the first place (McCourt and Ramgutty-Wong, 2003).

5.3 Summary

The experience of organizations in developing countries shows that the SHRM model has something to offer to countries outside the industrialized countries where it originated. However, the comparison between Nepal and Mauritius shows that the applicability of this model, probably in common with other management models, will be contingent on the circumstances of particular organizations and countries.

Study task 3: applying SHRM in your own situation

Finally we would like to give you the chance to spend some time thinking about the application of the HRM model in *your* country. To what extent are conditions conducive or not conducive there? To what extent does your country resemble China as Warner has analysed it? Again you may find Table 2.5 helpful.

Table 2.5   Application of the SHRM model in your country

HRM element	Condition(s) conducive to application of element	Condition(s) not conducive to application
Strategic integration		
Commitment		
Flexibility/adaptability		
Quality		
Line manager ownership		

5.4   HRM in the public sector

In the terms that we introduced in Chapter 1, up to now we have been addressing the national dimension of difference. Let us now briefly discuss the other, sectoral dimension of difference; that is, differences between different sectors of the economy, using a study of HRM in the UK public sector.

Box 2.4   Convergence and divergence in the public sector

The application of the SHRM model in the public sector is the subject of an analysis by John Storey. Storey considers four HRM elements: strategic integration, commitment, line manager ownership and individualism (by which Storey means the tendency for the management of organizations to strengthen their relationship with their staff as individuals, through the practice of the HRM activities like performance management and appraisal, at the expense of the relationship with their staff as a collective group, represented by trade unions).

After noting the factors that favour the introduction of the HRM model, such as a widespread recognition that a greater investment needs to be made in human resource development, Storey considers the individual elements in turn. To take just strategic integration as an example, Storey notes that, just as in the private sector, attempts have been made in some parts of the public sector to derive the direction of staff management from corporate objectives. This has been facilitated by the creation of the post of chief executive in local authorities, which for the first time has made a single person responsible for the overall management of the local authority. More generally, Storey notes the influence of national bodies like the UK Audit Commission, which have promoted management practice, again facilitating the adoption of a strategic approach.

However, Storey also notes a number of factors which act as constraints on the introduction of SHRM. For instance, he points to the difference between strategic planning in the private and public sectors: in the public sector, planning means responding to signals from politicians through the political process, rather than signals from the market through the economic process.

See Storey (1989).

We should note that the UK experience is distinctive. As with the experience of the other countries discussed in this chapter, you will have to 'translate' Storey's analysis to the situation in your own country.

6   Conclusion: SHRM as a model for managing people and for thinking about HRM

We now come to the end of our review of models of ways in which organizations manage people at work. We began by looking at the personnel management model before presenting the SHRM model, with the key concept of strategic integration, in both its vertical and horizontal aspects, and the other items on the 'new agenda' of commitment, flexibility, quality and line manager ownership. We reviewed evidence about whether SHRM is actually being practised, and that 'good' HRM leads to organizational success, before finally looking at the SHRM model in an international context, with studies from the Asia/Pacific region, China, Mauritius and Nepal.

Our view, in the end, is that SHRM does represent a genuine step forward. There is no need to regard everything that went before the formulation of the SHRM model as the Dark Ages, and there have been negative trends that have accompanied the introduction of SHRM, such as in the increased insecurity that many workers have experienced as the pace of competition (a common factor, as we saw, in all the accounts of SHRM) has increased. But given that work organizations are distinctive essentially in the way they exist to achieve a particular purpose, it makes sense that an approach to managing staff that aligns itself with the organizations' overall purpose must be a potentially powerful one. Moreover, the SHRM model has given us a partial framework for organizing the material that we present in this book, and it gives you a framework for organizing your thinking about HRM issues, both in your study and in real life.

Notes

1   In our experience the 'clerk of works' role is one with which many HRM practitioners from developing countries identify.
2   Please put out of your mind any other associations that these two terms may have for you. It is exclusively in the sense employed here that we will use them in this book.

3 Human Resource Planning

Derek Eldridge and Willy McCourt

What this chapter is about

This chapter introduces human resource planning (HRP) as an organization-level approach to managing staff. The key framework we will use is the notion of a *human resource plan*, which we show in Figure 3.1. The process starts with a forecast of likely future demand for staff – what we call *demand forecasting* – which we can do in terms of the organization's overall strategic objectives. We then look at the supply of labour available to meet the demand we have identified – what we call *supply forecasting*. Thus the eventual plan is a statement of how, given our current staffing, we can match labour demand and supply in order to achieve our strategic objectives.

Alongside this 'Big Planning' approach, we suggest that there is also a more modest role for HRP as a way of solving discrete staffing problems. This relates to the discussion towards the end of this chapter about where HRP works and does not work, and how we can adapt it to suit the circumstances of particular organizations.

The chapter contains activities which require you to make simple calculations for which you will need a calculator (specimen answers are provided).

What you will learn

By the end of the chapter you should be able to:

- explain how human resource planning can contribute to achieving the organization's overall strategic objectives;

- carry out a demand forecast;
- carry out a supply forecast;
- advise on an approach to human resource planning which is appropriate to your organization or one with which you are familiar.

1   Introduction: what is human resource planning?

1.1   Taking a long-term view

Human resource planning (HRP) is an activity that allows us to take a view about the overall staffing needs of the organization.[1] For a lot of the time the HRM specialist is preoccupied by tactical questions: do we need to fill *this* post; how can we improve the performance of *this* employee? HRP allows us to step back from these day-to-day concerns and take a long-term view, identifying trends in our overall staffing. For example, is the number of staff we lose every year (what we will call the *turnover index*) going up, so that we are having to fill more posts overall? Likewise, when we look at the personal profile of our staff as a whole (what we will call the *human resource inventory*), have we got so many managers who have a professional qualification in management that we no longer need to run basic management training courses?

1.2   Why plan?

But do organizations need to have a human resource plan? How do those organizations that do not plan, yet somehow or other survive, make their overall staffing decisions? Let us take the example of an organization adopting a plan to staff a new divisional suboffice. It probably has three alternatives to choose from: precedent, analogy and sheer judgement.

Precedent
When we last opened a divisional suboffice, how did we staff it? Large, well-established organizations may or may not have formal HRM plans, but they almost certainly have *custom and practice*; that is, they have evolved staffing policies incrementally, whether written down or not. Precedent oils the wheels of bureaucracies, often determining what will happen in the future. If we staff our new suboffice rationally, without reference to precedents, we may create a salary anomaly, for instance, which staff in other suboffices may not find acceptable. So it might make sense to say: we opened a suboffice in another district five years ago, and all we need do is reproduce its staffing structure.

Analogy

Where precedents do not exist, we may fall back on analogies. Thus we have never had suboffices before, and are establishing this one as a first step towards decentralizing our activities, so no precedent exists. But might we not view staffing the suboffice by analogy with the structure of one of our headquarters departments, and relate the staffing establishment to that? This may be a 'felt fair' solution, that is, one where the interested parties are satisfied that the staffing outcome is equitable. So it might make sense to say: the work of the suboffice is roughly on the same level as the work of a headquarters section within a larger headquarters department – let us reproduce that.

Individual managerial judgement

Even the largest, most stable and well-established organizations have to make a leap in the dark from time to time. We might just make an intuitive judgement. Such judgements should not be despised. There is a long-standing interest in them that goes back to Vickers' (1965) seminal work. The judgement of an effective manager is based on his or her accumulated experience and tacit intelligence, expressed in problem-solving skills that he or she has developed over many years. It can be imaginative, and informed by an instinctive political sense (for example, about how key stakeholders will respond) and a shrewd intuition about the future.

'Market forces'

A fourth way in which organizations deal with staffing needs is to say: the market will do our planning for us. 'Thousands of jobs are locked away every night in the filing trays of local authority Planning departments,' said Michael Heseltine in 1980, when he was a minister in the Conservative government in the UK, expressing the hostility to planning which has been a feature of right-wing politics over the last couple of decades. The influential right-wing economist Friedrich Hayek (1944) had argued that a planned economy along the lines of the Soviet Union was incompatible with individual liberty. Thus, as the capitalist model of the economy has spread to more and more countries following the collapse of Communism, many organizations have declined to plan, either because they cannot plan because market conditions are unpredictable, or because they do not wish to for ideological reasons.

1.3   From precedent to planning

A lot of the time, precedent, analogy or judgement are all we need. However, they often are not enough, for instance when we are faced with

- big organizations,
- complex staffing needs,
- a changing environment,
- financial constraints,

where we need to generate a range of options, and to generate dialogue between stakeholders, which together will lead to a shared commitment. It is in situations like these that we need to plan.

1.4 HRP as problem solving

Presenting HRP as a method for taking a long-term view of overall staffing needs is the mainstream view. However, you can probably see already that HRP done in this way is elaborate and expensive. It will not suit every organization. Many organizations, especially in developing and transitional countries, lack the resources to carry out HRP on this lavish scale. But it is also possible to use HRP techniques on a more modest scale to solve discrete staffing problems. Here is an example.

An international NGO is in the middle of producing a five-year plan for one of the countries where it operates. It has adopted a policy of appointing more nationals of the country to senior positions, rather than the expatriates that it has mostly relied on in the past. Given the work that it expects to do in the next five years, how should it set about obtaining those people? Are people with the skills it needs available in the labour market? If they are, they can be obtained through normal recruitment channels. Alternatively, are the skills it is looking for so specific that the external labour market cannot provide them? If they are, then perhaps the NGO should consider developing its existing staff so that they can acquire them; or possibly it should recruit staff as 'trainees', with the expectation that they will acquire skills they lack over a period before becoming fully effective in the job that is needed.

In this example, the NGO is, in effect, using HRP to solve a particular problem, which we could pose like this: *how can we increase the number of nationals in senior positions?* In terms of the 'adopt – adapt – reject' model presented in Chapter 1, using HRP in this way is an example of how we can *adapt* a textbook good practice technique to suit the circumstances of particular organizations.

Here are some other examples of problems that an organization may use HRP techniques to try to solve:

- Should we be worried about our rate of staff turnover?
- What are the staffing implications of our new decentralization policy?
- Is it time to start a graduate recruitment programme?
- What can we do to get more women into senior positions?

In this chapter we are going to present a 'classic' model of HRP (what we call 'Big Planning') a model that assumes that we are trying to take a long-term, overall view of the organization's staffing needs. As we work through the model, keep reminding yourself that the more modest use of HRP that we have just outlined is also possible. We will return to it towards the end of the chapter.

2 A framework for human resource planning

2.1 Developing the framework

So let us agree that we need to carry out human resource planning at least some of the time. How do we do it? In a nutshell, Figure 3.1 answers this question.

The figure is one of those flow diagrams that people who write management textbooks are addicted to: one management writer compared his to the plumbing in an ancient Scottish castle! We hope it will give you a framework for organizing your thinking about what we cover in this chapter. There are three general points to make about it now.

A strategic model
The first thing to say is that the figure represents a strategic model. Notice how it establishes the links between overall strategic objectives (cell 1.1 in the figure) and labour demand.

There are a few things that we know by this stage about strategic models. One thing we learnt in Chapter 2 is that a strategic approach to HRM means integrating the organization's overall strategy with the way it conducts HRM activities: we called this *vertical integration*. How might it apply to the link between overall strategy and HRP? Let us take the example of British Airways, one of whose strategic objectives following privatization in the 1980s was to get closer to the customer. Privatization could have several implications for HRP. One might be to move more of its staffing resources into jobs where there is direct contact with the public, like check-in staff and in-flight attendants. Another one, which the airline actually implemented, was to set up a huge programme of customer training for its entire staff.

Strategic integration has a second aspect, which we called *horizontal integration* in Chapter 2, referring to the way we link the individual HRM activities to each other. It is also present in the figure, at the 'implementing' stage of the HRP process, represented by cells 11 to 14, where we see our human resource plan having implications for other HRM activities like recruitment and selection and learning and training.

Something else we learnt about strategy is the need to be wary of 'blueprint' strategic models, models where organizations make plans that are set in cement, far too rigid to cope with the inevitable changes that occur after the plans are complete. This is something you will have to be on your guard for as you develop your understanding of HRP. It is the easiest thing in the world to slip into a mechanical approach to HRP, producing annual statistical updates on staff turnover and so on in a vacuum, with no reference to the organization's strategic needs. But just as we saw that there is a more flexible way of approaching strategic management, so there is a more flexible way of approaching HRP. We will see what we mean by that later in the chapter.

Labour demand and supply
The second point we want to make about our model of HRP is that it is based on the notion of reconciling *labour demand and supply*. You are probably aware of the way the relationship between demand and supply operates in the economy as a whole: if demand for a product is greater than supply, the price goes up; if supply is greater than demand, the price goes down. An example that was current at the time of writing is the price of coffee. The supply of coffee on the world market was greater than the demand early in the twenty-first century, partly because, in the 1990s, Vietnam, with encouragement from the World Bank and the IMF, had begun to produce and export large quantities to earn foreign exchange. This forced the price down. An opposite example is the price of oil. OPEC (the Organization of Petroleum Exporting Countries) exists to regulate the supply of oil onto the world market so that it does not greatly exceed demand, in order to keep the price stable and, if possible, high.

We have the same notion of demand and supply in the labour market. It is no use for a Ministry of Health to produce a human resource plan that specifies the recruitment of a large number of doctors (*demand*), if those doctors are not available in the marketplace (*supply*). Where that is the case, the ministry has a choice between taking action on the demand side – for example, reducing its demand for doctors by recruiting health auxiliaries ('barefoot doctors') instead – or by taking action on the supply side – for example, by training more doctors, or making it harder for the doctors it trains to go and work overseas when they have finished their training.

Thus two major elements of HRP are forecasting demand (cells 1–3 of our diagram) and forecasting supply (cells 4–7).

A planning process
The final thing to say about Figure 3.1 is that it represents a *planning process* which has five stages, based on Bramham (1988). We outline them in the next section.

2.2   Stages of the planning process

Investigating (cells 1–2, 4–6)
Building up awareness of the HRM situation, in particular identifying key problems, opportunities and staff groups which should take precedence in planning work.

Forecasting (cells 3 and 7)
Making predictions through examining possible courses of action based on different assumptions. Our key task is to reconcile demand with supply. This is the stage where we produce a draft document with questions/options for discussion by managers. We may find that we need to go back to the investigating stage for further analysis.

Planning (cells 9 and 10)
Agreeing an approach and translating it into plan targets. Targets require timetables, resources to implement them and criteria for monitoring implementation. We also have to check our approach across a range of areas to make sure that it is consistent before we move on to implementation.

Implementing (cells 11–14)
Deploying resources within the specified timetable to meet our targets.

Monitoring and evaluating (cell 15)
Checking the progress of implementation against our criteria and reporting to managers.

The next section concentrates on the demand side of forecasting and its methodology, together with issues of staffing costs, and the volume and quality of work that will be required.

Figure 3.1   A framework for human resource planning

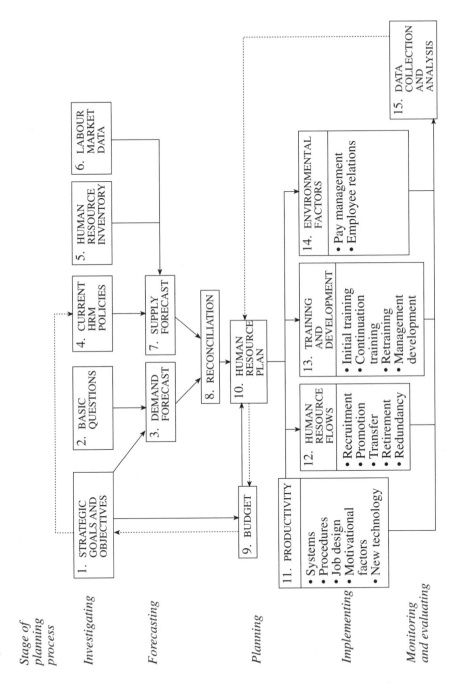

3   The demand side: forecasting demand

3.1   Why demand forecasting is valuable

In the real world, organizations usually start from where they are now. That is, they will first produce what we call later on a 'human resource inventory': a listing of the staff that they already have, and of their qualifications, skills and so on. But as an HRM inventory is, logically speaking, part of the business of supply forecasting (which is why it appears as cell 5 in our diagram), we will leave it until later. Instead, we start from the logical starting point in the HRP framework that we have outlined in Figure 3.1, a forecast of demand.

As its name indicates, demand forecasting aims to predict future demand for staff. This is useful for three reasons:

- it gives us a way of prioritizing staffing areas which are particularly important for achieving our strategic objectives;
- it helps us to maximize the contribution that each job and each employee makes to the achievement of our objectives; or, to use current management jargon, the 'value' that each job and each employee 'adds' to the organization;
- it provides a 'mediating tool' which helps managers to resolve dilemmas such as (a) the conflict between ideal staffing levels and limited staffing budgets, and (b) the conflict between long-term human resource development needs and a short-term financial squeeze: this may, for example, militate against developing younger staff to replace staff who will be retiring in five years' time.

3.2   Assumptions in demand forecasting

While demand forecasting does derive from a rational calculation of demand, it is by no means an exact science. We have to make many assumptions, and demand forecasting is only as good as the assumptions it is based on. What kind of assumptions? Box 3.1 gives a few examples, but also some constraints. Listing constraints is a way of saying that our assumptions may be affected by factors that we do not completely control.

3.3   Basic questions (cell 2 of Figure 3.1)

Forecasting demand entails answering three basic questions at the investigating stage in our planning process:

Box 3.1   Assumptions in demand forecasting

Private company

- level of sales aimed at,
- level of production necessary to support projected sales,
- product development plans,
- return on investment needed.

Constraints: shortage of materials and machine capacity, and of staff and management ability.

Public agency

- levels of activity projected based on legislation, political objectives or community needs (in terms of services, client groups and projects).

Constraints: a change in political objectives; difficulty of coordinating activity across public agencies responsible for different aspects of activity; uncertainty about future staffing budgets.

---

1 What factors determine workload?
2 How can we measure staff performance?
3 How can we improve performance? Whose support will we need to do so?

Table 3.1 shows how we answer them, and some techniques that will help us.

We have to admit that the techniques are a bit of a jumble, but their haphazard nature inadvertently makes the point that there is no mechanical formula for assembling the data on which our demand forecast is based. There is plenty of room for creativity here.

3.4   'Disaggregating' demand and the role of job analysis

As we move to the level of detail that we will need to answer the questions posed in Table 3.1, we find that the answers are very different for different kinds of jobs. A demand forecast will either be *selective*, concentrating only on jobs that are a priority (so that we might decide to concentrate on recruitment of health auxiliaries, where we know we have a problem, and ignore all other jobs in the Ministry of Health); or, if our forecast is comprehensive, then *the whole will be the*

Table 3.1   Basic questions at the investigating stage

Investigating stage	Relevant techniques
1 What factors determine workload?	Interviews with staff and managers
2 How can we measure staff performance?	Questionnaires to managers
• Can we identify an indicator that gives a realistic measure of work output for the average postholder or for critical elements of the job?	Observation of staff at work/use of basic recording techniques, including process mapping
3 How can we improve performance? Whose support will we need?	Search of files related to work performance
• Does the work that staff are doing now contribute to achieving strategic objectives?	Analysis of statistical returns on performance over time
• Is the average staff member producing enough output in the specified time?	Job analysis
• How well do staff in relevant work units work together?	Inter-plant/office comparisons
• On the whole, do existing staff members have the appropriate knowledge and skill to do the job well?	In the public service, staff inspection (if this function exists)
• Are staff using equipment, materials and other inputs effectively?	Reference to corporate plans/budgets
• What changes in managerial/supervisory methods do we need to make staff more productive?	Survey of client views

sum of the parts, that is, our overall forecast will be the sum of our forecasts for all the different categories of staff that we have in the organization. Certainly we can ask the same questions in relation to any job. It is just that we will get different answers each time we ask them, and different actions may follow from them. So if we take health auxiliaries as an example, the action that might follow from a forecast might be to increase recruitment onto the training courses that are run at regional Primary Health training centres. In contrast, the action that might follow from a demand forecast for doctors might be to offer them better incentives to resist the temptation to go and work overseas.

To get the level of detail we need, job analysis may be a necessary prior step. It can contribute to removing inadequacies in individual performance, and encourage staff to be as productive as possible. It can provide a basis for deciding future job requirements in the organization, and the average workload expected from them. A list of staff categories derived from job analysis can form the basis for demand forecasting. (We present job analysis in Chapter 4.)

3.5   Choosing a demand forecasting method

As we move to the forecasting stage in our planning process (cell 3), we have to choose a demand forecasting method which will be appropriate in the light of the answers we obtained to the three basic questions at the investigating stage in the planning process. Table 3.2 shows how we do this.

3.6   Applying the framework

We can now put all the data together. In Table 3.3 we have applied the model to two important posts in local authorities in Tanzania. The table lists the kinds of data on which a forecast might be based. In line with what we said earlier about the need to disaggregate, you will notice the differences between the data required for the two posts.

3.7   Using consultation to obtain forecasting data

Strategic planning is inevitably a 'top-down' activity. The dangers are that the planners will lose touch with actual working conditions, resulting in unrealistic plans, and that line managers will not implement the plans with any enthusiasm because they have not been involved in making them.

It should go without saying that the HRM planner will need to consult. Getting data requires discussion amongst the managers and staff who do the work. Their experience of working practices, technology and staff productivity is important. The manager's responsibility for managing staff performance and considering future staffing needs is particularly critical.

Consultation may also involve a wider range of stakeholders, including clients, managers from other parts of the organization, trade union representatives and outside experts, especially when major changes in

Table 3.2   Choosing a demand forecasting method

Forecasting stage	Techniques from Table 3.1, plus:
• What method should we use to forecast the number of posts we will need?	Reference to human resource planning literature Benchmarking data
• Will we need the same type of work in the future? • What total level of organizational/work unit activity, related to the work of the staff group, do we expect in the plan period?	Market research (in the private sector) Investigating possible changes in government policy including amendment of existing programmes to make services more responsive to client needs (in the public sector) Understanding the impact of development plans Survey of forecasting literature
• Could changes in working practices, systems, procedures or investment in equipment increase the productivity of the average postholder/work system?	Application of systems analysis/ process mapping techniques/ business process re-engineering Drawing on experience from elsewhere Incorporating the ideas of managers and staff Survey of project appraisal reports
• Should the existing category of staff be more clearly defined for forecasting purposes?	Using the results of job analysis Using standard classification systems
• What timescale is appropriate for the forecast?	Analysing the lead times for learning and training Obtaining data on the rate of technological change Obtaining data on possible market trends
• What level of detail do we require in the forecast?	Estimating the data needs of managers to make effective decisions and obtain adequate managerial control
• What external factors may upset the forecast?	Making an appraisal of political, economic and environmental trends affecting the work of the organization and the degrees of uncertainty prevailing

Table 3.3   Demand forecasting in local government in Tanzania

	Medical assistant	Revenue collector
What factors determine workload?	Number of patients registered Number of beds in hospital Size of population to be covered Number of supporting staff Types of common disease	Types of revenue source Size of area of operation The target of revenue to be collected The response of taxpayers
How can we measure staff performance?	Number of patients attended in a given period Number of deaths Number of patients discharged Time taken to treat a patient Punctuality of staff	Amount of revenue collected in relation to target Audit approval
How can we improve performance? Whose support will we need?	Improved diagnosis and more timely treatment (all staff) Organizing and motivating staff better (Medical Officer)	Overcoming problems in revenue collection (revenue collectors) Training is needed (District Treasurer) Better system of estimating (District Treasurer)
What method should we use to forecast the number of posts we will need?	Number of posts should be related to population	Number of posts should be related to: • types of revenue source • size of revenue source

technology and working practices are contemplated. It may be structured and systemic, perhaps involving the use of questionnaires or other process mapping methods.

There is always a danger in relying too heavily on data provided by line managers and other stakeholders. Each of them has an interest of their own, or at least sees the world from their own point of view. For example, managers may be so entrenched in existing working practices that they fail to see ways of improving productivity, such as the use of new technology. Alternatively, they may see the planning exercise mainly as an opportunity to lobby for extra staffing for their own departments.

Figure 3.2   *'Top-down' versus 'bottom-up' in demand forecasting and its resolution*

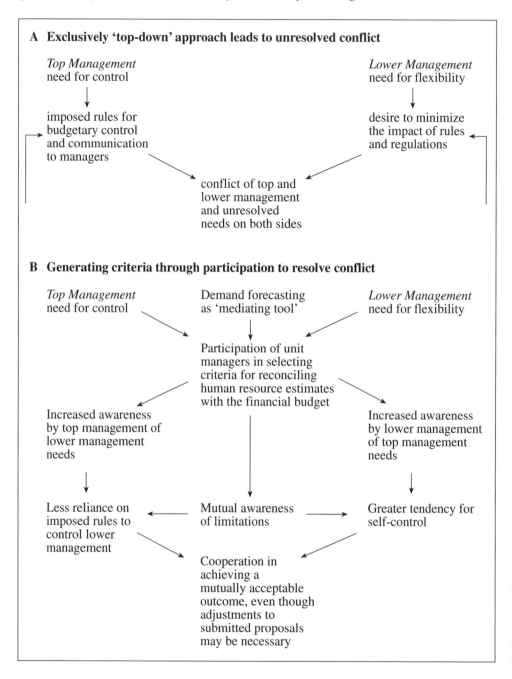

Source: Institute for Employment Studies (adapted).

Thus there is a tricky choice between excluding line managers and other stakeholders, with the result that planning becomes remote and fails to win managers' commitment, and being swayed by managers' special pleading, with the result that staffing resources flow to the managers who are most powerful, and managers succeed in resisting change that threatens the staffing status quo in their departments.

One way to resolve the dilemma is through a process that generates criteria for carrying out demand forecasting. The process is shown in Figure 3.2, and particularly in the lower half of the figure (the upper half shows what happens when planning is exclusively 'top-down'). Such criteria may result from detailed demand forecasting work to establish options on staffing levels and associated costs. This allows demand forecasting to become a 'mediating tool', as we called it earlier, providing managers with helpful data to resolve possible conflicts. The criteria agreed should meet the need of top management to maintain overall budgetary control, while allowing line managers room to respond to local needs.

Examples of criteria for reconciling staffing forecasts and resource availability are:

- administrative staff costs not to exceed 20 per cent of total staff costs,
- staff costs not to exceed 60 per cent of total costs.

Making this work entails a planning cycle that enables participation at key decision points, and builds commitment to a common interest in meeting organizational needs. This may also allow a full discussion of trade-offs between budgetary targets and longer-term human resource development needs (see below on the issue of budget constraints).

Study task 1: forecast of child health care assistants in Beleriand

It is now time to give you the chance to put all of this together and try a bit of forecasting yourself. Our case study involves the use of a demographic indicator, linking the projected size of a client group with the number of posts required. This is a very useful indicator in planning public services, for example, in ratios such as one teacher: 30 pupils, one extension officer: 10 farmer groups, and one nurse: 20 hospital beds.

Beleriand's Seventh National Development Plan (Beleriand is the name of an imaginary country), commencing 1 January of Year II, incorporates a Ministry of Health initiative to reduce the incidence of chronic illness and mortality among very young children. The scheme involves the creation of a new post of Child Health Assistant, whose sole function is to provide regular medical care for all children aged three and under. Resources have been allocated for the recruitment, training and salary costs of the new group.

Doriath Region has been chosen for pilot implementation of the scheme because it has the highest incidence of chronic illness and mortality amongst very young children of any region in the country. A recent survey estimates the following mortality rates for young children in Doriath:

Under 1 year of age	12% of live births
1 and under 2 years of age	3% of those reaching the age of 1
2 and under 3 years of age	1% of those reaching the age of 2

The National Census produced an estimate of the population of Doriath of 2 481 000 on 1 January of Year I. Comparing that figure with the census figure for five years earlier shows that (a) total population has increased by 9 per cent per annum, and (b) the crude birth rate, that is, the number of live births per 1000 of the population per year, is unchanged at 44. The Chief Census Officer advises that these two figures are accurate enough to be used for forecasting over the next four years (Years II, III, IV, V).

The Ministry of Health has decided that one Child Health Assistant can handle 3000 registered children aged 3 and under. This ratio is based on a well-established similar health scheme for young children in a neighbouring country.

It is intended to implement the Child Health Scheme from 1 January of Year V. This allows three full years, (II, III, IV) for detailed service planning and training the new staff required.

Forecast the number of child health assistant posts required in Doriath on 1 January of Year V. Assume that total forecast births in Year V are to be taken account of in the forecast. Use Table 3.4 to produce your answer.

✍

3.8 Summary

We have seen above what is involved in the demand side of human resource planning. We saw several reasons why demand forecasting is valuable, including the fact that it allows us to relate staffing needs to our overall strategic objectives. We saw that it is only as good as the assumptions on which it is based.

In operational terms, we can think of demand forecasting as an attempt to find answers to three questions at the investigating stage of the HRP process, namely: what factors determine workload, how can we measure staff performance, and how can we improve performance? As we look for the answers, we realize that we may have to consider jobs one at a time, and that we may need job analysis data

Table 3.4   *Forecast of child health assistants: working sheet*

Year	Population forecast 1 January	Live births forecast	Number of children reaching the age of 1	Number of children reaching the age of 2	Number of children reaching the age of 3	Total children in scheme 1 January Year V
I						
II						
III						
IV						
V						

67

when we do so. Finally, we make our choice of the forecasting method that we are going to apply in the light of the answers we have obtained to our three questions at the investigating stage.

4 The supply side: forecasting supply

4.1 The components of a supply forecast

We now move from the demand side to the supply side of the planning exercise. If you refer back to Figure 3.1, you will see that a supply analysis draws on several kinds of information:

- the impact of current HRM policies on the capacity and motivation of the workforce (cell 4),
- the details of current staff (cell 5),
- the influence of the labour market (cell 6).

4.2 Developing a human resource inventory (cell 5)

We said earlier that, in the real world, an organization is likely to start the HRP process with an inventory of its staff. If for no other reason, this is because the organization needs to have a basic record in order to pay them, to know when they joined the organization and so on. Let us look at what is involved.

A human resource inventory lists staff in terms of basic information such as occupation, grade, department, age, length of service, qualifications and gender. It is relevant to us because it tells us what staffing resource we already have to meet the needs that we identified in our demand forecast.

We get the data we need to compile a human resource inventory from a number of sources, such as

- human resource record forms or files,
- recruitment and selection forms,
- training and career records (training undertaken, promotions and transfers),
- performance management or appraisal records,
- salary statements.

A human resource record form or file is often the main source of information on an individual. It is useful if it summarizes essential information from the other sources listed. Typical contents are shown in Table 3.5.

Table 3.5   Typical contents of the individual staff record

Personal*	Present position
Name	Job title and code
Date of birth	Grade
Address and telephone number	Date appointed
Gender and marital status	
Date appointed	
Location	Career history
Department	Positions
Section	Dates
Qualifications	Remuneration and benefits
Academic	Conditions of service
Professional	Basic pay
	Superannuation
	Leave entitlement
	Other benefits
Training received	Date of resignation
	Reason for leaving

Note: * It is important that personal records are not used improperly. For example, it would be discriminatory to use information on staff's gender and marital status to make promotion decisions.

Computerized human resource information systems make inventory compilation a lot easier. Manual systems require much time-consuming clerical effort to extract data from individual records.

4.3   Using the human resource inventory to forecast supply

Supply forecasting relies on the ability to *aggregate* data from the human resource inventory, for instance the number of staff in an occupational group or the number of leavers in a year. We can use this aggregate data to show changes in total staff employed by category, age structure, male/female ratio and so on over relevant time periods. Trends can be identified which we would otherwise miss.

In particular, the inventory can be used to establish trends in staff *wastage*, categorized according to avoidable and unavoidable reasons for leaving (assuming these were reliably stated by the leavers and recorded properly), reasons such as:

- personal improvement,
- wages,
- location,
- relationships with supervisors and fellow-workers,
- dismissal,
- retirement,
- ill-health,
- death,
- pregnancy.

Avoidable wastage is obviously of interest, particularly if it affects staff who have important skills which are in short supply in the labour market. Identifying the rate of wastage stimulates discussion of the reasons for wastage. Are staff leaving because of

- pay that is not competitive with that of other employers?
- overstaffing and resultant staff boredom?
- understaffing and resultant stress?
- poor job design?
- poor management?
- unsuitable recruitment?
- inefficient training?
- unsatisfactory working conditions?

To improve the quality of information about why staff leave, some organizations have individual *exit interviews* with leavers, especially if they are in a key staff category. We say more about exit interviews in our discussion of job analysis in Chapter 4.

4.4   Wastage measures

For forecasting purposes, a crude *wastage rate*, as used in Study task 2, is often enough. It is defined as

$$\text{Crude wastage rate (\%)} = \frac{\text{No. of leavers in year}}{\text{No. of staff in post at the beginning of the year}} \times 100$$

Box 3.2 explains two more sensitive measures of wastage.

Box 3.2   Calculating the turnover rate and the stability index

The *turnover rate* is usually calculated at year-end to summarize staff wastage during the year.

$$\text{Turnover} = \frac{\text{number of leavers in the year}}{\text{average number of staff employed in the year}} \times 100$$

The turnover rate gives an impression of staffing changes in an organization or department, but it can be misleading. Consider, for example, three similar departments that employ 100 people:

- Department A loses every employee at the beginning of the year, and each is replaced by someone who stays until the following year.
- Department B loses half its employees at the beginning of the year, and their replacements also leave before the end of the year, hence they need replacing.
- Department C loses only four employees at the beginning of the year, but their jobs are filled by a succession of people each of whom stays only two weeks.

In each case, the turnover is 100%. However, department A has lost all its skilled staff, department B has lost only half, and department C has lost only four.

To present a more realistic picture of staff wastage, an alternative measure, the *stability index*, can be used.

$$\frac{\text{Stability}}{\text{index}} = \frac{\text{number of staff with one or more years' service}}{\text{number of staff at start of year}} \times 100$$

Here is an example of how the turnover rate and the stability index are calculated:

Staff at start of year	Leavers during year	Recruits	Net change	Staff at year end
400	45	35	−10	390

(i)   Average number of staff employed during year = (400+390) ÷ 2
                                                                              = 790 ÷ 2 = 395

(ii)   Staff with one or more years' service = 400 − 45 = 355

(iii)   Turnover rate = (45 ÷ 395) × 100 = 11.4%

(iv)   Stability index = (355 ÷ 400) × 100 = 88.8%

> The staff turnover and stability indices can be used to compare patterns of staff mobility
>
> - across departments,
> - across time,
> - by skill factors,
> - by gender,
> - by age.

Based on Bramham (1988).

To establish trends or average values for key HRM variables used in forecasting work requires data on staff over a number of years. The incompleteness of a new inventory is inevitable until relevant time series data are built up.

4.5   The effect of current HRM policies (cell 4 in Figure 3.1)

An important part of supply forecasting is finding out how effective current HRM policies are in closing gaps between demand and supply, and whether current policies are likely to be adequate in the future; and also revising policies to ensure adequate supply. Our policies could have a bearing on any of the following:

- high wastage rates,
- high vacancy rates,
- persistent skills shortages,
- high overtime levels,
- problems related to organizational contraction,
- unmet staffing needs due to organizational expansion or changed goals,
- shortage of suitable recruits,
- shortage of suitable promotees.

For example, are we losing a lot of doctors because we are not paying them enough to stay? Or is it because we do not have any restriction on their going overseas once they have finished their training? It is possible to model the effect of various alternative policies on the labour supply.

What we are essentially doing here is generating options for ensuring the future balance of demand and supply. Managers can choose the most viable option and work out its operational implications. As with demand forecasting, our supply forecasting options are only as good as the assumptions they are based on. You will have a chance to see what that means in our next Study task.

4.6   Internal staffing flows

Forecasting stock levels in a staff category (such as teachers) at particular future dates requires predicting future flows. One staff category, as represented in Figure 3.3, can have up to eight distinct flows affecting its stock level.

Figure 3.3   Staffing flows in and out

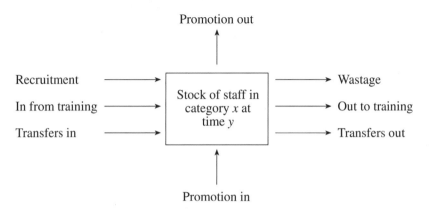

In practice, however, there are not usually more than three or four significant flows in a given period.

Table 3.6 is a simple framework for recording anticipated key flows.

Table 3.6   Staffing flows

Staff category	Stock at year start	Expected Flows During Year			Projected stock – year end
		Wastage	Promotion in	Promotion out	

Computerized supply models and spreadsheets can be developed for more sophisticated flow and year-end stock projections in more complex staffing structures.

4.7   The external labour market (cell 6)

All the factors we have discussed so far are internal, and the organization has some control over them. With the external labour market, the organization has less control, and it is a matter of becoming aware of how it affects the availability of staff to join the organization from outside.

Factors that govern the labour market are local and national, and also international for a growing number of organizations.

Local factors
People in manual and clerical jobs, and most professional people as they get older and put down roots, look for work mainly in the local travel-to-work area. Factors that affect the local labour market include:

- unemployment levels;
- degree of competition for staff with other employers in the area;
- output of people from the education system (schools and technical colleges) and the basic qualifications/skills available;
- local transport facilities;
- local housing or accommodation at appropriate prices.

National factors
Professional people, especially early in their careers, are often thinking in terms of a national job market: they will be ready to travel to get the job they want. Organizations may find that they are competing for these staff in a national market. National factors include:

- population movement related to the distribution of income/job opportunities;
- effects of government legislation, particularly on employment conditions;
- impact of development planning, particularly the location of economic zones such as Export Processing Zones, which many developing countries like Mauritius and Sri Lanka have set up to attract employers to particular areas;
- government training schemes, particularly those related to key skills provision.

International factors

Some organizations, usually at senior levels, operate in an international labour market. This is true for high-level jobs with international organizations like the United Nations. It is sometimes also true for some less well-paid jobs, for example the market for domestic workers in Malaysia, where workers may come from Indonesia or the Philippines.

Information from previous recruitment drives is usually available in the organization, and this may help in understanding the labour market. Additionally, data may be obtained from agencies concerned with labour market conditions and trends. Data may also be available from a Ministry of Employment or Human Resources, or from private employment agencies.

It is worth keeping an eye on the labour market. Early identification of constraints on recruiting the staff the organization needs can stimulate ideas about alternative HRM strategies before serious problems arise.

Tight and loose labour markets

The last paragraph implies that the organization may have to take active steps to attract candidates from outside. A market where the jobseeker selling his or her labour is in a strong position – perhaps because there are few people with a particular skill (information technology and financial skills have been examples in recent years) – is a 'tight' market; or, to put it differently, a *seller's market*. A market, on the other hand, where the buyer is in a strong position, perhaps because there are many people chasing few jobs (most manual jobs would be an example), is a 'loose' market; or, to put it differently, a *buyer's market*. There are obvious implications here for HRP. We say more about tight and loose labour markets in Chapter 6.

4.8 Summary

We draw on several sources of data when we make a supply forecast. There is the Human Resource Inventory, compiled from staff's personal records: we can use it to identify trends in the movement of staff, using calculations of (in ascending order of precision) wastage and turnover rates and the 'stability' of the workforce. Such calculations of internal factors enable us to predict staffing flows with some certainty, since the organization has some control over them. That is not the case with the external labour market, where it is a matter of the organization trying to understand the market it is operating in, whether that is a local, national or international one.

5   The human resource plan (cell 10 in Figure 3.1)

In a way, everything we do in the other activities that we discuss in this book, like recruitment and selection and learning and training, derives from a comparison of demand and supply forecasts. This section aims to bring together many of the concepts used in the chapter so far to understand how a human resource plan is prepared. After learning about supply forecasting methodology, and types of HRM plans, you will do a forecasting exercise using the Nargothrond teaching hospital case study (Study task 2).

Of course managers can reject all the options we present: they may prefer their own 'judgement'. But even if they do, they can still use our forecasts to explore alternative possibilities. Thus forecasting can stimulate institutional learning, whether managers select one of the options that the forecasting has generated or not.

5.1   Plan elements

At last we reach the planning stage itself, the point where we can put our demand and supply forecasts together to make a human resource plan. Its elements will be the HRM activities, notably the major ones like recruitment and selection and learning and training which we cover in this book. In other words, we can think of the plan as representing a list of the HRM actions that we will take to deal with the implications of our demand and supply forecasts.

What the list will contain, of course, will vary according to the needs of particular organizations. However, it is likely to be drawn from the possibilities that we have outlined in cells 11 to 14 in Figure 3.1. In practice, not more than three of those possibilities listed in cells 11–14 are usually relevant to a given planning objective. The positioning of cell 11 suggests that considering productivity and human issues is fundamental. We will explore some of the items that we have listed in cell 11 in Chapter 4.

5.2   Implementing the plan

In the light of those possibilities, we list typical actions in Table 3.7 below.

Table 3.7   Implementing the human resource plan: possible actions

Action area	Strategy/ plan element	Example of action
Productivity	Systems	Increase per capita workload for clerical workers by 10% in 2003
	Procedures	
	Job design	
	Motivational factors	
	New technology	
Human resource flows	Recruitment	25 fully trained fitters to be recruited in every quarter
	Promotion	37 staff in Grade A to be prepared for promotion to Grade B by 31 Dec. of this year and promoted to Grade B as vacancies arise next year
	Transfer	No more than 5% of total staff to be allowed transfers
	Retirement	10 staff who reach retirement age to be offered one year contracts to continue employment
	Redundancy	20 staff to be offered terms for voluntary redundancy this year, at least 12 months before they are required to depart
Training and development	Initial training	At quarterly intervals, 25 fully trained fitters recruited from the labour market, to be given one week's training on the company's method of working
	Continuation training	50 sales staff to be given training in this year on new product ranges to be introduced next year

Table 3.7   continued

Action area	Strategy/ plan element	Example of action
	Retraining	20 staff in Department X to be retrained for work in Departments Y and Z
	Management development	15 middle managers to be identified for promotion to senior management, and individual development plans to be agreed by 30 June of this year
Environmental factors	Pay management	5% pay rise to be awarded to all staff (on agreed settlement date) 30 staff in Grade J who complete 10 years' service to be redesignated Grade K
	Employee relations	Proposals on improved working procedures in Department N to be agreed with trade union

5.3   The budget and the plan

There is just one final input left to add: a costing of the activities we are proposing. We should not expect that everything we propose will be accepted: our proposals will have to take their chances alongside the proposals of colleagues from other departments, in the context of the organization's overall budget (cell 9 in Figure 3.1). That being so, it will be helpful if we:

- put the costed proposals in priority order, so that at least the most important ones are likely to be implemented, even if it is not possible to implement everything;
- indicate where a proposal is urgent, and where it can be postponed for a year or more;
- recognize that cheap proposals, and proposals that save rather than cost money even more, are most likely to go through: even important HRM activities like introducing a new performance appraisal scheme can cost little money – unlike, for instance, capital construction projects.

Study task 2: matching demand and supply in the Nargothrond teaching hospital

Our second activity gives you the chance to practise making the simple calculations that are part and parcel of a human resource plan.

1 *By completing Table 3.8, which follows the case study information below, make a forecast of the numbers of nurses that need to be recruited in each of the years 2003, 2004, 2005, 2006 and 2007.*
2 *When you have completed the forecast, ask yourself what issues the managers to whom you present your forecast might raise, and how you would respond to them. (This question is intended to put you in the shoes of the general manager who will look at your analysis from a non-numerical, 'common sense' point of view.)*

The University Teaching Hospital is situated in Nargothrond, the capital city of Beleriand. It has freedom to manage its own nursing staff in terms of recruitment, training and conditions of service. The hospital recruits students with good secondary school certificates into a four-year training scheme leading to a nursing qualification, but increasingly relies on direct recruitment of qualified nurses from the labour market into the standard nursing grade.

The hospital is about to expand its number of in-patient wards and new posts are being created in the standard nursing grade. Senior management, however, is worried about the hospital's ability to recruit and retain skilled nurses, and has decided to carry out a five-year forecast so that it can look more closely at its training and recruitment policies for nurses in the standard grade.

It is now early December 2002 and the planning has to be completed over the next few weeks so appropriate decisions can be made. Data are available which result in the following assumptions being adopted for the forecasts to be made in Table 3.8 below.

(a) Of existing nurses currently employed by the hospital, it is estimated that 300 of them will be available for work on 1 January 2003 (item 1 in Table 3.8).
(b) Existing work requirements on 1 January 2003 will result in the need for 300 nursing posts at the standard grade (item 6).
(c) The following numbers of secondary school leavers entered the nurse training scheme at the dates stated:

1 January 1999	20
1 January 2000	30
1 January 2001	35
1 January 2002	50

It is anticipated that 50 trainees will enter the scheme on 1 January 2003.

The training scheme lasts four years and newly qualified nurses become available on 1 January of the fifth year after entering training (item 2). They are allocated posts during this fifth year.

Table 3.8   Forecasting nurse recruitment in Nargothrond Hospital

Item	2003	2004	2005	2006	2007
1 Number of existing nurses available on 1 January (in post)					
2 1 January output from training scheme waiting to take over posts					
3 Total number of nurses available on 1 January (add items 1 and 2)					
4 Reduction during year: (i) Statutory retirements (ii) Early retirements and deaths (1% p.a.) (iii) Discharges (2% p.a.) (iv) Promotions (5% p.a.) (v) Voluntary resignations (10% p.a.) Total forecast loss of nurses (add (i) to (v))					
5 Total number of nurses available at end of year (item 3 minus item 4)					
6 Number of nursing posts required on 1 January to meet existing work commitments					
7 Forecast of additional nursing posts required for new work arising during the year					
8 Total requirement for nursing posts on 31 December (add items 6 and 7)					
9 Additional number of nurses needing to be recruited (item 8 minus item 5)					

The letters S U P P L Y appear vertically in the left margin beside items 1–5, and D E M A N D beside items 6–9.

(d)   The following numbers of nurses will reach the statutory retirement age in the year stated, and retire (item 4(i)):

2003	10
2004	8
2005	12
2006	20
2007	25

(e)   In any year, each category of staff reduction from the standard nursing grade, except statutory retirement, is determined by a *percentage of the numbers in post at the beginning of the year* (item 1) as follows:

Early retirement and deaths	1%
Discharges	2%
Promotions	5%
Voluntary resignations	10%

Assume no wastage from recently trained nurses about to take over posts (item 2), or from those on the training course.

(f)   Expanded ward facilities are likely to give rise to the need for additional nursing posts in each year as follows:

2003	50
2004	10
2005	15
2006	0
2007	0

(g)   It is possible to recruit all the required nurses for any year, and they will be in post by 1 January the following year: that is, the demand forecast for 31 December any year (item 8) = the number of nurses available at the beginning of the next year (item 1).

Hints

- For (e) apply percentages to item 1.
- Work through the 2003 column first and then look at (g) above in order to understand how to start the 2004 column, and similarly for subsequent years.

As the implementation of the plan proceeds, it may be 'rolled forward' every year or so. Thus, when it gets to December 2003, the hospital may roll its plan forward to include the year 2008, resulting in a new five-year forecast 2004–2008.

5.4   Monitoring and evaluating plan performance (cell 15 of Figure 3.1)

Those responsible for human resource planning cannot afford to sit back and hope for the best. Once our plan has been implemented, we need to collect and analyse data to monitor progress and assess whether corrective action is necessary. These data are gathered in different ways according to the needs of managers at different levels in the organization. An overall reservation about monitoring is that we should be careful not to overload the system with demands for information which divert energy from delivering the service that the organization exists to provide.

Line management level
Line managers can review progress on an hourly/daily/weekly basis, according to the nature of the work, to ensure that targets, including budgetary ones, are met. Immediate feedback to those concerned should ensure corrective action when necessary. Unless things are going badly, line managers and staff are usually able to take any corrective action necessary by themselves.

Strategic level
Senior management keeps itself informed of the progress of operational plans, according to a few key indicators directly related to organizational goals and objectives.

Naturally, monitoring by 'level' in this way is affected by the nature of organizational and reporting structures. The flatter the organization, the easier it is for everyone to inform others about performance, and to be informed themselves.

That completes our discussion of the stages of the planning process up to the production of the human resource plan. In terms of Figure 3.1, we move on finally to discuss how we might monitor and evaluate the success of the plan.

6   'Big planning' and appropriate planning

6.1   Planning contingencies

At the start of the chapter we said that what we called the 'classic model' of HRP, or 'Big Planning', is not appropriate everywhere.

Organization types
The first of these contingencies invokes a typology of organization career systems devised by the American scholars Sonnenfeld and Peiperl (1988). They identified four kinds of organizations:

- *The fortress* is an organization in a struggle for survival; staff are hired and fired as the market dictates.
- *The baseball team* places a premium on innovation, and lack of employment security heightens the pressure for creativity.

- *The club* views security and membership as the essence of commitment and typically operates in a monopoly situation, whether in the public or the private sector.
- *The academy* sees professional growth as a personal goal and even a community obligation, and it seeks to develop and retain its own talent.

The four types are shown in Table 3.9. Which of them is your organization closest to?

Table 3.9 *A typology of organization structures*

Fortress	Baseball team
Hotels	Media
Retail	Entertainment
Textiles	Advertising
Publishing	Law firms
Natural resources	Consulting firms
	Software development

Club	Academy
Utilities	Consumer products
Museums	Cars
Government agencies	Electronics
Airlines	Pharmaceuticals
Military	Office products
Banks	

Source: Sonnenfeld and Peiperl (1988).

The most interesting feature of Sonnenfeld and Peiperl's model for our purposes is how they characterize HRM systems corresponding to each of the organizational types (Table 3.10). They suggest that organizations that represent each organizational type will tend to have different approaches to key HRM decisions. They categorize them in terms of how staff join the organization (*entry*), how their career progresses within it (*development*) and how they leave it (*exit*).

The implications of Table 3.10 for the way organizations conduct human resource planning are shown in Table 3.11.

To translate Sonnenfeld and Peiperl's analysis into the language of our HRP model, what they are saying in effect is that different organi-

Table 3.10   HRM systems, by different organization types

Fortress: retrenchment	Baseball team: recruitment
Entry	*Entry*
• passive recruitment	• primary HRM practice
• drawn in by own interests or background	• emphasis on expertise
• selective recruitment	• all-career recruitment
Development	*Development*
• retain core talent	• on-the-job
	• no formal training
	• no succession planning
Exit	*Exit*
• lay-offs frequent	• high turnover
• respect seniority	• cross-employer career

Club: retention	Academy: development
Entry	*Entry*
• early career	• early career only
• emphasize reliability	• ability to grow
Development	*Development*
• as generalists	• job-specific training
• slow paths	• sponsor 'stars'
• required steps	• elaborate career path
• emphasize commitment	
Exit	*Exit*
• low turnover	• low turnover
• retirement	• retirement
	• dismissal for poor performance

Source: Sonnenfeld and Peiperl (1988).

zation types are likely to emphasize different activities from our lists in cells 11 to 14 in Figure 3.1. To take one example from Table 3.11, their analysis suggests that 'baseball team'-type organizations, rather ruthlessly, will not waste time on developing their staff: their motto might be the American phrase 'shape up or ship out'.

Table 3.11   The implications of organization type for the scope of human resource planning

Organization type	Planning for		
	Recruitment	Development	Succession
Fortress	'core talent' only	'core talent' only	'core talent' only
Baseball team	major activity; opportunistic; headhunters.	x	x
Club	major activity, but not valued	planned transfers	taken for granted?
Academy	yes, very much so; scope for tests	yes, very much so	yes

Source: Sonnenfeld and Peiperl (1988).

Size

Another possible contingency is size. HRP is particularly appropriate for big organizations, whose economies of scale mean that they can afford to employ specialist staff, and to bear the other costs of gathering and analysing planning data. Smaller organizations that are expanding can benefit from HRP, but are less likely to spend the large amounts of money and time, relative to their small size, that 'Big Planning' requires.

Degree of (de)centralization

This issue is closely linked to the issue of size. Planning is affected by the *centrifugal* trend in organizations across the world, that is, the trend to decentralize managerial responsibility. Traditional models of HRP, which assume *centripetal* organizations where planning is centralized, are not well equipped to cope with decentralization. Is decentralized planning a contradiction in terms? The Abbey National bank, one of the UK's largest financial institutions and one that has devolved a lot of responsibility to its line managers, suggests to its managers that they should:

> give as much time to planning resources as we would give to the planning of other resources. In this way we will be better prepared to recruit, retain, motivate and deploy the staff that are most appropriate for the achievement of corporate goals. If one organization plans, and subsequently uses, its human resources more effectively than another, the resultant strategy

will give that organization a competitive advantage. (Quoted in Storey and Sisson, 1993: 127)

Thus we should not assume that HRP has no relevance in a decentralized organization. In general, however, we can expect that organizations that have taken 'line manager ownership' to its logical conclusion by decentralizing staffing decisions will be less likely to invest in HRP.

Stability
Planning is about making predictions based on present knowledge. It cannot work where the environment is so unstable that meaningful projections are impossible. If demand for a company's products is volatile, possibly in a fast-changing market such as the market for fashion clothes (see our case study of Benetton in Chapter 9), or, in the public sector, where there are frequent changes of government, HRP will have little value.

Strategic capacity
We have emphasized that effective HRP must be closely linked to an organization's overall strategic plan, but we also know that organizations do not always have an overall strategy. It is unlikely that organizations lacking strategic planning in other areas will make an exception for human resource planning. Only two-thirds of organizations in a British survey were prepared to say that they had any human resource plan (Torrington and Hall, 1991: 54).

Moreover, the HRM function must have some strategic capacity of its own. It is true that some of the most interesting human resource planning systems have been line manager initiatives (Storey and Sisson, 1993), but, in most cases, organizations will only carry out HRP if HRM specialists take the initiative.

6.2   Appropriate planning: HRP as problem solving

Any of the above contingencies can affect the application of HRP, but they need not rule it out altogether. Certainly they may mean that we cannot do Big Planning – taking that long-term view of overall staffing needs which is the essence of what we called the 'classic model' of HRP. But selective use of HRP techniques to solve particular problems is still a possibility. You will remember the example at the start of the chapter of the international NGO which was trying to increase the number of country nationals in senior positions. Attempts to answer questions such as these are examples of HRP playing a consultancy role, helping the organization to clarify a problem and drawing on available expertise to suggest ways of solving it. The role is problem- rather than technique-oriented. That is, rather than having a routine set of HRP procedures, such as calculating turnover rates, which are customarily carried out whether asked for or not, the consultant views HRP as a repertoire of techniques which he or she draws on in order to solve a particular problem.

Taking this flexible problem-solving approach has other advantages as well. For instance, you know already that it is increasingly line managers who are responsible for managing jobs and people (we called this *line manager ownership* in Chapter 2). HRP helps line man- agers make decisions about the acquisition, deployment, utilization, development and retention of the people they manage.

All this illustrates the use of HRP techniques to solve discrete prob- lems. No doubt you can see how this problem-solving approach rep- resents an 'adapted' approach in terms of our 'adopt – adapt – reject' model. We would just like to note, finally, that the HRM specialist who takes this problem-solving approach will need to have good consul- tancy skills. As well as specific knowledge of HRP techniques, the HRM specialist will need the distinctive consultancy abilities of ask- ing questions, diagnosing, working with managers to understand their problems and so on.

7   Summary and conclusion

Most of what we have covered in this chapter is outlined in Figure 3.1, which acts as a visual summary of the main elements of HRP. We have presented HRP as a process that begins with an investigation and culminates in implementation of a human resource plan, whose progress we can monitor and evaluate.

Certainly there are organizations whose size or instability, among other things, preclude elaborate planning techniques. But equally there are many organizations, especially large ones whose staffing needs are complex, which can benefit. Moreover, even a small organization can use HRP techniques selectively as a way of solving a particular problem that it faces, such as the difficulty it has in retaining a particu- lar group of specialist staff. As with strategic management, the strate- gic thinking and institutional learning processes that HRP stimulates can be as valuable as the actual product of the strategic thinking in the form of the comprehensive human resource plan.

All in all, for the HRM specialist who may find himself or herself working in both large and small, volatile and stable organizations in the course of an HRM career, HRP remains an important part of the repertoire of techniques, one that allows the specialist both to see the 'Big Picture' and to solve discrete staffing problems.

Note

1   You may have come across the notion of 'national' or 'sectoral' human resource planning. These terms refer to the way governments make national plans, for example for the number of schools that will be needed to educate the number of children which the government's demographic projections show will be going to school in, say, four years' time. The techniques used are pretty much the same as the techniques that organizations use. In line with our focus in this book on HRM at the level of the organization, we will not discuss this aspect of planning.

4 Job Analysis

Derek Eldridge and Willy McCourt

What this chapter is about

This chapter moves us from the organization level at which we discussed human resource planning in Chapter 3 down to the job level, focusing on job analysis, a set of techniques for identifying the content of jobs (the *job description*), the knowledge, skills and duties that will be needed to do them well (the *person specification*) and the standards by which we judge their contribution to the organization's objectives (the *performance indicators*). After highlighting some basic 'tensions' in job analysis, we review the main methods, taking care to show how job analysis can be used 'appropriately'. We also discuss the implications of job change, and how jobs can be designed in ways that will increase workers' satisfaction and possibly also their efficiency.

What you will learn

By the end of the chapter you should be able to:

- list the steps in carrying out job analysis;
- write job descriptions and person specifications;
- state some implications of teamworking, job change and job design for job analysis;
- recommend an approach to job analysis that will be appropriate to your organization or one with which you are familiar.

1   Introduction

1.1   Tensions in job analysis

What would you say is the basic unit of work in an organization? Some people, especially in the last 20 years, and in Japan most of all, have started to say that it is the team, and that we should not try to go down any lower, because we risk losing cooperation between team members. We will consider their argument later on. But for most people, what we might call the 'atomic level' (and the word 'atom' comes from the Greek άτομος, 'atomos', which means 'indivisible') is the level of the job. Job analysis is the set of techniques that has grown up over almost a century to identify the content of jobs, and the knowledge, skills and abilities that people will need to do them well.

Whether the basic unit is the job or the team, why should we be interested in the way it is organized? To the manager, the answer is obvious: to make work more efficient. If we can clarify the elements of jobs, we can organize them more efficiently. That, if you like, is the *unitarist* view as applied to job analysis, understanding its purpose on management's terms. But there is another answer: to make work more satisfying. According to this view, if we can clarify the elements of jobs, we should be able to organize them in a way that makes work more satisfying – more varied perhaps, or giving the worker the chance to express himself or herself. If we recognize the legitimacy of a concern with job satisfaction, then right at the start of our discussion we are plunged into the *pluralist* world-view, where we have two competing purposes for job analysis (efficiency and job satisfaction) that we will have to reconcile.

A pluralist point of view leads to a recognition of workers' *ownership* of the jobs they do, or in other words the right they have, within reason, to do their jobs in their own way. Yet this cuts across the classic approach to job analysis. Traditionally, job analysts have borrowed the expert's 'white coat' from the organizational dressing-up basket in order to assume the right to get involved in the minutest details of work, even to the extent of studying the body movements that a factory worker makes to perform some repetitive task. More recently, though, some have suggested that job analysts (and for that matter managers in general) should shift their emphasis from managing the *inputs* of work (the tasks the worker performs) to managing the *outputs* (what the worker achieves by performing those tasks). Take care of the outputs, they suggest, and the inputs will take care of themselves. This has the effect of giving the worker more discretion over how they do their jobs, even if it is not the reason why the shift of emphasis has taken place.

Our discussion has introduced three 'tensions' in the practice of job analysis, which we can represent like this:

- The *level* of job analysis: jobs versus teams
- The *purpose* of job analysis: efficiency versus job satisfaction/ownership
- The *focus* of job analysis: inputs versus outputs

For most of its history job analysis has been one of the most practical, and least controversial, areas of human resource practice. On the one hand, this means that it offers the HRM specialist a simple but powerful set of techniques that has a wide range of application, and most of us agree on how to use them. On the other hand, it means that job analysis has sometimes been just a little *dull*, lacking the lively debates that we have about employee relations, for example. In this chapter we are going to try to hang on to that valuable practical orientation, but inject some interest by dropping our fishing line into some holes in the ice, in the form of the 'tensions' we have listed, that job analysts usually prefer to try to skate over.

1.2   What is job analysis?

Job analysis involves collecting, analysing and presenting information about the content of jobs. Information is gathered from various sources, but primarily from the jobholder and those she/he directly works with, to establish the following:

- the quantitative and qualitative contributions of the job to end results, and how the job is done (the *job description*);
- the competencies necessary to do the job effectively (the *person specification*);
- the value added to the organization as a result of jobholders' efforts (the *performance indicators*).

Thus the job description describes the job, including its main purpose, responsibilities and key tasks, while the person specification lists the knowledge, abilities and other attributes that the jobholder needs to do the job well, and the performance indicators represent the contribution that the job is supposed to make to the performance of the organization.

1.3   What is job analysis for?

If you have a particularly good memory you know the answer to this question already. In Chapter 2 we used job analysis as our example of the SHRM concept of 'horizontal integration'. We chose job analysis as our example because it occupies a *pivotal* place in the sequence of HRM activities. We use the word 'pivotal' advisedly because so many of the activities use job analysis data as their starting point. You should look again now at Table 2.1 in Chapter 2.

The strength of the connections between job analysis data and other HRM activities shows us what job analysis is for: it exists to place the other HRM activities on a firmer footing, giving them a basis in systematic data. Jobs are not just the 'basic units' of work, but also the building blocks for the other HRM activities.

2   The process of job analysis

2.1   The process

The process of job analysis is shown in Figure 4.1. We have just seen how job analysis can be carried out for a variety of purposes, so it is important to identify the purpose of the analysis on any given occasion (this is point **(a)** in the figure).

We also need to use the most suitable approach (point **(b)**). For example, job analysis to design a selection procedure concentrates on the qualities that the successful candidate will need, in other words on the person specification, whereas job analysis to make decisions about gradings and pay concentrates on the level of work that the jobholder will do, in other words on the job description. Moreover, since job analysis can take a lot of time and money, we need to decide how thorough our analysis is going to be. Sometimes a 'quick and dirty' analysis is perfectly adequate.

Before we start our study, we need support from everyone affected (point **(c)**). First, senior management's commitment can add momentum, and also help to overcome any suspicions that staff have about the exercise. Second, we need the participation of relevant line managers to determine acceptable standards of work performance and to prepare job descriptions. Above all, we need the cooperation of jobholders themselves if we are to get full information about their jobs and, later on, if they are to act on the findings of our analysis. Finally, we may also want to keep trade union representatives in the picture.

Figure 4.1   The process of job analysis

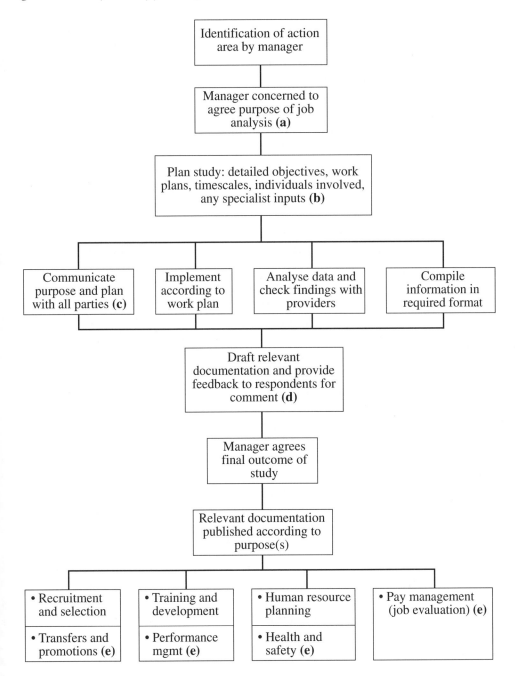

If we do not do all these things, staff suspicion and opposition may grow. Unless we communicate what we are doing actively, there is the risk that rumours will spread, for example that the job analysis exercise is a prelude to a redundancy programme.

Whatever the purpose of a job analysis, we will need to present its results, certainly to managers, and possibly to jobholders as well (point **(d)**). This ensures that our analysis is accurate, and that we have not missed anything important. Once all this is done, our analysis is complete, and we can go on to use the data for whatever purpose we have gathered it (point **(e)**).

2.2 'Big' and 'appropriate' job analysis

The process outlined assumes that job analysis is a formal and quite elaborate exercise. This is typically the case when a large number of jobs are included in the study, perhaps in more than one department. But sometimes managers do more informal ad hoc job analyses in their own sections or departments. Such studies, costing little or nothing other than the time they take, can be just as useful in their own way as a formal study. They give managers and staff the opportunity to collaborate to identify elements of cooperation between jobs, and to match the key tasks of their jobs with those of the work unit as a whole. They are one way of addressing task issues at the level of the team, something we return to later in the chapter. Job analysis thus becomes a means of organizational development, as well as a data source for HRM decisions. (You have probably noted that the distinction just made between formal, organization-wide job analysis and an ad hoc exercise carried out by an individual manager is akin to the distinction between 'big' and 'appropriate' planning that we made in Chapter 3.)

3   The job description

3.1 Techniques for identifying and mapping job elements

Job analysis aims to break jobs down into their constituent parts: the main activities or duties (the job description) and the knowledge, skills and abilities that jobholders need to do them (the person specification). Thus it implies that there is a 'subatomic' level (to continue our physics analogy) consisting of discrete particles that together make up the job. Seen in this light, job analysis is a set of techniques for identifying those 'discrete particles' and mapping them in some coherent way. In this section we will look at some techniques that we can use to identify duties and map them in a job description.[1] None of them is really self-sufficient, and it is always desirable to use at least two techniques so that we have two points of view on the job. In section 4 we will look at a technique (repertory grid) that we can use to identify knowledge, skills and abilities and map them in a person specification. Unlike the job description techniques, it can be self-sufficient.

3.2   Observation

The most obvious job analysis method is observation: observing the jobholder at work. A complete work cycle is observed and recorded in a standard format. The analyst then asks the employee to clarify any points that were not understood, and to identify any activities not observed. The method is relevant to simple, repetitive, short-cycle, unskilled or semi-skilled types of work, like those of machine operators, assembly workers and service personnel dealing with routine operations. Observation familiarizes the analyst with the materials and equipment used in the job and with working conditions and hazards.

There is no doubt that observation gives us information that we cannot get in any other way. For example, one of us was involved some years ago in identifying the training needs of staff who work in unemployment benefit offices in Birmingham in the UK. Managers were concerned that officers were not providing the unemployed people who were their clients with a good quality of service. We spent some time observing how benefit officers interviewed unemployed people who were claiming benefit. (So as not to disturb them unduly, we filmed the officers on video.) The immediate impression was that officers were indeed remote from the claimants they interviewed: there was little eye contact between officers and claimants. But this did not mean that the officers were aloof. On closer inspection, it became clear that, for both the officer and the unemployed person, the interview was largely a means to an end, the end being the completion of the benefit claim form – it was the form, and not the officer, that was the star of the show. Successful completion of the form was the key that unlocked the benefit that the claimant wanted. Thus both the officer *and the claimant* (one could equally have accused the claimant of being remote from the officer) directed their attention to the form. That was why there was so little eye contact, and so little sense of a relationship between the officer and the claimant.

Since observation is a fundamental job analysis technique, there are many approaches. Table 4.1 is an example of the way a sequence of behaviours can be recorded (in this case, the behaviours of a salesperson dealing with a new customer).

Table 4.1   Behaviour sequence – salesperson

Behaviour	Behaviour Sequence												
	1	2	3	4	5	6	7	8	9	10	11	12	13
Establishing needs		x							x				
Benefit statement			x							x			
Feature statement					x	x	x	x					x
Supporting				x									
Disagreeing												x	
Seeking information	x										x		

Source: Rackham and Morgan (1977).

Limitations of observation

Observation does have three limitations.

1 It is time-consuming: it takes much longer for an analyst to watch work being done than for the worker to describe to the analyst how he or she has done it.
2 It can be disruptive: the act of observation may affect how the job is performed. (Just think about a job analyst observing a police officer interviewing a suspect.)
3 Many jobs, especially senior ones, include cognitive activities that cannot be observed. There is a serious argument that the most important activity of a manager is mental – the manager reflecting on his or her job, possibly having brainwaves, like Archimedes, in the bath – and therefore unobservable (Carroll and Gillen, 1987). The Hungarian writer Arthur Koestler (1964), in his seminal book *The act of creation*, describes a scientist who had such a dramatic flash of inspiration that it made him fall off his bicycle on his way to his laboratory. What a job analyst would have observed was the scientist pedalling his bicycle. But it was not the observable activity of cycling that was part of the scientist's job; it was the unobservable activity of thinking.

3.3   Observation in work study and time and motion study

'Work study' represents one very specific and detailed application of observation (for the purposes of our discussion we can treat work study and time and motion study as different terms for the same thing). It grew directly out of Frederick Winslow Taylor's 'scientific management', which we referred to in Chapter 1. Figures 4.2 and 4.3

Figure 4.2   Serving dinners in a hospital ward (I)

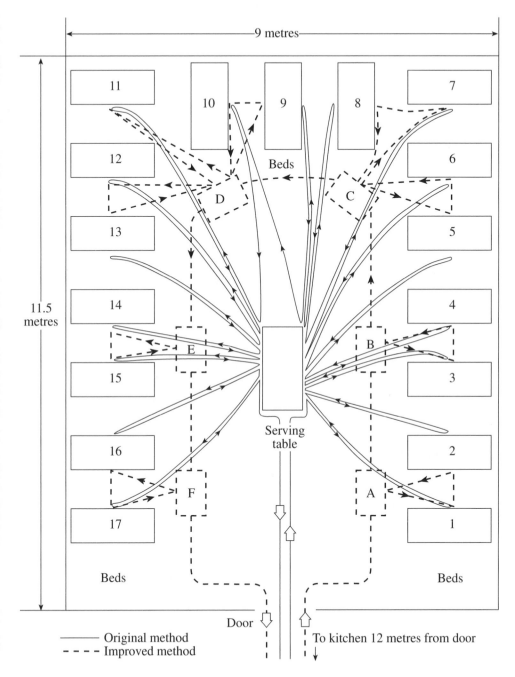

Source: Kanawaty (1992).

Figure 4.3   Serving dinners in a hospital ward (II)

Flow process chart			Worker type		
Chart No. 7 Sheet No. *1* of *1*			Summary		

Subject charted: *Hospital nurse*	Activity	Present	Proposed	Saving
	Operation ○	34	18	16
	Transport ▷	60	72	(–12)
Activity: *Serve dinners to 17 patients*	Delay D	–	–	–
	Inspection ▢	–	–	–
	Storage ▽	–	–	–
Method: Present/Proposed	Distance (m)	436	197	239
Location: *Ward L*	Time (work-h)	39	28	11
Operative(s): Clock No.	Cost	–	–	–
	Labour	–	–	–
Charted by: Date:	Material (*Trolley*)	–	$24	–
Approved by: Date:	Total (*Capital*)		$24	

Description Original method	Qty. (*plates*)	Distance (m)	Time (min.)	○	▷	D	▢	▽	Remarks
Transports first course and plates –									Awkward load
kitchen to serving table on tray	17	16	.50						
Places dishes and plates on table	17	–	.30						
Serves from three dishes to plate	–	–	.25						
Carries plate to bed 1 and returns	1	7.3	.25						
Serves	–	–	.25						
Carries plate to bed 2 and returns	1	6	.23						
Serves	–	–	.25						
(Continues until all 17 beds are									
served. See Figure 4.2 for distances)									
Service completed, places dishes on									
tray and returns to kitchen	–	16	.50						
Total distance and time, first cycle		192	10.71	17	20	–	–	–	
Repeats cycle for second course		192	10.71	17	20	–	–	–	
Collects empty second course plates		52	2.0	–	20	–	–	–	
Total		436	23.42	34	60				
Improved method									
Transports first course and plates –									Serving
kitchen to position A – trolley	17	16	.50						trolley
Serves two plates	–	–	.40						
Carries two plates to bed 1: leaves one;		⌈ 1.5 ⌉							
carries on plate from bed 1 to bed 2;	2	0.6	.25						
returns to position A		⌊ 1.5 ⌋							
Pushes trolley to position B	–	3.0	.12						
Serves two plates	–	–	.40						
Carries two plates to bed 3; leaves one;		⌈ 1.5 ⌉							
carries one plate from bed 3 to bed 4;	2	0.6	.25						
returns to position B		⌊ 1.5 ⌋							
(Continues until all 17 beds are served.									
See Figure 4.2 and note variation									
at bed 11)									
Returns to kitchen with trolley	–	16	.50						
Total distance and time, first cycle	–	72.5	7.49	9	26				
Repeats cycle for second course	–	72.5	7.49	9	26				
Collects empty second course plates	–	52	2.00	–	20				
Total	–	197	16.98	18	72				

Source: Kanawaty (1992).

show how meals are delivered to patients in a hospital ward. The format is confusing, but what is going on is straightforward.

Figure 4.2 shows the work study analyst's analysis of how the work is being done at present, with the analyst's breakdown of how it could be done better superimposed on it. The single continuous line shows how the work is done at present. It shows the server entering the ward at the bottom, putting the meals on a central serving table, and then walking backwards and forwards to each bed in turn (shown by a double line), delivering one meal at a time. How the work could be done better is shown by the broad dotted line. It shows the server entering the ward with the meals on a trolley, which she (let us assume the server is female) 'parks' at points A, B, C, D, E and F as she moves round the ward. As she does not have to walk as far from the trolley to the bed as from the serving table to the bed, she can carry two meals at a time. So the meals get served more quickly. Apart from being more efficient for the server, there is a better chance of the meal still being warm when the patient gets it.

Figure 4.3 shows how the analyst recorded all this on a standard form. You will see how it records in minute detail the *time* the server took as well as the movements, or *motions* she made: hence 'time and motion study'.

Detailed information as in the salesperson and meals server examples we have just discussed can be the basis for a precise job description, which can be used to monitor the performance of the employee. Gareth Morgan (1986) gives the example of a checklist for a counter assistant in a fast food restaurant (Table 4.2).

3.4   The 'tension' between efficiency and job satisfaction and ownership

At this point you are probably starting to feel a bit uneasy. Should we be prescribing to workers how they should do their jobs in such detail, as if they were robots? If you do feel uneasy, you are in good company, for if you have come across work study or time and motion study already, it is probably as something that your organization used to do, but does not do any more. Work study has suffered the same fate as the practice of 'scientific management' as a whole from which it derives. Gareth Morgan (1986), and even Brannick and Levine (2002) in their job analysis textbook, criticize it for treating people like machines: Morgan sardonically suggests that scientific management was actually ahead of its time, being

Table 4.2 A management observation checklist

Greeting the customer	Yes	No

1 There is a smile.
2 It is a sincere greeting.
3 There is eye contact.
Other:

Taking the order	Yes	No

1 The counter person is thoroughly familiar with the menu ticket (no hunting for items).
2 The customer has to give the order only once.
3 Small orders (four items or fewer) are memorized rather than written down.
4 There is suggestive selling.
Other:

Assembling the order	Yes	No

1 The order is assembled in the proper sequence.
2 Grill slips are handed in first.
3 Drinks are poured in the proper sequence.
4 Proper amount of ice.
5 Cups slanted and finger used to activate.
6 Drinks are filled to the proper level.
7 Drinks are capped.
8 Clean cups.
9 Holding times are observed on coffee.
10 Cups are filled to the proper level on coffee.
Other:

Presenting the order	Yes	No

1 It is properly packaged.
2 The bag is double folded.
3 Plastic trays are used if eating inside.
4 A tray liner is used.
5 The food is handled in a proper manner.
Other:

Asking for & receiving payment	Yes	No

1 The amount of the order is stated clearly and loud enough to hear.
2 The denomination received is clearly stated.
3 The change is counted out loud.
4 Change is counted efficiently.
5 Large bills are laid on the till until the change is given.
Other:

Thanking the customer & asking for repeat business	Yes	No

1 There is always a thank you.
2 The thank you is sincere.
3 There is eye contact.
4 Return business was asked for.
Other:

Source: Morgan (1986: 21)

particularly suited to robot production, such as most car factories now use.

This issue relates to the second of the 'tensions' that we pointed to at the start of the chapter, between job analysis being used to increase efficiency as opposed to job satisfaction and ownership. It is easy to see that imposing a rigid job description like that in Table 4.2 could reduce job satisfaction, with many workers resenting their loss of autonomy. The same might apply to the hospital meals server's job in Figure 4.3: even if she could recognize that the new arrangement was more efficient, she might be unhappy, once again, that she had lost 'ownership' of her job because this working method had been imposed on her.

Yet there must be something to be said for reorganizing work so that patients get their meals while they are still warm, as in the example we looked at earlier. When we were writing this chapter, a colleague told us that a children's hospital in London had realized that some children who had suffered an accident were dying simply because of the length of time it took to get them from the Accident and Emergency department to the recovery ward. They therefore asked the British Williams Formula One motor racing team to help them organize this stage in the treatment. Why a motor racing team? If you have watched motor racing on TV, you will realize that motor racing teams are incredibly skilful in changing car tyres when a car has to go into 'the pits' (the area where cars are serviced) in the middle of a race: the whole operation can be done in a matter of seconds. The hospital was hoping that Williams would be able to apply the same skill to the way they organized treatment of accident victims. And probably all of us would agree that any time and motion study that would lead to children's lives being saved is a very worthwhile activity.

In short, the application of work study methods based on very detailed observation may have fallen out of fashion, partly owing to the ethical distaste that they have inspired, but they still have a lot to offer to the analysis of complex, frequently repeated work processes that cannot be mechanized. But they must not be conducted in a way that is to workers' detriment, if only because they will get such a bad reputation if they are that it will be impossible to continue with them. Thus, very ironically, this job analysis method, which has been so hostile to workers' interests in the past, must in future be carried out in a way that respects workers' sense of 'ownership' of their jobs and that does not detract from their job satisfaction, if it is to survive and realize its potential contribution to work efficiency.

3.5   The Critical Incident technique

Background

'Critical Incident' is one of the oldest, and possibly the best known, job analysis techniques. It grew out of job studies carried out in the US armed forces in World War II. It is associated with J. C. Flanagan (1954), whose seminal article is still widely quoted.

It is simple in essence. The 'incidents' are events which a jobholder or other stakeholder who knows the job well is asked to identify. They are 'critical' in the sense that what the jobholder did in the event in question was critical to successful performance in the post. The technique is, therefore, incisive and *qualitative*. There is an implicit prioritizing of tasks which we may not get from the more mechanical, *quantitative* methods which focus on quantifiable aspects such as the amount of time a jobholder spends on different duties.

On the other hand, Critical Incident paints a deliberately selective picture of a job: a jobholder might not refer to the duty that she spends most of her time carrying out. For example, a train conductor might refer only to incidents where she had to deal with abuse or the threat of violence from a passenger, ignoring the mundane business of checking tickets. Thus Critical Incident data do not stand alone, and need to be complemented by data from some other source. A second disadvantage is that there may be a *recency effect*: that is, the interviewee may concentrate disproportionately on recent and vivid incidents. Further, because it is backward-looking, it cannot be used to analyse new jobs. Finally, jobholders may be reluctant to volunteer critical incidents which show them in a bad light.

Carrying out a Critical Incident interview

Critical Incident works like this:

1 The interviewer asks the jobholder (or manager or other stakeholder), 'Can you give me an example of an incident that was critical to work performance? This could be either something that went very well or something that went badly wrong.'
2 In response to the interviewee's reply, the interviewer presses for more detail. For example, she or he might ask, 'Can you tell me *exactly* what happened in this situation?'
3 Having completed discussion of one critical incident, the interviewer goes on to ask about others. (It is a matter of judgement or common sense at what point to close the interview. You will sense when the interviewee has started to repeat her/himself, or has nothing more to say.)

(Note that it is not necessary to pursue each incident in great detail. Going into greater detail will mean going into the *behaviour* of the interviewee. While this will shed useful light on skills and abilities, it will duplicate work you will do later on when you come to draw up a person specification, especially if you use a technique like a repertory grid.

Note also that it is more useful to have superficial information about a fairly large number of incidents than detailed information about a small number.)

4 The interviewer goes on to conduct more Critical Incident interviews. It is important to do a minimum of two, to guard against getting an idiosyncratic picture of the job painted by one individual. Again, it is a matter of common sense how many you will do. One consideration is that you may want to interview the important stakeholders so that their views are represented.
5 Having completed your interviews, the next stage is to process the material. It is recommended, rough-and-ready though this might sound, that you clear a big space in front of you, and put all the critical incidents down. (It helps if you can jot a 'title' for each incident onto a slip of paper.)
6 You then group the incidents into piles.
7 You have now come to the end of the Critical Incident process. At this point you should combine the Critical Incident data with data from other sources (exit interviews, existing job descriptions and so on).

3.6 Exit interviews

Exit interviews are, very simply, interviews conducted with a member of staff who has recently left, or who is about to leave, a job or an employer. Their purpose always includes asking the jobholder why they have left. Unlike the Critical Incident technique, exit interviews have not been developed in the context of job analysis. They are used primarily as a way of getting feedback for the organization on why someone has left a job. There may, for example, be an unacceptably high turnover in the job, and we do not know why. Exit interviews may give us the answer.

The value of exit interviews
Box 4.1 gives a real example.

Box 4.1   Understanding high turnover

A former colleague worked with mentally handicapped adults in a Social Services Day Centre in England. She was the 'key worker' for a 23-year-old woman who came to the Centre during the day to give her family a break. This woman had very difficult behaviour. For example, if unable to get her way, she would tear her hair out or tear at her flesh. If restrained by a member of staff, she might then try to tear at the staff member's flesh. My acquaintance discovered some time after she had started the job that her two predecessors in the post had left after a short time as a direct result of their inability to cope with this client.

Although in one sense the client's behaviour was well known to other staff in the Centre, in another sense it was not known at all: when my acquaintance was recruited, no mention of this client was made to her, and there was no indication that Centre managers were aware that the client was the reason why they were losing staff. A system of exit interviews would almost certainly have revealed the reason why staff were leaving.

Exit interviews are, so to speak, a way of putting a finger on the pulse of an organization. They provide information about the health of the organization which probably cannot be obtained in any other way. One reason for this is that a departing jobholder is much more likely to feel free to criticize his or her boss when they have another job to go to, since the boss now has less power over them. Thus their value lies in the simple fact that no one knows as much about a job as the person doing it. When that person leaves the organization, a unique source of information is lost. The nature of the job may have changed gradually over time, in a way that has not been noticed by the supervisor. The jobholder may have built up informal networks or contacts who can help get the job done more smoothly. These are two examples, and no doubt you will be able to think of others.

Conducting an exit interview

In what follows we have given a step-by-step guide to conducting an exit interview, and to processing the information which the interview generates.

1 Set up a procedure where a jobholder's resignation triggers off an invitation to an exit interview. Contact the individual directly. Explain the purpose of the interview as explicitly as you can (there may well be suspicions about what you are up to). Stress that the interview is voluntary, and that the information from it will be confidential, although you may use it without attributing it to its source.

2 Follow an interview structure such as the following one.

   (a) *General remarks.* How did you find the job? Which parts did you particularly like? Which did you particularly dislike?

   (b) *Job description* (if one exists, even if it is only an outline). How accurate is this as a statement of what you did in the job?
        You should go on from discussion of the job description to develop a more accurate picture of the job, as follows.

   (c) *Principal duties.* You should establish with the interviewee which are the principal duties. If the jobholder comes up with a very long list, you should encourage him/her to group items under headings. There should be not more than about nine separate headings.

   (d) *Work quantity.* Having established the principal duties, you should ask the jobholder to estimate the proportion of his or her time that was spent on each of them.

   (e) *Work quality.* Ask the jobholder if there are duties which took little time but which were disproportionately important. (And conversely, perhaps, duties which took a lot of time but which were disproportionately unimportant.)

   (f) *Priority of items.* Now ask the interviewee to place the items in a priority order, giving due weight both to the amount of time (*quantity*) that he or she spent doing them, and their relative importance (*quality*).

   (g) *The future.* Jobs are never static. Ask the jobholder to look over the material you have recorded up to now. Then ask him or her to say what changes are likely to come about in the foreseeable future in the way the job gets done.

   (h) *Any other business.* Finally, give the jobholder the chance to say anything else that may occur to him or her which is relevant to the task of putting together a job description.

   (i) *Further interviews.* When using an exit interview as part of a job analysis, you will normally only interview the departing jobholder. It is, however, possible to complement the data from that interview by conducting a second interview with someone who left the post some time ago but is still in the organization. This is possible in organizations which promote from within, and where it is likely that there will be a previous jobholder or jobholders working in another department.

Using the interview data

You will be aware from other parts of this chapter that no job analysis technique should be used in isolation. After the interview you will therefore have to combine the data from your exit interview, or interviews, with data from other sources, such as a Critical Incident interview.

3.7   Questionnaire methods

Questionnaires provide structured information in a way that takes much less of the job analyst's time, and their results can be analysed statistically. They are cheap when large numbers of jobs are involved in a study. Box 4.2 contains a checklist for designing your own questionnaire.

Box 4.2   Checklist for preparing questionnaires

Objectives
1 Have you clearly identified the problem to be tackled by the analysis?
2 Have you established the objectives of the questionnaire?
3 Have you determined what information you need?
4 Are you sure the information does not already exist in some other form?

Practicality
5 Have you established the necessary validation procedure?
6 Do you intend to computerize the information?
7 Will the layout allow you to edit and code responses?
8 Have you worked out the collating procedures?
9 Will answers to the questionnaire be kept confidential? (If they will, say so in the heading; if not, ask respondents to state any information which should be kept confidential.)
10 How many questionnaires do you need to get filled in to give you an adequate sample?

Question content and wording
11 Are there any unnecessary questions?
12 Is the questionnaire longer than is absolutely necessary?
13 Will respondents have the information they need to give accurate answers?
14 Will respondents be able to answer any non-factual questions?
15 Are the questions precise?
16 Are there any open-ended questions which could be turned into multiple choice questions?
17 Are there technical words and jargon which respondents will not understand?
18 Have you tried to put yourself in the respondent's shoes?

Validation
19 Do you need to administer the questionnaire to a test sample to validate its design?
20 Do you need to pre-test alternative versions?

See Local Government Training Board (undated).

3.8   Other techniques for drawing up a job description

We have by no means exhausted all the relevant techniques, but, in view of pressure of space, we will now briefly review the main features of just four more of them, following the account given by Pearn and Kandola (1993, ch. 3).

Self-description diaries or logs
Jobholders are asked to keep a record using a suitable unit of time, such as hour-by-hour or half-day by half-day. Pearn and Kandola give the example of asking the managers of English pubs to keep a daily record of their activities.

Interviews
Interviews are flexible and participative. We say more about them in Chapter 6.

Checklists/inventories
These are prepared lists of job tasks which mean that the job analyst does not have to start from scratch, but can ask jobholders or their managers to indicate whether the jobholder does a particular task, and possibly also how often he or she does it and how important it is. They are useful where we want to get information from all jobholders in the case of a job that is done by a large number of people. Table 4.3 is an example of a checklist, used to identify the tasks carried out by a training specialist in one area of their work.

Hierarchical task analysis
This enables the jobholder to break a job down into a 'hierarchy' of key tasks, support tasks and other tasks. Jobholders use their knowledge to build a model of their own jobs, entering each task on a card. The cards are laid out in front of the jobholder in a hierarchical arrangement, with the main tasks at the top. As the analyst asks probing questions about job content, cards can be moved until the most realistic assessment of the job is achieved. New cards may be added, to show tasks that are not in the current job description. Performance standards can be added to each task statement, and the knowledge and skills demanded by each task can be written on the back of the respective card when a person specification is drawn up.

3.9   A job description format

We conclude this review of methods with two job descriptions which use a typical format (Figures 4.4 and 4.5). Both come from public

Table 4.3   Job analysis checklist

Work area 1: Identifying training/learning needs – gathering information

Listed below are the tasks included in a 'task group'. Add at the bottom any tasks you do which are not listed.	Indicate how often you do each task by placing a tick (✓) in the appropriate box.			
Task group	Never	Sometimes	Often	Very often
1 Design surveys				
2 Design questionnaires				
3 Carry out surveys				
4 Construct trainee nomination forms				
5 Interview line managers				
6 Interview potential trainees				
7 Attend meetings with managers				
8 Design job description formats				
9 Carry out job analyses				
10 Carry out task analyses				
11 Write job descriptions				

Source: Adapted from Morgan and Costello, quoted in Pearn and Kandola (1993: 37).

agencies in a developing country in Africa. The format is concise, with all the information contained in less than two A4-size pages.

4   The person specification

4.1   The importance of the person specification

Having said what a job consists of, the logical next step is to say what attributes the jobholder will need to do it well. This is the stage of job analysis that we would like you to try for yourself. In one form or another, most of us are familiar with the notion of a job description. The person specification, however, may be new to you.[2]

The point of the person specification is that there are some HRM decisions for which we need to know, not so much the duties of the job that they relate to, as the personal qualities the jobholder will need to do those duties well. This is particularly true for recruitment and selection,

Figure 4.4   Job description (library assistant)

Name of postholder (if applicable)	. . . .
Prepared by	. . . .
Job title and grade	Library assistant (small research institute library)
Department/section	Library
Responsible to*	Librarian
Responsible for*	(No subordinate staff)
(*Titles of posts)	
Liaison with	Chief administrative officer of the institute (for financial arrangements, acquisitions, database hardware etc); other library assistants
Purpose of job	To operate the library systems on a day-to-day basis in the interests of users

Main activities (in priority order)

Title of activity	Purpose of activity
(Max. 6 words)	(To . . . .)
Serving the needs of borrowers	To check in and issue books to borrowers, giving advice as necessary
Dealing with requests	To write recall notices, manage the reservations file and issue collect notices to borrowers
Managing stocks	To organize and maintain library shelves according to classified order on a daily basis
Adding new materials to stock	To receive, classify and place new acquisitions in library
Providing database info. to users	To conduct on request searches of the database to identify specific items for borrowers
Journal contents distribution	To photocopy and display photocopies of contents pages of journals

which is the subject of Chapter 6: as you will see, we are most likely to get the best person for the job when our selection is based on the person specification. But we may also use the person specification in performance management, to compare an individual's current skills with the

Figure 4.5   Job description (principal human resource officer)

Name of postholder (if applicable)	. . . .
Prepared by	. . . .
Job title and grade	Principal Human Resource Officer, level II
Department/section	Public Service Department, Section PM.1
Responsible to*	Chief Human Resource Officer
Responsible for*	Two senior HRM officers
(*Titles of posts)	
Liaison with	Chairman of the Public Service Commission; human resource officers in departments; senior line managers
Purpose of job	To develop human resource policies and manage senior employee resourcing to meet the strategic needs of the public service; to manage employee relations in the best interests of the service

Main activities (in priority order)

Title of activity	Purpose of activity
(Max. 6 words)	(To . . . .)
Human resource policy	To advise the Chief Human Resource Officer on major changes required in the General Orders to clarify existing procedures and to meet the emergent needs of the Service, bearing in mind the need for consistency and equity
Staff management	To manage staff in Section PM.1 to meet the objective of the Public Service Department, taking into account the abilities, personal needs and development potential of staff
Recruitment and selection	To manage the recruitment and selection process for vacancies and new posts arising at levels 7–10, in all departments, ensuring that professional standards are maintained
Induction	To design induction programmes for newly appointed officers at levels 7–10, so they are oriented to the goals and values of the service and performing in their jobs to the required standard within two months
Conditions of service	To review and decide on the interpretation of General Orders on cases in doubt referred by departmental human resource officers, where necessary making reference to the Public Service Commission, drawing a fair balance between the interests of the Service and of individuals
Information circulars	To provide guidelines on the contents and design of internal circulars relating to a range of staff matters, so that staff are kept fully informed of new developments

skills we believe the job ideally needs, and in learning and training, where our plans for an individual's development may be based partly on the gap between an individual's current skills and, once again, what the job ideally needs (we call this the 'performance gap').

A personal anecdote will illustrate this last point. When one of us moved in 1986 from adult education into an organizational training job with a large English local authority, his boss drew his attention to the need for consultancy skills. An organizational trainer needs to be able to operate as an internal consultant, working with managers and departments to identify their training needs and designing a learning and training programme to meet those needs – you may know this already. This was not the most important part of the job, but it was certainly the one where the gap between his performance and the ideal performance that the job required was greatest! His experience up to that point had given him no experience of operating in this way. His boss identified a four-day 'trainer into consultant' training course which helped him to develop the role.

So we think it is important to spend some time in this chapter on the person specification. We are going to present just one technique, so-called 'repertory grid', but we are going to look at it in detail.

4.2   Using repertory grid to draw up a person specification

Background
Repertory grid is a technique for eliciting how individuals 'construe' some aspect of the world they live in. It is called 'repertory grid' because it reveals an individual's 'repertory' of ways of looking at a particular aspect of their world and because, in its most detailed application, it maps them in a grid. It reveals what it does by establishing the categories that individuals use when they think about that aspect of the world. One can establish, for example, that a certain person thinks about other people in terms of their sense of humour and their intelligence. Such an individual, when talking about other people, will typically make remarks like 'He's very boring', or 'She's very bright'.

The technique derives from Personal Construct theory, first developed by the American psychologist George Kelly in his careers advice work with young people in the United States (Kelly, 1955). It assumes that everyone has their own distinctive personal 'constructs' for viewing the world. While one person may think about other people in terms of their sense of humour and their intelligence, another may think mainly in terms of their dependability and whether they are hardworking or not.

The point of repertory grid is to make these construct systems explicit. This is reckoned to be valuable because most of us are not fully conscious of the 'constructs' that we use. Thus, for example, a young person choosing a career might not realize that being able to work on his own is more important to him than anything else, more important even than job security or being able to earn a lot of money. To put it in repertory grid jargon, 'working on your own' is a prominent construct in his construct system for 'the ideal job'. Rather than finding that out the hard way through working in jobs that are well paid but which he cannot stand because he hates taking orders from someone else, repertory grid might help him to recognize and act on his strong preference at the start of his career.

Repertory grid as a job analysis technique

Over the last 30 years the technique has been applied in a variety of settings. Therapists, for example, have used it in their work with people who are mentally ill. In the recent past it has grown in popularity as a job analysis technique which helps the analyst to get a very clear picture of job requirements. It does this by drawing on the categories – the 'construct systems' – that individuals already have in their minds when they think about jobs.

What follows is a step-by-step guide to using repertory grid to draw up a person specification.

Using repertory grid to draw up a person specification

1   Identify a person who knows the job and whom you can interview about it. (This can be any 'stakeholder': the person doing the job now, that person's supervisor, a colleague, a client, and so on.)
2   Ask the person to think about three[3] people who have done the job and whose performance the interviewee has some knowledge of. The first two should be people who have done the job well; the third should be someone who has done the job (relatively) poorly.
3   Ask the person to bracket in their minds the two people who have done the job well. Ask, 'What did they have in common that made them good at the job?' Write down the replies on separate slips of paper.
4   Now ask, 'What made the third person poor at the job?' Write down the replies.

Table 4.4 sets out the replies we got from a Careers Officer when we interviewed her about a clerical assistant post in her office.

The table contains the raw material of a person specification, but as it stands it is a jumble of skills, personality traits and behavioural statements. Some of the items are clear (for example, 'rarely took time off;

Table 4.4 Raw data from repertory grid interview

Clerical assistants who are both good	Clerical assistant who is poor
• conscientious • personal pride • wanted to do well • willing to learn: keen to pick things up • rarely took time off; punctual • fitted in very well and quickly • able to pick things up • willing to ask if not sure • had experience of work • willing to learn and accept supervision • initiative: thinks about what she's doing • welcoming, pleasant, cheerful manner • reliable, punctual • keen • integrated into office	• inability to pick up things (e.g. postcards filled in wrongly) • unable to admit having made a mistake • slow • immature: came to work late because of row with father • not suited to clerical work

punctual'), some are not clear, either because they are vague ('not suited to clerical work') or because they represent personality traits that could mean different things to different people ('conscientious'). There is also some repetition ('keen'). So we need to refine the list, which we do as follows:

5 For any item which is unclear, ask: 'What did you see the person *doing*[4] that gave you the evidence to say that he/she was good at the job/poor at the job?'[5] (You may obtain one or several statements at this point, depending on how much your interviewee has to say.) Once again, write down the replies on separate slips of paper.
6 If possible, go on to a second 'triad' of people that the interviewee has seen doing the job and repeat the above stages. If that is not possible – probably because the interviewee does not know three more people who have done the job – you can get complementary data by using one of the 'alternative approaches' which we outline below.

Two alternative approaches to using repertory grid
Although we have only reached the halfway point in the repertory grid process, we interrupt our description to explain that there are a couple of other ways that we can reach it.

In our experience, the approach we have just outlined is the most powerful, because most of us find it easier to talk about real human beings than about abstract job duties; hence the enduring appeal of gossip and TV 'soap operas'. However, your interviewee may not know enough people who have done the job to make the above approach possible. This could be because the interviewee is new to his or her job and so has only come into contact with the job in question recently; or because there are only one or two people who do the job; or because the job is a new one. If so, you can conduct the repertory grid interview like this:

I   Ask your interviewee to:

- write the (not more than 10) key duties of the job on slips of paper (he or she can use a job description if one already exists)
- take out two at random and say what knowledge, skills or abilities are needed to do both of them
- take out a third and say what knowledge, skills or abilities are needed to do it which are not needed for the other two
- repeat the process by 'shuffling the pack' one or more times until your interviewee has nothing more to say.

(You will notice that we preserve the 'triad' structure here [see note 3]: the only difference is that the contrasting elements are job duties rather than people who have done the job.)

II   Alternatively, you can ask him or her to talk about their ideal jobholder, contrasting that imaginary person with the interviewee's idea of the worst possible jobholder.

Whichever approach you have used up to this point – and repertory grid is flexible enough to be used in different ways – you should now have a large mound of slips of paper that is beginning to look like the raw material for a person specification. The next stage is to sort it. You do it like this:

7 Ask your interviewee to group the slips into piles in whatever way makes sense to him or her.
8 Agree with your interviewee a title for each pile (you may need to help him or her with this).
9 Lastly, ask the interviewee to put those titles into priority order.

That is the end of the repertory grid interview. Before moving on to draw up your person specification, however, you should carry out at least one more repertory grid interview, in order to get a second opinion on what the job requires (your first interviewee may well have had an idiosyncratic view of some aspect of the job). If you have personal knowledge of the job, you might 'interview' yourself!

Processing the repertory grid data
Once you have completed at least two interviews, you will have two (or more) lists of personal attributes in priority order, representing the 'titles' that your interviewees listed, with each attribute supported by a number of separate behavioural statements (these are the slips of paper that your interviewees grouped into piles). The next step is to combine the items in the two (or more) lists. We tend to do this mechanically, giving a weighted score for each item depending on how high a priority each interviewee gave to it.

Once you have a single list in priority order, it is only a matter of finding a suitable format for the person specification. The format we like to use comes from Smith and Robertson (1993). Figure 4.6 is a person specification which one of us drew up for the post of lecturer using this format, based on repertory grid interviews with two of his lecturer colleagues. You will notice that it 'fleshes out' the person specification items (consultancy skills and so on) by listing 'positive and negative indicators' ('relates well to clients and learners', 'relates badly to clients and learners' and so on). This was done by drawing on the behavioural statements which were originally written down on separate slips of paper in the two repertory grid interviews. The items are also listed in priority order, reflecting the priority that the two interviewees gave to them.

4.3   Further points on person specifications based on repertory grid

So that is what a person specification produced using repertory grid looks like. We hope you agree that it gives us a rich picture of what someone needs to do a job. There are just three further points to make about it.

The relevance of qualifications and experience
The first is about an inherent limitation of the repertory grid method. What we usually obtain is a rich list of the knowledge, skills and abilities that a job requires. As a rule, the list does not include professional or academic qualifications, or even previous relevant work experience. Thus, although our lecturer colleagues have qualifications that go from a simple undergraduate degree (in the case of two recently retired colleagues) to a PhD (the majority of us), 'a higher

Figure 4.6   Person specification (lecturer in Human Resources)

Negative indicators	Positive indicators
Consultancy Skills Relates badly to clients and learners: overpowers, or fails to respect their views	Relates well to clients and learners: recognizes primacy of client or learner; listens to them
Counselling Skills Is self- rather than client-centred in dealing with clients and learners. Insists on own agenda, emphasizes own knowledge at the expense of the client/learner's	Demonstrates core counselling qualities: unconditional positive regard, empathy, congruence and genuineness
Feedback Skills Retains information; assumes that client/learner understands; feedback is shoddy or obscure	Gives clear, appropriate and timely feedback; checks understanding; invites questions and handles them skilfully
Facilitative Style Dull, self-centred teaching style induces passiveness and boredom in learners and clients	Emphasis on learners' and clients' learning leads to enthusiasm and interest
Presentation Skills Presentations and lectures are unprepared, unclear, disorganized and/or woolly	Presentations and lectures are well-prepared, clear, well-organized and incisive
Team Skills Works in isolation from colleagues; prefers to complete projects unassisted	Engages colleagues in discussion about teaching and research; works collaboratively
Subject Knowledge Knowledge is stale; conveys view that subject is static and has fixed boundaries	Teaching and research are informed by recent developments; draws on new ideas in teaching and research
Analytical Skills Thinking is directionless and disordered; wrestles ineffectually with problems	Establishes and communicates clear analytical frameworks; resolves knotty problems
Mental Agility Thinks on tramlines; pursues line of thought doggedly or overcautiously; impervious to new ideas suggested by research or by clients and learners; does not publish	Changes direction when new ideas require it; seeks out new ideas; takes risks; writes for publication
Energy and Commitment Squanders time; works slowly; is discouraged by setbacks; lags behind clients and learners; neglects commitments	Works quickly; takes initiatives; 'moves up a gear' when necessary; honours commitments

degree' is not one of the attributes listed in the lecturer person specification. This is simply because neither of the colleagues on whose repertory grid interviews the person specification was based thought that it was part of the difference between good and bad lecturers (likewise previous work experience).

Now this is very different from the experience most of us have of applying for jobs. Usually employers place a lot of weight on formal qualifications and work experience. Indeed the tendency of many employers, especially in developing countries, to place *too much* weight on qualifications, distorting education so that it becomes a 'paper chase' for school and university certificates at the expense of learning, has been labelled the 'diploma disease' (Dore, 1997). Similarly, at levels beyond the school leaver or fresh graduate levels, employers usually emphasize work experience.

What the person specification format we are using here implies, however, is that what really matters is *knowledge and skills*. It is not that qualifications and experience do not matter, but rather that they are useful to employers to the extent that they have enabled applicants to develop the knowledge and skills they need to work effectively. And, as all of us will agree, it is possible to develop knowledge and skills on the job rather than by doing a formal course. It is possible, for example, to have good consultancy skills without doing a course, just as it is possible to do a course but still come out the other end with bad consultancy skills.

All well and good, we hope: we will explore the implications of the point we have just made for learning and training in Chapter 8. But our iconoclastic view creates a problem. For it is actually impossible to use a person specification like this at the recruitment and selection stage to draw up a 'shortlist' of five or six people from a large number of applicants. We simply cannot identify candidates' *skills* from a written application form. (Just think about 'energy and commitment' as an example here.) Thus, if you are using a person specification for recruitment and selection, and you need to carry out a 'shortlisting', you will need to list some qualifications and/or experience in the person specification that will enable you to choose between the written applications you receive. (We discuss shortlisting in Chapter 6.)

Essential and desirable requirements
The second point is that person specifications usually make a distinction between essential and desirable requirements. We define an *essential requirement* as one without which a person is simply unable to do the job. Required professional qualifications (for example, in medicine) are an example, as are in certain jobs, simple but important things like the ability to drive a car or to work at weekends. We must reject out of hand any candidate who fails to meet an essential requirement, however strong they may be in other areas.

We define a *desirable requirement* as anything that contributes significantly to effective performance but is not essential. We decide whether something is a desirable requirement by applying this rule of thumb: *other things being equal, is someone who meets this requirement likely to be better at the job than someone who does not?*

Not more than nine separate items

Finally, a person specification should contain no more than nine separate items. This is because very long person specifications are unwieldy to use in other HRM activities, especially recruitment and selection (we will see why that is in Chapter 6). The fact that the repertory grid technique enables us to prioritize the items is helpful here.

4.4   Short cuts

The greater the effort, the better the job analysis. But time is not always available, and we must not allow 'the best to be the enemy of the good'. Moreover, we may need an 'appropriate' rather than 'big' job analysis method that we can recommend to a non-specialist line manager. The next activity (Study task 1) asks you to review the format of an 'appropriate' person specification, for the post of Library Assistant in a developing country research institute. It complements the job description you looked at earlier. You will notice that the relevant knowledge, skills and abilities are simply inferred from the job duties as listed in the job description.

Certainly this person specification has some weak points, but it is worthwhile if the alternative is to have no person specification at all.

4.5   Summary

In this section we have explained the importance of the person specification and why it is distinct from the job description. We presented the repertory grid technique as a way of generating a rich person specification, but we also saw that there are some short cuts we can take if we are in a hurry.

5   Performance indicators

At the start of the chapter we referred to three 'tensions'. The third of them was to do with the *focus* of job analysis, and the trend in recent

Study task 1: what are the strong and weak points of the person specification in Figure 4.7?

Figure 4.7   Person specification (library assistant)

Name of postholder (if applicable) . . . .

Job title and grade . . . . Library Assistant . . . .

Specification prepared by . . . .

Title of activity (from JD)	Knowledge	Skills (SK)
Serving the needs of borrowers	Principles of issuing system How library is arranged	Communication skills Pleasant but firm disposition Ability to work under pressure Operation of database
Dealing with requests	How reservation system works	Willingness and ability to interpret requests Writing recall/collect notices Keeping reservations file in order
Managing stocks	Classification: understanding of decimal ordering	Tidy, orderly approach
Adding new materials to stock	Understanding of arrangement of author catalogue	Word processing skills
Providing database information to users	How database is organized, and how documents are keyworded Finding your way through the menu system Knowledge of subject matter and stock	Able to deal with complex requests Logical mind Interest in technology Word processing skills
Journal contents distribution	How to operate photocopier and use manual	Dealing with minor breakdowns and maintenance

management thinking to make outputs the focus of attention and to give employees a good deal of freedom to achieve them in their own way. This has given rise to an emphasis on broad performance indicators, representing standards against which employees' contribution to the organization can be judged.

Peters and Waterman (1982), the authors of the best-selling management book of the 1980s, *In search of excellence*, suggested that 'excellent' organizations have, among other things, 'simultaneous loose–tight properties'. The 'loose' half of that formula referred to allowing employees a lot of freedom. In Peters and Waterman's model, the 'tight' half of the formula referred to the strong cultural norms which are supposed to be a more effective and more humane way of governing what employees do than traditional management control. But we could think of performance indicators as doing the same job in a different way, especially if the performance indicators are the outcome of some participative process in which employees themselves have a say.

Table 4.5 provides some examples of performance indicators.

Table 4.5   Examples of performance indicators

Job category	Performance indicator
Office cleaner	Floor area cleaned per standard shift
Assembly line worker	Units assembled per hour, per standard shift or per day
Immigration officer	Inward passengers dealt with per hour
Loan administration officer	Number of loan applications processed per week or per year
Craft worker	Value of output per standard shift or per day
Train driver	Locomotive miles driven per shift
Sales representative	Value of sales achieved per year
Delivery truck driver	Tons delivered per driver hour
Servicing engineer	Number of units installed and/or serviced per shift or per year
University lecturer	Contact hours with students per week

You will notice that many of these indicators are for manual or clerical jobs, but arguably performance indicators are even more appropriate in senior and professional jobs, since, as we saw earlier, such jobs typically have a strong cognitive content which is unobservable, and also because it may not be easy to break them down into discrete duties in the way that traditional job analysis assumes.

A second advantage of performance indicators is that their flexibility makes them easy to adapt to team performance. In principle it is as easy to set indicators for a team as for an individual. (See our discussion of job analysis and teams below.)

Performance indicators fall into a number of basic types, which are shown in Table 4.6.

Table 4.6   Types of performance indicators

Type of Indicator	Definition
Performance	Measure of performance/output expected from one jobholder per standard time period
Time	Time required in one post to complete a set number of standard tasks (plus time for travel between tasks and so on)
Demographic	Number of people in a client group served by one post
Production	Number of machines of type x operated by a jobholder with skills y
Location	Number of locations served by one post
Supervisory staff	Number of staff that can be directly managed or supervised by one post (span of control)
Support staff	Number of staff that can be internally 'served' by one support post

Indicators should be:

- quantifiable;
- comprehensible for employees and managers;
- suitable for negotiation with staff about reasonable performance levels, based on data easily accessible in the organization's information systems.

It is true that performance indicators can be seen as an example of 'Management by Objectives' (MbO), a 1970s management fashion which has faded from view (we discuss it in Chapter 7). But MbO *was* based on a sound principle: the research evidence about the value of objectives and performance indicators in improving individual performance is among the strongest that we have about any management practice. The principle remains intact, even if its particular application in the form of MbO was faulty. In fact the use of such indicators has, if anything, strengthened over time, as organizations have learnt how to avoid the problems of rigidity and imposition from above which robbed workers of their control over their jobs and which led to the demise of MbO. Organizations do this in practice by using performance management to generate performance indicators through a dialogue between managers and employees, leading to a greater sense of ownership of the performance indicators on the part of employees.

However, there is one cautionary note that we need to sound. There is a saying that organizations get the behaviour that organizations reward. Performance indicators need to be handled lightly. Otherwise there is the danger that employees will concentrate on their performance indicators to the exclusion of all else.

A crude obsession with meeting performance targets has even led to the fall of a government on one occasion. In the mid-1970s, the Congress government in India, led by Mrs Indira Gandhi, decided that it was time to get tough with family planning. With Mrs Gandhi's son Sanjay in charge, local officers were given ambitious targets for carrying out male sterilizations, and it was made clear that no excuses would be accepted if the targets were not met. Since offering inducements such as free transistor radios was not always enough, some zealous officers had men sterilized against their will. The resulting public outcry contributed to the downfall of the Congress government in January 1977, and was a setback for family planning from which India, arguably, has still to recover.

You may have noticed that one of our examples of a performance indicator for a delivery truck driver was the 'tons delivered per driver hour'. In order to see how such an indicator could become counterproductive, read Box 4.3 below.

6   Job analysis in practice

Now that we have reviewed some of the main job analysis methods, let us consider a brief example of how they can be used. Box 4.3 is based on a case study in Pearn and Kandola's (1993) useful guide. It shows how job analysis can get to the bottom of an organizational problem, and demonstrate that the 'obvious' solution to the problem might actually be the wrong one.

Box 4.3   Using job analysis to find out what is *really* going wrong

The transport division of a large company was concerned about the high level of damage to its vehicles, which ranged from specialized building equipment to heavy goods vehicles. Accident repairs were taking up 18 per cent of its workshop time. Most worryingly, the cause of 50 per cent of the accidents was 'unknown'. The company's first reaction was to assume that they had employed bad drivers, and that they ought to train them. But they decided to carry out a job analysis to get more information.

They used the following job analysis methods:

- Observation, where drivers were accompanied and informally observed. It was difficult to arrange this, and only seven hours of observation in total took place.
- Critical incident interviews, lasting up to two hours, with 18 individual drivers to identify good and bad (or dangerous) driver behaviour. Drivers were asked to describe in detail incidents they had seen themselves or that they had heard about.
- Repertory grid interviews. Drivers were given 'triads' such as 'safe general vehicle driver' – 'safe heavy goods vehicle driver' – ' duty supervisor'. These elicited constructs such as 'sticks to the regulations' – 'doesn't stick to the regulations'.

The analysts found that it was not lack of driver skill that explained the high level of accidents. Instead, it was the interplay between aloof managers and frustrated, unsupervised drivers in a stressed and noisy environment where doing work *fast* was all that mattered, and where no one felt personally responsible for vehicles, leading to a 'vehicle bashing culture'. Training would have been a waste of time. Instead, there was a need to make organizational and management changes, including clarifying the company's policies.

See Pearn and Kandola (1993).

7   Job analysis for teams

7.1   Teams and cultures

We now come to the last of the 'tensions' that we outlined at the start of the chapter, between job analysis at the level of individual jobs and job analysis at the level of teams. Job analysis assumes that it is the duties carried out by the individual employee that are the 'atomic level' in the organization. There are those, however, who believe that we should go no lower than the team, because going down to the level of the individual job risks destroying the fragile cooperation which is the essence of successful teams, in which the team 'whole' is greater than the sum of its parts.

This issue also has a cultural dimension. Hofstede's research on national differences in work styles has given us strong evidence of an important difference between employees in different countries. In some countries, workers tend to see themselves as autonomous individuals (this is what Hofstede calls an *individualist* orientation); in others, as interdependent team members (this is what Hofstede calls a *collectivist* orientation). It is very significant that the United States, where job analysis developed as a practical application of Taylor's 'scientific management', appears in Hofstede's research as a strongly 'individualist' country. It is equally significant that Japan, where the emphasis on teamworking is particularly strong, is a strongly 'collectivist' country.

An article in the American journal *Personnel Psychology* reported a clash between American and Japanese cultures in this area. The authors were invited to carry out a job analysis for the job of assembly worker in a factory being opened by a Japanese company that manufactured car parts. Since the factory was new, there were no jobholders to interview. Kevin Love and his colleagues therefore went to Japan to do the job analysis in a factory owned by the same company. The excerpt from their article in Box 4.4 shows what happened. As you read it, focus on the nature of the problem they faced, and on what they did to solve it.

Thus the problem that Love and his colleagues faced was that they could not use job incumbents as a source of data because 'employees did not feel free to express individual opinions', so that 'a traditional job analysis based on task characteristic ratings from supervisors and incumbents was not possible'. Their solution was to dispense with the job incumbents and rely exclusively on the 'subject matter experts' and on videotapes.

Box 4.4   Job analysis across two cultures

Due to the fact that this selection system was to be developed to select American workers according to a Japanese management philosophy, several culturally related problems were encountered while conducting a traditional job analysis. According to the steps outlined by Levine (1983),[6] a typical job analysis consists of collecting job-related data from job incumbents and other subject matter experts (SMEs), developing a task taxonomy, and then measuring task characteristics using a questionnaire which asks job incumbents and supervisors to report the frequency and importance of each dimension. However, because the plant did not exist during the selection system development, actual jobs, equipment and materials were not available for analysis. In addition, the only job incumbents were located in Japan. Thus, no input from current job incumbents could be obtained. Japanese managers were available during the job analysis; however, due to the language barrier, they could not be interviewed. Thus, the job analysis was primarily based on observations of videotapes of Japanese workers performing the job and American managers who had completed an extended period of training in Japan. In addition, manuals, drawings, product specifications and other printed materials were reviewed.

Through discussions with SMEs a series of critical incidents were generated that distinguished between effective and ineffective assemblers. These were based on their actual experiences in observing and/or managing assemblers in the Japanese plant. Using these critical incidents, following traditional job analysis procedures, a questionnaire was to be developed to rate task characteristics using the input of Japanese job incumbents and their supervisors. However, we were unable to distribute such a questionnaire because the Japanese managers did not understand the concept of using a questionnaire to solicit employee opinions. In Japan there exists a strong desire to develop and maintain harmony in all types of relationships – familial, co-worker, and supervisor–subordinate. Based on the Shinto notion of *joge*, group activities and views are preferred over individualistic action and opinions (Maher and Wong, 1994). Personal interests are subordinate to those of the society as a whole or the corporation. Thus, employees do not feel free to express individual opinions until they have discussed it with fellow workers and their supervisor. As a group they will then proceed to develop the correct or acceptable answers to any questions. Thus, in Japan public opinion polls are unusual, and individual employees rarely offer personal views to management. Based on these cultural norms, a traditional job analysis based on task characteristic ratings from supervisors and incumbents was not possible. This questions the plausibility of traditional job analysis procedures within a Japanese management climate (Love, 1990). A culture geared to minimizing differences between people, especially at the same social level (i.e. workers), renders the measurement and public identification of applicant differences unacceptable. Moreover, within the context of typical worker and supervisor selection procedures in Japan, measurement of individual differences is the responsibility of the training or educational institution, not the employer (Maher, 1985). Corporations submit requests for a specific number of workers or supervisors to various trade schools, universities and so forth. The educational institution matches the characteristics of the student with the demands of the corporate position and provides a list of prospective employees. Open recruitment, testing and selection of applicants is rare.

In light of these roadblocks, in order to continue with the job analysis it was necessary to modify the task-based approach and rely exclusively on the SMEs and observation of the videotape (approximately 90 minutes). Using these sources and an importance rating scheme, a total of 140 critical behaviors were identified which covered the sequence of steps in assembly, quality control checkpoints and related plant operations.

See Love *et al.* (1994: 837–8).

This is interesting, but we do not have to take Love *et al.*'s analysis at face value. First of all, we are personally suspicious of all cultural generalizations such as 'Based on the Shinto notion of *joge*, group activities and views are preferred over individualistic action and opinions.' We know that there can be as much variation between individuals and groups within a culture as there is between two cultures as a whole. Such generalizations can easily lead to negative stereotyping. Secondly, the excerpt arguably says as much about American culture as about Japanese culture. What we mean is that the realization that these Japanese workers preferred to think in terms of the team rather than of individuals appears to have come as a shock to the American analysts, robbing them of their ability to make the kind of *creative adaptation* of a western method that we have been trying to recommend throughout this book. For instance, we cannot see why they could not have arranged a meeting, in the style of a quality circle, so that individuals could give their view of job requirements as members of a team. Also, we cannot see why the reluctance of Japanese workers to participate in the 'measurement of individual differences' needed to become a roadblock, given that the selection of workers for the new factory, which the job analysis was designed to facilitate, was going to take place in America, not in Japan.

Most importantly for our discussion, Love and his colleagues seemed unable to treat the problem as an opportunity, and switch their attention from the level of the individual job to the level of the team as a whole. This is probably an example of what is sometimes called a 'learned inability', in that it is precisely the exclusive emphasis in traditional job analysis on the individual job that has imposed 'blinkers' on the job analysts' vision.

The need for techniques for analysing the duties of teams is clear, but such techniques are still thin on the ground. However, Table 4.7 shows an example of an attempt to work at this level.

7.2 Summary

In this section we have explored the tension between the job and team levels in job analysis, and we have seen that it is related to an important national dimension of difference, that between individualist cultures like the United States and collectivist cultures like Japan. The clash of cultures that we saw in Love *et al.*'s study highlights some assumptions on which job analysis is based. In particular, there is the assumption that it is the level of the job and not the team that is the 'atomic level' in organizations. This need not be the case, and it may even be damaging in some situations to insist that it should be.

8   Job change and job analysis

How has your job changed since you started doing it? Are you doing the same job that your predecessor (if you have one) used to do? Do your colleagues do their work in the same way that you do? Our jobs as lecturers have changed in several ways in recent years. The most dramatic has been our launch of distance learning: the idea that we might do some of our teaching through on-line tutorials rather than face-to-face classes had not occurred to any of us as recently as the late 1990s.

A real difficulty for job analysis is that jobs can be a moving target, continually changing as events change and jobholders innovate. Nicholson and West's (1988) research demonstrates the extent to which managers' jobs change simply because of the way in which the individual approaches the job. This is an important disadvantage of a fixed job description.

From the management perspective, organizations will want to retain flexibility so that the jobholder can be asked to take on new duties

Table 4.7   Generic teamwork skills

Interpersonal KSAs[a]

A.   Conflict resolution KSAs
1.   The KSA to recognize and encourage desirable, but discourage undesirable team conflict.
2.   The KSA to recognize the type and source of conflict confronting the team and implement an appropriate resolution strategy.
3.   The KSA to employ an integrative (win–win) negotiation strategy, rather than the traditional distributive (win–lose) strategy.

B.   Collaborative problem-solving KSAs
4.   The KSA to identify situations requiring participative group problem solving and to utilize the proper degree and type of participation.
5.   The KSA to recognize the obstacles to collaborative group problem solving and implement appropriate corrective actions.

C.   Communication KSAs
6.   The KSA to understand communication networks and to utilize decentralized networks to enhance communication where possible.
7.   The KSA to communicate openly and supportively, that is, to send messages that are (a) behavior or event oriented, (b) congruent, (c) validating, (d) conjunctive, and (e) owned.
8.   The KSA to listen nonevaluatively and to appropriately use active listening techniques.
9.   The KSA to maximize the consonance between nonverbal and verbal messages to recognize and interpret the nonverbal messages of others.
10.   The KSA to engage in small talk and ritual greetings and a recognition of their importance.

Self-management KSAs

D.   Goal setting and performance management KSAs
11.   The KSA to help establish specific, challenging, and accepted team goals.
12.   The KSA to monitor, evaluate, and provide feedback on both overall team performance and individual team member performance.

E.   Planning and task coordination KSAs
13.   The KSA to coordinate and synchronize activities, information, and tasks between team members.
14.   The KSA to help establish task and role assignments for individual team members and ensure proper balancing of workload.

---

[a]   KSA = knowledge, skill and ability.

Source: Reprinted with permission from Stevens and Campion (1994).

(and that is why the last item on a job description is often a catch-all phrase such as 'or any other duty which is consistent with the grade': it can be frustrating for a manager to be told by an employee that something that needs to be done is 'not in my job description'). From the employee's perspective, the jobholder himself or herself will want to retain flexibility so that he or she has scope to develop the job and to innovate. In short, job analysts need to resist the temptation to carve job descriptions in letters of stone: they must leave room for change.

9   Job design

9.1   An anecdote

When one of us, in the early 1980s, worked for the Education section of a UK-based NGO that sends people to work as volunteers in developing countries, one of the things he found most satisfying was being able to follow applicants right through the recruitment process. He would read their application forms, then sit on the interview panel that appointed them, then post them to a developing country, and finally train them on the two-week teacher training courses that they attended before going overseas. He got friendly with many of them, and continued to write to them while they were overseas.

Shortly after he left, the NGO brought in a firm of management consultants to make work more efficient. It observed, correctly, that staff, being mostly returned volunteers themselves, were not experts in any of the above activities. It restructured the organization, making one group of staff solely responsible for applications, a second for recruitment and selection, a third for posting and a fourth group for training. The intention was to increase efficiency by allowing people to specialize. The effect was that staff dealt with only one part of the process, and lost the ability to build up a relationship with volunteers. We cannot say whether efficiency increased, but many staff became frustrated and even angry: they felt reduced to cogs in a machine. Staff turnover, traditionally high, became even higher. Several years later, the NGO restructured again, this time back to the original structure.

A job design that seems efficient can be deeply dissatisfying for the jobholders. A pessimistic view is that this is inevitable. The American writer Chris Argyris (1974) has argued that, while individuals have an inherent urge to become autonomous and independent, organizations require them to submit to external control. To put this in terms of the 'tension' that we pointed to at the start of the chapter, Argyris is saying that, in determining the purpose of job analysis, efficiency will always triumph over job satisfaction and ownership. But there is a tradition of *job design*, by contrast, that seeks to design jobs that will provide job satisfaction while maintaining, or perhaps improving, employee performance – a tradition that asserts that we can have our cake and eat it, as the saying goes. Job design arose out of the 'Human Relations' school that charted the ways in which employees' informal work norms can subvert organizations' attempts to force them into uncongenial ways of working. It grew up in conscious opposition to scientific management's attempt to impose a narrow and unnatural efficiency on workers.

9.2 Job enrichment

One important version of job design arose out of Herzberg's Motivation/Hygiene Theory. In Herzberg's original research, accountants and engineers in Pittsburgh (USA) were asked to describe times when they felt satisfied and dissatisfied at work. They tended to be satisfied when they experienced things like recognition, responsibility, advancement, growth, the intrinsic nature of the work itself and achievement. This led Herzberg to develop what he called 'job enrichment', which aimed to address some of the following:

- increasing individuals' responsibilities;
- giving them more scope to vary the methods, sequence and pace of their work;
- giving a person or work group a complete unit of work, reducing task specialization;
- removing some controls from above while ensuring that individuals or groups are clearly accountable for achieving defined targets or standards;
- allowing employees more influence in setting targets;
- giving employees control of information they need to monitor their own performances;
- encouraging employees' participation in planning, innovating and reviewing work;
- introducing new and more difficult tasks;
- assigning specific projects to individuals or groups.

9.3   The job characteristics model

Perhaps the most succinct statement of the principles of job design is that of Hackman and Oldham (1975), who identified five 'core dimensions' which they found to be positively related to job satisfaction and negatively related to absenteeism and staff turnover. Can you see how they relate to the NGO's experience?

- *Skill variety:* the extent to which a job requires a number of different activities which use a variety of different skills.
- *Task identity:* the extent to which a job requires a complete unit of service which can be identified by the staff member, making the job more meaningful.
- *Task significance:* the extent to which a job has significant effects on others – jobholders find work more meaningful when they understand that the results of their work connect with the work of others, whether inside or outside the organization.
- *Autonomy:* the extent to which a job offers independence, self-control and freedom at work.
- *Feedback:* the extent to which the results of their work are communicated to employees who can then reflect on their performance.

In a word, the NGO's mistake was to ignore the satisfaction that staff got from doing work that was varied, that constituted 'a complete unit of service', following volunteers from their initial application right to their departure overseas, and that offered staff some autonomy in how they did their jobs.

There is one qualification that we need to make on all of this. Job design is based on motivation theories like that of Herzberg, but most psychologists these days prefer 'expectancy theory', which suggests that we are motivated to the extent that we believe that work will give us what we want. Not everyone is motivated by variety, for example. Some of us are positively reassured by a job where there are few surprises, and where someone makes the big decisions for us. Some of us may be motivated exclusively by money: it has been suggested that this motivation predominates in developing countries, though that is almost certainly an oversimplification. Still, it is safe to say that, while some of us are happy to be cogs in a 'scientific management' machine, the Human Relations school is right to point out that many of us are not.

9.4   Implications for job analysis

The implication of job design for job analysis is simple: it reinforces the importance of avoiding a narrow and alienating approach to job content, while suggesting design principles that we can use to design satisfying jobs. But the application is more complicated: as so often, we HRM specialists are left with the difficult task of reconciling the efficiency needs of the organization and the satisfaction needs of the employee, something that perhaps we can only do on a case-by-case basis. But it is perhaps better to struggle to reconcile these things than to bury our heads in the sand and pretend that the problem does not exist.

Summary and conclusion

In this chapter we have listed the steps in carrying out job analysis, seen what is involved in writing job descriptions and person specifications, and reviewed some implications of teamworking, job change and job design for job analysis. In doing so we have tried to show how job analysis, which does have a monolithic appearance, can be used flexibly in ways that will be appropriate in different organizations.

At the start of the chapter we recognized that job analysis grew out of Taylor's 'scientific management', and that its most rigid application, the work study approach exemplified in the hospital meals service, has acquired the same bad name that scientific management itself has acquired. In the end, though, the level of the job is the 'atomic level' in most organizations, and jobs remain the basic organizational building blocks. We hope that we have shown that it is possible to do job analysis in a flexible way that respects employees' ownership of their jobs by ensuring that jobs contain enough variety and so on, and that recognizes that employees work as team members as well as individuals. Probably most informed practitioners these days will agree with this view. But the methods that the long history of job analysis has bequeathed to practitioners are still tainted by their scientific management origins, and are less flexible than we would like them to be. HRM specialists should not take them at face value, but should be ready to adapt them so that they can deliver the efficiency improvements which these methods promise while not alienating the employees without whose cooperation such improvements will not materialize.

Notes

1   At the risk of stating the obvious, the first data source to which we should always refer is the existing job description, if there is one.

2   Sometimes employers combine the job description and person specification for convenience in a single document. The point we want to make is that the two are distinct, whether employers treat them as separate documents or not. As you will see, they also require different formats.

3   This group of three 'elements' in which two 'elements' are contrasted with the third is called a 'triad' in repertory grid jargon.

4   The word 'doing' is important, because it will elicit behaviours that are *observable* and *measurable*.

5   Breaking down the initial interview responses into more detailed statements is called 'laddering' in repertory grid jargon. It is the 'laddering' stage that, done properly, provides the precise information that makes a person specification based on repertory grid so rich and detailed.

6   This is an earlier edition of Brannick and Levine's (2002) textbook.

5   Managing Pay

Willy McCourt

What this chapter is about

After outlining some concepts and approaches, we discuss how pay issues have been handled by organizations, and the problems that organizations have faced. We then discuss attempts by organizations to reform the ways in which they pay their staff. We look at two widely-used techniques: job evaluation and performance-related pay. Finally we look at the issue of equal pay between women and men.

What you will learn

By the end of the chapter you will be able to:

- outline basic techniques for managing pay;
- assess some of the measures which governments have taken to reform pay;
- state how job evaluation and performance-related pay operate, and assess the issues which organizations face in implementing them;
- explain how gender bias occurs in pay management, and how it can be prevented.

1   Introduction

It is not difficult to demonstrate the importance of pay among the human resource issues that confront the manager. Pay is at the core of the employment relationship: the organization pays its staff in return for their labour. Indeed for many of us work is only work when it is paid (a notion that has the incidental effect of ignoring the contribution of unpaid work to the economy, in particular the contribution of women's household labour and of subsistence agriculture). But the distinction between paid and unpaid work is still an important one. It is one of the principal differences between Non-governmental Organizations (NGOs), often staffed partly by unpaid voluntary workers, and other kinds of organization. Moreover, it goes without saying that, from the employees' point of view, pay, which determines their standard of living and that of their dependants, may be the most important of all the topics we deal with in this book. Employees typically take a good deal more notice of their employer's pay decisions than they do of decisions about say, appraisal or training.

Yet pay decisions, important as they are, are often made crudely. Pay decisions have usually been rudimentary, amounting merely to the percentage pay increase that staff will receive in the coming year. Decisions have typically represented incremental adjustments to an otherwise unchanging system whose origins may be lost in the mists of time. The idea that there are alternative ways of designing pay systems appears almost as fantastic as to suggest that the monuments of ancient Egypt might perhaps be cubes rather than pyramids.

2   Conventional pay systems

2.1   Why do different staff earn different amounts?

The simplest form of pay system would be one in which all staff earned the same fixed rate of pay, subject only to an annual adjustment to take account of changing circumstances, notably inflation. Such a system was in fact operated up to the early 1980s by the management of London's largest arts magazine, *Time Out*, which began life in the late 1960s as a cooperative with a highly participative management structure (we shall discuss worker participation in Chapter 10). In most, if not all, organizations, however, there is a *hierarchy* of pay rates: some staff earn more than others. Why, in such a traditional system, do different staff earn different amounts? There are essentially three reasons:

- because of the nature of the jobs they occupy;
- because of their length of service in the organization, their age or their qualifications;
- because of their different levels of performance.

Let us discuss them in turn.

The nature of the job

The fundamental feature of traditional systems is that *individuals are paid firstly for the job they occupy, and only secondarily, if at all, for their individual performance*. Let us assume that two gardeners and a gardening supervisor joined a Ministry of Works on the same day. The two gardeners will be paid the same amount, even though one may be doing the job more effectively than the other. On the other hand, the hardworking gardener will earn less than his or her supervisor, even if the latter is working ineffectively. In other words, there will be a pay difference, or *differential*, between the two jobs, based on a judgement about their relative importance; and it probably will not be qualified by the difference in the two individuals' performance.

But that may not be the only difference between the ways the gardener and the supervisor are paid. In many countries, the gardener will be appointed on a 'spot rate', and that amount will only change in line with the annual pay award, which of course applies to all staff. The supervisor, however, may be appointed on a grade, which is a pay range comprising a number of points rather than a single amount.

In order for this traditional pay system to operate, there must be a system of jobs, and some way of estimating their relative importance. Organizations can exist, exceptionally, without a system of jobs: some computer firms in the United States, including the very large computer manufacturer Apple, do not have job designations, preferring to recruit staff and allow them to determine where they can best make a contribution to the firm once they have started work. But the computer industry is a fast-moving business. In the vast majority of organizations, which change more slowly, fixed job designations continue to be the norm.

The body of techniques which can be used to determine the content of jobs is, of course, job analysis, which we discussed in Chapter 4. The body of techniques which can be used to estimate the relative importance of different jobs is called *job evaluation*. It is built on job analysis, and we discuss it later in this chapter.

Length of service in the organization, age and qualifications

Our gardening supervisor was appointed on a grade rather than the spot rate on which the two gardeners were appointed. We defined a grade as a pay range with a number of points. Those points are usually known as *increments*. Staff who are appointed on a grade may start on the bottom point, or they may receive credit for their age or their educational qualifications, and therefore start on a higher point. Subsequently, progression from one increment to the next is normally annual until the ceiling of the grade is reached or until the individual is promoted to a higher grade. In this way staff in an organization earn different amounts of money because of their different lengths of service, ages or qualifications.

Performance

The third reason why different staff earn different amounts is that the employer judges that some are performing more effectively than others. (Pay based on a judgement of performance is the exception rather than the rule.) For manual workers like the two gardeners, that judgement could be exercised through bonus schemes, where an assessment is made of what a normal day's work should be, and staff who exceed it qualify for an extra payment. For supervisory, professional or administrative staff like the gardening supervisor, the judgement is often made through the annual appraisal (Chapter 7). Progression to the next increment is usually subject to a satisfactory annual appraisal report. In many organizations, especially in the United Kingdom and the United States, an attempt is made to link pay more directly to performance, as we shall see.

2.2   Designing a grade structure

We have seen that supervisory staff like the gardening supervisor, and also administrative and professional staff, are normally appointed on a grade consisting of a number of increments. How many grades will there be? And how many points will there be within each grade? Such questions of design need to be addressed by the architect of pay systems just as other questions of design had to be addressed by the architects of the pyramids. Let us look at some examples of pay structures to show the effect that those design decisions have.

A simple graded pay structure

Graded pay structures involve a number of design issues concerning non-overlapping and overlapping structures, size of increments, differentials and number of grades.

Non-overlapping and overlapping structures   In the example in Figure 5.1, there are seven grades. Staff on any grade will always earn more than staff on the lower adjacent grade. Even someone on the highest increment of the lower grade will still earn less than someone on the lowest increment of the higher grade. This is a *non-overlapping structure*.

Often, however, an organization will have at least some grades which have a large number of increments (so that the grade has a *large pay*

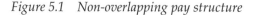

Figure 5.1   Non-overlapping pay structure

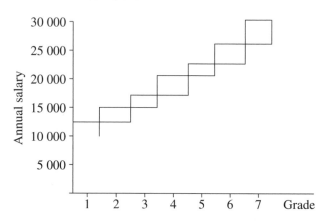

range). These may be 'main professional grades', where there is an expectation that staff will spend many years in the grade, and this is reflected in the quite large number of increments. Grading of teachers' salaries in many countries is an example. When someone occupying a teacher's grade is promoted to a higher grade, for instance as head of department in a secondary school, she may initially earn less than someone on the lower grade with long service and who has reached the top of that grade. More simply, if the organization has at least several grades that have a large pay span, it may only be possible to fit them into the overall range between the lowest and the highest paid worker in the organization by overlapping them. Armstrong and Murlis (1994: 187), the authors of the standard British textbook on pay management, say that an overlap of 30–40 per cent is typical in British organizations.

Such a structure is shown in Figure 5.2. Notice that it may give rise to a situation where a more senior staff person (like the head of department in a school) supervises the work of someone (like a long service teacher) who earns more.

An overlapping pay structure
Size of increments   Of course it is possible to have a large number of increments within a small pay span if the size of the increments is small. A grade that stretches from £20 000 to £30 000, so that there is a pay span of £10 000, could contain five increments of £2000 each, or 10 increments of £1000 each. It is simpler to decide on the size of a pay span first (for example, £10 000) and then the number of increments desired (say, five) to obtain the size of increment within the span (thus £2000). In practice, however, the range of the pay span is often deter-

Figure 5.2 Overlapping pay structure

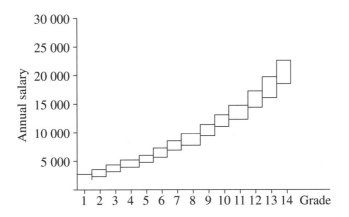

mined by previous decisions about the number and size of increments.

Differentials Earlier we mentioned the notion of a *differential*, which we can now define as the mean difference between two grades (or, for manual workers who are paid on a spot rate, the difference between two spot rates). Differentials are an important topic in pay management, as Box 5.1 illustrates.

Box 5.1 Relative pay and absolute pay

Do workers invariably want to earn more? Not always, at least not if earning more is at the expense of losing a differential advantage over another group of workers.

In a research study, a group of workers was offered a hypothetical choice between a large and a small pay increase. Workers were told that, if they opted for the large pay increase, another group of workers which currently earned less than they did would receive an even larger increase and would overtake them as a result. The majority of the workers opted for the smaller increase, preserving their differential.

Armstrong and Murlis (1994: 186) suggest that a differential of 15–20 per cent is normally appropriate. Differentials larger than that make it difficult to accommodate all the grades within the overall pay range; differentials smaller than that lead to arguments about marginal cases from staff on lower grades who think that their jobs should be regraded to higher grades. (It is a fact of life that payroll budgets tend to increase quite apart from annual pay increases, because from time to time individuals or groups of staff convince the organization that their jobs should be upgraded. British local government pay budgets include an amount to cover this eventuality. This phenomenon is known as *grade drift*.)

The size of differentials determines a ratio which is common to all organizations, but which is strangely absent from most industrialized country discussion about pay management: the *compression ratio*. The compression ratio refers to the ratio between the wages of the lowest and the highest paid staff of an organization. As we shall see later in our discussion of pay management in developing and transitional countries, the question of an appropriate compression ratio has been central to attempts to reform public sector pay.

Number of grades   Many organizations have *steep pay structures* where there are many grades (or, for manual workers, many pay rates) with relatively small differentials between them. The advantage of this is that there are many opportunities for promotion, an important factor in career development (see Chapter 4, section 4.2). But there are some disadvantages. Many grades means small differentials, leading to the problem of grade drift. A second disadvantage is that it leads to a proliferation of job designations whose main purpose is to provide an opportunity for promotion.

Box 5.2   Steep pay structures and job proliferation

One of the authors used to work as a training officer in a British local authority with a steep pay structure. The authority had a programme of supervisory management training courses. Staff whose job descriptions contained an element of staff supervision were eligible to attend a course. A difficulty in running the training was that many participants actually had no real experience of management. Their only supervisory responsibility was to 'deputize for the section manager in his or her absence', in other words, to take charge of the section or office when the manager was sick or on leave. Naturally, any important decisions such as the recruitment of a new member of staff were always deferred until the manager recovered from sickness or came back refreshed from leave. These supervisory terms basically existed to provide a promotion opportunity.

This example shows how a grade may be almost meaningless in terms of its content. A second way in which this happens is where promotion to a higher grade is automatic; that is, where staff normally progress to the higher grade once they reach the ceiling of the lower grade. This is a feature of pay administration in many developing countries, notably the French-speaking countries of West Africa. As a result, when the government of Senegal reduced the size of its civil service between 1983 and 1985, automatic progression meant that the net result was only a reduction in the annual growth rate of the wage bill from 14 to 9 per cent (Nunberg, 1994: 134).

Awareness of the above problems has led to a movement towards *flatter pay structures*, that is, structures with relatively few grades. Thus in the late 1980s the Department for Education in England and Wales introduced a 'main professional grade', that collapsed four previous teaching grades into one. Movement towards flatter structures has often been part of a conscious attempt to reduce the number of levels in the management hierarchy, especially in the private sector. This lay behind Ford Motors' decision to reduce the number of separate job categories at their UK plants from no fewer than 516 in 1986 to 45 in 1988. This may be part and parcel of the introduction of participative working methods (which we discuss in Chapter 10) or simply a device to reduce the size of the overall pay bill.

Making a decision about numbers of grades entails making a decision about *grade width*: the number of different job designations that a grade contains. A grade can be narrow because it contains only a few job designations, or broad because it contains many. Suppose a local authority employs both accountants and auditors, and the authority believes the post of auditor is slightly more responsible than that of accountant. The authority must then decide whether the two jobs will be within a single grade or in two different grades, with the auditor job on the higher grade. The placing decision may be arbitrary, although job evaluation potentially provides a systematic basis, as we shall see later. (Placing both jobs within a single grade would produce a relatively 'broad' grade.)

Box 5.3   Organizing pay in a tight labour market

Singapore's tight labour market, a consequence of its rapid economic growth, has had an impact on pay in the public sector, and it allows us to focus on how a traditional pay structure operates in practice, as well as on the changes that Singapore made to its pay structure to take account of the tight labour market.

Jobs in the Singapore public service are grouped into four 'divisions'. These correspond to what are called 'cadres' in many developing countries, especially former British colonies. Cadre in this sense refers to a category of staff. Each cadre has its own 'scheme of service', the conditions of employment which apply to it only; they include separate pay arrangements.

Singapore has a graded pay structure which is broadly in line with our description. There is a system of grades, grouped within four divisions. There were no fewer than 183 separate grades, so this is an extremely steep structure, especially bearing in mind that there were only 61 650 civil servants in 1991. The scales are incremental.

Grades overlap in some cases (for example, between the Permanent Secretary and Principal Assistant Secretary grades), but not others (for instance, between the entry grade of the clerical service and the entry grade of the administrative service). Probably this reflects the four-division structure: the latter two grades are actually in different divisions. What we called the 'compression ratio' earlier is high, at least relative to the countries of South Asia. Pay rates are not based on job evaluation.

A further feature of public sector pay in Singapore is the way that Singapore uses comparisons with private sector pay rates. The private sector is much more developed in Singapore than in many developing and transitional countries, and government needs to be aware of its pay rates in order to retain civil servants. (We are told that, during the late 1970s, the discrepancy between public and private sector pay led to many civil servants leaving to work in the private sector.) Thus the principle of private sector *comparability* is the basis for public sector pay decisions.

Singapore has avoided the problems faced by other developing country governments in the 1970s and 1980s, where relatively large wage bills were at the expense of the materials – such as teaching materials and transport – which public servants needed to do their jobs effectively. The relatively small proportion of wages in government expenditure as a whole is a reflection of the small size of the civil service relative to South Asian countries such as Bangladesh.

See Chew (1997).

2.3   Designing pay structures: summary

In this section we have looked at the design of a traditional pay structure common to many organizations, especially in developing and industrialized countries. We have covered

- the basis of different pay rates,
- the link between job content and pay rates,

- non-overlapping and overlapping pay structures,
- increments,
- differentials,
- decisions about number of grades, including grade width and the distinction between steep and flat pay structures.

3   Reforming pay

3.1   Pay implications of 'success' and 'failure'

In Box 5.3 we made comparisons between Singapore and other developing countries, notably the countries of South Asia: Chew draws on his own study of civil service pay in that region, which appears in the list of references at the end of the article. Chew implies that those countries have faced considerable difficulties in pay management. We now move on to discuss some of those difficulties, and also some of the proposed solutions to them.

Singapore's approach to public sector pay in recent years has been a response to the problems created by economic success. While this has been a feature of public sector pay policy in a number of East and South-east Asian countries, elsewhere the pressing need has been to respond to economic failure.

Study task 1: Economic influences on pay

As we embark on our discussion of pay reform, we need to emphasize the economic context in which reform efforts have been made. From what you have studied so far in this book, and from your own experience, answer the following questions.

- What effect do you think that the economic context has had on public sector pay in your own country?
- Has it created pressure on organizations to pay their staff more?
- Has the public paybill become unaffordable because of economic difficulties?

Write down some suggestions.

In general terms, we can distinguish between problems of success and problems of failure. Singapore, where civil service wages have risen sharply, represents a response to success. By contrast, the response of the government of the Republic of Korea (South Korea, where economic growth has also been high) has been to hold down public sector wages, partly in an attempt to use low public sector pay rises as a moderating influence on private sector pay increases. Although public wages have therefore fallen behind private wages, the high status of public employment in South Korea means that the public sector has continued to attract and retain good staff; the quality of public administration appears not to have suffered (Park, 1997).

Many countries, however, are struggling with problems of economic failure. Inflation and low levels of government revenue have eroded the value of public pay, as governments simply lack the money to maintain its value, let alone increase it. Low pay has a number of consequences. It contributes to the corruption which we discuss in Chapter 6 in the context of recruitment and selection. Although the evidence is anecdotal, it has probably also affected employees' commitment to their work. This is summed up in the pithy saying current in the transitional countries of Central and Eastern Europe during the Communist period: 'You pretend to pay us, and we pretend to work' – a saying whose truth would still be recognized in many developing and transitional countries, where the link between effort and financial reward has been weakened by economic problems. Public agencies have also found it hard to retain staff who have a skill which is in demand elsewhere.

One specific reason why employees' commitment lessens is that employees are forced to find other sources of income to make ends meet. 'Moonlighting', carrying out other paid work in addition to one's main employment, is a common response. Where low pay persists over a period of years, moonlighting becomes institutionalized, with many employees openly absent for several hours of the working day. It is difficult for a supervisor to criticize an employee's poor attendance record when the supervisor knows that it is almost forced on the employee (and supervisors are probably in the same position themselves). In Zimbabwe, moonlighting became so prevalent in the 1980s, including in a fast-growing number of private colleges staffed predominantly by serving public employees, that the government decided in 1992 to relax the ban on outside working, although they retained the prohibition on doing outside work during office hours (Ncube, 1997).

A Ugandan government report summed up the bleak situation like this:

> The civil servant had either to survive by lowering his standard of ethics, performance and dutifulness or remain upright and perish. He chose to survive. (Report of the Public Services Salaries Review Commission, 1982; quoted in Lindauer, 1994: 27)

To the extent that such public sector pay problems are a consequence of national economic difficulties, an economic response is needed: macroeconomic problems require a macroeconomic solution. Uganda's ability to raise the pay of its civil servants in recent years, and thus to tackle the problems that its salaries commission highlighted in 1982, derives partly from its good recent growth performance. Macroeconomic performance is outside the scope of this book, but the pay problems that developing countries face are not exclusively economic: they have human resource aspects that are relevant to us here.

3.2   Human resource aspects of pay problems

Overstaffing
If the cake will not get any bigger, reduce the number of slices. There is a close yet paradoxical connection between increasing pay and reducing the number of employees. Attempting to reduce the number of employees is an aspect of job reduction, which is the subject of Chapter 9, so we shall not discuss it in detail here. Earmarking some of the savings from reducing the number of employees to increase the pay of those who remain has often been used to win the support of employees for job reductions. In South Africa, an agreement in 1996 between the government and the trade unions made the connection explicit: roughly half of the amount budgeted for pay increases was to come from job reductions.

Certainly it is possible for such a trade-off to be made successfully. Figure 5.3 was given to the authors by staff of the Ministry of Public Service in Uganda, where it is used to show how reducing staff numbers can free resources for increasing pay.

Figure 5.3   Staff reduction and pay reform in Uganda

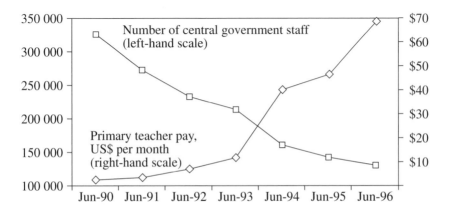

So in Uganda the trade-off worked: real pay did increase (and, while the increase for primary teachers was particularly dramatic, the increase for other categories of employee was also substantial). But there is a danger in making the link too explicit: expectations may be raised that government fails to fulfil. In Tanzania, as in Uganda, civil servants were promised a pay rise which was to be financed by job reductions. There was a dramatic improvement in civil service salaries in 1993/4, when monetary pay tripled in value. However, Tanzanian public servants to whom we spoke in 1996 had no recollection of any such dramatic increase. This was partly because some of the increase was swallowed up by inflation; partly because improvements were being made from such a low base that increases did not make a significant impact; and partly, too, because the rhetoric of civil service reform raised expectations to an unrealistically high level. Even in Uganda, in early 1997, one of the authors frequently heard civil servants complain that government had failed to deliver on its promise of a substantial pay increase, despite objective evidence that there had been a significant increase in percentage terms.

Imbalance between wage and other expenditure

It occasionally happens that the size of an organization's pay bill puts pressure on other areas of expenditure. In Tanzania, the need to service the government wage bill put pressure on government expenditure, so that extension workers could not go to work because of lack of transport, and teachers lacked the books they needed to teach. As recently as 1997, the Tanzanian government was setting up a 'primary teacher human resource plan', one of whose objectives was to shift the ratio of teacher wages to other recurrent expenditure from 93:7 to 80:20. It aimed to do this by transferring teachers from areas of surplus to areas of deficit, and also by making teachers redundant. (Again, redundancy is discussed in Chapter 9 in the context of job reduction.)

Allowances, benefits and the principle of 'transparency'

In many organizations, and especially in public agencies, the non-wage element in employees' remuneration can be substantial. Table 5.1 shows the composition of civil service remuneration in five developing countries.

In all five cases the non-wage element is substantial. It takes different forms in different countries. There can be allowances for transport, or for housing, or for living in remote areas, or even (in India) a 'dearness allowance' intended to compensate for the effects of inflation. We shall look in more detail at the relationship between allowances and other remuneration shortly, when we study the operation of civil service pay in the Sudan.

Table 5.1   Composition of civil service remuneration, selected countries, various years

Country	Year	Benefits as a percentage of total compensation	Salary as a percentage of total compensation
Bolivia	1982	70	30
Cameroon	1987	19	81
Central African Republic	1984	38	62
	1987	41	59
Gambia, The	1982	12	88
	1988	22	78
Senegal	1980–85	25	75
	1989	43	57

Source: Lindauer and Nunberg (1994: 143)

In Chapter 6 we will argue that a good selection process is transparent in the sense that the basis for selection decisions is clear to applicants and selectors. Transparency has become an important principle in pay management as well in recent years. Pay reformers argue that a system with numerous allowances and benefits which supplement the basic wage is opaque, because it is complex and hard to understand. This is particularly so because not all the benefits are 'monetized'. One striking example is where employees receive free housing. Very often the housing is of a high standard, dating sometimes from the colonial period, and could not be afforded by civil servants if economic rents were charged. Because in many cases no rent is charged, economic or otherwise, the value of the benefit to the employee is unclear, or 'opaque'. Reformers recommend 'monetizing' all these allowances and benefits, and consolidating them into a single salary package in the interests of transparency.

However, salary is taxable whereas allowances often are not. Therefore reformers usually also recommend increasing the basic salary to compensate for the extra tax that employees now have to pay. The bad news for the employee is that tax is liable on his or her entire remuneration package; the good news is that the pension entitlement, or severance payment for redundancy, may increase dramatically, since pensions and severance payments are usually based on final salaries.

Salary compression

We noted that the economic difficulties afflicting many developing countries have elicited the paradoxical recommendation that civil servants' pay should be increased. A more refined version of the recommendation is that some salaries need to rise, while others may actually need to fall. An even greater paradox is that the recommendation frequently is that the salaries of the highest paid should rise, while those of the lowest paid should fall. In David Lindauer's academic words: 'More disaggregated treatment of government pay levels reveals that while some wages (usually of the least skilled) may still be "too high", other wages are now "too low" (Lindauer, 1994: 25). Paraphrasing the Christian Bible, to them that have more, more should be given.

How is that recommendation supported? Lindauer and other writers invoke the concept of the compression ratio, which we mentioned in our earlier discussion of differentials. In Table 5.2, evidence is presented that the compression ratio has reduced in 10 of the 21 countries listed, and has increased in only three. Lindauer infers that this reduction must have a negative effect on the retention and performance of

Table 5.2   Salary compression ratios

Country	Earliest period	Latest period	Reference period
Argentina	4:1	–	pre-1990
Burundi	17:1	–	1984
Cameroon	22:1	–	1989
Central African Republic	9:1	9:1	1985–88
Gambia, The	8:1	6:1	1985–88
Ghana	6:1	10:1	1984–92
Guinea	9:1	5:1	1985–89
Guinea-Bissau	5:1	4:1	1988–89
Laos	3:1	7:1	pre-1988–1988
Malawi	33:1	30:1	1975–83
Mali	16:1	–	1985
Mauritania	7:1	3:1	1975–85
Mozambique	2:1	9:1	1985–90
Niger	18:1	15:1	1975–85
Nigeria	18:1	9:1	1975–83
Senegal	8:1	6:1	1980–85
Sudan	13:1	9:1	1975–84
Togo	12:1	–	1985
Uganda	6:1	–	1983/84
Zaire	47:1	–	1985
Zambia	14:1	7:1	1975–84

Source: Lindauer and Nunberg (1994: 145).

senior civil servants, and indirectly on the performance of the staff whom they supervise.

The subjective nature of this recommendation becomes apparent, however, as soon as one asks, 'What is the right compression ratio?,' to which the most precise answer is, 'Larger than it is just now.' Some of the data used to support the recommendation is suspect. For instance, Lindauer (1994: 24) bemoans the fact that, whereas an assistant director in Zambia received 17 times what the lowest paid employee received in 1971, by 1986 that ratio had declined to 'a mere 3.7:1', and gives the British economist Christopher Colclough as the source of his data. But Colclough himself points out that the higher compression ratio in the earlier period was a hangover from the colonial period, when there were separate salary grades for African and non-African (that is, British) employees: he characterizes the gap between those grades as 'inappropriately wide' (Colclough, 1997: 82).

Can we get any help on this point from the human resources literature, as distinct from the economic development literature? Unfortunately, as we have mentioned already, the concept of the compression ratio is not found in that literature. We saw earlier, however, that Armstrong and Murlis in their textbook on pay management believe that a differential of 15–20 per cent between grades is normal, although they suggest that the differential might reasonably be as low as 15 per cent at the bottom end, and as high as 30–40 per cent at the top end, to reflect the greater influence that senior staff are said to have on organizational performance (1994:186). If we take an eight-grade structure (a typical number of grades according to Armstrong and Murlis), where there are differentials of 15 per cent between the bottom three grades, 35 per cent between the top two, and 20 per cent between the grades in the middle, this yields a compression ratio of 3.8:1 – by a remarkable coincidence the figure in Zambia in 1986 that Lindauer condemned!

Moreover, the concept of the compression ratio applies only to salary differences: differences in allowances are excluded. It is likely that the allowances that senior staff receive are worth much more than junior staff allowances (an example of the kind of opaqueness which pay reformers are seeking to move away from). It must also be said that the picture that Lindauer and others present, of a senior cadre of staff who earn only marginally more than their junior colleagues, is not often recognized by the junior colleagues from a wide range of developing countries with whom we have discussed this question.

One final point to make about salary compression is that decompressing salaries is likely to increase pay inequality between women and men, since senior staff in most organizations are predominantly male while junior staff are predominantly female. (We shall say more about equal pay later in the chapter.)

Box 5.4   The remuneration package in the Sudan

An analysis by the Oxford economist Derek Robinson illustrates very well the problem of calculating the total remuneration package. Robinson calculated that by 1986 the basic salary for a graduate entering the Sudan civil service on grade 9 had fallen to a mere 24.5 per cent of its 1975 value, after allowing for inflation. However, once he included allowances to which staff on that grade were entitled (for housing, transport and 'nature of work'), its value rose to 50.4 per cent. (Robinson called this figure the *real gross salary.*) Allowances, in other words, were worth as much as salary.

The picture was further qualified by the fact that grade 9 was an 'incremental scale', so the graduates got an annual pay increase. Taking this into account pushed the figure up to 60.4 per cent of the 1975 value. (Robinson calls this the *real non-promotion salary index.*) Finally, Robinson looked at the actual earnings of the graduates who joined the civil service in 1975 (he calls this the *real actual gross salary index*) and found that it was on average 121.5 per cent of the 1986 value. This was because many of the graduates were promoted during the period.

Thus the complete picture was as follows:

Basic pay on Grade 9 in 1975:	100.0%
Basic pay (allowing for inflation) in 1986:	24.5%
Gross pay (including allowances):	50.4%
Real non-promotion salary index (including increments):	60.4%
Real actual gross salary index (including promotions):	121.5%

While the basic pay of new graduate entrants to the civil service in 1986 was worth only 24.5 per cent of what their counterparts received in 1975, by 1986 the average actual pay of those counterparts had risen to 121.5 per cent of what they received when they joined in 1975.

See Robinson (1990).

Pay devolution

In a number of countries, including the UK and (very recently) Singapore, organizations have taken steps to transfer responsibility for pay determination from the centre to individual departments. Those organizations argue that transferring responsibility in this way allows pay levels to match the circumstances of the individual parts of government, so that, if an Information Technology department, for instance, has difficulty retaining its specialist staff because their skills are in demand in other companies, it can pay them more without any implication for staff in other departments. Pay devolution is an aspect of the general movement towards administrative devolution. We discuss it in Chapter 9.

3.3 Summary

The distinctive features of pay management and reform we have discussed in this section are

- the effects of the economic context on public sector pay: low pay, corruption, 'moonlighting' and so on;
- overstaffing: the connection between pay reform and employment reform (the subject of Chapter 8);
- imbalance between wage and other expenditure, so that employees lack the resources they need to do their jobs;
- the contribution of allowances and benefits to the total remuneration package;
- the possible negative effect of salary compression;
- devolution of pay determination.

4 Job Evaluation

In the rest of this chapter we look at two distinctive approaches to pay management: job evaluation and performance-related pay. Both have been proposed as solutions to some of the problems we discussed in the last section: Robinson noted that the absence of job evaluation in the Sudan contributed to an overemphasis on qualifications in determining pay; he also suggests productivity bonuses as a way of increasing efficiency. Chew explained how performance-related pay operates in Singapore as an incentive to greater productivity. Both approaches are widely used in industrialized countries, so we have a lot of experience to draw on. We now look at job evaluation in some detail, and then consider performance-related pay more briefly.

4.1 Definition and types of techniques

Smith defines job evaluation as 'the determination of the relative worth of jobs as a basis for the payment of differential wages and salaries'

(Smith, 1983: 69). It is one of the best-established HRM techniques, with a history that goes back at least a hundred years, and extensive applications in both industrialized and non-industrialized countries.

Techniques subdivide into two kinds: qualitative and quantitative (sometimes also described as non-analytical and analytical, respectively). Qualitative techniques rely heavily on subjective judgements by the job evaluator, and are therefore simple but crude. Quantitative techniques set up numerical systems that reduce the possibility of bias: they are therefore rich but difficult to operate. The distinction between the techniques is blurred, and you are likely to come across hybrid versions in practice. We shall illustrate them by looking at one representative example of a qualitative technique, *job classification*, and one representative example of a quantitative technique, *points factor rating*.

Study task 2: advantages and disadvantages of job evaluation techniques

While you study the discussion of the different techniques, you should use the following table to make notes about their advantages and disadvantages.

Method	Advantages	Disadvantages
Qualitative		
Quantitative		

✑

4.2   A qualitative technique of job evaluation: job classification

The process of job classification is shown in Figure 5.4, which follows the description in Thomason (1980: 62–4). Notice the importance of job analysis data, giving us a further example of horizontal integration (Chapter 2).

Figure 5.4   The process of job classification

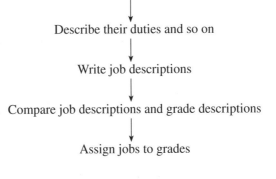

Establish grades: how many are to be recognized in the job population?
'Benchmark' jobs may be used as anchor points here

Describe their duties and so on

Write job descriptions

Compare job descriptions and grade descriptions

Assign jobs to grades

Box 5.5 displays a set of grade definitions for managerial staff based on job classification.

Box 5.5   Grade definitions for managerial staff

Grade 1
Senior supervisors in charge of a large group or section in which the work is mainly routine; or assistant to grade 2 specialists.

Grade 2
Senior supervisors in charge of a large group or section where some of the work is non-routine; or specialists giving advice or services or carrying out research work when a professional qualification or its equivalent is required.

Grade 3
Managers of medium-sized departments consisting of several sections where the work is mainly routine; or senior specialists leading a section or team of grade 2 or grade 1 specialists.

Grade 4
Managers of large departments consisting of several large groups or sections where the work is mainly routine; or managers of medium-sized departments where a considerable amount of non-routine work is required; or managers of small specialized departments entirely engaged on high-level professional, technical or scientific work.

Grade 5
Managers of very large departments consisting of a number of large units, each carrying out similar but mainly routine work and headed by grade 4 managers; or managers of large departments where the work is mainly non-routine,

or heads of specialized functions providing advice or services for a division.

Grade 6
Managers controlling a number of different functions headed by grade 5 managers; or heads of major functions providing services throughout the division and contributing to the formulation of divisional policies and plans.

Grade 7
Divisional directors accountable for the results achieved by major activities or functions of the division and for the formulation and implementation of divisional policies and plans for their area of responsibility; or heads of group functions providing advice and services throughout the group and advising on group policies and plans.

Grade 8
Chief executives of medium-sized divisions; or group directors responsible for coordinating functional services throughout the organization or for formulating group policies in relation to a major service function.

Grade 9
Chief executives of major divisions accountable for the results achieved by their division; or senior group directors in charge of major functions and responsible for formulating group policies and plans in key operating and financial areas.

Grade 10
Group chief executive.

4.3 A quantitative technique of job evaluation: Points factor rating

Job classification is a systematic technique, but can be grasped by the non-specialist. However, its outcomes are often crude, and may be difficult to defend if challenged by a strong trade union or if a formal legal challenge is brought (for instance, a complaint alleging gender discrimination in pay, a possibility we address towards the end of this chapter). For any of those reasons, an organization may seek a more rigorous, quantitative technique.

Quantitative techniques are complex, and it is unlikely that a HRM specialist will try to use them without the help of a specialist consultant. For that reason we do not discuss them in detail here. We confine ourselves to outlining how such a technique works, using the so-called 'points factor' method as our example.

In this method, jobs are broken down into factors. Points are allocated for each factor, and then added together to give a total score. Pay for the job is based on the score: the higher the score, the higher the pay. Factors can be

- *inputs* (the personal characteristics, including qualifications, needed to do the job);
- *processes* (the working methods needed to do the job, such as dealing with people, difficult working conditions and mental effort); and
- *outputs* (the contribution that the job makes to the overall performance of the organization).

If factors are not all of equal importance, a 'weighting' can be used where some factors have a higher value so as to reflect their greater importance. Box 5.6 presents an example of a factor scale for a single job factor, dealing with a job *process*.

Box 5.6   An example of a factor scale

Factor 6: contacts
This factor considers the requirement in the job for contacts inside and outside the organization. Contacts may involve giving and receiving information, influencing others or negotiation. The nature and frequency of contacts should be considered, as well as their effect on the company.

Level 1   little or no contacts except with immediate colleagues and supervisor (10 points);
Level 2   contacts are mainly internal and involve dealing with factual queries or exchange of information (20 points);
Level 3   contacts may be internal or external and typically require tact or discretion to gain cooperation (30 points);
Level 4   frequent internal/external contacts, of a sensitive nature requiring persuasive ability to resolve non-routine issues (40 points);
Level 5   frequent internal/external contacts at senior level or on highly sensitive issues, requiring advanced negotiation/persuasive skills (50 points);
Level 6   constant involvement with internal/external contacts at the highest level or involving negotiation/persuasion on difficult and critical issues (60 points).

See Armstrong and Murlis (1994: 105).

4.4   Implementing job evaluation

As we have seen, job evaluation has existed for quite some time, and techniques have been refined considerably over the years. However, there are still some practical issues that organizations face when they try to implement it, and in this section we shall review some of them. First of all, it is a good idea to think about what implementation issues you can foresee in the light of what we have said so far. Study task 3 gives you a chance to do this.

Study task 3: issues in implementing job evaluation

Given our presentation of job evaluation in this chapter, what issues do you think that an organization will face when it tries to implement job evaluation? (You will find it useful to refer back to the notes you made on advantages and disadvantages of job evaluation exercises.)

Here we deal with three issues: reasons for using job evaluation, the expertise needed to carry it out, and the skills necessary to implement it successfully.

Reasons for using job evaluation
Apart from the standard use of job evaluation to determine pay, reasons advanced for its use in more recent years have included the following:

- as a tool for contributing to any strategy involving changes in the values of an organization (Bowey *et al.*, 1992: 95);
- as part of an integrated HRM system, with links to appraisal and development;
- as a way of facilitating the introduction of performance-related pay (PRP) (Davies, 1991: 52–3);
- as a way of promoting equal pay for women (Gray, 1991);
- as a consequence of an organizational restructuring (Riley and Baker, 1987).

Job analysis expertise
The need for expertise will be particularly strong if the organization decides to use one of the more complex quantitative techniques. If so, there is a case for using specialist consultants. Even if you want to produce a tailor-made scheme for your own organization – possibly because you feel that your organization has a unique set of jobs and duties – the outside viewpoint that a consultant provides can

still be useful. Naturally you can only use consultants if you can afford to.

The skills of job evaluation

In order to implement job evaluation successfully in an organization, it is not enough for the HRM practitioner to have an exhaustive knowledge of this rather technical subject. Good personal skills are also needed.

- *Analytical skills*: the organization suggests that there is a problem, and that job evaluation is the answer. But have we formulated the problem correctly? Are there other ways of tackling it? What do we stand to lose, as well as to gain, from implementing job evaluation?
- *Negotiating skills*: like any other new specialist approach, it may be necessary to 'sell' job evaluation to your organization: there is likely to be resistance to it, and the ability to negotiate is important (we discuss negotiation in Chapter 10). You will also need negotiating skills in the narrower sense if you get involved in appeals by individuals against the gradings to which job evaluation has assigned them.
- Your *ability to persuade* will also be in demand, as will your *coaching skills*, when you come to brief line managers and staff representatives on what their role will be.
- Lastly, *persistence* is always going to be needed. Job evaluation takes a great deal of time and effort. You may well reach the point where you realize that you have the option of quietly dropping the whole thing, and that no-one will be very sorry if you do. Your ability to complete this lengthy and complex task may well be crucial.

This list is by no means exhaustive. The important point to remember is that it is not enough to know all about job evaluation. You can only use your knowledge if you have the personal skills to deploy it.

4.5   Summary

This section introduced job evaluation as a systematic approach to making pay decisions. We divided job evaluation techniques into two categories, qualitative and quantitative, and provided one example of each: job classification and points factor rating, respectively. We went on to look at the issues involved in conducting job evaluation, and discussed the reasons why organizations might use it, and the knowledge and skills that the HRM specialist needs in order to use it.

5   Performance-related pay (PRP)

We noted earlier that a disadvantage of graded structures is that they do not recognize the contributions that different individuals make, and we saw that a major objection to job evaluation is its failure to recognize different individual contributions because of its emphasis on the job rather than the jobholder. An agency which specializes in monitoring pay trends in the UK made this comment:

> The most damning charge against job evaluation for employers and employees alike, is that it simply measures the wrong things. The idea that the focus should be measuring the job, not the jobholder, runs counter to the way work is increasingly organized. (Income Data Services, quoted in Armstrong and Murlis, 1994: 109)

The increasing concern with the productivity of individual employees has led to a growth of interest in how pay can be used to increase productivity. Using pay in this way has come to be called *performance-related pay*. It is to be contrasted with traditional bonus systems, often known as payment by results (PBR), of the kind we referred to in our discussion of the gardeners and the gardening supervisor.

5.1   What is PRP?

PRP is one approach to using pay to provide an *incentive* to individuals to work more effectively. Armstrong and Murlis (1994: 258) use it to refer to schemes that 'base additional financial rewards on ratings of performance, contribution and competence'. They go on to describe it as 'the main method of determining pay progression for non-manual workers'. PRP, they say, 'has now largely replaced the fixed incremental pay systems introduced in the private sector during the 1970s.'

5.2   How does it work?

PRP in practice can be seen as an extension of appraisal. Where appraisal includes objective setting, the determination of pay can follow from the setting of objectives. In other words, objectives are set for the individual member of staff and performance against them is linked to pay. How this operates is shown in Figure 5.5.

Once objectives have been set, the individual goes about meeting them. The supervisor monitors and helps the individual during the year, and at the end of the year there is a formal review of perform-

Figure 5.5   The PRP process

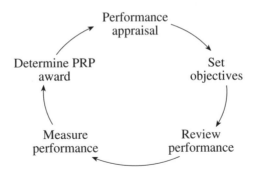

ance in the light of the objectives. The PRP award then reflects the extent to which objectives were met. This leads on to a setting of fresh objectives, and the process begins again.

Box 5.7   PRP in the UK Inland Revenue

The Inland Revenue is the official body responsible for the collection of taxes in the United Kingdom. PRP was introduced for managerial grades in 1988 as an element in the annual pay agreement between the Revenue and the Inland Revenue Staff Federation, the union that represents managers.

As in Figure 5.5, PRP was linked to the appraisal scheme. (This 'open appraisal' approach was in contrast to the 'closed', confidential system which was used for scientific and professional officers in the civil service at large.) First there was an annual discussion of individual work objectives (the 'job plan') for the coming year between each member of staff and his or her immediate superior, the 'reporting officer'. Second, there was supposed to be frequent review of achievements in relation to this job plan, which in turn might lead to the plan being revised. Finally, the reporting officer was asked to rate the performance of the staff member at the end of the year according to as many as 13 work-related criteria. These ratings, plus impressions from discussions about the job plan, provided a basis for the overall rating of the employee. The marking was then vetted by the reporting officer's superior, the 'countersigning officer'.

Ratings were on a scale of 1 to 5, and awards were restricted to staff who got 1s or 2s. Staff who got a 'Box 1', the top marking, received an accelerated increment if they were not already at the top of their scale, and an additional increment if they were. Staff who got two consecutive 'Box 2s' received half an increment, but only if they were already at the top of their scale. For tax inspectors, the maximum award for sustained outstanding performance was 12 per cent of salary.

The 1988 pay agreement which introduced PRP also set a ceiling on the total amount that could be awarded (para. 13 vi): 'It is expected that ... the cost will not exceed (nor fall substantially short of) the cost of giving 25 per cent of the staff in the grades covered an increase on the (scale) on which they are on.'

See Marsden and Richardson (1994).

For many employees a system like that described in Box 5.7 has an intuitive appeal. It does seem unjust that two individuals should receive the same pay even though one is doing better. Many employees are also motivated by clear objectives. (We will see in Chapter 7 that there is strong research evidence that working to objectives does improve performance.)

Box 5.8   Performance-related pay in Malaysia[1]

While PRP has been widely discussed as a possible solution to problems of performance and low motivation in developing country public sectors (it was one of Robinson's proposed solutions in the Sudan), it has been adopted in relatively few countries – Singapore is one of them. Another country which has adopted it enthusiastically is Singapore's nearest neighbour, Malaysia, where PRP has been an integral part of civil service reform. The basic process is that PRP awards are made following appraisal, and are based on a manager's assessment of performance against objectives (called 'work targets' in the Malaysian system) which have previously been set jointly by manager and employee.

There are three major differences. First, there are some features which relate the operation of PRP to the SHRM model which we discussed in Chapter 1. PRP has been introduced in an attempt to achieve a 'shift in the work culture' of civil servants. Objectives ('work targets') for individuals are set only after objectives have been set for the department in which the individual works as a whole. This is an example of vertical integration: there is clearly an attempt here to ensure that appraisal and pay determination contribute to the achievement of the organization's strategic objectives.

The second major difference is how criteria for appraising performance are prescribed (in the Malaysian system these have the bland title of 'aspects of appraisal'). Some of them, particularly those under the heading of 'personal traits', appear to invite the problem of subjectivity in appraisal ratings which we will discuss in Chapter 7. It is also unclear how assessment of performance against work targets fits into the system. In theory, it should come under assessment of work output; in practice, the manager and the employee might lose sight of it amongst all these very elaborate 'aspects'.

The third major difference is the way salary progression is determined following the appraisal rating, with outstanding employees enjoying what is called a 'diagonal' progression, and exceptionally weak employees suffering a 'static' progression. While it is unclear what exactly these different salary progressions – 'diagonal', 'horizontal' and so on – represent, it is clear that the intention is to give larger pay increases to high-rated employees. Quotas are placed on the number of employees who can enjoy accelerated salary progression: a manager's rating of an employee as outstanding may not be endorsed if the department's quota has been exceeded.

This last feature may appear strange, but it has almost certainly been introduced to control the inflationary tendency of PRP, a result of the 'leniency bias' which we discuss in Chapter 7 as one of the problems associated with appraisal rating. However, failure to endorse the salary progression of an employee whose manager has rated him or her as outstanding seems unlikely to motivate the employee as PRP schemes are supposed to do (and we have anecdotal evidence of complaints from Malaysian civil servants on precisely this point).

5.3   Does it work well?

Malaysia's PRP system (Box 5.8) is broadly recognizable in terms of our description, but contains potential problems. Box 5.9 gives an example of a PRP scheme introduced in a British public enterprise (subsequently privatized) which was reported as a success.

Box 5.9   Performance related pay in British Rail

When Trevor Toolan took over as managing director (Personnel) at British Rail in 1986, he inherited a situation where all BR's managers were represented by trade unions, and received an annual percentage increase in July each year which was common to all BR's staff. There were 21 different grades for managers alone. Each manager also received a merit award in January based on a rudimentary performance appraisal system, which entailed appraisers ticking a box from one (unsatisfactory performance) to five (excellent), with each box carrying a fixed merit award. However, managers already at the top of their grades – and there were many of them, since grades were narrow – did not qualify for merit increases.

After negotiations with unions reached an impasse, BR offered individual contracts to all 9000 managers, most of whom accepted. In the
new system, managers and subordinates agreed a set of around five
objectives (interestingly, these were mostly unquantifiable; in the old
system the objectives had been pre-set and quantifiable) and the
means by which performance would be assessed. In November, they
met again to reach an interim performance rating. Finally, the meeting
in the following May determined the performance rating, and the PRP
award.

A survey shortly after the scheme was introduced showed that 50 per
cent of employees felt that the new system would motivate managers
to improve their performance, although 30 per cent believed it was too
early to judge.

See Personnel Management Plus (1990).

Some contrasting evidence comes from the operation of PRP in the UK
Inland Revenue, the national tax collection agency which introduced
it in 1988. In 1991 a survey was carried out to assess its effects, with
2423 managers participating. Tables 5.3 and 5.4 give the results.

You will notice that the material from the two surveys is contradictory.
Why do you think this might be? One reason might be that the Inland
Revenue survey was an independent study, whereas the British Rail
survey was conducted under management auspices. But examples of
both success and failure have been reported, suggesting the possibility that the success of PRP schemes is contingent on specific conditions in the organization.

So what conditions are necessary for PRP to work successfully?
Armstrong and Murlis (1994) suggest the conditions displayed in Box
5.10.

Table 5.3   Views of Inland Revenue managers on the impact of PRP on their staff

Performance-related pay has:	Agree (%)	Disagree (%)
Caused many staff to work beyond the requirements of their job	15	79
Led many staff to give sustained high performance at work	14	77
Helped to increase the quality of work of many staff	10	82
Made many staff more committed to their work	12	79

Table 5.4   Views of Inland Revenue staff on some effects of PRP on staff as a whole

Performance-related pay has:	Agree (%)	Disagree (%)
Led me to improve the quality of my work	12	80
Led me to improve my sensitivity towards colleagues	14	63
Helped to undermine staff morale	55	25
Caused jealousies between staff	62	21
Made staff less willing to help colleagues	28	53

Source: Marsden and Richardson (1994).

Box 5.10   Conditions for successful PRP

PRP should be linked to the performance management (or appraisal) process. We saw two attempts to do this, in Malaysia and in the Inland Revenue in Britain.

PRP should be tailored to the particular needs of the organization. There are many 'ready-made' schemes which can be bought from consultants who specialize in pay management, but they may be incompatible with the organization's working practice, for instance in assuming pay differentials which do not exist, or prescribing criteria which are inappropriate.

Balancing PRP criteria. Criteria for making PRP awards should be a mixture of output factors, in terms of the individual's work performance, and 'input' factors in terms of the individual's skills, possibly including evidence of educational qualifications. The latter factor should not be exaggerated: we saw in the case of the Sudan how the pay system there was distorted by an overreliance on qualifications as the main factor for determining pay.

Flexibility. Ideally there should be room to make awards in different ways, perhaps on occasion making lump sum awards rather than simply increasing the overall salary. (We saw how Malaysia uses both kinds of awards.)

Teamwork. Credit should be given for working as a member of a team, so as to avoid an exclusive concentration on the individual as the unit of performance, which might lead to unhealthy competition between colleagues. (We made a similar point about job analysis in Chapter 4.) At one extreme, individual bonuses might be shared equally among the members of the team: this was what the education advisory service did in one British education authority in the early 1990s. Less ambitiously, contribution to the overall performance of the team would be one of the performance criteria on which the PRP award was based.

Avoiding short-termism. The criteria used to determine PRP awards become a sort of definition of effective performance. If the criteria refer exclusively to short-term objectives, how employees do their jobs may become too narrow. Some important work objectives take years to complete. For instance, in a large Tanzanian local authority the updating of staff personnel records may take three years. In such a case annual work objectives should include progress towards meeting longer-term objectives, as well as completion of objectives which can be achieved within a year.

Involvement in the design process. Employees should be able to participate in the design of the PRP scheme. The British Inland Revenue's scheme was the outcome of the annual pay negotiation between management and the trade union.

Getting the message across. Thought should be given to the way in which the scheme will be communicated to staff, including how it should be launched.

See Armstrong and Murlis (1994: 273–4).

5.4   Is PRP 'appropriate'?

I have no choice but to come to town because I need money. Why should a man undergo such hardship for any other reason? I must help my family. If that means working every day... I will do it. I cannot let my family suffer.
(Kenyan nightwatchman, quoted in Blunt, 1983: 39)

I work five days a week, man, loading crates down on the dock,
I take my hard-earned money, and meet my girl down on the block.
Monday when the foreman blows time,
I already got Friday on my mind.
(Springsteen, 1980)

These two quotations, the second from a well-known American song-writer, illustrate an *instrumental* work motivation. It is sometimes suggested that the motivation of workers in developing countries is mainly instrumental; that is, that they value work because of the rewards that they get from it rather than for its own sake. It would follow that developing country employers should give exclusive attention to improving pay and other benefits in order to motivate staff. However, research summarized by Blunt (1983: 39–41) suggests that an instrumental motivation is found among low-status workers wherever jobs are scarce, whether in a developing country or anywhere else: workers value work principally for the material rewards it provides, which they can use to improve their lives outside work (like the docker in Springsteen's song). On the other hand, workers in high-status occupations, such as managers, are more likely to be *intrinsically* motivated; that is, they value work for itself rather than for the rewards that work offers, which they may take for granted when those rewards are sufficient. (Alternatively, perhaps it is not so much the status of the work as the autonomy and pride in craftsmanship: arguably the workers in a bicycle repair cooperative have more of those than a relatively well-paid insurance salesperson.)

Such differences between occupational groups need to be taken into account when designing pay systems, as do differences between organizations. The pay system that is appropriate for a small, growing private sector company will probably not suit a large, well-established organization in the public sector. However, we should be careful not to assume that a particular pay system is 'culturally appropriate' simply because it is well-established. Often the system that is regarded as 'appropriate' was inherited from the former colonial power. Such a system is certainly *familiar*. It may or may not be *appropriate*. Moreover, we should be alert to the many other factors as well as pay that can affect staff motivation: for example, how much staff are able to participate in decision making and the extent to which they receive support from their managers.

6 Equal pay

Pay management has an important equal opportunities dimension especially where gender is concerned. In most organizations in most countries (industrialized, developing and transitional) women earn less than men. The discrepancy is glaring in the UK: in the 1990s, women in the UK earned on average only 77 per cent of their male counterparts' earnings, up to 10 per cent less than women in other European Union countries (Metcalfe, 1994). The main reason for this is that women are concentrated at the lower end of the management hierarchy. It follows that the main remedial action needed is in the areas of recruitment and selection and career development, to ensure that there are no unreasonable barriers to women's career progression, and that they are equipped with the skills they need to progress, especially where their education has failed to give them those skills. But there can also be unfairness built into the pay system which compounds gender inequality. And that unfairness can operate even where approaches like job evaluation and performance-related pay are used.

6.1   Job evaluation and equal pay

While the application of any good technique should make matters at least a little better, there is a particular difficulty with qualitative job evaluation techniques, which tend to perpetuate the status quo. The prejudices in society and in organizations which cause gender discrepancies in the first place are likely to be reproduced in the judgements that evaluators make in qualitative approaches, where judgement is subjective. So in this section we will examine how discrimination can occur in the operation of job evaluation, and later on how it can occur in performance-related pay.

Equal pay for equal work is the essence of equal opportunities in pay. In order to assess whether two jobs are in fact equal, a systematic approach such as job evaluation is needed: in the UK, job evaluation has received a fresh impetus in recent years from equal opportunities concerns. But although introducing job evaluation can contribute to pay equality between women and men through providing a systematic basis for comparing jobs, job evaluation can itself be a source of bias.

Now work through the following study task, which will help you to understand how discrimination can creep into job evaluation, and what can be done to prevent it.

Study task 4: equal pay

UK law allows cases to be brought claiming discrimination in pay. Such cases often hinge on the way in which the employer applies job evaluation to two different jobs, one carried out mainly by men and the other mainly by women. Here are some job evaluation data based on such a case. The data present how a company 'scored' the jobs of maintenance fitter (a job traditionally carried out by men) and company nurse (a job traditionally carried out by women). Study the data and answer the following questions:

1   *In what way might this job evaluation discriminate against the women who have the job of company nurse?*
2   *How could the job evaluation method be revised so that it operates fairly?*

Factors (each factor is scored on a scale from 1 to 10; for simplicity no weights have been applied)	Maintenance fitter	Company nurse
Skill		
Experience in job	10	1
Training	5	7
Responsibility		
For money	0	0
For equipment and machinery	8	3
For safety	3	6
For work done by others	3	0
Effort		
Lifting requirement	4	2
Strength required	7	2
Sustained physical effort	5	1
Conditions		
Physical environment	6	0
Working position	7	0
Hazards	7	0
Total	65	22

UK case law arising out of cases like this one indicates that only a quantitative scheme will provide an adequate defence against a complaint of pay discrimination. This strengthens the argument for using such a procedure, although of course the complexity of quantitative methods and their consequent expense are barriers to their use, especially in small organizations.

The UK's Equal Opportunities Commission also points out that, where factor weighting is used, discrimination can creep in if the actual weightings used are biased towards male characteristics (or, conceivably, female characteristics: discrimination refers to unfair treatment on grounds of gender, against either women or men). A heavy weighting on either physical activity or working conditions would probably work against the female job.

Equal pay between women and men is not universally legislated for (it has only been fully recognized in the UK in the last 10 years, following pressure from the European Union), so the question of whether to take equal pay seriously may well be an *ethical* rather than a legal one for you. Of course there is still the issue of the quality of information that you will obtain by using a qualitative technique.

PRP and equal pay

In theory PRP should be neutral in its impact on pay equality between women and men. In practice, however, just like job evaluation, PRP decisions can be unequal if the criteria on which they are based are discriminatory. Box 5.11 below, on the experience of one British public development agency which introduced PRP, shows how this may happen.

Box 5.11 PRP and equal pay in a British development agency

A British government development agency introduced PRP in the mid-1990s. The scheme was well designed, being firmly rooted in the agency's performance appraisal scheme, and having an objective-setting procedure. It applied to all staff.

Human resource specialists responsible for operating the scheme reported to one of the authors that it tends to discriminate against women, because the criteria that the agency prescribes for assessing performance apply more readily to senior than to junior staff. For instance, managers are expected to rate subordinates on 'initiative'. Managers sometimes give a low or a zero rating for this to their secretaries. Their justification is that their secretary merely does the work that he or she is asked to do, so there is no question of them showing initiative. Since, as in most organizations, the majority of senior staff are male and the majority of junior staff are female, this means that women tend to receive disproportionately low PRP awards.

Another way in which PRP may disadvantage women is if the scheme applies only to senior staff, who are predominantly male. Many PRP schemes do apply only to senior staff, in fact.

7 Summary and conclusion

In this chapter we have covered:

- a typical pay structure;

- the economic background to pay reform, and the issues that organizations face in reforming their pay structures;
- a critical account of two distinctive approaches to pay management: job evaluation and performance-related pay;
- how employers can promote equal pay between women and men.

Reforming pay structures may be a little like redesigning the pyramids, as we suggested at the start of this chapter, because pay structures, once established, are highly resistant to change. However, the pressures on wage bills, and the availability of distinctive approaches to pay design, may create opportunities for change from which organizations can benefit.

Note

1   We are describing the scheme as it operated in the late 1990s. In 2002 the Malaysian government was carrying out a detailed revision.

6 Recruitment, Selection and Equal Opportunities

Willy McCourt

What this chapter is about

The chapter starts with a review of the stages in a good practice selection process, before considering the problems that can arise in recruitment and selection and the importance of issues of 'equal opportunities'. The concepts of race and gender discrimination, positive action and positive discrimination are explained, and illustrated in practice. The chapter then addresses the role that different interest groups play in influencing the conduct of selection, and lastly suggests alternatives to conventional procedures of recruitment and selection.

What you will learn

By the end of the chapter you should be able to:

- apply a good practice model of recruitment and selection;
- apply several good methods of selection;
- identify how nepotism and favouritism can operate in recruitment and selection;
- identify race and gender discrimination in selection;
- state how the interests of different stakeholders can best be accommodated;
- apply alternative methods of filling staff vacancies.

1   The selection process

Just about all of us have experience of recruitment and selection. You may have sat on an interview panel or screened applications for a job. Almost certainly you have been a candidate yourself. Your experience in this area is the subject of Study task 1.

Study task 1: your experience of the selection process

Think of the most recent appointment you were involved in or know about, and make brief notes on the following.

1   What information did the selectors (or the candidates) have about the contents of the job and the attributes which the successful candidate would require?
2   How was the job advertised to potential candidates?
3   What procedure (if any) was used to reduce the number of applicants before inviting them to the final selection stage?
4   Was an interview used at the final selection stage?
5   Were other selection methods used at this stage? If yes, which?
6   What information (if any) did the selectors seek from people who had personal knowledge of the candidates' abilities?

• Now make a brief assessment of how well these aspects of selection were managed

  – from the selector's point of view?
  – from the candidates point of view?

• How might you improve any of these procedures?

1.1   Stages of the selection process

You may have noticed that the questions you have completed in Study task 1 correspond to the various stages of the selection process. These stages are summarized in Table 6.1.

In the rest of this section we elaborate on these stages of the selection process, and then examine in more detail some important aspects that are often overlooked.

The selection panel

What practical arrangements facilitate the implementation of selection as an integrated process? Typically organizations think in terms of an interview panel which meets to interview and to appoint at the final

Table 6.1   Stages of selection

Selectors	Applicants
Form selection panel	
Job particulars (Person specification)	Advertisement Further particulars
Shortlisting (References)	Applications
Interview (Assessment centre)	Interview (tests etc)
References	
Final decision	

stage of selection: preceding stages in the selection process are viewed as merely a means to an end, necessary to get the candidates to the final selection stage where 'the real decisions' are made. However, from a process point of view, the organization needs to think in terms of a *selection panel*, which first meets to carry out the job analysis, or to ratify a draft job analysis which has been done on its behalf, and to agree the content of the advertisement. It meets a second time to carry out shortlisting, using the selection criteria of the person specification for the post. It meets a third and final time to make the actual appointment, typically at the end of an interview.

In practice, it may be difficult for the panel to operate in this way. There may be problems of diary coordination, and the vagaries of leave, transfers, sickness and so on all have to be accommodated. More problematically, this integrated approach probably cuts across organizational boundaries, especially in a large organization: one central section may be responsible for writing and placing advertisements, for example. An adequate solution, not wholly satisfactory, is to have at least one member of the panel (typically a chairperson) who can play an active role at every stage of the process, and guide other panel members who are unable to do so.

The person specification
The starting point is when the organization decides that an appointment is to be made, what exactly the job is to consist of, and what kind

of person is needed to do it. As you saw in Chapter 4, this involves job analysis, with its twin products, the *job description* and the *person specification*. In recruitment and selection, it is the person specification that is crucial, and is in fact the basis for all selection decisions. It should also be the key document given to candidates in the 'job particulars'.

The distinction we made in Chapter 4 between *essential* and *desirable* requirements in the person specification is important. An essential requirement, you may remember, is defined as *a requirement without which the postholder would be unable to do the job*. Examples, for certain jobs, are required professional qualifications and the ability to travel around the area in which the post is located. A desirable requirement is *a requirement which contributes to effective performance, but which is not essential*. You should avoid listing requirements as essential if they are not strictly that. There is a real danger of discrimination here, one that we come back to later in the chapter.

As we said in Chapter 4, not more than nine separate items should be listed. This is because selection at later stages in the process becomes unwieldy if there are too many items.

There is, of course, a backward linkage from the person specification to the job description, since the person specification presents the abilities which the postholder will need to carry out the duties of the job description. But there are also forward linkages. The advertisement should, in part, reflect the contents of the person specification. When we move on to shortlisting decisions, and then on to the eventual decision to appoint, our decision should be based on the items of the person specification which provide *selection criteria*. The design of the final selection stage should, ideally, incorporate those same criteria. These forward and backward linkages are shown in Figure 6.1 below. (You should note that the selection process should be *integrated* in much the same way that the sequence of HRM activities as a whole ought to be.)

Advertising

The next stage in the selection process is the advertisement. Again, most of us are familiar with it: the newspaper advertisement, the notice on the organization notice board, the card in the office of the employment service or careers centre. Those who make enquiries in response to the advertisement will receive some written material, often described as the *further particulars* of the post. They normally include an application form. They may also include information about the job. The job description and person specification are obvious docu-

Figure 6.1   Forward and backward linkages in the selection process

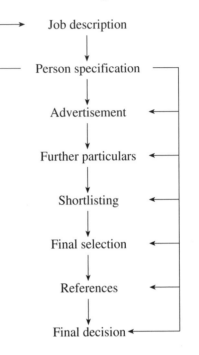

ments to include. Information about the organization, the department or office in which the job is located, and other information relevant to the needs of applicants, may also be included.

Shortlisting

Where there are more applicants than can realistically be seen face-to-face, organizations use a *shortlisting* procedure to whittle them down to a manageable number. This may be a simple matter of excluding those who do not have required qualifications, but, as we shall see below, a more elaborate procedure may also be used, using selection criteria derived from the person specification.

Final selection

Usually a small number of applicants is invited to the *final selection stage*, although large organizations, notably government agencies, such as a Civil or Public Service Commission responsible for recruitment into the Civil Service, may invite most applicants to sit a qualifying test which becomes the penultimate stage in the process. Final selection may comprise a number of different elements, of which the one probably most familiar to you is *the selection interview*. Often the interview is the only element, but it may be complemented by other methods that we discuss below (indicated by 'Assessment centre' in Table 6.1).

References and final selection

Following the final selection stage the organization is in a position to make an appointment. Before the appointment is confirmed, organizations normally ask candidates to nominate reliable informants who can provide an opinion in writing – usually called a *reference*, or testimonial – based on their personal knowledge about the candidate's suitability for the post. Organizations usually take up references either when the candidates are invited to the final selection stage, or following the final selection stage for the candidate recommended for appointment (both possibilities are shown in Table 6.1).

How does this discussion compare with your answers to Study task 1? Possibly some of the elements we have touched on were absent from your experience. The proper use of a person specification, for example, is still quite rare. Similarly, at the final stage it is likely that the interview was the only selection method you noted, despite the availability of additional (and effective) selection methods.

Having outlined the selection process as a whole, we now look in more detail at the following important stages: attracting suitable candidates, shortlisting and final selection.

1.2 Attracting candidates: labour market conditions

You may find it strange that an organization needs to make an effort to attract candidates. Many developing countries have very large numbers of unemployed people. In Bangladesh, for example, the number of candidates applying to join the civil service is so great that at times there has been a two-year delay in processing their applications. But even in countries where unemployment is high, HRM specialists and managers often understand that able candidates, especially for specialist jobs, are at a premium, and that some jobs will be hard to fill.

This is due to conditions in the labour market. Chapter 3 introduced the concept of the labour market with its supply and demand sides. We saw that, in a loose labour market, the employer can afford to pick and choose from among applicants, while in a tight labour market the employer needs to make an effort to attract applicants. Even in a loose labour market there are likely to be, as it were, knots of tightness, areas where skilled workers are scarce, for example workers with computer skills or entrepreneurial skills. Alternatively, there might be areas – they may be remote or have a difficult climate – where many jobseekers do not want to live, despite a relative availability of jobs.

Study task 2: loose and tight labour markets

Make some notes on the following questions.

1 Would you describe the labour market in your country as generally loose or tight at the moment?
2 What was the position 10 years ago?
3 How do you expect the situation to change in the next five years?
4 In what skill areas or geographical areas is the market relatively tight?
5 What measures might be used to 'loosen' those areas of tightness?

The approach which an employer takes to attracting candidates should vary in line with labour market conditions. Very often, however, employers are not sufficiently sensitive to those conditions. They may continue to assume that they will have a steady stream of candidates for finance positions, say, even when demand for such candidates from the private sector has risen as a consequence of economic liberalization. Alternatively, a civil service may continue to operate a system of guaranteed entry to public sector employment long after the supply of qualified applicants in the form of secondary school or university graduates has far outstripped demand (the case until recently in certain countries in sub-Saharan Africa).

Now read Box 6.1, which outlines measures used by employers in Singapore to deal with the problem of labour shortage.

Box 6.1   Singapore: a response to demographic change

In Singapore, changes in the demographic and labour supply factors have also caused a tightening of labour markets (reflected in the government's approach to public sector pay, which we discussed in Chapter 5). Although the following discussion focuses mainly on Singapore, similar problems are encountered in several other South-east Asian countries where economic development has been rapid.

Recruiting foreign workers. Singapore employers are responding to the current labour shortage by hiring foreign workers who have been attracted to Singapore by high pay. However, their attempts to recruit more foreign workers is constrained by the Ministry of Labour which imposes a foreign worker levy as well as a quota based on a local:foreigner ratio.

In recent years, Malaysian employers have also become increasingly dependent on foreign workers, especially those from neighbouring

Indonesia. Recently, the Malaysian government has also introduced a foreign worker levy on employers.

Intensifying recruitment efforts through advertising campaigns and posters, liaising with employment agents in neighbouring countries.

Strengthening liaison with schools and polytechnics by participating in industrial attachment schemes and providing work experience opportunities for students.

Enhancing career development. In order to retain existing workers, many employers are now providing better training facilities; job restructuring/multiskilling; career development programmes; better promotion prospects; and employee participation through quality circles and the like.

Women. In order to attract more female workers, some Singapore employers are experimenting with flexible hours as well as part-time work.

A problem facing many employers is the lack of child care facilities, which obliges many women to stop working when they have a baby. While highly paid female professionals can afford to employ maids to help them in household chores and child care, lower paid women may have to stay at home with their children.

Older workers. Some Singaporean employers have extended the retirement age from 55 to 60. Some have introduced flexible retirement arrangements to retain their older employees.

Students. Some companies employ students on a part-time basis. This is common in restaurants and shops.

See Torrington and Huat (1994: 43).

1.3 Shortlisting

Employers can manage demand for jobs to some extent in both tight and loose labour markets, but such strategies are inevitably a blunt instrument. Moreover, for political reasons an employer may be obliged to cast the net widely, even in a loose labour market. Many governments in former British colonies, as far apart as Malaysia and Botswana, have a central agency responsible for civil service recruitment, usually known as either the Public or Civil Service Commission. That agency may be obliged, often by an act of parliament or a provision in the national constitution, to advertise widely for entry to the civil service, perhaps even to invite all eligible candidates to sit an examination, even though there may be thousands of candidates.

Where large numbers of candidates apply, and it is impractical to invite all of them to a final selection stage, employers often use a shortlisting procedure to reduce applicants to a manageable number for interview. Usually they do so by using written application forms. An application form asks for basic biographical details, information about previous education and paid work experience, and the names of referees; there should also be space for the candidate to write a statement which addresses the items listed in the person specification.

Shortlisting decisions should be based on the selection criteria stated in the person specification. If selectors consider other factors such as previous knowledge of the candidate, there is scope for bias, particularly in the form of nepotism and favouritism, as we shall see.

It is also necessary not to pay too much attention to *presentation* of an application at the expense of its content. How does the research reported in Box 6.2 relate to your experience of the way candidates are

---

Box 6.2   Applications: presentation and content

Paying too much attention to the presentation of the application is likely when selectors have no guidance on how to carry out shortlisting, and rely on their own intuitions about what makes someone a good employee. In a study of the decision processes used to assess application forms by graduate recruiters in six UK companies, Herriot and Wingrove found that one in five comments related to presentation rather than to the evidence which candidates presented about their job-related abilities: 'He hasn't written much on the form, and what there is I can't read' and 'Terrible spelling' were typical comments.

Reflecting on their findings, Herriot and Wingrove say, 'The development of a decision aid to enable recruiters to summarize an area and record it seems desirable. Such an instrument might, for example, require the recruiter, after he or she had read the section on academic qualifications, to rate the applicant in terms of probability of successfully completing training, or of patenting a new invention within three years. It would relieve recruiters of the need to call upon their conceptual armoury of implicit personality theories and inferential logic in order to reduce information load on working memory.'

See Herriot and Wingrove (1984).

selected for interview using the information written on an application form? Can you suggest a better way of going about it?

To produce the 'decision aid' that Herriot and Wingrove recommend, it is necessary to draw up a *scoring scheme*. We take each of the selection criteria identified in the person specification, and score them from 1 to 10. Since some criteria are more important, we use a weighting to reflect their relative importance, as shown in Box 6.3.

Box 6.3 Shortlisting in a Tanzanian local authority

Among the criteria for the post of personnel officer are:

- counselling skills;
- knowledge of the Personnel Code (the conditions which govern employment in local government in Tanzania);
- relevant qualifications (either an advanced diploma in public administration or a degree from the University of Dar Es Salaam).

'Counselling skills' is the most important of these three criteria, and is weighted (multiplied) by a factor of 3. 'Knowledge of the Personnel Code' is also important, but less so than counselling skills, so it is weighted (multiplied) by a factor of 2. 'Relevant qualification in administration' or 'degree from the University of Dar Es Salaam' is scored from 1 to 10 like the other criteria, but is not weighted. The merits of two applicants (A1 and A2) could thus be compared, as shown in the following scores.

Criterion	Raw Score		Factor	Final Score	
	A1	A2		A1	A2
Counselling skills	8	5	×3	24	15
Knowledge of the Personnel Code	3	6	×2	6	12
Advanced diploma or degree	10	10	—	10	10
Total score				40	37

Selectors should try to use the full length of the scoring scale: they should be ready to award 0 out of 10, or 10 out of 10, if the candidate deserves it, rather than just clustering their scores within a narrower range. They should also mark each criterion separately, rather than mark on their general feeling about the candidate (what Herriot and Wingrove called 'implicit personality theories'). With each criterion they should base their score on the evidence they have of the candidate's ability in that area. Finally, if more than one selector is involved in shortlisting (which is desirable to control bias), they should score independently, and stick to their scores.[1]

When shortlisting is based on scores, the decision about whom to invite to interview is straightforward: we simply add up the scores, and the highest scoring candidates are invited to interview. A record of the scores should be retained. It will be valuable if the selection decision is challenged, either through an organization's internal grievance procedure or through a court of law. This is increasingly common in many countries, and a written record helps a successful defence against such challenges.

1.4   Final selection

Inviting candidates to the final selection stage

Candidates who have been shortlisted are invited to attend the final selection stage. This is a convenient point to introduce an important management principle, that of *transparency*. Candidates should receive as much information as possible about how selection is managed and how the organization will reach its decision. We said earlier that it is desirable that all applicants should receive a copy of the job description and the person specification. When shortlisted candidates are invited for final selection, their letter of invitation should contain information about the design of the final stage. If there is going to be a test, for example, candidates should be briefed on what kind of test it will be. They should be told approximately how long the interview will last, and who the members of the panel will be.

There is a civil liberties argument in favour of transparency: that candidates who provide confidential information about themselves should know how the organization will use it. Moreover, organizations should be able to account for their decisions. Apart from that, there is a strong practical case for transparency. To make an informed decision at the end of the selection procedure, we need as much information as possible about our candidates. We are more likely to obtain it if candidates know why we need it, and have had time to prepare it. In the interview, for instance, the candidate who knows in advance that there will be some questions about the requirements stated in the person specification is able to prepare to answer those questions fully.

The interview

The interview is the most widely used *and* the most heavily criticized of all selection methods. Most of us have taken part in one, either as selector or candidate. Sometimes defined as 'a conversation with a purpose', it is a meeting, usually lasting anything from five minutes to one hour, between a representative or representatives of the employer who asks questions, and a candidate who has to answer them – though he or she may be allowed to ask a few questions too.

The interview is the classic selection method, and in most countries there is a huge urban mythology about what happens in it, and about experiences that friends and relative have suffered. It plays a prominent part in the great Indian film director Satyajit Ray's film *Mahanagar* (The Big City) where the hero has to endure a succession of dreadful interviews in his desperate search for work. The low point is reached when one interviewer asks him, 'What is the specific gravity of the moon?' At this point the hero gets up and walks out!

Study task 3: advantages and disadvantages of the interview

Drawing on your own experiences, make a short list of the advantages and disadvantages of the selection interview. You can then compare your views with those listed in the specimen answer at the back of the volume. ✍

Designing an 'assessment centre'

In the final stage, the basic principle of selection design is highlighted. It is expressed in the question: *What selection methods should be used to obtain evidence to assess candidates against each item of the person specification?*

To explore its practical implications, we can return to the earlier example of the person specification for a personnel officer working in a Tanzanian local authority, from which we extracted three criteria: counselling skills, knowledge of the Personnel Code, and an advanced diploma or degree. Let us now add three further criteria: experience of personnel work, report writing ability, and presentation skills.

The relevance of previous experience of personnel work is self-evident. Report writing ability is important because personnel officers have to write reports for council meetings; presentation skills are important because officers have to present those reports, and also to make presentations on other occasions to staff groups.

Table 6.2 is a *selection grid* designed to provide the evidence we need.

Table 6.2   Selection grid

Criterion	Form	Interview	Written test	Presentation
Counselling skills		x		x
Report writing ability	x		x	
Presentation skills		x		x
Experience of personnel work	x	x		x
Knowledge of Personnel Code	x	x	x	
Advanced diploma or degree	x			

The left-hand column lists the selection criteria. The other columns represent four methods for obtaining evidence for each criterion. We can take the application form (column 2) and the interview as given in our design: in some shape or other they are probably inevitable elements. A written test has been added to provide evidence of candidates' report writing ability; likewise, a presentation has been added to provide evidence of candidates' presentation skills.

There are two other principles at work here. First, *there should preferably be at least two separate sources of evidence for each major criterion* (evidence is inevitably conditioned by the method we use to obtain it, therefore it is desirable to have more than one method or source); second, *the design should be parsimonious*: each method should yield evidence for more than one criterion.

In the table there are two sources for each criterion, with the exception of 'advanced diploma or degree', for which the application should provide adequate evidence, and each method provides evidence of at least two criteria. Thus the table conforms to the two principles stated.

Suppose that the written test asks candidates to write a report on the implications of integrating a group of central government staff, following decentralization of a central government function to local government. If knowledge of the Personnel Code is a desirable but not essential criterion, we would need to set an alternative task which does not require prior knowledge in this area, so that candidates who do not have that knowledge (those from outside local government) will not be penalized.

The approach we have taken to design of the final stage of selection, combining a number of methods, is sometimes called an *assessment centre*. The name is a little confusing, since it refers to a group of selection methods rather than to a place. It was first developed in the

German, American and British armed forces before and during World War Two, for the selection of officers and of specialist personnel such as aircraft pilots. It is still widely practised in the armed forces in many countries, and its use has spread to civil service recruitment, and also to recruitment into senior and specialist positions in large private sector firms. There is a substantial literature dealing with assessment centres, and a body of skills for acting as an assessor in them (for example, observing a presentation to obtain evidence for specific criteria of selection) for which specialist training is desirable.

Notice the role of the interview in this process: rather than acting as the only method of final selection, it is one element or method among others in the selection procedure. Like other elements, it is used to obtain evidence for specific criteria; it is not used to provide a final summary judgement on candidates. In practical terms, the methods we have noted can be employed alongside each other on the final selection day (or days: assessment centres can extend over two or even three days). Thus one candidate might be giving a presentation while another is attending the interview, and so on. Following the completion of all the elements, a review session, sometimes called a 'wash-up' session, is held in which evidence obtained by different methods is pooled and a final decision made.

Written tests and presentations are two examples of assessment centre activities which are widely used. Other methods include various group activities: candidates as a group may be given a problem to solve, or may be asked to attend a meeting in which each candidate is given a specific role to play, perhaps to argue a particular point of view on an issue. Such activities provide evidence of *interpersonal skills* and *problem-solving ability*. A further method is the 'in-basket exercise': candidates are asked to deal with a series of items representative of the work of the post for which they are being considered. Such an activity provides evidence of ability to *organize a workload* and of *analytical skills*.

Selection tests may also be used: we will discuss them a little later.

Rehabilitating the interview
Research shows that the assessment centre is a powerful method. Although it is not always practical to implement such a comprehensive design, we can still use its underlying principles to improve existing practices. For example, while the interview might remain the major element in the final selection stage, it might be supplemented by a short written task. Otherwise, an interview can be designed to stimulate some of the features of an assessment centre. This has been

termed *behavioural interviewing*: candidates are asked questions designed to elicit information about things they have done (behaviours) which are relevant to each selection criterion in turn.

Critics of the interview have long argued that decisions reached by interview fail to predict subsequent job performance. One very widely quoted study found that interviewers often made up their minds within the first four minutes of the interview. (Presumably they spent the rest of the interview finding evidence to support their prejudices.) Interestingly, more recent studies (undertaken because of the persistence of organizations in using interviews for selection) have attempted to specify ways of improving interviews, and the ability to predict performance of candidates appointed after interview. One article which reviewed a large number of separate research studies (Conway *et al.*, 1995) found that the following simple improvements dramatically improved the predictive value of the interview:

- *standardizing interview questions* (in other words, asking everyone the same questions);
- *mechanical combination* (in other words, making a selection decision by simply adding the scores given by interviewers to each candidate interviewed, and choosing the candidates with the highest aggregate score);
- *job analysis* (in other words, basing the interview questions on a job description or, preferably, a person specification);
- *interview training* for the interviewers.

Despite these very encouraging findings, the interview must remain imperfect. Conway *et al.* also note that, once the above improvements have been made, predictive ability reaches a ceiling. There is still a case for using other selection methods to supplement the interview.

1.5   Using tests in selection

Recognition of the limitations of the interview has led to the development of other selection methods which can be used to increase the quality of evidence that selectors have about candidates. Research has shown that some methods are more likely to predict job performance accurately, which after all is usually the main purpose of selection. (The technical term for this is *predictive validity*). Generally speaking, the method with the highest predictive validity is the *ability test*. Ability tests take different forms. Selection tests for manual workers, for example, may test manual dexterity by timing how long it takes candidates to place a large number of pegs into holes on a board (this is supposed to be suitable for selecting staff to work in electronics assembly plants). Tests for selecting clerical staff, for example, may measure skills of verbal checking by assessing how many deliberate mistakes of spelling and grammar in a page candidates manage to identify.

Advantages of tests like this include the following:

- they have gone through a rigorous process of test development, so that the test results are highly reliable;
- they have test manuals which give instructions on how the tests should be used, and technical data which the HR specialist can use to decide if the test is appropriate;
- recent test manuals have information about the relative performance of women and men, which the selector can use to help interpret test results and avoid discrimination.

Some disadvantages:

- published tests are expensive, and are only available in countries where the test agencies have representatives;
- access to the published test is restricted to staff who have received specialist training, which again is expensive;
- tests are seen as threatening by many candidates, and insulting by others (research suggests, for instance, that tests which are accepted as normal by German or British candidates may be resented by French or Italian candidates, whose countries use tests much less in selection).

The problem of access is a particularly serious one. The need for an 'appropriate technology' of testing has not been addressed by the test agencies, which are run mainly as commercial companies more concerned with generating profits than with widening access. Tests are used more widely in developing and transitional countries in education than in occupational assessment, so you may be able to get advice from an educational testing specialist, such as an educational psychologist.

Creativity in testing: the cloze test
There is one kind of test which is widely used in education, which is potentially suitable for use in organizations, and which is easy to design, administer and score. This is the so-called 'cloze test'. A cloze test consists of a passage of written language at the appropriate level from which every *n*th word – typically every seventh word – has been deleted. The candidate has to supply the missing word, and receives a

mark only if the exact word has been supplied. (There are variations of practice, but this method is the simplest and possibly also the best from a technical point of view.) It can be used for any language.

Try the following test.

Study task 4: a cloze test

Prison and the authorities conspire to _____ each man of his dignity. In _____ of itself, that assured that I _____ survive, for any man or institution _____ tries to rob me of my _____ will lose because I will not _____ with it at any price or _____ any pressure. I never seriously considered _____ possibility that I would not emerge _____ prison one day. I never thought _____ a life sentence truly meant life _____ that I would die behind bars. _____ I was denying this prospect because _____ was too unpleasant to contemplate. But _____ always knew that someday I would _____ again feel the grass under my _____ and walk in the sunshine as _____ free man.

I am fundamentally an _____. Whether that comes from nature or _____, I cannot say. Part of being _____ is keeping one's head pointed towards _____ sun, one's feet moving forward. There _____ many dark moments when my faith _____ humanity was sorely tested, but I _____ not give myself up to despair. _____ way lay defeat and death. ✍️

Source: Mandela (1994).

Suggesting the use of cloze tests, which are easy to design, administer and score, enables us to make a final point about the standard model of good practice in recruitment and selection. Precisely because it is systematic and exists to curtail freedom to make arbitrary appointments, there is the danger that we will come to believe that there is no room for initiative. On the contrary, our cloze test example shows how we can be creative. While operating systematically is important, we do encourage you to experiment with new activities as part of your selection design.

We have now completed our review of the standard model of good practice in recruitment and selection. To help you to consolidate your understanding of its stages and the methods available to the selector, you should now do Study task 5, a case study of selection in a management consultancy firm in Argentina.

Study task 5: applying the good practice model

Imagine you are a human resource specialist in the firm, and you are concerned about its high rate of staff turnover.

In the light of the model of good practice which we have just presented, identify the problems in the recruitment and selection system and recommend how they might be resolved.

Recruiting staff into a management consultancy firm in Argentina

Following many years of military government and the restoration of multi-party government in the mid-1980s, a new market for political and socioeconomic surveys emerged in Argentina as organizations sought to obtain updated market information. Anticipating the emergence of this new trend, two well-known sociologists opened a consulting firm with three other young professionals. Within 10 years business had increased considerably and the permanent staff had risen to over 30. Once the firm had a well-established reputation in the market, the partners decided to widen the scope of their business to other areas such as macroeconomics and marketing. By 1996, the company was employing 60 permanent employees and another 50 as external surveyors.

The firm recruits its staff by advertising in Argentinian universities. Rising unemployment in recent years has increased the number of applications, and dozens of applications were arriving every day, resulting in a mountain of applications to be sifted through. The first step was to reduce this mass of applications to 30. Applications were sifted informally on the basis of good performance at university, computer and statistical skills and professional interests.

The next step was an unstructured interview conducted by one of the partners and a senior manager in an attempt to select 15 candidates who would take part in a two-day course to be held by the company. This course consisted of a presentation of the organization's activities by different managers, some training sessions on the skills needed to carry out surveys through different stages, and a final session to integrate concepts and give feedback to the participants. Candidates were individually evaluated by each of the professionals giving the courses. After pooling their evaluations they selected the final candidates.

Around seven or eight new staff were appointed in this way every year. However, the firm found that many newly appointed staff left as little as three months after joining. The reasons were unclear, but it appears that they had a false perception of the nature of the work. They had been led to expect that they would perform a specific, challenging job, but in practice in the first few months after appointment they were used mainly to pick up excess work of more experienced staff. ✍

How does your answer compare with that of the human resources specialist who actually undertook the study? Given our earlier discussion, you should have spotted the importance of basing the selection on good job analysis data, and providing training for the selectors. But it is possible that you have also made different recommendations. You might, for example, have moved the interview to later in the process, where it would contribute to the final decision of which candidates to appoint, rather than merely to the initial decision of which candidates to invite to the assessment centre. You might have suggested including an ability test as one of the elements in the assessment centre, rather than as a stand-alone initial sifting device. Different answers, of course, are possible. But we hope that the case study has helped you to consolidate your understanding of the 'good practice' model of recruitment and selection, and helped you to see how it can be applied in practice.

2   Nepotism, corruption and discrimination

2.1   Good practice and favouritism

Why should organizations take the trouble to introduce the model of good practice outlined above? The argument in the specialist literature is that it will improve the performance of organizations by improving the quality of staff who work in them. But there are other reasons too. In this section, we suggest that applying good practice is particularly appropriate to confront problems of nepotism, favouritism and discrimination.

- Nepotism or favouritism is the tendency to ignore considerations of merit by giving preference to members of one's own family, ethnic group or geographical region, or to individuals whom we favour for some other personal reason (because they support the same political party, for example, or because they have offered us a bribe)
- Discrimination is the tendency to give preference to one gender (usually men) or to one ethnic group, and to disregard the merits of the other gender or of other ethnic groups.

The satirical cartoon below appeared in *The Herald*, a Zimbabwean newspaper, in 1985, and suggests three ways in which appointments (and promotions) can be made.

Nepotism, favouritism and discrimination are so prevalent in many countries that we must spend a little time considering them before we see how good practice can contribute to eradicating them.

Robert Wade, a development economist based at the University of Sussex in England, has given an exceptionally detailed account of how corruption can operate in staff management (Wade, 1989). He

Three ways of getting to the top.

Source: *The Herald* 1985.

describes the system of promotions and transfers in the irrigation department of a state government in southern India, and shows how corruption has become institutionalized to the extent that the price paid for different jobs is semi-public knowledge. He argues that the system of frequent transfer within the department, introduced originally to prevent nepotism, has the opposite effect because transfer posts are bought and sold corruptly to increase the earnings of senior staff of the department.

One comes away from Wade's article with a pessimistic impression of the difficulties of fighting corruption when it is so thoroughly entrenched. Wade quotes the German sociologist Max Weber's view that merit administration can exist only where social sanctions are present to support it, and comments that such sanctions are almost entirely absent in India. However, Wade also distinguishes between the corruption of the transfer system and the honesty of recruitment and promotion. Elsewhere, Wade refers to 'the avowedly elitist and public service ethic of the examination-recruited cadres such as the Indian Administrative Service'. It is hard to see how such an ethic can exist in the absence of Weber's convention of merit administration. We shall discuss later what this contradiction implies for the manager concerned to make good, fair appointments. First we turn to a more specific example of bias in recruitment and selection.

2.2   Ethnic discrimination

The favouritism which Wade discusses in the southern Indian context can take more specific forms, leading to the favouring of one ethnic group over another, what we call *ethnic* (or race) discrimination, or to men over women (and rarely to women over men) which is what we call gender discrimination. Britain has a long history of both kinds of discrimination. The British experience is well documented, and provides useful material for considering what the HRM specialist can do about discrimination.

A pioneering book by David Smith (1977), *Racial disadvantage in Britain*, is still one of the most convincing treatments of the subject. The research on which Smith's book is based contributed to the passing of the Race Relations Act and the Sex Discrimination Act, two major pieces of social legislation introduced by a Labour government in office from 1974 to 1979. Before Smith carried out his research, it was often stated publicly that racial discrimination in employment was rare in Britain, whereas it is now widely accepted that it does occur, and that government has a responsibility to act against it. Although Smith's research is almost 30 years old, periodic replications show that the incidence of discrimination in Britain is remarkably stable. Smith's findings, and his perceptive analysis, are still relevant.

Using a simple methodology which has been widely imitated (and which perhaps some reader of our book will try to use in their own country), Smith submitted bogus pairs of applications for jobs. The applications were identical, except for the name and place of birth of the applicants: one was identifiable as white while the other was identifiable as non-white. Thus, for example, non-white applicants might be called 'Asif Mirza' (a Pakistani name), while white applicants might be called 'Binelli' (an Italian name: Smith wanted to see if there was discrimination against white foreigners such as Italians as well as against non-white foreigners). Smith took care to ensure that it was clear that the applicants were fluent in English, and had identical British qualifications.

Smith found that, in 30 per cent of cases, employers were willing to invite the white applicant to an interview, but not the non-white applicant. In other words, 30 per cent of employers discriminated against the non-white applicant. Moreover, he points out that his research probably understated the extent of race discrimination, since he focused only on the application stage. It seemed likely that some of the non-white applicants who were invited to interview would still have suffered discrimination at the interview stage.

Acting against discrimination

Smith's research prompts two sets of questions for us to answer. The first is for you to ask yourself: to what extent is there discrimination against members of particular ethnic (or religious) groups in my country? Would a study like Smith's produce similar or different results? Only you, of course, can answer these two questions. But there is a further question that we can examine together: given the evidence that Smith presents, what kind of action might be needed in any country to overcome discrimination on the scale that he identified?

Many people would argue that discrimination can never be overcome while dominant ethnic groups (or men as the dominant gender) have negative attitudes about other ethnic groups (or about women). Smith, however, believed that deliberate action by governments and employers to curtail discrimination would, over time, create a more positive climate of opinion: attitudes would, eventually, come into line with the new situation. It was not necessary for governments and employers to promote a 'change of heart': instead they should change working practices. 'If we look after the facts,' Smith (1977: 330) said, 'the attitudes will look after themselves.'

2.3   Gender discrimination

There are similarities between the workings of race and gender discrimination, but they are not the same. We can again illustrate this from the British experience, this time by reporting in Box 6.4 a legal case brought under the Sex Discrimination Act (one of the two major legal Acts to which Smith's research contributed). This was a landmark case which led to the British civil service changing its age limits for recruitment in most areas of activity.

To understand the court's judgment, we need to explain the distinction between *direct* and *indirect* discrimination. Direct discrimination means directly favouring a man over a woman simply because he is a man, and for no other reason. Indirect discrimination is more subtle. It means applying a condition or requirement to both women and men which has a *disproportionate adverse impact* on women – that is, women find it harder to meet the requirement – and which cannot be justified in terms of the need of the job (*justification* is crucial in the definition of indirect discrimination). The civil service's age limit of 28 years constituted indirect discrimination because, although it applied equally to both women and men, it was hard for women to comply with (so there was a disproportionate impact) and it was not necessary for the efficient recruitment of executive officers (so it was not justifiable).

Box 6.4   Gender discrimination and recruitment age limits

The case concerned a woman called Belynda Price, who applied to join the British civil service as an executive officer (a junior management grade) and was rejected because she was above the age limit of 28 years, the national limit imposed by the civil service at that time. The civil service claimed that it was justified because there were roughly equal numbers of men and women in the population under 28, and also in view of the need to achieve a balanced age structure within the civil service workforce, and in particular to ensure a future supply of suitably experienced candidates for higher grade posts.

The court found in favour of Ms Price. In practice, they said, a smaller proportion of women than men could comply with the requirement. This was because many women between their mid-twenties and mid-thirties were prevented from working because they were raising children. However, such women usually returned to work in their thirties once the children had grown up. But by then they would not be eligible to join the civil service, because they were above the age limit.

See Equal Opportunities Commission (1985).

Please note that it is equally possible for a man to argue that a condition or requirement discriminates against him as a man *in exactly the same way*, even though in practice the incidence of discrimination against men is probably lower than discrimination against women in every country of the world.

So there is a two-stage test of indirect discrimination: does the condition or requirement have a disproportionate effect, and is the condition or requirement justified by the needs of the job? It is quite possible for a requirement to have a disproportionate effect but still be justifiable. For instance, some manual jobs could have a requirement that staff need to be able to lift heavy weights. This would be harder for the average woman to comply with than for the average man. But the requirement would not be discriminatory as long as the employer could show that it was necessary in terms of the duties of the job. (Notice that this would not be a reason to exclude all women applicants. Some of them would be able to lift heavy weights, just as some men would not.)

In our earlier discussion of the person specification, we said that the manager should be careful to avoid listing items as essential unless they are absolutely necessary, and we commented that there is a risk of indirect discrimination if this is not done. You should now be able to see why. Imposing an arbitrary age limit, or a requirement that staff be able to lift heavy weights, could indirectly discriminate against women if in either case there was a disproportionate effect on women and *if* the requirement was not justified.

After discussing problems of discrimination, you may now feel that selection is a minefield that managers enter at their peril. Certainly indirect discrimination is a subtle concept, and many selection criteria which organizations have used for years without question will turn out to be discriminatory on closer inspection. But there is a simple rule of thumb which will help you to avoid discrimination: *Think carefully before you make any paid work experience or any qualification essential.*

Employers are most likely to discriminate when they require particular paid work experience or a particular qualification, because experience shows that men are more likely than women to have certain kinds of work experience and qualifications (and the same may be true where some ethnic groups are concerned). On the other hand, there is less difficulty in listing criteria under the headings of skills as essential, since individuals can acquire skills in different ways. For instance, management skills are necessary in many senior jobs. But while such skills can be gained through paid work experience or by study, they can be gained in other ways too. A woman who has been active as a voluntary member of a Parent Teacher Association, or of a self-help credit union, may have developed sophisticated skills, for example in managing budgets or chairing meetings.

It is also possible that she has developed skills through running a household, or by growing crops and marketing the produce. The economic importance of women's role in the household economy and in the economy at large has often been overlooked in the past. We should not compound that error by overlooking the skills that women have developed through those economic activities.

2.4 The implications of favouritism and discrimination for the HRM specialist

We believe that human resource good practice can contribute to overcoming such problems as nepotism, favouritism, corruption and discrimination. You will have noticed Smith's conclusion that the best remedial action to combat discrimination is structural change rather than changing attitudes. Human Resource good practice has a contribution to make to such 'structural' solutions.

3   Beyond non-discrimination: positive discrimination and positive action

By eliminating discrimination and introducing good practice we aim to create a 'level playing field' where all the 'players' compete in equal conditions. But this ignores the fact that players come onto the field with different advantages which are the product of their different experience of education and of opportunities to learn skills. Nepotism and the other -isms on the scale that Wade and Smith discuss have deep social roots and it would be naïve to suppose that a simple injection of human resource 'good practice' will be enough to eradicate them. It is beyond the scope of this chapter to consider the social forces which lead to the existence of the problems in the first place. However, more farsighted organizations have tried to address some of those deeper causes of disadvantage, and we shall discuss the methods that they have used.

3.1   The stubborn nature of discrimination

Study task 6: eliminating discrimination

Let us frame a typical question which the well-intentioned but frustrated manager might well ask: why, despite all our efforts to eliminate discrimination, are more members of disadvantaged groups not being appointed? Assuming that discrimination has been eliminated (a difficult assumption to make), what possible reasons do you think there could be for this state of affairs? Spend a few minutes writing some down. ✍

Organizations which want to do something about these problems have a choice between intervening on the demand or on the supply side of the labour market. We consider demand side interventions first.

3.2   Overcoming disadvantage I: demand-side interventions

Members of disadvantaged groups do not meet essential requirements: using positive discrimination
Generally speaking, appointments to senior positions in organizations are made from a pool of applicants who have many years of experience in that agency. If for historical reasons that pool consists mostly of men, or (male) members of one ethnic group, then women, or members of other ethnic groups, are effectively excluded. When the

African National Congress government was elected in South Africa in 1994, it inherited an administration whose senior civil servants, appointed during the apartheid period, were white. In the normal way it would take many years before black candidates would be eligible for senior positions. Similarly, in the early 1990s, the British Labour Party had relatively few women Members of Parliament, and feared that it would take many years to change this unless specific action was undertaken.

In such circumstances, one possible short cut is to consider only members of the disadvantaged group for the next vacancy, or to reserve a *quota* of vacancies for them. This is sometimes called *positive discrimination*, which we can define as *selection which is wholly or partly on the basis of membership of a disadvantaged group*.

That is more or less what the British Labour Party did, by introducing a policy of all-women shortlists for selection of candidates in certain parliamentary constituencies. As a result many more women contested seats in the 1997 general election on behalf of Labour than in any previous general election.

Where the problem of underrepresentation of ethnic groups and/or women is very great, organizations may resort to positive discrimination. A number of countries have taken similar measures to give disadvantaged ethnic groups better access to jobs and university places. In India and the United States there are, or have been, quotas for disadvantaged ethnic groups (what are known in India as 'scheduled castes') to enter higher education.

Such action may appear to be a simple solution. But can you see any difficulties? There appear to be at least four.

1 The action may be struck down by the law courts as being in breach of a specific law, or in breach of constitutional guarantees of equal treatment for all. Thus the United States Supreme Court in the early 1980s overturned the policy of a medical school in California which had lower entrance requirements for black applicants. The Public Service Commission in one South Asian country decided against introducing similar measures aimed at recruiting more female civil servants, because they believed that this would breach the national constitution.

2 It may cause dissatisfaction among precisely those groups whom it was intended to benefit: members of the disadvantaged group may resent the implication that they were appointed because of their membership of that group, and not on merit.

3 It may simply not be possible: only qualified doctors can be appointed to medical positions, only qualified engineers to engineering positions, and so on.

4 For the employer it may conflict with the obligation to provide the best quality of service possible. Positive discrimination is only invoked, after all, when we want to appoint someone who is not in other ways the best person for the job. Admittedly there are instances where one might argue that only a member of a particular group can do the job effectively (this is what we call a *genuine occupational qualification*). For instance, it seems reasonable that female nurses should care for female patients where there is a requirement of privacy. Customers might reasonably expect the cook in an Indian restaurant to be Indian. But in most situations where positive discrimination is invoked, the argument is not about the effective performance of that particular job, but about the overriding need to have representation of a particular disadvantaged group in the workforce or in education. In such cases, in effect there is a choice, or trade-off, between more jobs for members of a disadvantaged group and better service.

The problems of positive discrimination can be so great that many agencies look for alternative policies to encourage the employment of members of disadvantaged groups. There are a number of actions which employers have taken. Their common feature is that, while they aim to assist disadvantaged groups, they all stop short of discrimination at the point of selection. They are known as *positive action* to distinguish them from positive discrimination.

Applicants believe that we still discriminate: positive action and publicity

The second reason why we may still fail to appoint members of disadvantaged groups, even after we have eliminated discrimination, is that they simply do not apply. The organization which has had a 'change of heart' and which genuinely wants to eliminate discrimination may find that the public is unaware of the change, or believes cynically that it is purely cosmetic. In this case, the agency can simply advertise its new approach. This need not be expensive: one simple action is to add a short phrase to its normal advertising material. The University of Manchester in the UK adds the phrase, 'An equal opportunity employer welcoming applications from all sections of the community' to all its job advertisements.

Eligible members of disadvantaged groups cannot comply with the conditions of the job: help for working parents

In most societies, women play a major role in bringing up children. Very often, women stay at home while their children are small, returning to outside work only after they have started school. Even then, it is often the mother who is responsible for getting the children to school and fetching them from school at the end of the day. If working hours clash with school hours, the mother may be unable to work. (There is often a relative or neighbour who can take care of the children for the crucial period – which may be no more than half an hour – in the morning or in the afternoon. But as more people move to cities and towns, extended family and informal social arrangements weaken.)

Of course one solution would be for fathers to share child care responsibilities. But employers can help in a number of ways. The former socialist countries of Central and Eastern Europe pioneered policies which provided child care for working parents. In Box 6.5 below we list the actions taken by one British local authority.

Box 6.5   Help for working parents in a British local authority

Introducing 'flexi-time', so that staff can fix their own working hours, as long as they work the specified number of hours in a week; this allows parents, for example, to leave children at school on their way to work.

Setting up a workplace nursery, where parents can leave children below school age while they are working.

Introducing 'job sharing', so that two members of staff can share a single job, enabling both to spend more time with their families.

Introducing a 'career break' scheme, so that staff with children have a period of leave without pay for up to three years while children are very small.

Notice that, with the exception of the nursery (for which parents themselves may have to pay), none of the above measures has a financial cost. Indeed, one can argue that there is an efficiency gain: in the case of job share, for instance, the employer gets two heads for the price of one. Such arrangements need not be confined to junior posts which carry no management responsibility. For example, in the late 1990s, the post of senior health advisor, with overall responsibility for health policy in the development agency of the government of Switzerland, was shared by a husband and wife team.

3.3   Overcoming disadvantage II: supply-side intervention

Even with the above measures (and putting aside positive discrimination), there may still be many members of disadvantaged groups who are not eligible to apply for vacancies, for example because they lack the required qualifications. Another way of putting this is to say that we have reached the limit of what we can achieve through demand-side interventions; that is, through interventions which affect the employer's demand for labour. For example, when Royal Nepal Airlines Corporation, the national airline of Nepal, advertised for aeronautical engineers in 1995, almost all the candidates who applied were male. No women were appointed.

Historical patterns of disadvantage often mean that members of disadvantaged groups reach the point of selection without the necessary qualifications or experience. In such cases, employers may provide special training aimed at the disadvantaged groups as a way of bridging the gap (this is sometimes called *positive action training*). This is a supply-side intervention, which affects the skills and attributes which jobseekers offer to employers. Thus, when the Local Government Service Commission in Tanzania organized professional training for senior personnel specialists working in local authorities, they set aside some places on the training courses for more junior personnel staff who were female so that they would be qualified for promotion to senior positions when posts became available later on.

3.4   Summary: beyond non-discrimination

Let us summarize what we have covered in this section. We began by stating the problem that, even with active measures to eliminate discrimination, many members of disadvantaged groups may still be excluded. Organizations wishing to tackle this problem have a choice of possible actions. On the demand side of the labour market, they are positive discrimination, publicity aimed at disadvantaged groups, and altering conditions of work. On the supply side, positive action training can be provided.

4   Beyond the standard model

4.1   Beyond the standard model I: stakeholders in selection

Now we can return to our discussion of recruitment and selection, which we interrupted to discuss the special problems of nepotism, favouritism and discrimination.

We argued that the good practice model, discussed earlier in the chapter, is a powerful safeguard against those problems. Apart from that particular advantage, the evidence for the technical superiority of the good practice model of selection (following the stages outlined above) is very impressive. All recent research points in this direction, including 'utility analysis' which claims to calculate the 'dollar value' of selection to organizations. As long ago as 1981, two of its practitioners calculated that the introduction of improved selection practices by the United States federal government would save US$16 billion annually (Schmidt and Hunter, 1981).

However, we must confront an awkward fact. Despite the professional consensus about selection methods, and the powerful arguments for their use in combating nepotism and so on, they are not actually used very widely. Survey after survey of organizations in the United States and Europe shows that the methods most favoured by selection specialists – the methods with the highest predictive validity – are not the most widely used, not even by selection specialists themselves. Indeed, one survey even found a negative statistical correlation between usage and validity of –0.25: in other words, the better the method, the less likely it was to be used. Although formal survey evidence does not exist for developing and transitional countries, the situation is probably the same.

The tendency of the selection specialist, perhaps like any specialist, is to blame the amateurs: 'We have not adequately preached the virtues of our best selection methods to the heathen ... the habits of the ages, and the exhortations of the charlatans, have more influence than science,' says one of the gurus of modern selection practice (Guion, 1989: 113). Such explanations, while patronizing to managers, should not be dismissed out of hand. But they imply that the problem is extrinsic: in a word, they blame the customers.

Can you think of other reasons why the model of best selection practice is not used more? One simple but compelling reason is that the model is expensive: a two-day assessment centre will cost money. But there are other reasons. One quite subtle reason is that introducing this model of good practice disturbs the balance of power in an organization. How, after all, are appointments made in the absence of a properly designed and integrated selection process? As often as not, by managers who exercise discretion to appoint the candidates they favour. In this situation, introducing systematic good practice limits their discretion. It may also represent a transfer of power from the line manager to the human resource specialist with expert knowledge about selection practices, and to whom the line manager may now have to defer. (Incidentally, it is probably for this reason, as well as for more professional reasons, that HRM specialists are often such enthusiastic advocates of good practice.)

The specialist literature on recruitment and selection is very technical in nature. Specialists are preoccupied by fine differences between the predictive validity of different methods. The literature thus has a strangely impersonal character, implying that it makes no difference who makes an appointment – any disinterested specialist can do it. By contrast, the *stakeholder* concept (see below) offers a different perspective. Although originally proposed in the context of the private sector, it is equally relevant in the public and NGO sectors, given the complex relationships which the public or NGO manager has to negotiate with elected politicians, citizen groups, professional associations and others.

The problem identified by the stakeholder approach is that the standard model does not consider the interests of different parties involved in recruitment and selection. As in other areas of management practice, there is an assumption that there is 'one best way' of doing selection. The extract in Box 6.6, based on McCourt (1999), argues that the stakeholder concept provides a useful framework for taking account of the interests of different parties involved in selection, and suggests practical ways in which it can be used to improve the quality of staffing decisions. Notice the following points in the argument:

- the definition of the stakeholder concept and its application to staffing decisions;
- the list of possible stakeholders;
- how the stakeholder concept leads to a 'responsive evaluation' approach to evaluating the success of a staffing decision.

Let us take a simple example. Suppose we want to fill a typist post. Who are the stakeholders? One possible answer is shown in Figure 6.2. This is what is sometimes called a 'stakeholder map', and it is a visual method of identifying the stakeholders who have an interest in an appointment (or, for that matter, who have an interest in any organizational decision).

Box 6.6   Involving stakeholders in staffing

The stakeholder concept at the organizational level of analysis may be helpful in showing how to take account of the interests of the different parties involved in individual staffing decisions. Freeman, the first to elaborate it in a management context, defined a stakeholder as 'any group or individual who can affect or is affected by the achievement of the organization's objectives' (1984: 46). His argument is that, in the turbulent conditions of modern business, businesses that address the concerns of their stakeholders will be successful. This has been taken up by other writers such as the well-known American management writer Rosabeth Moss Kanter. Although the model was developed in the private sector, it is possible that it is even more relevant to the public sector, where public managers have to negotiate quite complex stakeholder relationships, for example with elected politicians and community groups.

The stakeholder concept offers a mechanism for dealing cooperatively with competing interests; it comes into its own most strongly with senior or specialist appointments, where complex stakeholder systems operate. For example, an American analysis of the appointment of a new college dean identifies faculty members, alumni and administrators as important players.

Identifying stakeholders. It is likely that identifying stakeholders in this context is contingent, as Freeman suggests is the case with organization level stakeholders. For instance, we would expect the Personnel Department to be an important stakeholder, given our earlier discussion, but this will depend on the role which Personnel plays in the larger organizations. Nevertheless, there are some stakeholders who can be expected to figure in many appointments. It is plausible that *the boss* will be one: the commitment of a good boss to working with a bad appointee can shape him/her into a good member of staff. Although the progressive transfer of responsibility for shopfloor appointments from the supervisor to the Personnel department was a feature of the bureaucratization of recruitment, the importance of involving the line manager in selection is recognized in the recent HRM practitioner literature. Similarly, the line manager is identified as a key influence on transfer of learning from a training course to work. Peers may also have an effect on the success of an appointment, given the importance of the informal organization established by various studies. So too may *subordinates*: research carried out by an American writer on leadership, Fred Fiedler, found that leaders who fail to get on with key subordinates dwell on their troubled relationships and fail to capitalize on their abilities (1967: 246). There is a case for considering *candidates'* interests, and Freeman himself highlights the importance of *clients*, both internal and external, as a final stakeholder group.

Figure 6.2   Typing post: stakeholder map

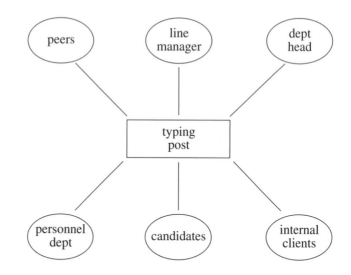

Source: Based on Freeman (1984).

The stakeholders who appear in this map are, of course, not the only ones who might have an interest in our typist appointment. The list of stakeholders will vary from one organization to another. For example, many organizations do not have a Personnel Department, which means that Personnel cannot be one of the stakeholders. So a different list of stakeholders would be justified, as long as you could show how they can affect, or are affected by, the appointment (remember Freeman's definition).

To summarize: we have suggested that it is not enough to choose the most sophisticated selection method. We must tailor our choice to the character of the different stakeholders involved. It is better to use a method which is less sophisticated if the stakeholders will be more committed to the appointment. As in other areas of HRM practice, the 'good practice' solution, by which we mean the practice which appears to be the most 'rational' or the most technically sound, is not always the best one. The HRM specialist or manager still has to exercise judgement, balancing the need to address the interests of the different stakeholders against the need to use methods which are technically robust enough to safeguard against such problems as nepotism, favouritism, corruption and discrimination.

Culture and selection
In our opinion recruitment and selection is the area of human resource practice where the case for the 'one best way' is strongest. We can see no reason to believe, for example, that there is any country or sector of

the economy where a structured interview is not better than an un-structured interview. However, even this area, where we have a single monolithic model of good practice, is not wholly exempt from cultural influences. Ryan *et al.* (1999) found that countries high in 'uncertainty avoidance' – a concept coined by the Dutch scholar Geert Hofstede to refer to the way in which managers in some countries have a prefer-ence for working in a strandardized, structured and rule-based way (France, Greece and Japan are examples of countries which are high in this, while Denmark, India and the UK are examples of countries which are low) – prefer more objective data, such as test results, on which to base their selection decisions. It follows that it would be easier to introduce highly structured selection methods in Greece than it would be in India.

4.2 Beyond the standard model II: staffing alternatives to a selection process

Failure to address stakeholders' interests is not the only reason why good practice methods are not used more widely. Sometimes, when an organization needs to deal with a vacancy, a selection process is not the right response. The technology of recruitment and selection is so highly developed that we can lose sight of what selection is. Stripped of its techniques, it is no more than a special case of organizational decision making, for which 'individual staffing' is often a more appro-priate label than 'personnel selection'. The decision in question is about the deployment of a person who we hope will meet a perceived organizational need for a certain expertise.

There are several ways, apart from the standard selection procedure, in which a modern organization might satisfy the staffing need in ques-tion. Some have always been available. Others are becoming more avail-able as organizations increasingly delegate responsibility for budget management to line managers. A line manager responsible for a staffing budget has more options than a line manager who must simply take what headquarters offers. At the level of the organization, human re-source planning models recognize that organizations can address staffing needs in other ways, for instance through learning and training, as you will see in Chapter 8. Strangely, however, the flexibility that is part and parcel of human resource planning is absent from most discussions of recruitment and selection, and we need to bring some of that flexibility into discussion of individual staffing decisions.

An advantage of looking at staffing decisions flexibly is that it allows us to take account of one important reality in organizations in developing and transitional countries today: that many organizations are more concerned with shedding existing staff than with recruiting new staff. The number of employees in organizations is shrinking rather than growing (is that the case with your country?). The following methods may be more relevant to that situation than the traditional recruitment and selection methods, which were developed when employment was expanding.

So what alternatives are there to the standard selection process? Here are some.

Reallocation of duties

When a post becomes vacant because of a departure of a member of staff, an organization or an individual line manager may prefer simply to spread the duties of the post among other staff in the same unit. Perhaps changes in the work of the unit mean that some of the duties of the post are no longer carried out. Perhaps there is a freeze on recruitment which means that the manager simply will not get permission to recruit, and must therefore make the best of a bad job.

Transfer

Wade's analysis of India showed how many posts are filled by internal transfer rather than recruitment and selection. Of course, in the case which Wade studied, this system of transfer had got out of control. However, there can be good reasons for transfers. For instance, many organizations have graduate development or other staff development programmes, with certain posts earmarked to be filled on a temporary basis by an employee on the programme.

Redeployment of a supernumerary

Organizations trying to reduce posts often redeploy a member of staff in a redundant post in another department as an alternative to making him or her redundant. For example, the government of Tanzania decided in 1996 to abolish the regional structure of administration and reassign its duties to Tanzanian local authorities. At the same time, it announced that all staff previously employed in the regional administration would be reappointed to other central government ministries or to the local authorities. Thus a line manager will be asked to accept someone from a 'redeployment pool' as an alternative to advertising a vacancy in the normal way.

'Outsourcing'

An aspect of the so-called New Public Management is the contracting out of public services. For example, a private firm may carry out refuse collection on behalf of the public organization responsible for the service. Contracting out is also widespread in the private sector: an airline might use a specialist firm to provide meals for passengers. The same thinking applies to filling jobs. Thus a line manager with control of a staffing budget may find it cheaper to use a secretarial agency to recruit a secretary than to fill the post in the normal way. (Of course, this also allows the manager to get rid of the secretary without having to go through the lengthy procedure necessary if the secretary was a permanent member of the organization's staff.)

Appointment of a previously identified successor

Some organizations may have formal succession planning programmes, where an 'understudy' is identified who will automatically step into a post (usually a very senior post) when its incumbent retires or comes to the end of his/her contract. In private companies in some OECD countries, there are elaborate formal succession planning programmes where the 'understudy' goes through a development programme to prepare for taking over the incumbent's duties. In the public sector, succession planning is usually done more informally. For example, when a new deputy head was appointed to the Social Services department of one British local authority, the elected councillors who made the appointment were aware that she would almost certainly become department head when the current head retired three years later, and this was made clear to the woman appointed.

Now that we have discussed and illustrated a variety of approaches to recruitment and selection, see how you can apply what you have learned in this chapter by doing Study task 7.

Study task 7: selecting staffing options

1   Outline the staffing options available to the staff training unit in the airline below.
2   Present an argument to support your preferred option.

An airline in one of the newly independent states of the former Soviet Union has recently been privatized, and is now coming under increasing pressure from its new shareholders to improve profitability. This has had an impact on staffing decisions in three ways.

- *Pressure to cut staff costs*   A redundancy programme has started. Although most of the redundancies so far have been voluntary, some compulsory redundancies have been made in areas such as catering where outside contractors are beginning to be used.
- *Redeployment*   Some staff have also been offered redeployment as an alternative to redundancy, and a central redeployment pool has been established.
- *Need to justify decisions to recruit*   Line managers are expected to provide a convincing justification for the recruitment of new staff, although top management has recognized that there are some priority areas which should be protected. For instance, there is a great deal

of public concern about the airworthiness of the airline's ageing fleet of passenger aircraft which was inherited from the former Soviet airline, Aeroflot. The programme of regular maintenance was disrupted by the events surrounding the country's independence, and there was a major crash last year which safety inspectors attributed partly to poor maintenance of the aircraft involved. Thus top management has protected spending in the aircraft maintenance division, including spending on staff.

Another area which might also be regarded as a priority is the staff training unit. Top management has signalled a commitment to staff training, influenced by the experience of other airlines privatized earlier. For example, following its privatization in the early 1980s, British Airways embarked on a major programme of 'customer care' training for a large proportion of its staff. British Airways believed that improvements in customer service were partly due to this programme. The staff training unit has recently been delegated a great deal of financial control, including control of the unit's staffing budget.

The airline's staff training unit now has a vacancy for a training officer, created by the retirement of a very experienced member of staff. That person had been responsible for a long-established programme of supervisory training which has been declining in popularity in the last three years. ✍

We have seen that an organization, or a unit within an organization, has a number of alternatives to the traditional process of recruitment and selection when it deals with a vacancy. While the traditional process probably remains suitable for the majority of vacancies, the increased discretion available to managers as their organizations change means that they should consider those alternatives carefully, whether that change is a consequence of decentralization (as in Tanzania), privatization (as in the former Soviet republic) or of some other process.

5   Summary and conclusion

In this chapter we have

- presented a good practice model of recruitment and selection,
- reviewed several good methods of selection,
- discussed how nepotism and favouritism can operate in recruitment and selection,
- discussed race and gender discrimination in selection,
- determined how the interests of different stakeholders can best be accommodated,
- reviewed alternative methods of filling staff vacancies.

Good practice in recruitment and selection need not be difficult. If a systematic approach is taken, and good methods are used, then organizations in developing and transitional countries can expect to see the quality of appointments start to improve. This is worthwhile in itself, but has the additional benefit of giving organizations a way of tackling seemingly intractable problems of nepotism, favouritism and discrimination. These problems have deep roots, and actions of different kinds will be necessary to eradicate them. But it is reasonable to expect that good practice will have an impact and that, over time, it will serve to increase public and customer confidence in the integrity and efficiency of organizations.

Note

1   We provide more detail on scoring in Chapter 7.

7 Performance Management and Appraisal

Willy McCourt and Derek Eldridge

What this chapter is about

In this chapter we begin by justifying the expense of time and money that appraisal requires,[1] before reviewing the different approaches that have evolved in the last 50 years, starting with the Annual Confidential Report and working through Management by Objectives and performance appraisal to reach the current 'state of the art', performance management. We provide a summary of research findings as a yardstick for evaluating the different approaches. Last of all we discuss a case study that highlights the interaction between appraisal good practice and the particular context in which it is applied.

What you will learn

At the end of this chapter you should be able to:

- justify the time and money that appraisal requires;
- use research findings to evaluate different approaches;
- appraise the annual confidential report, Management by Objectives, performance appraisal and performance management approaches;
- introduce appraisal successfully in the particular context in which you work.

1   Introduction

1.1   Formal and informal appraisal

Do we need performance management and appraisal? Appraisal is so well established in the HRM literature that some of us have to make an effort to remind ourselves that many organizations manage without it, and that many – perhaps even most – managers believe that their day-to-day, informal communication gives them all the information they need about their staff. Against this, Randell (1994: 221) defines appraisal as 'the *formal* (our emphasis) process for collecting information from and about the staff of an organization for decision-making purposes'.

Why have a formal process? Most fundamentally, introducing a formal appraisal scheme gives a powerful message to managers, possibly for the first time: *you* are responsible for the performance of the staff you manage, and you must take active steps to help them do their jobs well. While we should take managers' objections to formal appraisal seriously, and avoid, for example, overloading them with complicated forms to fill in, we may also suspect that part of the problem is that some of them would rather leave staff to sink or swim by themselves.

Moreover, what happens where there is no formal scheme? We agree with Clive Fletcher (1993: 1–2):

> No matter how hard it is to devise a satisfactory performance appraisal scheme, there is no real alternative to turn to. Appraisal will take place in an unstructured and perhaps highly subjective form wherever and whenever people work together. They will automatically form judgements about their own performance and that of their colleagues. To try to deny this is foolish … Organizations that try to avoid the issue by not having an appraisal scheme will simply end up having the same processes occurring without them being open to scrutiny or to control, with all the potential for bias and unfairness that this holds.

1.2   Managing individuals and managing systems

One serious argument against formal appraisal is that it allows managers to blame employees for problems which are really the fault of the organization's overall system: this demotivates employees and does nothing to improve production. Deming (1986), the guru of Total Quality Management (TQM), argues this case forcefully. To him, appraisal is one of the 'seven deadly sins' of management. In a TQM approach, problems are tackled at the level of the system, not the individual.

Certainly employees are constrained by their situations: a district officer cannot get around her district if a vital bridge is swept away by floods. Moreover, Deming's emphasis on the team rather than the individual level is one reason why his ideas have been so popular in Japan, where managers generally prefer to think of the team as the basic unit of production, as we saw in Chapter 4. But there is no reason for system, team and individual levels to be mutually exclusive. Even after system problems have been dealt with, there will almost certainly still be some individual issues left, just because individuals work differently and have their own aspirations. We can also adapt appraisal techniques to deal with a team's performance.

All in all, while most managers will probably agree that appraisal is a 'good thing' in theory, we can see why Latham and Wexley (1993: 1) remark wryly that 'Appraisal systems are a lot like seat belts. Most people believe that they are necessary, but they don't like to use them.' Perhaps you can also see why the organizational landscape is strewn with the carcasses of discarded appraisal schemes. HRM specialists may well have to convince managers and staff that appraisal is a good use of their time.

2 What makes appraisal work

2.1 Research findings

Appraisal, like recruitment and selection, has been around long enough for some research findings to have built up. A lot of the research has been done by organizational psychologists, since appraisal is one of the two main areas where organizations assess their staff (the other is recruitment and selection), and expertise in assessment is 'the jewel in organizational psychology's crown' (Herriot, 1995). Psychologists' rigorous research methods make their findings a powerful yardstick for comparing different approaches to appraisal.

2.2 Appraisal and organizational performance

If appraisal were everything it is cracked up to be, we would have clear evidence of a link between appraisal and individual and organizational performance. But we don't. Although 'formal performance appraisal' is one of the HRM elements which Huselid correlated with organizational performance (see Chapter 2), two separate studies commissioned by the UK's Institute of Personnel and Development in the 1990s found little positive evidence. The authors of one of the studies suggest that 'Our failure to prove the case can be attributed, at least in part, to the lack of systematic evaluation and the incredible diversity of actions that take place under the banner of performance management.' (Armstrong and Baron, 1998: 442).

Given the multiple purposes which appraisal typically serves (see below), this is a reasonable, though disappointing, conclusion. However, we do have some evidence about individual aspects of appraisal. We begin with two areas of research that represent the fundamental theoretical rationale for appraisal: feedback and objective setting.

2.3   Feedback

The Scottish poet Robert Burns (1909) famously wrote,

> O wad some Pow'r the giftie gie us
> To see oursels as others see us.[2]

And that is the 'giftie' that feedback bestows, however imperfectly. 'The positive effect of ... feedback upon subsequent performance is a well-established if not one of the best-established findings in the psychological literature,' say Locke and Latham (1990: 173), and several studies discussed by Anstey *et al.* (1976) report this as the most important function of appraisal from the appraisee's perspective. The following is a summary of research on its value.

Feedback should be fair, and preferably positive
Meyer *et al.* (1965) found that the number of criticisms in an appraisal interview correlates positively with the number of defensive reactions shown by the employee. Even neutral feedback can be badly received: Pearce and Porter (quoted in Dulewicz and Fletcher, 1989) found that many appraisees were unhappy to be appraised as merely 'satisfactory'.

Mindful of such research, it is often suggested that feedback should be entirely positive or, where negative, strictly limited (Robbins, 1989). Positive feedback does appear to motivate and negative feedback to demotivate. However, Greenberg (1986), in his research on fairness in work evaluation, found that perceptions of outcomes and of procedural fairness are relatively independent. This is an important finding because it suggests a way of overcoming the pervasive difficulty of giving negative (albeit accurate) feedback. Dulewicz and Fletcher (1989: 656) also suggest that appraisee defensiveness is moderated by the pressure appraisees feel to 'be reasonable'. The suggestion is that, as long as the appraisee is satisfied that the feedback is fair, the appraisee may accept it with as good a grace as he or she can muster.

Feedback should be participative

But it is only possible to capture that elusive fairness if the manager involves the appraisee in the process. Metcalfe (quoted in Walker, 1989) found that the successful appraisers were those who allowed their staff to participate. Nemeroff and Wexley (quoted in Latham and Wexley, 1993) found that participation increases appraisee acceptance of the appraiser's observations. It follows that appraiser feedback should be *tentative*, and that any eventual judgement or rating should be negotiated to some extent.

Other insights on feedback

Other points cropping up in the literature include the following: feedback should be *timely* (note the implication that appraisal should be a continuous process rather than a merely annual event), *objective* and should *come from a valued source* (Podsakoff and Farh, quoted in Locke and Latham, 1990). What this last insight means is that the appraisee will only take feedback seriously if he or she respects the person giving it.

2.4   Objective setting

So the value of feedback is well established. Likewise the value of objective setting: referring to four literature reviews, Locke *et al.* (1991: 370) describe it as 'among the most scientifically valid and useful theories in organizational science'. Certain conditions must be present if objective setting is to be effective. Locke and Latham (1990), its principal proponents, list the following:

- *Objectives should be specific and challenging.* Locke and Latham found 51 out of 53 studies showing significant effects in favour of specific, hard objectives.
- *There should be commitment to objectives.* Many factors contribute to this, including the perceived authority of the objective setter and peer group pressure.
- *There should be feedback on performance towards reaching the objective.* We have discussed this already. Note the implication, which has a good deal of support in the literature, that the value of both feedback and objective setting increases if they are used together.
- *There should be support for the employee in reaching the objective.* This includes both resources and psychological support.

- *Appraisers should foster self-efficacy and expectations of success.* ('Self-efficacy' is a technical term that roughly means 'self-confidence'.) Employees are more likely to succeed if they believe that they have the ability to do so.

Research findings on objective setting are summarized fairly well by the acronym SMART: objectives, in other words, should be specific, measurable, achievable, relevant and time-bound.

2.5   Job analysis

Although actual appraisal forms often require managers to assess employees on personality traits like 'confidence' or 'honesty', psychologists have emphasized the importance of using job analysis to generate behavioural criteria (Dulewicz and Fletcher, 1989). A review of job analysis studies (Latham, 1986) favoured the critical incident technique for doing this, and the repertory grid technique is growing in popularity: we discussed both of them in Chapter 4.

2.6   Cognitive limitations and biases

If you are a manager appraising an employee's performance, you are engaged in a complex cognitive process. You must obtain data about an appraisee's performance, retain it in your memory, categorize it as relevant or not and, lastly, evaluate it. Having to draw on data that stretches back over the whole of the previous year, this being the normal period which an appraisal interview covers, only increases the complexity. The likelihood is that the appraisal judgement at the end of this process will be arbitrary, unless you have gone to some trouble to avoid it.

There are also specific cognitive biases at work. Managers do not give up the perennial human tendency to be prejudiced when they sit down to appraise. Duarte *et al.* (quoted in Latham and Wexley, 1993) found that 'in-group' employees in a telephone company were rated highly regardless of their actual performance. There is also evidence from the United States of appraiser bias against people from a different race (Landy, 1989).

2.7   Problems with rating

Appraisal systems which try to measure staff performance run into four problems (Smith and Robertson, 1993).

- *Leniency*: the tendency for appraisers to give a higher rating than the employee deserves. It is especially marked where the appraiser has a personal relationship with the appraisee.
- *Dispersion*: the tendency for appraisers to use only a limited range of a scoring scale. A typical example is where scores bunch around the middle of the scale, for instance at 4, 5 or 6 out of 10. (The latter phenomenon is known as *central tendency*.)
- *Halo effect*: the tendency for a good opinion of an appraisee in one area to leak into other areas. For instance, if I think an appraisee has good budget management skills, and this matters to me, that may influence me to rate her overall performance highly, ignoring any specific evidence to the contrary.
- *Contrast effect*: an appraiser may rate a merely adequate appraisee too highly if the appraiser has just appraised two inadequate members of staff.

These problems are common to all assessment systems, and apply equally to ratings in recruitment and selection and in training and development.

2.8   Multiple purposes

Last of all, we face as usual the contrast that we established in Chapter 1 between what experts say organizations ought to do (*prescription*) and what they actually do (*description*). Surveys of appraisal practice show that organizations use appraisal for quite different purposes, as Table 7.1 shows.

Where organizations try to do everything at once, and they often do, the different purposes may contradict each other, as Randell (1994) points out. For example, the manager needs the employee to be honest about his weaknesses in order to discuss how he can develop. But if the employee knows that the manager will decide how much to pay him at the end of the interview, he will probably play those weaknesses down.

Randell therefore suggests that organizations should be ruthless in restricting the purposes for which they use appraisal, cutting out development or pay as the case may be. Another reason for doing this is that surveys show – just as common sense would suggest – that 'line managers dislike appraisal because it creates a lot of paperwork' (Long, 1986: 63).) If organizations insist on using all the purposes, Randell suggests that they should handle them separately, having separate procedures for each main purpose. We will see in a case study later in this chapter that this is exactly what one company tried to do.

Table 7.1   Overall objectives of appraisal systems

Bank of Indonesia	Gambia Public Transport Corporation	Indian Administrative Service	London Docklands Development Corporation
Evaluate employees in terms of: - work achievement - behaviour - potential for promotion	Award annual increments to staff Review the pay and benefits of the staff, as necessary Apply rewards and sanctions for good and bad performance Assess the competence of any staff recommended to fill a senior position Select employees for career development in the corporation	Use confidential reports as a tool for human resource development Ensure that reporting officers develop officers so that they reach their full potential Carry out a developmental review of officers' performance rather than a fault finding one Report shortcomings in performance, attitudes or overall personality of the employee	Reinforce effective interpersonal communication between the reviewing manager, the manager and subordinate/s Improve unit/team results by building on strengths and remedying weaknesses Identify training and development needs related to potential Agree on key tasks targets for the next 12 months Report on overall assessment of job performance in the previous 12 months: – against general performance criteria – against achievement of the jobholder's key targets

2.9   Summary: implications for appraisal practice

Research on appraisal has clear implications for the way organizations ought to carry it out. The list below sums them up.

- Use behavioural criteria derived from job analysis rather than psychological traits.
- Set SMART objectives.
- Provide feedback which is tentative, fair, participative, mainly positive, frequent and timely, objective, and comes from a valued source.
- Be aware of cognitive biases and limitations.
- If rating is used, be aware of common problems.
- Restrict purposes for appraisal, or handle different purposes separately.
- Minimize paperwork required by managers.

3   Appropriate appraisal: early approaches

Of all the HRM activities that we cover in this book, it is probably easiest for practitioners to get practical examples of good practice in appraisal, including examples from the Internet. Yet, paradoxically, this is an area where the problem of appropriateness, which we discussed in Chapter 1, is very great: organizations that try to apply a standard good practice model without considering whether it suits their circumstances are likely to fall flat on their faces. It is important not only to grasp good practice models, but also to be aware of what will be involved in adapting them to specific contexts.

As usual, it is helpful when we choose an appropriate model to have a range of models to choose from. The history of appraisal gives us just that. We will now review the way in which appraisal has developed, starting with the 'annual confidential report' (ACR) approach which is still practised in the public sector in many developing countries.

3.1   The annual confidential report (ACR)

The ACR procedure is of considerable antiquity, having been bequeathed by the British government to its former colonies at independence from the 1940s onwards. As its name indicates, the report is written once a year by a senior manager on each of the employees for whom he or she is responsible. It is essentially a way of checking that staff have not gone 'off the rails'. In public organizations that use it, where promotion is mostly internal and based on seniority, progression to the next increment or grade usually depends on getting a satisfactory report. Thus the audience for the report is not the employee who is its subject, but rather the agency which makes pay or promotion decisions. Since those decisions are usually made at the centre of government, this is a highly centralized system. Moreover, because the report is 'confidential', the assumption is that the manager will not discuss it with the employee. The rating of the employee in an ACR is based on an overall impression, or at best on psychological traits. A bank in Pakistan used the following three factors: 'irreproachable', 'honest and straightforward' and 'living within known means of income'.

The ACR's limitations will be obvious. In terms of the research findings that we discussed earlier, the total non-participation of the employee means that there is no provision for giving feedback or setting objectives, and reliance on psychological traits makes it easy for bias to creep in. Despite those limitations, the ACR is still practised in countries as far apart as Swaziland in southern Africa and Sri Lanka. Sheer organizational inertia is one reason, as always, but there are some positive reasons too. Some governments prefer a centralized system as a way of controlling favouritism by limiting line managers' discretion to reward cronies and punish enemies: in this sense the ACR is an aspect of the 'clerk of works' model of HRM that we discussed in Chapter 2. Similarly, trust between managers and employees can be so low that it is prudent not to reveal a confidential rating, because the employee will refuse to believe that even a neutral rating is based on anything firmer than the manager's negative bias (we discussed this in Chapter 1). Finally, the particular rating traits that the bank in Pakistan used had the useful function of reminding staff that the bank was determined to crack down on corruption.

3.2 Management by objectives (MbO)

The MbO (Odiorne, 1979) stage in the development of appraisal is an object lesson in what can happen when a good idea is taken to its logical conclusion (logicians call this *reductio ad absurdum*, a Latin phrase that means 'reduction to absurdity'). Based on the firm theoretical foundation of goal-setting theory, MbO elevated the useful technique of objective setting into *the* method for managing employee performance, with quantified objectives cascading downwards from the top of the organization to the individual employee, so that the organization became a giant machine for achieving objectives. This MbO became a monomania, where nothing except the objectives mattered, with the result that all too often the objectives, let alone unquantifiable goals like job satisfaction, were not achieved. This brought the whole practice of objective setting into disrepute, and for a while the baby went out with the bathwater. But it was not objective setting itself that was at fault, but rather the *process* of setting objectives, in which typically the employee did not participate, and the disregard of other factors like feedback that also contribute to performance.

4   Performance appraisal

4.1   Involving the employee

One insuperable problem that faces the manager writing an annual confidential report is that the person who knows most about an employee's performance is the employee himself or herself. After all, the manager mostly does not know what the employee is doing – she cannot be there all the time. Moreover, even when she does know, she does not know *why* the employee is doing it, and there could be a good reason (such as, possibly, 'Because that's how you told me to do it – remember?'). For his or her part, the employee wants (but also fears) feedback, an answer to the question, 'How am I doing?'

Performance appraisal seeks to improve on the ACR and MbO procedures by improving the quality of the data on which a manager bases an appraisal judgement, while at the same time providing feedback to the employee on his or her performance. In effect it takes account of the research finding that feedback is a key element in appraisal. It does so by making an annual interview between manager and employee the centrepiece of the procedure. An unintended, but benign, consequence is that there has to be at least one occasion in the year where the employee gets the manager's undivided attention, and is able to raise strategic or personal issues that are hard to raise in the normal course of events: it is that *quality* of attention that employees often appreciate, as much as anything else.

In introducing performance appraisal we need to concentrate on what matters most. Organizations spend a lot of time on the design of appraisal forms and on the minutiae of rating scales, yet 'Many appraisal systems have failed simply because staff people responsible for planning the systems have become engrossed in trying to achieve technical perfection' (Whisler and Harper, quoted in Randell, 1994: 225). We tend to agree with Randell (1994: 238) that 'With a skilled observer/interviewer as a manager, all the paperwork support that is required … is a blank sheet of paper.'

This is only a slight exaggeration: the manager and employee will certainly need a formal record of the meeting, especially if objectives are set and there are other action points at the end of the meeting. But certainly it is the skill of the manager, especially in the conduct of the performance appraisal interview itself, and not the design of the system that is crucial. Thus the emphasis in developing appraisal should be on developing managers' appraisal skills, something that probably requires a training course lasting at least two days to allow time for skills practice. Organizations are usually reluctant or unable to spend the time and money that this requires, but the Daletel case study later in this unit will show what happens when they do not do so.

4.2   The appraisal interview

The skills the manager needs centre on the manager's conduct of the appraisal interview. The appraisal interview seeks to assess, as honestly as possible, where performance has succeeded, where it has not, and why. It assumes that employees, with guidance and encouragement, can identify and deal with their own shortcomings. Thus appraisees should be able to communicate without fear of unhelpful blaming, and without inhibition due to the appraiser's higher rank. However, we know that organizations differ a great deal in the degree of openness that is possible. For example, in Malaysia a subordinate would be unlikely to raise a personal problem – a family problem, say – even if it had affected the subordinate's performance, and a manager would probably be very uncomfortable if the subordinate did raise it. In the UK, on the other hand, many people would find this acceptable, and the subordinate might feel that the manager was cold and unhelpful if the manager brushed the family problem aside. So the communication style has to be acceptable to both parties, in a way that reflects national and organizational culture.

Preparing for the appraisal interview is important. For the manager this means summarizing all that he knows about the appraisee's performance, and preparing questions on areas where he is in the dark. It may also mean consultation with other managers, including the manager at the next level up who may be the 'countersigning officer'. The preparation stage allows the manager to compare the appraisee with other staff for whom the manager is responsible.

The appraisee also needs to prepare, reflecting on what she has achieved and why. Appraisees have to be honest with themselves, especially in identifying personal factors that affected their performance. Such factors may indicate weaknesses in knowledge or skill that should be addressed in the interview.

Sometimes an appraisal system has a self-appraisal form to prompt recall and (self-) diagnosis before the interview. The form may be for the use of the individual only or may have to be submitted to the appraiser.

The importance of preparation and the organization of relevant data can be seen in Box 7.1. Notice that we have highlighted 'views of other colleagues on appraisee's performance', as this represents the justification for '360 degree appraisal', which we will discuss a little later.

Box 7.1   Appraiser and appraisee perspectives

	What appraisee knows	*What appraisee may not know*
What appraiser knows	• personal data of individual • current responsibilities • outcomes of joint performance discussion as work proceeds	• emergent organizational perspectives • work plans for next period • who is to succeed to more senior posts in the organization
What appraiser may not know	• work aspects that (dis)satisfy appraisee • personal views on recent achievements/ failures • appraisee's career ambitions • strengths/potential of appraisee • development needs	• **views of other colleagues on appraisee's performance** • appraisee capacity for specific roles • development options available to appraisee

---

The skills of the appraiser include careful questioning, avoiding an accusatory style, and counselling, so that appraisees can identify concerns about their performance and personal development. The appraiser needs to help the appraisee select from alternative courses of action with a view to improving performance. The appraiser should also be ready to suggest changing factors in the environment that affect the appraisee, including the appraiser's own behaviour.

The interview style should thus be constructive, encouraging learning and improvement, and should follow the guidelines below.

1 Establish ownership by encouraging appraisees to talk about their attitudes and feelings as well as performance: what they feel they do well; what worries they have; which parts of the job are easiest, hardest or monotonous; why it is important to work in a particular way; and anything that stops them from doing so.

2 Strengthen rapport by asking questions like 'How do you think this could be improved?' 'What about actions in this area?' 'How would that affect the situation?' Point appraisees in the right direction for them to discover practical solutions, rather than telling them what to do.

3 Give skilful feedback, focusing on behaviours rather than personality traits. Telling an appraisee that she is 'insensitive to clients' is less helpful than giving behavioural examples of this insensitivity. When necessary, ask the appraisee to rephrase in his or her own words a point you have made, to check whether it was understood.

4 Avoid emphasizing problems over which appraisees have no control.

5 Encourage appraisees to ask questions.

6 Present information so that appraisees do not feel devalued or blamed. Otherwise, they may reject the information altogether, or distort it so that it reinforces current behaviour instead of encouraging a new way of doing things.

The appraiser must be ready to receive feedback in return. This increases trust, as well as helping the appraiser to realize the effect of his or her behaviour on others. This is important because performance improvement by the appraisee often requires some facilitating change in the manager's behaviour, and the appraisee must feel confident that it will occur.

In some cases, for example when dealing with a poor performer, a fully open dialogue just is not possible, and the appraiser has to adopt a 'tell and listen' strategy. This means giving the appraisee information in areas where he is incapable of identifying his own weaknesses, and then waiting for reactions before responding to them to find solutions together. With very difficult appraisees, a 'tell and sell' strategy may be necessary: telling appraisees their weaknesses and selling the remedies to them. Such appraisees' commitment is probably low already, and 'tell and sell' may reinforce their rejection of evidence of their poor performance. It is therefore an approach of last resort, possibly a last attempt to persuade the appraisee to change his ways before going into a disciplinary procedure.

Box 7.2 summarizes the key points of good practice in appraisal interviewing that we have discussed.

Box 7.2   The effective appraiser

The appraiser should be

open
value-free
constructive
sensitive to personal issues which may affect performance
receptive to feedback from the employee
aware of his or her own biases

The appraiser should

look forwards rather than backwards
identify the parts of the job which make the appraisee feel (dis)satisfied
evaluate the appraisee's work
compare it with the job description and any objectives previously set
discover the reasons for performance at this level
identify and deal with constraints outside the employee's control
agree objectives for the coming year
identify development and training actions arising from the interview

---

4.3   360° appraisal

We said earlier that performance appraisal is superior to the ACR procedure because it adds the employee's perspective to that of the manager. But even the manager and the employee together do not have the complete picture: that is what the highlighted item in Box 7.1 represents. 360° appraisal (so called because in geometry, a circle has 360 degrees – the idea being that we are getting an 'all-round' picture of the employee's performance) addresses that fact by adding the perspectives of other stakeholders, notably peers, subordinates and external or internal customers. Their feedback is usually recorded on a standard form (Figure 7.3 at the end of this chapter is an example). Thus, when the manager and employee sit down for the annual appraisal interview, they have additional information about the employee's performance.

Box 7.3 is an excerpt from a 360° feedback report of a senior manager at a UK bank.

You will notice that the report is based on feedback from no fewer than 18 people. Clearly the information in such a report is worthwhile. However, as Armstrong and Baron (1998) note, if the informa-

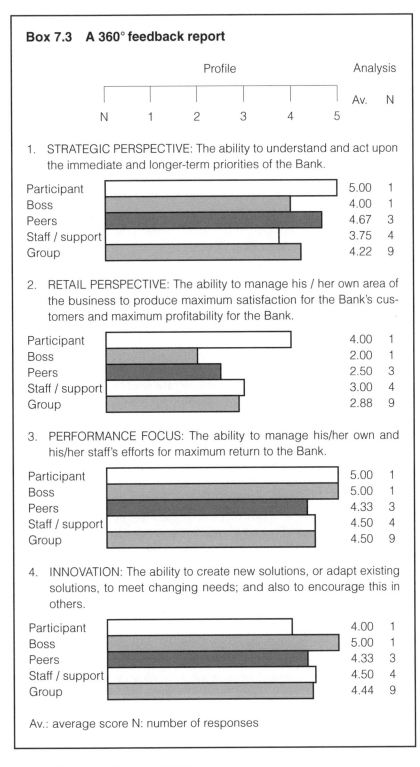

Box 7.3   A 360° feedback report

1. STRATEGIC PERSPECTIVE: The ability to understand and act upon the immediate and longer-term priorities of the Bank.

	Av.	N
Participant	5.00	1
Boss	4.00	1
Peers	4.67	3
Staff / support	3.75	4
Group	4.22	9

2. RETAIL PERSPECTIVE: The ability to manage his / her own area of the business to produce maximum satisfaction for the Bank's customers and maximum profitability for the Bank.

	Av.	N
Participant	4.00	1
Boss	2.00	1
Peers	2.50	3
Staff / support	3.00	4
Group	2.88	9

3. PERFORMANCE FOCUS: The ability to manage his/her own and his/her staff's efforts for maximum return to the Bank.

	Av.	N
Participant	5.00	1
Boss	5.00	1
Peers	4.33	3
Staff / support	4.50	4
Group	4.50	9

4. INNOVATION: The ability to create new solutions, or adapt existing solutions, to meet changing needs; and also to encourage this in others.

	Av.	N
Participant	4.00	1
Boss	5.00	1
Peers	4.33	3
Staff / support	4.50	4
Group	4.44	9

Av.: average score N: number of responses

Source: Stafylarakis *et al.* (2002).

tion obtained is voluminous and contradictory, the manager and employee may not actually use it, leading all concerned to see the whole exercise as a time-consuming paper chase. Also, although feedback from peers and others can be given anonymously, the manager and the employee have to give their own views openly. This can be stressful (it caused particular problems in the case study that we discuss later in this chapter) and it can oblige the manager to make just the negative judgements that we advised against in the last section. With those problems in mind, some organizations have started to use '180° feedback', getting the views of perhaps two or three key stakeholders only, not including the manager and employee themselves.

4.4   Appraisal rating

Although we are sceptical of the value of rating employees' performance, we realize that many organizations practise it, especially where employees can only move on to the next increment or grade if they have a satisfactory rating. It is, in fact the only major feature that is common to all appraisal approaches, as Table 7.2 shows. Box 7.4 reproduces the guidance given by one UK government department to its managers on how to rate overall performance. You should read it alongside the advice we gave on rating in the section on research findings earlier on.

Box 7.4   Guidance on rating

1 '*Outstanding*'
   A score of 1 should only be awarded to the jobholder who has consistently attained an outstanding level of performance compared to what you would normally expect from someone in the grade. The jobholder may have shown certain exceptional strengths, or worked very hard over an extended period to a consistently high overall standard. The expectation is that only a very small proportion of staff will receive a score of 1.

2 '*Performance significantly above requirements*'
   A score of 2 should only be given for a high standard of performance that is significantly above what one would normally expect in the grade. The mark can be appropriate only to a minority of staff in each grade, taken across the department as a whole.

3 '*Performance fully meets normal requirements of the grade*'
   A score of 3 should be used to denote a fully acceptable and effective performance overall. Think of the standard that you would

normally expect from a good performer in the jobholder's grade and give a score of 3 if the performance matches that. It is the appropriate mark for most good performers doing good work, and is the mark which a majority of staff in each grade, taken across the department as a whole, should receive when managers apply the scale correctly.

4   *'Performance not fully up to requirements, some improvement necessary'*
A score of 4 means that there are weaknesses in the jobholder's performance such that it falls short of the level of performance which would normally be expected of the grade. A mark of '4' can be used in several circumstances:

- when there are too many specific weaknesses to justify a score of 3, but where there is clearly scope for corrective action, through guidance, positive supervision or training, as a result of which performance is expected to improve to an acceptable level in the next reporting period;
- when performance is deteriorating and is likely to attract a score of 5 on the next report.

A score of 4 is a warning that action is required – by the jobholder to improve his or her performance and by you, to help the jobholder attain that improvement. You must also take particular care to follow the correct procedures so that if, despite best efforts, performance continues to decline, steps leading to dismissal can be taken.

5   *'Unacceptable'*
A score of 5 means that performance is consistently below the standard required from the grade. The mark can be awarded following a previous score of 4, if there has been no subsequent improvement in performance despite management efforts to assist, or can be awarded even if there has been no preceding score of 4 if performance has fallen away very sharply during the period. Dismissal proceedings are likely to result.

See Department of Trade and Industry.

5   Performance management[3]

A weakness of performance appraisal is that it is too easy for managers and employees to collude in the notion that it is the one and only time in the year when they have to discuss performance. Against that, it is sometimes said that one sign of effective management is that there are no surprises in the annual appraisal interview, the idea being that the manager has discussed problems with employees as they have arisen, so that the interview represents a summary of the whole year's activity. Certainly making an *annual* interview the centrepiece of the procedure flies in the face of the research finding that good feedback is frequent and timely: if a manager waits to discuss an employee's failure to produce, say, an annual budget statement on time until months after the event, the employee is likely to feel that it is so much 'water under the bridge'.

A second weakness of performance appraisal is that it takes place in an organizational vacuum, without reference to the organization's overall strategy: it is 'unstrategic' in the sense in which we used that word in Chapter 2. A third weakness is that the emphasis on the face-to-face encounter in performance appraisal has to some extent been at the expense of setting objectives: objectives are not always set at the end of an appraisal interview, despite the strong research support that objective setting enjoys. The recent development of performance management aims to rectify those three weaknesses.

We can, therefore, see performance management as applying the principles of Management by Objectives and annual performance appraisal to current staff management in a strategic context. Table 7.2 shows similarities and differences between performance management and the other approaches to appraisal that we have outlined in this chapter.

Table 7.2   Comparing approaches to appraisal

Feature	Annual confidential report	Management by Objectives (MbO)	Performance appraisal	Performance management
Link with organization mission or objectives	X	✓	X	✓
Individual objectives	X	✓	Sometimes	✓
Inclusion of feedback	X	Sometimes	✓	✓
Time period	Annual	Annual	Annual	Continuous
Rating of performance	✓	✓	Sometimes	✓
Basis of ratings	Traits	Performance on objectives	Traits or behaviours	Performance on objectives
Employee participation	X	X	✓	✓

6   Good practice and appropriate practice: the Daletel case study

Now that we have reviewed what is meant by good practice, it is time to explore the issue of appropriateness, which in appraisal is acute. The case study you are going to read kills two birds with one stone, as it illustrates both how performance management is supposed to operate in practice (the case study company had moved from a performance appraisal to a performance management model, just as the prescriptive literature recommends) and how good practice can fail in the wrong context.

Study task 1: performance management in 'Daletel'[4]

What went wrong, and what could the company have done about it? Answer the following questions as you read the case:

1 *To what extent did Daletel follow 'good practice' as we have presented it in this unit?*
2 *To what extent was the model of performance management that Daletel adopted appropriate to it, and particularly to its Chinese subsidiary, in terms of both organizational culture and national culture?*
3 *What could Daletel have done to make performance management succeed?* ✍

The case concerns the Chinese subsidiary of an international telecommunications infrastructure company, which we will call Daletel. At the time of writing, Daletel was a North American company operating in many countries, including several in Asia, such as India, Japan, Pakistan and Malaysia, as well as in China, where our case study takes place. It marketed fixed line service, wireless and enterprise systems to large commercial customers rather than directly to individual phone users. Daletel had operated in China since 1981, and had built up a significant share of the market. It operated in a fast-moving environment where competition was fierce, and staff were under pressure to meet tight deadlines. Human resource policies originated in its North American headquarters, and were relayed via Daletel's Asian headquarters in Hong Kong.

Up to 2000, Daletel had had a standard performance appraisal scheme based on an annual meeting between a manager and an employee. As in many North American companies, the scheme included a performance-related pay element (we discussed this in Chapter 5): following the meeting, the manager gave a rating which might lead to a 'merit pay' increase. In 2000, the company switched to a performance management procedure, in which managers and employees were expected to meet at least three times a year. The new procedure had an employee development orientation. Staff in Daletel's Chinese operation were told that this was because the company was operating in a fast-changing business where employees needed to update their skills continuously. The performance-related pay element was consequently taken out of the procedure. Instead, the company simply gave managers a pot of money, and discretion to decide in any way they pleased how large an increase to give to the staff in their departments.

The performance management procedure followed a cycle which is outlined in Figure 7.1. (The actual performance management forms which Daletel used appear below.)

Figure 7.1   The performance management cycle in Daletel

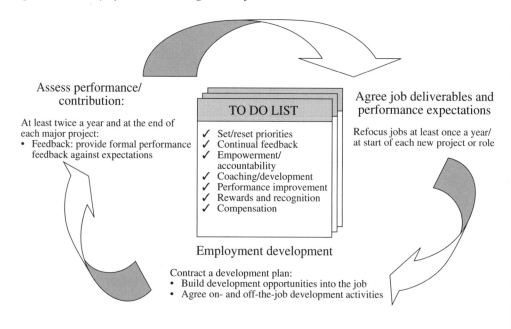

Assess performance/
contribution:

At least twice a year and at the end of
each major project:
• Feedback: provide formal performance
  feedback against expectations

TO DO LIST

✓ Set/reset priorities
✓ Continual feedback
✓ Empowerment/
  accountability
✓ Coaching/development
✓ Performance improvement
✓ Rewards and recognition
✓ Compensation

Agree job deliverables and
performance expectations

Refocus jobs at least once a year/
at start of each new project or role

Employment development

Contract a development plan:
• Build development opportunities into the job
• Agree on- and off-the-job development activities

Daletel's performance management cycle had three stages. At the start of each new project or role, and subsequently once a year, managers and employees were expected to agree what Daletel called 'job deliverables and performance expectations', and also the 'metrics and timing' that would be used for assessing delivery later on. The 'deliverables and expectations' should represent the 'job value add to business'. They should also take the form of 'SMART' job performance objectives.

The second stage was the 'contracting' of a development plan, building development opportunities into the job and agreeing off-the-job development activities. The purpose of this was to 'identify how to better leverage employees' strengths in their jobs', and to 'identify critical gaps between the employee's performance/behaviour and the job requirements'. All of this was recorded on the 'performance expectations' form, which appears as Figure 7.2.

The third and final stage was when managers assessed employees' performance, at least twice a year and/or at the end of every major project. The assessment was supposed to be informed by feedback from other 'stakeholders', using the Feedback Form (Figure 7.3). The outcome was supposed to be recorded on the Performance Evaluation Summary form (Figure 7.4), which fed into what the company called a 'talent segmentation scheme', where staff were divided into 'top performers', 'core contributors' and 'low performers'. Once the final stage was completed, the manager and employee returned to stage one for the start of the new year or the new project.

The process for introducing the scheme was that the Asian headquarters in Hong Kong informed the HR department in its Chinese subsidiary that the company was replacing the old performance appraisal scheme with the new scheme. The HR department then invited managers in China to attend a meeting at which they were briefed on the new scheme. Most (but not all) managers attended. The HR department also organized briefing meetings for employees, although only a minority attended. In both cases, briefings consisted of providing essentially the outline that we have given you.

So far, so good – except for one tiny problem: very few managers actually used the new system in anything like the way the company intended. Managers and employees – and even the HR department – tended to see the whole exercise as nothing more than an exercise in bureaucratic form filling, and did not take it seriously. Consequently, it was impossible to use performance data in the 'talent segmentation scheme', as the company had intended.

7   Summary and conclusion

In this chapter we have tried to justify the expense of time and money that appraisal requires. We have reviewed four major approaches: the Annual Confidential Report, Management by Objectives, performance appraisal and performance management. We summarized relevant research findings to give us a yardstick for evaluating the four ap-

Figure 7.2 Performance expectations

Name: _____

Project/Team/Function Name: _____

Global ID #: _____

Revised On: _____

Project/Team Role ☐

Functional Role ☐

Business/Team/Project Objectives	*What is the purpose of the overall work?*	This Role	*How does this role contribute to the business/team/project objective?*

What Will Be Achieved?	*What specific outcomes/deliverables am I committed to? Are these mine individually (I) or are they shared with others (S)?*

I/S	Required Outcomes	Timing	Evaluation		
			Missed	Met	Surpassed
			☐		☐
			☐		☐
			☐		☐
			☐		☐
			☐		☐
			☐		☐

How Will Outcomes Be Achieved?	What key behaviours/performance dimensions are expected in achieving the outcomes listed above?	Evaluation		
		Below Expectations	As Expected	Beyond Expectations
Performance Dimensions (Please indicate mastery level if necessary)		☐		☐
		☐		☐
		☐		☐
Productivity Conditions	What resources (e.g. equipment, materials, facilities, people) would help me to do the job well?			
Personal Development	What coaching, training, mentoring or education would help me do the job well?			
Feedback Timing and Methods	How will I get feedback on my performance (who, how often)?			

Manager's signature _____   Date

Employee's signature _____   Date

Figure 7.3   Feedback form

Name:

Team/Project/Function Name:

Global ID #:

Revised On:

Team/Project Role ☐

Functional Role ☐

| Feedback Requested From: | _____ Peer | _____ Functional Manager | _____ Project Manager |
| | _____ Customer | _____ Direct Report | _____ Other (describe) |

Feedback Requested About: Feedback is requested on the following outcomes and behaviours/performance dimensions. (If appropriate, a Performance Expectations form with the relevant items highlighted is attached.)

To The Feedback Provider: Please provide observations, dates, and other details on the feedback requested above. Then place an 'x' on the matrix below that reflects the overall performance. Use the relevant tables in the Priorities Process Guide to help you.

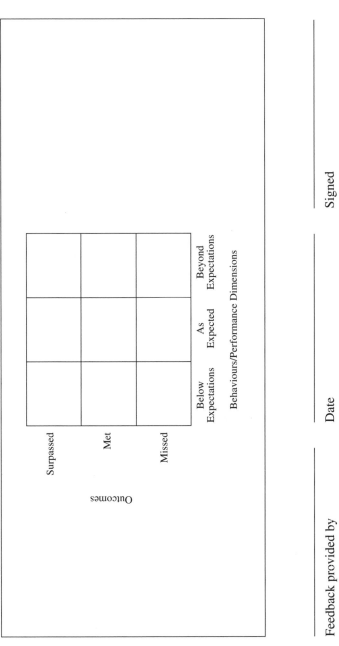

Feedback provided by   Date   Signed

Figure 7.4   Performance evaluation summary

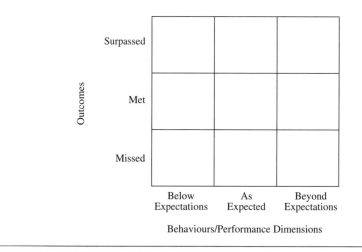

Name:

Project Completion ☐   Project/Team/Function Name:

Mid-year Review ☐   Global ID #:

End of Year Review ☐   Revised On:

Instructions

1. Collect all relevant *Feedback Forms*.
2. If this is an *End of Year* or *Mid-year Review*, collect any *Performance Evaluation Summaries* for specific projects.
3. Using this information, discuss a position on the matrix below that reflects performance over the duration of the project or time period being reviewed. Mark it with an 'x' (see *Priorities Guidebook* for more information).
4. Provide a written summary in the box below the matrix. Attach a continuation sheet if required.

Outcomes

Surpassed

Met

Missed

Below Expectations   As Expected   Beyond Expectations

Behaviours/Performance Dimensions

Summary of overall performance

Describe employee's overall contribution (e.g. targets achieved, complexity and scope of objectives, barriers surpassed, quality achieved). Summarize strengths and development needs in rellation to the agreed outcomes and PDs.

Employee may add comments in this section. A continuation sheet can be attched.

Manager's signature   Date

Employee's signature   Date

Employee signature does not imply agreement with the above information, only that the manager has reviewed the above with the employee.

proaches. Lastly, we discussed a case study that highlighted the interaction between good practice and the context in which it is applied.

In the end we continue to believe, with Fletcher (1993), that no matter how hard it is to devise a satisfactory performance appraisal scheme, there is no real alternative to turn to. But it is vital that the technical ramifications of rating schemes, form design and so on do not blind us to the overriding importance of an approach that is in harmony with the context in which we introduce it, or make us overlook the importance of developing managers' appraisal skills. Appraisal will stand or fall on whether we manage to do those two things properly.

Notes

1 We will use 'appraisal' as a shorthand for 'performance management and appraisal' in this chapter.
2 'Oh if only some power could give us the gift of seeing ourselves as others see us.'
3 Performance management is also used for managing the performance of organizations as a whole. In this chapter we confine ourselves to its use for managing the performance of individual employees.
4 I am very grateful to Ms Xiao Zhou for the material on which this case study is based.

8   Learning and Training

Derek Eldridge and Willy McCourt

What this chapter is about

This chapter presents the systematic learning model and explores its main stages: learning needs analysis, learning design and evaluation. Discussing the 'levels' of evaluation raises the issue of transfer of learning from a training course back to work. A case study of learning and training in a government ministry rounds off the chapter.

What you will learn

By the end of the chapter you should be able to:

- outline the systematic learning model;
- choose appropriate methods in order to carry out a learning needs analysis;
- design a learning programme, again drawing on appropriate methods;
- evaluate a learning programme at the four 'levels' of evaluation;
- state the implications of learning transfer for learning design and evaluation.

1   Introduction

1.1   Definition

In this chapter we turn our attention to learning and training, which we define as *a process which encourages learning to take place through planned and directed routes within an organizational context, and which*

236

'adds value' to an individual's personal development and to an organization's objectives.

1.2   The traditional model of training at work

Box 8.1   A traditional training design in Tanzania

In 1979, the President of Tanzania criticized the low level of performance in the public service and directed that a review of civil service performance should be carried out. The review found that top executives had received very little management training. As a result, the Ministry of Manpower set up a National Standing Team on Top Executive Training, comprising representatives from the four existing management training institutions. The team recommended a suite of four to six weeks' residential training courses. In due course they were held in a game lodge in a remote location.

Government commitment to the training meant that it was possible to release very senior managers, although many of them were sceptical about the value of the training. The report admits that it is not clear to what extent attendance in the programme affected personal and organizational performance, but anecdotal evidence exists that some improvements resulted. The fact that the participants were very senior was helpful in this respect: the report notes that lower-level participants often complain about not having the power to introduce positive changes after attending training programmes. Many participants commented that they found the opportunity to rest and relax very beneficial.

See Mutahaba (1986).

The above example shows the sort of process that an organization might go through to produce a training programme. First of all a *training need* was identified (in this case, by the late President Nyerere himself), then a training programme was *designed and implemented*, and finally there was an *evaluation* of the success of the programme, including the extent to which participants had used what they had learnt on the course. These are the main stages of the 'traditional' model of training that organizations have mostly relied on, and we shall work through them later on.

1.3   Limiting assumptions in the traditional model

Before we work through those stages though, we think we need to correct two limiting assumptions on which the traditional model was based: (a) if staff performance is a problem, training is the solution, (b) if staff need to learn something, they need to go on a course to learn it. We do not want to be unfair to practitioners of the 'traditional' model – probably no training practitioner would ever have insisted on either of those assumptions, if they were put to them in this bald way. But we do want to suggest that their actual practice was usually based on them. Let us look at the first assumption to see what we mean.

Performance deficiency = training problem?
Think back for a moment to the example of the company that was experiencing a high level of damage to its vehicles, reported in Box 4.3. Do you remember how the company's 'knee-jerk reaction' was to assume that they needed to train their drivers, whereas through job analysis they found that the real problem was the existence of what we called a 'vehicle bashing culture'? In our experience the company's assumption is a very common one.

But in fact there are many performance problems that are not amenable to training, as Figure 8.1 shows. To take just one example from the figure, an individual's performance may be deficient because of an *obstacle* in her path: for example, she may have been unable to visit rural health clinics for which she is responsible because the vehicle that she needs to use has broken down and not been repaired or replaced.

Thus the question of training only arises when we have discounted other explanations of poor performance. This point is particularly important for those of us who are training specialists, possibly working in a training department or in a consultancy company that specializes in training. For we will only add to an organization's problems in the long run if we accede to a request to provide training for staff in a situation where training is not the right solution.

Training and learning
The second assumption is equally limiting because, even where a performance deficiency *can* be rectified by the employee learning something, a training course might not be the best way to learn it. After all, how did you learn to do the job you are doing now? By going on a course that your employer organized? Or did you just pick the job up as you went along, maybe asking for occasional advice from your boss or your colleagues? Perhaps you already knew how to do it when you

Figure 8.1   Performance deficiency equals training problem?

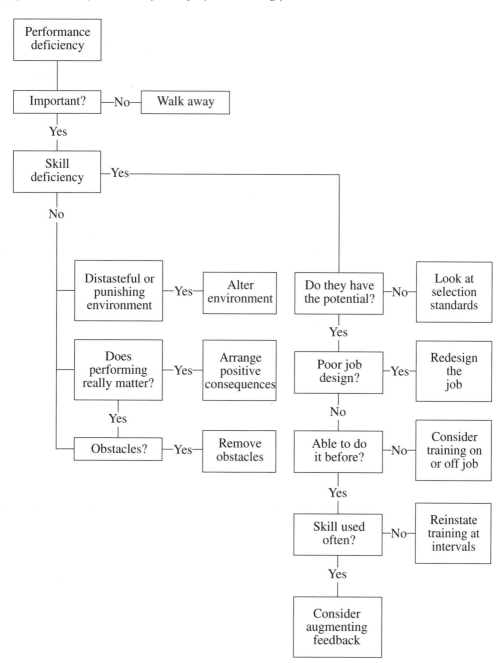

Source: Mager and Pipe (1970: 200).

started it. Maybe you did not learn it at all, but were born with the ability to do it.

The last point is not as daft as it sounds, since 'innate ability' was one of the things that managers said they relied on when John Burgoyne and Roger Stuart, researchers at Lancaster University in the UK, asked them where they had acquired the skills they needed to do their jobs. The answers Burgoyne and Stuart received are summarized in Figure 8.2.

You will notice from the figure that most of the managers said that the key source of learning was doing the job itself, not going on work-based training courses. In fact training courses were well down their list of sources of learning, behind such things as learning from other jobs (for three of the attributes) – and even from their parents (for one of the attributes). This of course is a far cry from the second assumption on which the Tanzanian management training course (and very many courses like it) was based: that if someone needs to learn something, they should go on a course to learn it. Burgoyne and Stuart's model implies a rather different approach to organizing and supporting employees as they learn to do their jobs better, and in particular to the way we design a learning programme. We shall discuss this later on, when we come to learning design in the learning process.

It is interesting to ask where the equation of learning with going on a training course comes from. We suspect that it derives from the experience that most of us have of formal education. All of us have spent many years in schools and colleges, and this has conditioned us to believe that, in order to learn something, we have to go on a course and be *taught* it. We continue to believe this even though, in practice, very few of us actually attend such courses once we have entered work (organizations have other spending priorities) and all of us do continue to learn while getting on with our jobs.

The influence of the educational model is pervasive, and also pernicious in a way. In reviewing the provision of in-service training in Botswana, Jackie Charlton (1992: 61) emphasizes the importance of moving 'from an organizational culture in which training is viewed as a route to promotion via paper qualifications to viewing training as an input into improving performance', and remarks that 'Like many developing countries, Botswana has valued education and training in proportion to the extent that it is paper based'. (What she describes is another manifestation of what we called the 'diploma disease' in Chapter 6.)

Although we will continue to use the term 'training', as we do in the title of this chapter, you should understand it from this point on as a

Figure 8.2   The nature, use and acquisition of managerial skills and other attributes

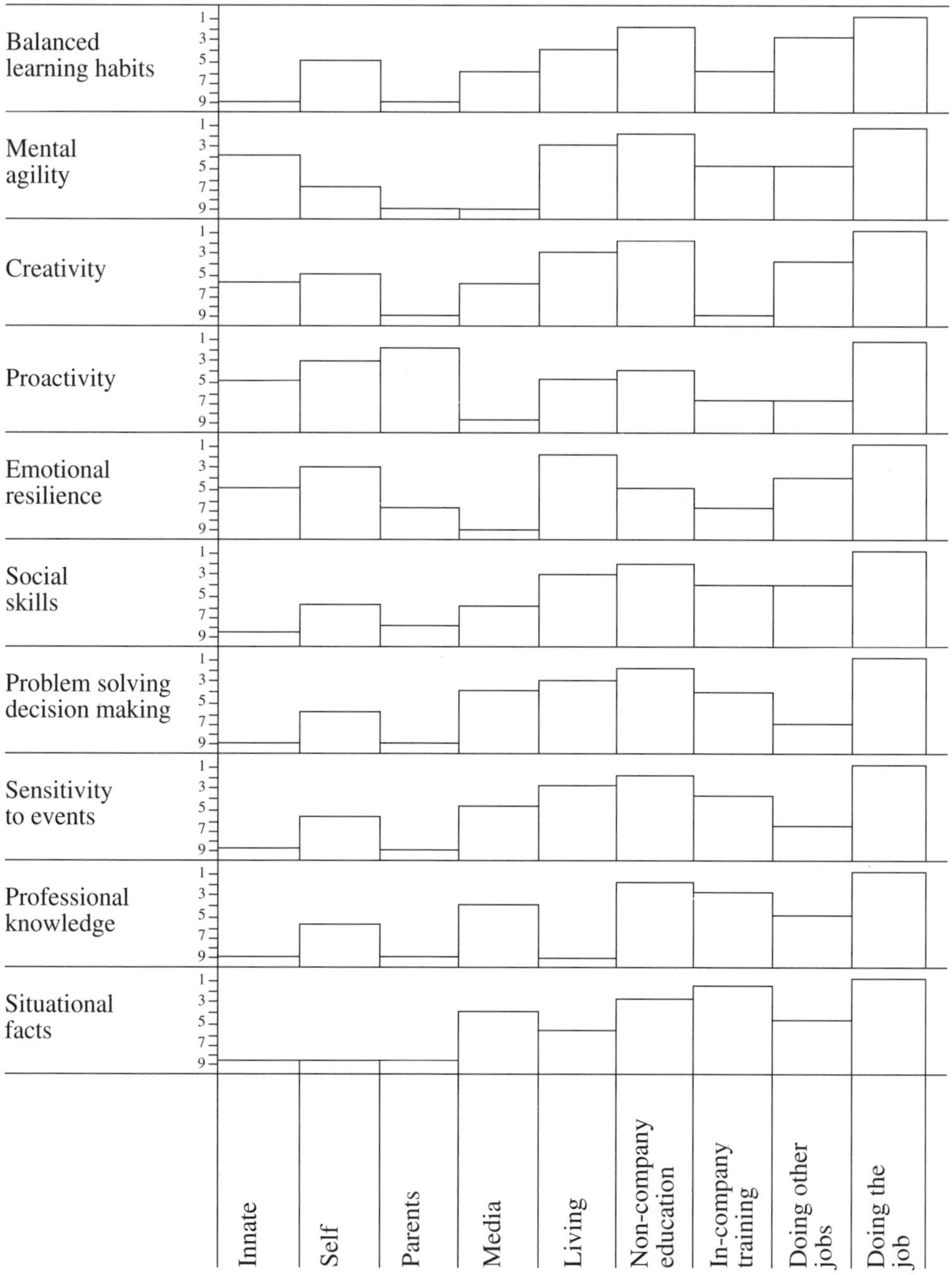

Source: Burgoyne and Stuart (1976: 27).

shorthand for 'any organized learning programme, whether it includes an off-the-job training course or not', except where the context makes it clear that we are talking specifically about an off-the-job training course.

Having discussed the two 'limiting assumptions' that we see as underlying the 'traditional' model, let us now look at the model itself, slightly modified to correct for those assumptions.

2 The systematic learning model

2.1 Features and application

The systematic learning model originated in the 1960s. At its heart is the idea that a learning programme should be related to the end results that the organization seeks to achieve. A programme based on this model can be defined as a planned programme based on

- an analysis of learning need,
- a designed learning plan, and
- an evaluation of the learning that actually occurred.

The definition allows for the fact that people are learning all the time in the ways that Burgoyne and Stuart listed. But learning of this kind, which Burgoyne and Stuart called 'natural learning', is unplanned and

Table 8.1   Systematic and unsystematic training

Features of systematic training	Features of unsystematic training
Training is part of the organization's overall planning process in pursuit of organizational goals	Training is not part of the planning process and arises on the basis of ad hoc needs
The organization has a training strategy which informs the approach to employee development	The organization has no training strategy and thus training is low priority
Skills are planned for and addressed systematically through formal training	Skills are learned 'as you go along'
There is a continuous cycle of training analysis, activity and evaluation	Training is carried out when an emergency arises, not based on needs analysis and not evaluated

haphazard when viewed against organizational requirements. The systematic model seeks to supplement 'natural learning' with a systematic intervention that relates to the organization's objectives (see Table 8.1).

The model is applicable across a range of development activities, which include:

- induction training for new employees;
- basic training for young employees;
- specific skills training at all levels;
  - manual,
  - clerical,
  - technical,
  - professional;
- safety training;
- management development.

It is important for you to dwell for a moment on the advantages of the systematic model. It certainly represents an advance on what went before: organizations introducing it give themselves for the first time a way of channelling individual learning so that it relates to the organization's demands. The value of this to any organization trying to manage strategically will be obvious.

2.2   The systematic learning model

The systematic model boils down to the process shown in Figure 8.3. As usual with such processes, we could also present it as a *cycle*, with an arrow going back from 'evaluate' to 'identify needs' in the figure, because our evaluation of the learning programme, at the end of the process, will have implications next time round for the way we identify learning needs and design the learning programme.

Figure 8.3   The learning process

Identify and analyse learning needs

Design learning programme

Implement the programme

Evaluate the learning

3   Learning needs analysis

3.1   Learning needs at the organization, job and individual levels

How do we identify learning needs, the first stage in the learning process? McGehee and Thayer (1961) suggest that it is helpful to think in terms of three levels as follows:

Table 8.2   Levels of learning need

Organization level	Needs derive from strategic objectives, human resource planning and organization-wide issues
Job level	Needs derive from job analysis
Individual level	Needs derive from performance management

In practice, learning needs can appear from anywhere and everywhere. A chief executive may decide one fine morning, after attending a slick presentation, that every manager needs to go on a time management training course. So we must be careful, as always, not to read the model in too mechanical a way. Still, it gives us a simple framework to organize our thinking about learning needs.

3.2   The organization level

In terms of the SHRM model (Chapter 2), the organization level is also the strategic level. This means that identifying learning needs at this level can be an example of vertical integration. The customer care training programme that British Airways introduced after privatization in the 1980s in an attempt to shift the airline from an armed forces culture to a customer culture is an example of a learning need that derived from the organization's strategic objectives.

At this level, learning needs may also arise from human resource planning, which as we know is the HRM activity that we carry out at the level of the organization as a whole. Remember that, at the start of Section 5 of Chapter 3, we said that, 'In a way, everything we do in the other activities that we discuss in this book, like recruitment and selection and learning and training, derives from a comparison of demand and supply forecasts.' Thus an organization might want to use its learning activities to take account of expected retirements, or transfer and career moves, or wastage trends. We saw in Chapter 3 how demand and supply forecasts might affect the training of revenue collectors (in Tanzania) or nurses (in the Nargothrond hospital case study).

However, learning needs at the organization level can also be pragmatic, deriving for example from performance problems that managers have identified. Here are a few examples:

- customers' complaints,
- delays arising in the work system as a whole,
- excessive maintenance costs,
- excessive waste,
- lack of cooperation between staff,
- ineffective management systems,
- absenteeism and unacceptable levels of short-term sickness,
- poor morale,
- high accident rate.

Remember, once again, the point we made earlier: a learning programme will not always be the right solution to these problems.

3.3   The job level

The job level is the level of job analysis. We focus at this level on the job description and person specification, identifying what tasks need to be done and what knowledge and skills are needed to do them. Typically we do this by identifying the needs of staff who share a particular job description – a group of principal administrative officers, for example. However, remember the first 'tension' in the practice of job analysis that we discussed in Chapter 4, between the individual and the team as the basic, or 'atomic', unit of work. We may wish to focus on the learning needs of a team, even if it consists of people who have several different job descriptions. We may be interested, for example, in how the group as a whole serves the interests of the other groups who are its internal clients.

3.4   The individual level

The classic mechanism for identifying the learning needs of individual staff is performance management and appraisal. What the manager and the individual member of staff do in this context is to identify what is called the *performance gap*, defined as the gap between actual and fully satisfactory performance of the job duties. Performance management is not the only means of identifying this, as Table 8.3 shows.

Table 8.3   Identifying the performance gap

Level	Primary method	Nature of performance gap
Managerial	Performance management and appraisal	Current performance measured – against targets – against required managerial competences
Skilled manual	Tests of competence	Result achieved compared to proficiency level
	Measurement of output	Quantity and quality of output compared to workplan requirements
Clerical and administrative	A mixture of the above	Selected from above, as appropriate

Bridging the performance gap is not the only way that we identify learning needs at the individual level. It is actually at this level that the development aspect of 'learning and training' comes into its own, since individuals may have development needs or aspirations which do not arise from their job descriptions. For example, someone who is working as a teacher may aspire to being promoted to a job in which she will manage staff. Similarly, an organization may be keen to encourage staff to look beyond the job they currently occupy as part of their career development. An individual manager may simply be keen to help a member of staff get to where he or she wants to go, even if that means leaving the organization. While of course such a need may be identified informally (the teacher might refer to it over a cup of tea in the school staff room) performance management is available once again as a formal mechanism for identifying such needs.

3.5   Who identifies needs?

The example of the teacher who aspires to become a manager raises the issue of who should be responsible for identifying learning needs. It is unlikely that either a manager or a training specialist would have identified the teacher's need: it was something that only she herself would recognize. Clearly the different stakeholders are likely to have somewhat different points of view on learning needs, as Figure 8.4 shows.

While some of the expectations are complementary – trainers' desire to give feedback to managers on training outcomes, for example, com-

Figure 8.4   Stakeholder expectations

Managers expect:
- individuals will relate learning needs to performance
- trainers will equip staff with knowledge and skills to improve performance
- training efforts will be geared to improving organizational performance
- relevant training

Individuals expect:
- managers and trainers to assist with their development
- a say in the type of training offered
- a suitable training environment
- support from managers to apply learning on the job

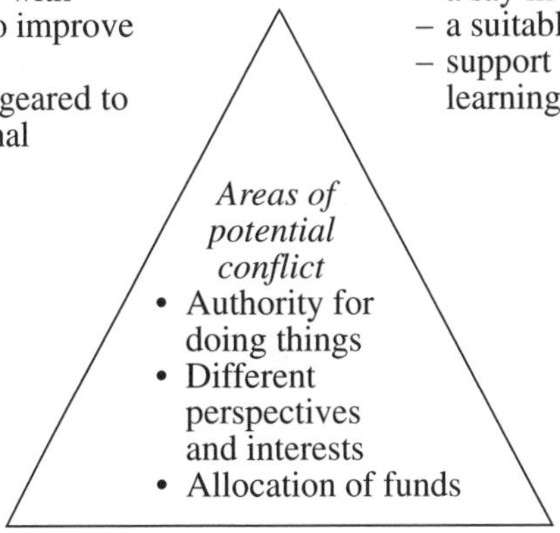

Areas of potential conflict
- Authority for doing things
- Different perspectives and interests
- Allocation of funds

Trainers expect:
- to develop training policy jointly with managers
- knowledge of future developments
- sufficient budget
- managers and learners to understand the role of training as a change agent
- trainees to be serious learners
- managers to be involved in training
- to give feedback to managers on training outcomes

plements managers' desire to see training that is relevant – some may be in conflict, as Figure 8.4 again shows. It is not easy to reconcile competing interests, as we will see in Chapter 10 when we discuss employee relations and the role of trade unions. But it should at least be possible to use learning needs analysis to become aware of what those interests are.

Such conflicts of interest take many forms. One of the authors had the experience of spending two weeks identifying the learning needs of staff employed in a legal empowerment programme by a large NGO in Bangladesh. Much of the time was spent in frustrating arguments between members of the team who had been trained in the United States, who had developed a preference for systematic, quantitative methods, and members who had been trained in the United Kingdom, who preferred a more impressionistic and qualitative approach.

3.6   Needs analysis methods

Our Bangladesh anecdote brings us on to the question of methods of learning needs analysis. Fortunately we can cover this quickly, as most of the methods that organizations use are the same ones that they use for job analysis and recruitment and selection, and we discussed them in detail in Chapters 4 and 6. We will list relevant methods here to refresh your memory, before discussing a couple of methods that we did not include in Chapter 4.

- Self-assessment, for example work diaries: valuable for getting the point of view of staff themselves.
- Interviews with target staff.
- Skill testing.
- Questionnaires.
- Observation.

Group discussion and brainstorming

This is self-explanatory. Brainstorming, where a small group generates a large number of ideas, is one approach to group discussion. A rule of brainstorming is that the group should not pause to evaluate the quality or relevance of the ideas, as this will slow down the flow of ideas.

Performance management and appraisal

We have, of course, discussed this already in Chapter 7. However, since it 'lies at the heart of training and development as it does of many other personnel processes' (Harrison, 1992: 303), we think we need to say a bit more about it here.

Appraisal forms often contain a section in which the learning needs of the appraisee are identified. The immediate supervisor can use it to address an individual's weakness, where this is the reason why he or she has failed to meet a performance target. Agreement between the supervisor and the employee on the nature of the training need, and how to address it, is sought in the appraisal interview.

In order to be effective in identifying learning needs, an appraisal system should have these components:

- stated and achievable work objectives;
- cooperative work arrangements between the supervisor and employee throughout the year;
- agreement on the knowledge and skills that are important.

With an effective performance appraisal system, learning needs can be collated across a range of employees to draw up an annual training plan. (As you will see later on in the Valinor case study, all this is easier said than done.)

4   Learning design

4.1   Learning objectives

Having established learning needs, the next stage in the learning process is to specify the change in behaviour that the learning programme is supposed to bring about. This is done by writing learning objectives, which state precisely the knowledge and skills learners need to acquire to bridge the gap and meet the demands of their jobs. Box 8.2 shows three types of objective.

Box 8.2   Typology of learning objectives

Thinking objectives	*Attitudinal objectives*	*Physical skills objectives*
Emphasize intellectual outcomes, such as knowledge, understanding and critical thinking	Emphasize feelings, emotions, attitudes and values	Emphasize physical dexterity and coordination
Example To be able to compile a department's budget in line with financial regulations and current spending guidelines	*Example* To act as a work team leader with emphasis on obtaining the best contribution from each individual	*Example* To be able to operate a photocopier including loading of paper, choice of copying mode and routine adjustment/ fault finding

---

By this stage in the book you will be familiar with learning objectives, as they appear at the start of every chapter. Notice how our objectives are always *behavioural*: we use 'action' words like 'state', 'describe', 'carry out' and so on, referring to activities which are in principle observable and measurable, rather than 'thinking' words like 'know', 'understand', 'be aware of' and so on, which are neither observable nor measurable.

4.2 Learning theory and learning design

Malcolm Knowles (1990) has suggested that the way we learn as adults (andragogy) is different from the way we learnt as children (pedagogy),[1] because adults have a greater ability to be *self-directed*, to draw on their experience as learners in facing situations, to have a personal learning agenda and to focus learning on life issues. His suggestion has important implications for the design of learning for adults:

- the trainer's role becomes to facilitate learners in finding their own direction and setting their own agenda;
- because experience and reflecting on experience are so fundamental for adult learners, experiential rather than didactic learning methods are appropriate to reflect adults' ability to draw on their experience;
- the learning programme should address real-life problems.

Contracting

Contracting is one example of how trainers can facilitate learners in setting their own agenda. At the start of a learning programme, trainers often confirm learning objectives, and also 'groundrules' for the programme, together with the participants. This is called 'contracting'. 'Contracting' covers objectives, but may also cover aspects such as the responsibilities of both participants and trainers, and what the group and individuals within it can do to support learning.

4.3 Kolb's learning cycle and Honey and Mumford's learning styles

David Kolb's very influential 'learning cycle', shown in Figure 8.5 below, is clearly an 'andragogical' model. Kolb's cycle implies that learners need to be active in all the stages of the cycle if they are to learn fully – and notably to be active in 'concrete experience', which is often neglected in traditional training course designs. That is the theoretical reason for the popularity of management development using the outdoors; and more generally it is the reason for the popularity of 'experiential learning'.

Honey and Mumford (1992) have extended Kolb's work by suggesting that the four stages in his cycle actually represent four learning styles, which different individuals will prefer to different degrees. They label the four styles *activist, reflector, theorist* and *pragmatist*. They

Figure 8.5   Kolb's learning cycle

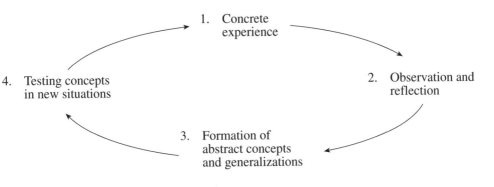

correspond to the four stages of Kolb's Cycle: 'activist' corresponds to 'concrete experience', and so on.

- Activists involve themselves fully and without bias in new experiences.
- Reflectors like to stand back to ponder experiences and observe them from many different perspectives.
- Theorists adapt and integrate observations into complex but logically sound theories.
- Pragmatists are keen on trying out ideas, theories and techniques to see if they work in practice.

Learning activities and learning styles
Honey and Mumford argue that people with a preference for a certain learning style tend to have a matching preference for certain learning activities (see Box 8.3).

4.4   Choosing learning activities

Trainers will need to have a wide repertoire of learning activities to cater for all the learning styles that Kolb and Honey and Mumford have identified. Table 8.4 is a list of possible activities, with a commentary on them. Notice that some of the activities are suitable for use in an assessment or development centre (see Chapter 6).

Box 8.3   Learning activities and learning styles

Activists tend to learn best from activities where
- they can immerse themselves in short 'here and now' activities,
- there is excitement/drama/crisis,
- there is a range of diverse activities to tackle,
- they have a lot of the limelight.

Reflectors tend to learn best from activities where
- they are allowed or encouraged to observe and reflect on activities,
- they can carry out some painstaking research,
- they have the opportunity to review what has happened,
- they can reach a decision in their own time without pressure and tight deadlines.

Theorists tend to learn best from activities where
- what is being offered is a model, concept, or theory,
- they have the chance to question and probe the basic methodology, assumptions or logic behind something,
- they can analyse and then generalize the reasons for success or failure,
- they are offered interesting ideas and concepts, even if they are not immediately relevant.

Pragmatists tend to learn best from activities where
- there is an obvious link between the subject matter and an opportunity to solve a problem,
- they are shown techniques for doing things with obvious practical advantage,
- they have the chance to try out and practise techniques,
- they are given immediate opportunities to implement what they have learned.

See Honey and Mumford (1992).

4.5   Learning at work

The growth of learning using the outdoors shows us that the traditional training course model is flexible enough to accommodate experiential, or 'andragogical', learning. However, another implication of Knowles' and Kolb's work is the shifting of the focus from the free-standing training course to the workplace itself as a source of learning. You should remember at this point how the managers in Burgoyne and Stuart's survey said that their key source of learning was doing the job itself, not going on work-based training courses.

Table 8.4   A guide to learning activities

Method	What it is	What it will achieve	Points to watch
Lecture	A talk/presentation where trainee participation is confined to asking questions.	Suitable for large audiences where learner participation must be limited. The trainer can control information to be covered and lecture timing.	The lack of participation limits feedback on learning achieved.
Team briefing	A briefing by a section manager. Employees may ask questions, and there may be brief discussion.	Suitable for putting across information to groups of not more than 20. Participation, though limited, retains learner interest.	Communication tends to be 'top-down': team briefing can be little different from a lecture.
Job (skill) instruction	A session during which a job or part of a job is learned in the following ways: • the learner is told how to do the job, • the learner is shown how to do the job, • the learner does the job under supervision.	Suitable for teaching skills. The job is broken down into parts which are practised separately. The whole skill is thus built up part by part, so learners are not overloaded. Suitable when a skill depends on the acquisition of much knowledge (e.g. many clerical skills).	Some skills need to be learned as a 'whole' rather than as discrete parts. Learners may be asked to absorb large amounts of information, and then shown what to do at length, before they have the chance to practise the skill.
Discussion	Knowledge, ideas and opinions on a particular subject are freely exchanged among the learners and the trainer.	Suitable where there is no 'one best way', and when attitudes need to be changed: learners are more likely to change attitudes after discussion. Also provides feedback to the trainer.	The discussion may become unfocused. Learners may become entrenched in their attitudes if discussion is not handled skilfully.

Table 8.4   continued

Method	What it is	What it will achieve	Points to watch
Role play	Learners practise a role which work requires. Useful for dealing with face-to-face situations e.g. manager/client, manager/team member. May be recorded on audio or video tape.	Learners can practise and get feedback in a safe situation. This gives confidence as well as offering guidelines. The learners get the feel of the pressures of the real life situation.	Learner confidence may be eroded if the situation is not handled well.
Case study	The Valinor case in this chapter is an example. Learners typically try both to diagnose and to solve a specific problem.	Allows detailed analysis of a problem in a lifelike setting. Case studies provide opportunities for exchange of ideas on a problem that learners face at work.	May exaggerate the importance of a 'cerebral' approach to problem solving, and make problems appear more cut-and-dried than they are in real life.
Exercise	Learners, singly or in groups, are asked to undertake a particular task prescribed by the trainer. It is usually a practice or a test of knowledge put over prior to the exercise. Exercises can check learners' current understanding before introducing new ideas.	Suitable when learners need to follow a particular formula. Learners are to some extent self-directed, and also active.	The exercise should be realistic and the expected result attainable by most learners to prevent loss of confidence and frustration.
Project	Allows learners to display initiative and creative ideas. The trainer prescribes the task but the learner is free to decide how best to achieve it. Data are drawn from a real situation, or at least extracted from relevant literature or project reports.	Suitable where initiative and creativity need stimulating or testing. Projects provide feedback on learners' personal skills as well as their knowledge and attitudes to a job. Like exercises, projects may be used as an informal test.	The project must engage the learner's interest and must be relevant to the learner's needs. If not, there could be a loss of confidence in the trainer.

Table 8.4   continued

Method	What it is	What it will achieve	Points to watch
In-tray exercise	Learners are given files, papers and letters which are the typical contents of a desk-worker's in-tray. Learners act on each item. The trainer marks the results.	Gives a snapshot of real-life problems and their solutions. 'High content reality' promotes transfer of learning. Gives feedback on learners' progress.	The contents of the in-tray must be realistic. Insensitive marking may decrease the confidence of a weak learner.
Business and mgmt. games	Groups are given different management roles to perform, based on written information about an organization. One group may be concerned with finance, another with production and so on. The task may be competitive.	Allows practice in dealing with management problems. Conveys the complexity of real life. The lifelike situation facilitates transfer of learning. Allows systematic assessment when used in an assessment or development centre.	It may be difficult to decide what is the 'right' answer. Learners may be dissatisfied if they do not accept the assessment of their decisions as fair.
Group dynamics	Learners are put in situations where the behaviour of individuals, or of a group as a whole, can be examined by trainers and learners	A vivid way for learners to find out how their behaviour affects other people. Group dynamics increases knowledge of why people behave as they do. This increases sensitivity in working with other people. Suitable for communication and team skills.	Learners may find out things about themselves that they would rather not know. They may then withdraw psychologically. It is important that the trainer nips problems arising within the group in the bud to prevent a damaging breakdown.

Source: Adapted from ILO (1972).

Using the workplace as a source of learning puts the spotlight on the role of the manager as trainer. There are many ways in which the manager might become a trainer. Table 8.5 presents some of them in relation to some of the major processes that Mumford discusses.

Table 8.5   The manager's role in on-the-job learning

On-the-job process	Manager's role
Secondment	Help the secondee to relate what he or she observes in the new organization to what happens in his or her own organization
Coaching	Use 'direct discussion and guided activity to help a colleague ... do a task better' (Megginson and Boydell's definition)
Mentoring	'Open doors' for and coach a less experienced colleague, usually one for whom the mentor has no direct responsibility

Other on-the-job learning methods include:

- a planned increase in job scope, activities and responsibility to increase individual self-confidence;
- acting in a deputy capacity for a senior;
- cooperating with others with similar needs in group/team training events;
- writing reports.

One further learning method that is widely used, including as far afield as Malaysia, is 'action learning'. We will also say a little more about it when we discuss transfer of learning.

Perhaps the most basic thing of all is to get the manager to recognize that staff development is first and foremost *their* responsibility: specialist trainers and training courses play a valuable, but merely supporting, role.

Problems with learning at work
But there are problems with learning programmes which have a significant workplace component. We recognized earlier that 'natural learning', while powerful, is also unplanned and haphazard when

viewed against organizational requirements. Learners are as likely to learn bad habits as good ones.

When one of the authors began his career with the British development NGO Voluntary Service Overseas (VSO) as an interviewer of candidates for overseas teaching posts, he picked up the skill of interviewing by watching how his more experienced colleagues on interview panels asked questions. This enabled him to function as an interviewer – but not very well! On one occasion he heard a colleague ask a candidate: 'What would you do if you were teaching on a Friday afternoon and two of the pupils at the back of the class were throwing balls of paper at each other?' The candidate gave a terrible answer, and the panel, inferring that he was unable to keep discipline in the classroom, came close to rejecting him.

So the next time the author was interviewing, he asked the same question himself. The result was just as he had hoped: the candidate failed to answer convincingly. But this time, after the candidate had left the room a (different) colleague turned to the author and demanded: 'Well, what would *you* have done?' Her point was that the question was unfair. Apart from being hypothetical, and hypothetical questions are usually bad questions, there was actually no right answer. So by observing his colleague in the first interview he was definitely learning from experience. Unfortunately, though, he was learning *the wrong thing*. As the American poet T.S. Eliot (1963: 208) put it in a different context, he 'had the experience but missed the meaning'.

So basing training in the workplace is not the automatic solution to all our problems, and this is without discussing practical problems such as how employees in a busy job are going to make time to try doing their jobs in a different way. If we are going to realize the potential of workplace learning, we will have to *design* workplace learning systematically in just the same way that we design a training course.

5   Evaluation and learning transfer

5.1   Levels of evaluation

Every discussion of learning and training includes something on evaluation. Yet that is not the case when we discuss the other HRM activities. Why are we so much more interested in whether training makes a difference than we are, say, in whether we have selected the right person? There are possibly two reasons. The first is that there is a longstanding tradition of evaluation in education, which organizational learning and training borrows from, so there are well established methods: all of us, in a sense, have been evaluated because all of us have done formal examinations. The second reason, we suspect, is that trainers know in their hearts that it is by no means obvious that training interventions make any difference at all.

Kirkpatrick (1959) identified four levels of evaluation which most training specialists accept. They are shown in Table 8.6. In terms of McGehee and Thayer's model of learning needs analysis, the first three levels correspond roughly to the 'individual level', while the fourth level ('impact on the organization') corresponds to the 'organization level'.

Table 8.6   Evaluating learning

Evaluation level	When conducted and by whom	Typical methods
Reactions learners' immediate reactions	At the end of the programme, led by the trainer	End-of-course questionnaires and discussions
Learning the extent to which learning objectives have been achieved*	At the end of the programme, led by the trainer	Tests and participants' own self-assessment
Behaviour the extent to which participants are doing their jobs differently	At work after the programme ends, led by the trainer, with participants and managers	Observation, managers' reports (including appraisal reports), participants' self-assessment
Results the extent to which training has contributed to achieving the organization's objectives	By trainers and senior managers	Organization-wide measures, such as: • client satisfaction • cost reduction • job satisfaction • work quality

* Notice here how learning should be evaluated in terms of the learning objectives. This approach is sometimes called *goal-based evaluation*.

Despite all the discussion of evaluation, anything more than the most basic approach is rare: 'The overwhelming impression from the literature is that most trainers are reluctant to practise evaluation and when they do attempt it they want the simplest possible method.' (Hoyle, 1984: 277).

How does evaluation of reactions work? Usually by means of a questionnaire, with items like this:

Session name: *Recruitment and selection*

1	2	3	4	5
very poor	poor	OK	good	very good

COMMENTS:

This is indeed basic, but still valuable, especially if results can be compared for a series of learning events.

Study task 1: evaluating reactions to a series of courses

Have a look at this summary of average scores on an end-of-course questionnaire for a series of training courses in which both the authors of this chapter were involved. (Do not worry if some of the item titles are unfamiliar.)

1 What do the scores tell you about the effectiveness of the training programme?

(Figures following each item under section 1 represent the average score on a five-point scale where 1 = very poor and 5 = very good. Items under section 2 were graded on a four-point scale.)

Item	Course III	Course II	Course I	Average score
1 Response to individual sessions				
1.1 Introductions	4.6	4.6	4.0	4.4
1.2 Contracting	4.3	4.1	4.0	4.1
1.3 Civil service reform	NA*	4.0	4.0	4.0
1.4 Local government & role of MMOs**	4.7	4.4	4.0	4.4
1.5 Procedures and the role of LGSC***	NA*	4.1	4.0	4.1
1.6 Human resource planning	4.4	4.6	4.5	4.5
1.7 Job analysis	4.8	4.7	4.5	4.7
1.8 Recruitment and selection	4.6	4.9	4.5	4.7
1.9 Introduction to action planning	4.2	4.2	NA****	4.2
1.10 Performance appraisal	4.6	4.6	4.3	4.5
1.11 Employee relations	4.3	3.9	3.9	4.0

Item	Course III	Course II	Course I	Average score
1.12 Training & development	4.4	4.5	4.4	4.4
1.13 Budgeting	4.2	3.9	4.25	4.1
1.14 Counselling	4.7	4.7	4.4	4.6
1.15 Personnel administration	4.6	4.6	4.35	4.5
1.16 Preparation of action plans	4.5	4.5	4.6	4.5
1.17 Quality of accommodation	4.1	4.5	4.1	4.2
1.18 Average score for 5-point items	*4.5*	*4.4*	*4.2*	*4.4*
2 Overall responses (4-point scale)				
2.1 The course objectives were clearly explained	3.5	3.8	3.6	3.6
2.2 The programme objectives were consistent with my needs, abilities and expectations	3.5	3.8	3.5	3.6
2.3 The methods used were appropriate	3.5	3.7	3.5	3.6
2.4 The programme was well structured	3.5	3.7	3.5	3.6
2.5 Time allocated was sufficient and effectively utilized	3.5	3.5	3.0	3.3
2.6 Training materials were used well and assisted my learning	3.6	3.9	3.5	3.7
2.7 The tasks presented were practical and relevant	3.5	3.8	3.75	3.7
2.8 Average score for 4-point items	*3.5*	*3.7*	*3.5*	*3.6*
2.9 Your overall impression about the programme (5-point scale)	*4.4*	*4.9*	*4.5*	*4.6*

Notes:
*   Sessions did not take place on course III.
**   Manpower Management Officers.
***   Local Government Service Commission.
****   This session was introduced in course II.

The value of evaluating any significant learning programme at all four levels will be obvious. Assessing only participants' *reactions*, for example through an end-of-course questionnaire such as the one on which Study task 1 is based, is clearly of limited value: participants often feel a sense of euphoria at the end of a course, or they may be reluctant to criticize the trainers. Reluctance may have a cultural component: Akin-Ogundeji (1988) describes how course participants in Nigeria, which Hofstede's research identified as a 'high power distance' society, hesitate to criticize trainers, who they see as authority figures. It is for these reasons that trainers sometimes call such end-of-course questionnaires 'happy sheets'.

Even if there is a formal test of *learning*, it will not show by itself whether participants are actually using what they have learnt at work. This may not matter to the participants, but should matter a great deal to any organization which is sponsoring the learning programme. Thus it is very desirable that any substantial learning programme should evaluate *behaviour change*, and ideally also what Kirkpatrick called *results*.

5.2   Learning transfer

Moving from evaluating reactions and learning to evaluating behaviour change and results raises the last important issue that we want to discuss in this chapter. Have you ever had the experience of going on a training course which you thought was excellent – well designed, well taught, informative and interesting – and yet, when you went back to work, you did not actually use anything you learnt? If you have, you are not alone: this problem of *learning transfer* is very common in learning and training, and is one that every training specialist needs to address.

What, after all, distinguishes work-based learning programmes from school- or college-based education? Mainly the fact that our involvement in a work-based programme is not an end in itself. We need continually to remember that such programmes are merely the vehicle that an organization has chosen for improving the skills of its staff. As such, they are valuable only to the extent that staff are able to apply back at work what they have learnt on the programme.

Binsted and Stuart (1980) have given us a model for thinking about learning transfer. They suggest that learning in this context has three elements: content (*what* the participants learn), process (*how* they learn it), and environment (*where* they learn it), any of which can have a 'high' or 'low' reality content. They further suggest that if learning is 'low reality' in any of these three respects, there is a learning transfer problem which the trainers will need to deal with.[2] Figure 8.6 shows what they mean. Which of the three types of learning event shown here has the most favourable learning transfer potential?

Clearly the action learning set has the most favourable potential. It is 'high reality' in terms of content because, in an action learning set, participants deal with their own issues which they bring with them from work. It is also fairly 'high reality' in terms of both process and environment because participants deal with their issues by discussing them with work colleagues (which is one of the ways in which we

Figure 8.6   Learning transfer: low and high reality training

	LOW REALITY		HIGH REALITY
	◄─────────────────────────────────►		
Content:	OL		ER AL
Process:	ER	AL	OL
Environment:	OL, ER	AL	

KEY: OL = outdoor learning event
      ER = lecture on employee relations
      AL = action learning set

Source: Binsted and Stuart (1980).

solve problems at work) and they usually discuss them in a meeting room at their place of work itself. No doubt you can see why action learning has become such a popular learning method.[3]

Does it follow that we should prefer action learning to just about any other learning approach? Not quite! We may deliberately design a learning event so that one or other of the three elements is low. We saw at the start of the chapter how the Tanzania course designers felt that they needed to get their participants away from work: in other words, to make the learning environment 'low reality', so that participants would have time and space to reflect. However, whenever any of the three elements is 'low reality', we create a problem of learning transfer that we will have to compensate for. If we do not, transfer of learning is likely to be low, however excellent the training may be in other ways.

5.3   The relationship between learning transfer and evaluation

What we have learnt in this section has an implication for the way we go about evaluation. It shows us that, if we are going to maximize behaviour change and 'results' (the impact that the learning programme has on the organization's overall effectiveness), we may need a radically different learning design from the one that most organizations continue to use. Beyond a certain point, it is probably useless to tinker further with the traditional training course model. Instead, we need to expand the model to include what happens in the workplace before and after the employee attends the training course. Such an 'expanded model' is shown in Box 8.4.

Box 8.4   An expanded learning programme model

Before the course

Learning needs analysis
Pre-course involvement of supervisor
Pre-course work by participants

At the course

Learning process matches work process
Action planning

After the course

Participants implement action plan
Supervisors support implementation
Review workshop
Organizational implications for work procedures
Revised learning design for future programmes

There is, as always, the practical objection that this model will take more time and money. That is true. We would argue, however, that, if the amount of time or money cannot be increased, it is better to reduce the number of learning programmes. A smallish programme where participants do actually use what they learn when they go back to work is better than a big programme which participants do not use.

5.4   Conclusion

Organizations often pay only lip service to evaluation. Even in the United States, an American Society for Training and Development survey found that, while almost everyone evaluated reactions, only 10 per cent of organizations evaluated behaviour change (quoted in Tannenbaum and Yukl, 1992). Evaluation is important, yet it can be just a way of shutting the stable door after the horse has bolted, as the English saying goes, in the sense that a faulty learning design, one that concentrates on what happens on a training course itself at the expense of what happens back at work before and after the course, is unlikely to make any difference in the long run. To realize the potential of evaluation in the learning process (see Figure 8.2 above), feedback from evaluation to learning design must affect not only the content of this or that training course session but also the overall learning design.

Study task 2: training in the Ministry of Land and Housing in Valinor

To round off the chapter, we look at a case study that raises many of the issues that we have discussed in a holistic way and in a real-world setting.[4]

The case highlights the problems faced by a government ministry in the imaginary country of Valinor (a tropical country whose economy has developed successfully to the point where it has been invited to join the Organization for Economic Co-operation and Development) because of its ineffective learning and training system. The Human Resources (HR) Department of the ministry had to respond to two challenges: a newly appointed Chief Executive Officer (CEO), who wanted an overhaul of the existing training function; and a new civil service policy on training, which stipulated a target of 15 training days per public officer by the year 2000 (see case study Annex 1). A consultant from the Civil Service Institute[5] was asked to assist in developing the training plan for the ministry. He quickly realized that the problems were more complex than he had expected. He wondered how he was going to suggest the necessary changes to the CEO.

This is a rich case study which touches on many issues. We suggest that you concentrate on aspects that we have covered in this chapter, and in particular on these questions:

1 *To what extent is the ministry's training 'strategic', and what could it do to make it more strategic?*
2 *How does the ministry analyse learning needs? (What use does it make of data from performance management and appraisal?)*
3 *What steps has the ministry taken, and what additional steps could it take, to ensure that staff transfer learning from courses to work?*
4 *How does the ministry evaluate the effectiveness of its training, and how could it do so better?*
5 *(A large but important question): how appropriate is the standard good practice model to this ministry?* 🖎

The Ministry of Land and Housing

Established in 1959, the Ministry of Land and Housing (MLH) existed to provide low-cost, affordable quality public housing to the general public. With a staff strength of 2900, it was one of the largest ministries in the civil service. Thanks to the many successful land projects started by MLH in the late 1960s and 1970s, 70 per cent of the population at the time of the case study now lived in public housing.

At the start of the new century, as Valinor strove to become a developed country, the public sector needed to take account of a public that was increasingly demanding of higher standards of service, and an economy that was increasingly outward-oriented, facing keener competition and faster technological changes. The public service would have to learn to anticipate demands, influence developments and meet needs with innovation. This was the context in which MLH now operated.

MLH was headed by the new CEO and was organized into three major divisions: Building and Development, Administration and Finance, and Land Administration (see Figure 8.7). Each division was headed by a director who had several departments reporting to him. The Administration and Finance Division consisted of four departments, namely Human Resources, Public Affairs, Management Services and Finance. Mr Abidin, the Assistant Manager of the HRM Department, reported to the Divisional Director, Mr Manmohan. The HRM Department was in charge of all personnel matters such as pay, welfare and benefits, leave/vacation administration, recruitment, termination and training.

Figure 8.7   The structure of the Ministry of Land and Housing

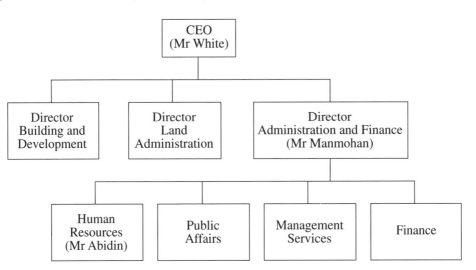

At the time of the case study, the distribution of the staff in the organization was as follows:

Division 1 (degree-holders and above)   37 per cent
Division 2 (diploma-holders)   30 per cent
Division 3 (all others)   33 per cent

The phone call

Mr Dennis Lee, a consultant with the Civil Service Institute, received a call from the Assistant Manager of the HRM Department in MLH. The latter, Mr Jonalis Abidin, had asked Dennis for assistance on developing a training plan and system for his ministry.

Jonalis: Mr. Lee I'm glad I reached you. I think we've got a problem here.

Dennis: How can we help you, Mr Abidin?

Jonalis: I've been in the HRM Division for the last 10 years and everything had been running fine until the latest circular that was issued. I'm sure you are aware of what the circular is about. By the year 2000, each ministry will have to meet the training target of 15 days per staff officer. In addition, a systematic training plan will have to be developed by each ministry. [*Note: this circular appears at Annex 1.*]

Dennis: Yes, I have heard of that. You need assistance in designing a training plan for MLH, I suppose?

Jonalis: Definitely, that's why I called you. We do not have one at the moment. But the problem is more than that.

Dennis: What's troubling you?

Jonalis: It's Mr Alan White, the new CEO who was appointed two months ago. He was adamant that the Human Resource Department look into 'people development'. He wanted us to develop new strategies to link training more closely with corporate needs as well as organizational performance.

Dennis: Well, we're talking about transfer of learning, right?

Jonalis: That's not all. The CEO's after my neck! He wanted me to work with CSI on this matter urgently and basically called for a drastic overhaul of the human resources practices in my department, particularly training. I have been here for so many years and this Mr White, who is only two months old in the Ministry, is telling me what to do. He speaks of developing a 'nurturing' organization. All this while, we have had no problems with training whatsoever. I don't understand why.

Dennis: (interrupting) Perhaps he was trying to adopt a more structured approach to staff development in MLH, if it had not already been done. Certainly, a systematic training plan will bring about greater effectiveness in training and in achieving better results. Sounds like you need a Training Needs Analysis.

Jonalis: I have told him doing a Training Needs Analysis would be a costly affair for MLH. He didn't listen. Anyway, with the release of the training policy circular, my department has got to come up with training plans and road maps for the entire organization. Mr White wants to increase training time for each staff officer from this year onwards. I really need your help.

That was a great class, but...

Following the telephone call, Dennis made an appointment to meet the CEO, Mr Alan White and Mr Abidin one week later. On 19 June 1997, he arrived at the MLH Headquarters situated at the prime commercial district in Shenton Way. As he made his way up to the 25th floor of the MLH building, he chanced to overhear a conversation in the lift that worried him.

'That was a great seminar wasn't it? That American management guru and his ideas – lots of entertainment and razzmatazz. But honestly, I won't get to use it,' said one officer to another.

Looking at their nametags, he recognized that they were staff officers from MLH. Dennis's ears pricked up, and he listened attentively to what the four men were to say. 'Well, with such a manager like yours, how could you apply what you've learnt into the workplace? That Mr Tan's a difficult manager who either didn't favour training or didn't understand training. He's an old-fashioned and conservative supervisor. Stayed too long in the organization, I think,' was one reply.

'The HQ management is not open to new ideas. How are we supposed to apply what we have learnt in the class back to work? What a waste of time!' cried one bespectacled officer. Another officer chipped in, 'You know, once I went for a course on learning that new software application and I was really enthusiastic about it. Guess what happened? When we returned to our offices and tried it, there were so many technical problems with the system. Bugs and memory failure! It took us nearly eight months to be able to use the system as it had to undergo repeated testing.'

The bespectacled officer spoke again, 'Every year, it's the same thing. Customer service, teams, empowerment, people management. Do you think a course would change MLH's culture? Are we living in a dream world or what? 'I'm a civil engineer, and they're telling me to be customer-focused. I'm here to manage projects and buildings, not people. And they have put me on the next workshop on "Handling Difficult People". I'm quite fed up with it,' said the officer, with a sense of frustration.

'Don't you have staff working under you? You will need to handle difficult staff. They're your customers too!' one officer replied, grinning.

'Yes, I'm sure that Mr Tan belongs to that category as well. So what's new on the training menu offered by CSI? What's the Flavour of this Month?' one officer quipped.

'I don't know much. One thing that's good in my section, I get to choose my own courses to attend. I'm going to sign up for that Internet course in CSI because I don't believe in those so called "management" courses. I can surf my way throughout the whole three days,' another officer said, smiling to himself.

Finally, a moustached officer, who had been quiet all this time, spoke gravely. 'The reason why all this training is a waste of time is that we don't seem to be able to connect what we've been taught to our jobs. It's what I call unaligned training.'

When the lift door opened, Dennis waited for the four officers to leave before stepping out. 'Unaligned training,' he repeated to himself. To him, it was clear that these four officers had become cynical towards training as a result of that. As he strode towards the office of the CEO, thoughts raced through his mind. He wondered what were the other training problems in MLH.

The meeting with Mr White

During his interview with Mr White, Dennis observed that he was a man who placed a great deal of importance on people development. He believed that, in an era of fast changes, technological advances and customer orientation, the competitive edge of an organization depended on its strategic use of its people. Henceforth, training and development were vital in enhancing the quality of the staff and achieving greater productivity and better business results. In his opinion, the key element in determining the progressiveness of an organization lay in the quality of the people.

The discussion with Mr White went as follows:

Mr White: And I am not saying it out of lip service. Now, the previous CEO, Mr Tong See Koon, did not look into the HRM Department seriously and, with the latest training policy, we've got to clean up a lot of mess. I have a vision of MLH being a dynamic, forward-looking and caring organization. I want to see MLH having greater motivation among its staff, improved staff retention rate and greater loyalty.
Dennis: How are your managers responding to your vision?
Mr White: I can sense that at least the middle managers are the ones who are reluctant to change their paradigms. Among other plans, I want to see every employee from all divisional status, in particular, all Division 3 officers, to be computer-literate by year 2000. My HRM Department, however, thinks that it's too ambitious a target. Now, with the policy of 15 training days by the year 2000, it would be an excellent opportunity to put training in its proper perspective.

Dennis: Has there not been a strategic and systematic approach in aligning training with business needs, career development plans of officers, and tracking the feedback of the training delivered?

Mr White: No, what we are sorely lacking is a total approach towards training. So far, it seems to me that the training has been a waste of time and money. Now, what I would need from CSI are some preliminary ideas and suggestions as to how I can improve the situation. I've instructed Jonalis and his team to work with you on this. Can you deliver that within a month?

Dennis: No problem. I will see Jonalis after this and submit a report and some recommendations in a month's time.

Finding out more

After he left the CEO's office, Dennis knew that he was facing a huge task. An observation he made was that neither Jonalis nor any other managers or directors were in the meeting. He made his way to the HRM Department to discuss the situation with Jonalis.

The HRM Department consisted of five senior officers and five clerks under the supervision of Mr Jonalis Abidin. Under the original establishment, there were 10 officers in the department, but currently only six posts were filled. Cynthia Low was responsible for the recruitment and hiring function; two officers, Razali Hakim and John Lim, were responsible for appraisal and promotion functions; one officer, Amy Yong, was in charge of wage policy, pay matters and benefits; and finally, a training executive officer named Patricia Quek was involved in the training function. Dennis hoped that his interview with Jonalis would bring some results.

Dennis: Jonalis, I've met your CEO and he has asked that we look into the current HRM practices and the training and development system, together with your team of officers.

Jonalis: Well, I think he only cared about meeting the training target of 15 days by the year 2000. It's a numbers game. Everyone knows that. My feeling is that ministries will be sending more staff officers to CSI for training because they're worried about not being able to meet the target.

Dennis: Mr White sounded serious about his plans on people development just now.

Jonalis: Well, that slave driver should realize we have been facing a shortage of officers in the department. Six officers are doing the work of 10 here. Already, my staff are complaining about being overworked. Now with the latest developments, it would be additional workload for us!

Dennis: Are you having difficulties in recruiting staff for your department? Has it been a perpetual problem? After all, you are the recruitment unit for the entire organization of 2900 and you should have no problems hiring for yourself.

Jonalis: These days, employees hardly stay in a job for more than two to three years here. That's precisely why in the era of job-hopping, investing in a worker is a liability. If he leaves the public service, the ministry will lose him and, worse, he may become our competitor. Just imagine the amount of training that will be wasted. I feel we should focus more on the immediate needs of the organization rather than investing an excessive amount in training and development.

Dennis: Besides your staff shortage, what other constraints have you been facing?

Jonalis: The question of funds. Our ministry was given only $800 000 a year from the Ministry of Finance last year. The training budget for each ministry differs according to its staffing size and factors such as training needs. It ranges between $100 000 for a small ministry of about 500 staff, to about $3 million for a large ministry of 30 000 staff. With 2900 staff under my charge, it's impossible to budget for even eight days of training per officer at the CSI!

Dennis realized that, since the introduction of Inter-Departmental Charging (see note 5), ministries were allowed to approach private sector institutions for training. Though CSI courses were priced at fees below market rates, many of its courses had been falling short of nominations and applications.

He understood the concerns of ministries about the limited training funds given by the Ministry of Finance. However, since December 1996, the Skills Development Fund (SDF), a semi-government organization responsible for giving training grants to private sector companies, had extended grants to ministries and government departments of up to 40 per cent of the training budget. However, to qualify for training grants, among other criteria, the organization had to draw up a Total Company Training Plan (TCTP) for its staff. Prior to drawing up a TCTP, it would need to do a Training Needs Analysis for the entire organization.

Dennis: Jonalis, perhaps you should apply to SDF for more funds. There would be sponsorship of up to 40 per cent of the training budget.

Jonalis: I am aware of that. But application for SDF requires a great deal of time, energy and staff to do that. It would incur a lot of administrative paperwork, such as filling in triplicate forms, getting them signed and approved by different supervisors and filling in the applicants' bio-data. That would be a tremendous task to undertake. I cannot afford to have my staff doing that. Besides, I know of no other ministries that have applied for SDF. Furthermore, my director, Mr Manmohan, was against the idea of committing so many resources and staff to doing that.

Dennis: What is Mr Manmohan like? I haven't heard you or Mr White mention your immediate boss before.

Jonalis: He's a busy man, being director of four departments – Public Affairs, Management Services, Finance and Human Resources. For the last five years while he was the director, he won the support of the middle managers in the organization. Compared to Mr White's auto-cratic style, he is much more dynamic and caring about his staff. That's why he is against the idea of overloading the staff with more administrative paperwork.

Dennis: Does Mr Manmohan have any problems working with Mr White?

Jonalis: They have had disagreements over several issues before. To be honest, they're not on really good terms with each other.

At this juncture, Patricia Quek entered the room and interrupted the conversation with some seemingly urgent matters for Mr Abidin.

A closer look at the training function

Dennis realized that he needed to ask for some data and information on training in MLH (see Table 8.7).

Dennis discovered that managers could nominate their staff to attend courses from the pre-approved list that had been recommended by the Training Steering Committee. All nominations for courses must be approved by the officer's immediate supervisor and supported by his senior manager. After receiving the two-tiered approval for the courses, it was Patricia Quek's job to put up the applications to the respective institutions. If an application was successful, Patricia would inform the officer concerned, as well as his immediate supervisor.

Interview with Patricia Quek

Dennis knew that his next step should be to interview Patricia to investigate how training functions were carried out in MLH. Through the subsequent interview he found out that Patricia was the person responsible for selecting the types of courses and workshops needed by MLH. The list, chosen from the range of courses offered by CSI, Construction and Building Training Centre (CBTC), a private sector training centre and other private sector institutions, would then be discussed with Mr Abidin and Mr Manmohan, together with the Train-ing Executive Officer, at an annual training plan exercise. The three-some, known as the Training Steering Committee, would submit the

Table 8.7 Training data for 1996

Category of courses/workshops	General Development	Technical Skills	Continuing Education
Course Description (Duration of each course is about 1–5 days)	Related to subjects on management, supervisory skills, Productivity-related skills, service quality-related, language, team building, communication, presentation and public speaking	Divided into housing design and construction management, IT-related, administration and finance, estate management, land administration, OJT etc	Usually month-long certificate programmes, overseas conferences attended by managers, retirement programmes etc
Total Training Days (approximate) and Participants' Profile	3690 days 2030 days (55%) – Div 1 1291 days (35%) – Div 2 369 days (10%) – Div 3	2440 days 1464 days (60%) – Div 1 732 days (30%) – Div 2 244 days (10%) – Div 3	540 days Mainly managers, Directors and above (all Div 1)
Budget Allocated (%)	40	45	15
Expenditure for 1996 (Total = $800 000)	$320 000	$360 000	$120 000

recommendations on the types of programmes to the Chief Executive Officer. The latter would then make the final decision.

Dennis: Patricia, could you tell me the basis on which the Training Steering Committee decides on the training programmes?
Patricia: Well, we more or less followed the same system that has been in use for the last five years. Sometimes we receive brochures and recommendations from the training officers at CSI and from other institutes to help us decide.

Patricia further explained that the suggested courses should fall under any of the three categories: (1) General Development, which focused on developing supervisory and interpersonal skills and some other core skills for the staff, (2) Technical Skills, where the courses were based on suggestions of CBTC, and (3) Continuing Education, such as overseas workshops and conferences, which were meant for higher management executives.

Dennis: How about the CEO and his role in this matter? By the way, what was the ex-CEO, Mr Tong like?
Patricia: Mr Tong was easy to work with. He hardly vetoed the recommendations of the Steering Committee. Judging from the fact that

he was a civil engineer, he was not really an expert in the field of training and human resource development. To be honest, I really had no idea how he decided on the courses.

Dennis: What was the percentage of training expenditure against total personnel expenditure, or payroll?

Patricia: It was an insignificant figure, about 0.67 per cent or so, of total personnel expenditure each year.

Dennis: How did the managers decide whom to nominate or send for the courses? Do you have any idea on that? Would the officers themselves have a say on the type of programmes to attend?

Patricia: Officially, their interests are indicated in the appraisal reports of the officers. At the end of the year, the officer would indicate what courses he wishes to attend in the following year, and his immediate supervisor would make a note or recommendation, to either approve or disapprove it. When the course dates are made known the following year, the supervisors are supposed to nominate their officers to attend.

Dennis: But in practice?

Patricia: Well, I don't really know. But my personal experience is that whether an officer manages to attend the course or not depends on the timing of the course, the current demands on time, availability of budget and so on. Sometimes, officers do not get to attend the courses recommended by us because the managers would put a stop to it, for some reason, thus ruining the officer's plan which he had set out in his yearly appraisal report.

Dennis: Could officers attend any 'new' or ad hoc courses other than those approved by the Committee?

Patricia: No problem. The officer concerned or his supervisor has to put in a report to justify his applying for the course. It would have to go through several levels of management approval, right up to the Chief Executive Officer, before it was fully endorsed.

Dennis: How about linking training to career development? Won't you have determined the types of programmes for each rung of the officer's career ladder? For example, some 'milestone' programmes at each grade of promotion? Is there a Career Development Committee here? I'm speaking of career development of the officers through training.

Patricia: Well, I believe it's a 'one-size fits all system'. I don't think the Career Development Committee monitors the training records of the officers, or their indication of interests for development.

Dennis: But how about their appraisal reports that had the training plans indicated in them?

Patricia: To be honest, the Committee and the appraisal board focus mainly on the officer's ranking in the yearly promotion exercise, not so much the training requirements. The section on Training and Development in the appraisal report is not taken seriously. We don't have a 'milestone' training programme for every grade of promotion. Just think, a graduate-entry officer has to wait for at least four years before he can be promoted to the next grade! I don't think people would stay that long in an organization though.

Dennis: How about induction programmes for new entrants?

Patricia: We have one-day induction programmes for all levels of staff. For that, we spell out the values, mission and vision statements of the organization.

Dennis: Is there any 'mentoring' scheme where newly recruited officers are assigned on-the-job mentors during their probation period?

Patricia: It is up to the individual department to suggest. The HRM Department is not involved in this. We would not know whom to choose as the right mentor for the new officer.

Dennis: Are you aware of how the departments choose the mentors?

Patricia: I'm afraid you're asking the wrong person. The role of the HRM Department stops after the one-day induction programme for new officers. I wasn't even assigned a mentor when I first joined four years ago. I don't think many of the departments bother anyway.

Dennis: How effective were the training programmes that the officers went through? How was the feedback regarding the trainers, course content, facilities and so on?

Patricia: Well, we have difficulties in organizing in-house programmes where 20 or so of our officers could attend at the same time. Hence individual officers were sent on public courses, where there were other participants from different ministries. The training institutions concerned would conduct evaluation for these courses, not us.

Dennis: But won't you have asked the institutions for the feedback?

Patricia: We never ask them. It would have been too much work on our part. However, we do encourage officers to give informal feedback, either through e-mails or phone calls, if the quality of programmes was questionable. I believe the training programmes have been fine. So far, we have not received any adverse comments on the CSI and CBTC courses.

Dennis: Don't the supervisors track the training impact on the officers, at both the individual and the organizational level? One final question, was there a kind of 'social contract' made between the supervisor and the officer on the results of the training?

Patricia: Not that I know of.

Writing the report

After the long interview with the various key persons, Dennis felt that he had sufficient information to furnish a report. He realized that the problems in the organization were more massive than he had thought initially. In the comfort of his own office, he carefully studied the circular on training policy that seemed to have ignited the whole chain of events in MLH. Aware of the tight deadline of one month, he pondered on how he would write his report and recommendations to the CEO.

Annex 1: government circular no. 346/97

Training policy for the civil service

Importance of training and development
1.   Training and development is a vital component in strategic management for the civil service. As we look at Valinor's future as a developed country, the challenge that lies ahead for the public sector is how well it can meet the increasing demands for higher standards of service, and cope with keener competition and technological change. A key way to meet this challenge is continual skills upgrading of the civil service. We have to train wider and higher as never before. Continuing training, continuous learning and continuous improvement are not just desirable but essential to assure lifelong employability.
2.   Training and development is essential for maximum effectiveness of our staff, not only for their current duties but also on a continuing basis for the future. Training will enable the public service to derive maximum benefit from the potential of its people both as individuals and as teams, helping the nation to enhance its competitive advantage through strategic maximization of its limited resources. Thus, though its number is limited, the civil service can enlarge its strategic capability through training skills, motivation development and continuous upgrading.

Current levels of training in the civil service
3.   The latest Productivity Survey carried out by NPB reveals that, on a national average, companies in Valinor spent 3.4 per cent of their payroll on training, of which 2.1 per cent was spent on off-the-job training and 1.3 per cent on on-the-job training. However, the current level of recorded training in the civil service is only 0.7 per cent of payroll (from figures provided by Budget Division, Ministry of Finance). This is inadequate in the civil service given the importance of training in the strategic maximization of its limited human resources.
4.   So far, there has been no target set on training requirements. Instead of relying on training expenditure, which is difficult to measure owing to hidden costs, it is agreed that a time target should be set rather than an expenditure target. For FY 94/95, the level of training in the civil service is 2.44 days per capita per year, with 1.4 days contributed towards CSI (Civil Service Institute) courses. This is 1.22

per cent of the available work hours. Compared to some private sector benchmarks, this is comparatively low.

Time target for training

5.   It is agreed that eight training days per officer per year is a realistic target to start with, rising to 15 days by the year 2000, as follows:

1997   8 days
1998   10 days
1999   12 days
2000   15 days

6.   Each ministry would have to reach the target of 15 days per officer per year to be achieved by the year 2000. The 15 days should also include structured on-the-job training as well as off-the-job training.

Plan for training and developing civil servants

7.   Although ministries and departments are already providing training, few have specific plans for staff development and training. In the ministries, nominations for officers to attend courses may be carried out by officers who are not specially trained or dedicated to do these functions. Sometimes consultants may approach departments and offer their services and, if a department has enough money, it may engage the consultant to conduct the training even though the training is already provided for by CSI at much lower cost. Therefore training can be a bottomless cost if it is not properly managed. The right persons may also not be chosen for training. In addition, if the training is not relevant to the officer's needs, training fatigue could easily set in.

8.   Each ministry should henceforth be responsible for designing a training plan to develop its own officers. It is recommended, though not compulsory, that the plan should include an induction programme plus four levels of training and developing for officers on the job, as follows:

(i)   First year of service – basic training,
(ii)   Second and third year of service – advanced training,
(iii)   Fourth to sixth year of service – extended training,
(iv)   Subsequent years of service – continuous training.

9.   Each officer should have a 'training road map' which shows clearly the types of training needed by the officer. This training road map could set out clearly the four components and it should be updated every year, and as part of his annual appraisal report, with a report of the training actually received in the past year and the training plan for the new year.

Responsibility for training

10.   Managers and supervisors should share the responsibility, together with their officers, for ensuring that what is learnt by the officer has a chance of being applied and reinforced in the organization. To achieve that, managers and supervisors would have a say in determining what training is needed by their officers. Their continued encouragement, reinforcement and organizational support are much needed to ensure the transfer of learning in the workplace.

11.   Every officer should also be responsible for seeking the necessary training so that they can constantly learn and upgrade themselves to keep up with changes in the environment and their jobs.

12.   Each ministry and major department should have a trained Human Resource Development Co-ordinator (who can work with CSI) to see that staff are trained to the level planned.

7   Summary and conclusion

In this chapter we have:

- outlined the systematic learning model;
- indicated how to choose appropriate methods in order to carry out a learning needs analysis;
- shown how to design a learning programme, again drawing on appropriate methods;
- suggested ways of evaluating a learning programme at the four 'levels' of evaluation;
- discussed the implications of learning transfer for learning design and evaluation.

Unless you are already a training specialist, you probably started the chapter with the idea that learning and training was about what happens on training courses away from work: about how to design exciting and dynamic training sessions and all of that. Now what happens on training courses is important, but most of us knew that already. What many of us did not know is that what goes on *around* the training course is every bit as important. Since this is not so widely known, we have chosen to spend a lot of time on it.

In the end, what we would like you to take away from this chapter is an emphasis on learning, not training, and the realization that this emphasis serves to highlight the importance of the learning skills that we have as individuals, and the potential of the workplace as a source of learning. Training courses away from work will continue to have a place, but, if they are to be effective, then once again it is the link with the workplace that matters most: the job of the trainer is not just to run relevant and lively training courses, but to build a bridge across which participants can carry learning from course to work. It is also the trainer's job to facilitate systematic learning in the workplace itself.

Notes

1 Both 'andragogy' and 'pedagogy' derive from ancient Greek. Ἀνδρος ('andros'), παις ('pais') and ἀγογός ('agogos') are Greek for 'man', 'child' and 'guide' respectively. Thus 'andragogy' is the art of guiding, or teaching, men, or adults; and 'pedagogy' is the art of teaching children.
2 The extent to which a learning programme is high or low reality overall is sometimes called 'transfer distance' (Laker, 1990).
3 As we completed this book in early 2003, we sadly learnt of the death of Professor Reg Revans, the founder of action learning.
4 We are grateful to our colleagues at INTAN, Malaysia's Civil Service Training Institute, and especially Ms Lee Meng Foon, and to Mr Gerald Lim, for providing the case from INTAN's case library (available on the Web at the time of writing at *www.intanbk.intan.my*).
5 The Civil Service Institute (CSI) at the time of writing was a public sector training institution in Valinor which offered training in such areas as management, public administration, supervisory skills, technical skills and IT skills. Operating on a system known as Inter-Departmental Charging (IDC), CSI acted as a quasi-private training institution, charging ministries for courses and training programmes. Each year, ministries received a certain budget for staff training and they had the option of approaching private sector training institutes if CSI was unable to meet their requests. The duration of courses offered at CSI ranged from one day to a maximum of five days.

9   Job Reduction

Willy McCourt

What this chapter is about

The chapter begins by explaining why job reduction is something that every HRM specialist should know about. In the light of a review of the experience of job reduction in developing countries, we present a strategic and systematic model of job reduction, starting with interventions which avoid the need to make staff redundant, and then working through job reduction methods in an ascending order of hardship to the staff affected, and culminating in voluntary and compulsory redundancy. We also discuss the advantages of controlling budgets rather than controlling numbers of staff. Finally, we review the steps that employers can take to reduce hardship of staff who are made redundant.

What you will learn

At the end of this chapter you should be able to:

- state the relevance of job reduction to the practice of HRM;
- summarize the experience of developing country organizations in this area;
- outline the steps which organizations can take to reduce jobs;
- plan how staff can be made redundant in ways that minimize hardship.

1 Introduction: the unpleasant reality of job reduction

1.1 Organizational contraction and job reduction

Armies on the battlefield do not always advance: organizing an orderly retreat is part of the art of war. Organizations in a capitalist market economy – in which, for better or worse, all of us increasingly live – do not always grow, and managers need to know how to organize contraction as well as growth. Contraction probably means job reduction, so HRM specialists need to know how to conduct it.

There are three reasons why contraction is an inevitable feature of the organizational landscape. First, new products constantly emerge to make old ones obsolete (think of what happened to 'clockwork' watches when digital watches came in), and new companies emerge to challenge the existing ones, in an unending process of 'creative destruction' (Schumpeter, 1947). Second, economies follow a cycle where a period of 'boom' will be followed by a period of 'bust', when the economy stagnates or even shrinks. Arguably the most surprising feature of the so-called 'East Asian crisis' of the late 1990s, when economies in Asia went into recession, was that there had been such a long period of uninterrupted growth before the downturn. Western economies suffered slowdowns in the late 1970s and early 1980s, and again at the beginning of the new century.

The third reason is that the number of jobs in an organization can reduce even while output is increasing. The spread of new technology means that fewer people are needed to carry out standardized tasks: sending bills to customers is one example.

Nor is all this confined to the private sector. Staff retrenchment has been the biggest human resource issue confronting the governments of developing and transitional countries in the last 20 years. It was a standard feature of the so-called 'structural adjustment' programmes imposed by the IMF and the World Bank in the 1980s and 1990s, a period when the World Bank was involved in no fewer than 68 of them (Nunberg, 1997). Retrenchment programmes were also carried out by 22 of the 27 member governments of the Organization for Economic Co-operation and Development (OECD). No other human resource policy was so widely practised.

So, one way or another, there is a good chance that an HRM specialist will be involved in a programme of job reduction at some point in his or her career, despite the subject's virtual invisibility in most HRM textbooks. This chapter is about what is involved in carrying out such a programme, and what can be done to make sure that it causes as little hardship as possible to the staff who are affected.

1.2   Is job reduction the only way?

Do 'creative destruction', the economic cycle and new technology make job reduction inevitable? Some say they do. Pearce and Robbins (1994) found that firms emerging from decline in the American textile industry which pursued a 'retrenchment strategy' (abandoning un-profitable businesses and the staff that went with them) were gener-ally more successful than firms which pursued an 'entrepreneurial strategy' (trying to generate new business while preserving their ex-isting business intact and retaining their existing staff). Their view would receive strong support in many corporate boardrooms. But there are alternatives. In the private sector, others suggest that firms can spend their way out of trouble, for example by investing in new product lines. Even some of those who accept the need for retrench-ment suggest that it should be seen as the first stage of a programme of corporate recovery, where emergency actions to cut costs ('decline-stemming strategies') lead to a second stage of strategic planning for the future, generating stakeholder support, strategic development of the organization's staff and so on ('recovery strategies') (Pandit, 1996).

In the public sector, meanwhile, some have argued that there could be more scope to reduce government deficits through higher taxation or improved revenue collection than through retrenchment (Dia, 1996). And governments have taken heed: for example, the City Council of Dar es Salaam, Tanzania's capital, was reported to have collected as much tax in the last quarter of 1996 as in the previous two years put together.

However, the fact remains that, whether wisely or foolishly, organiza-tions do decide from time to time that they have to cut staffing costs, and it is the job of the HRM specialist to show them how to do it. For the remainder of this chapter, therefore, we will assume that top man-agers have already made that decision, even though we know that other decisions might have been possible. We will first review the experience of organizations that have decided to cut their staffing costs in the past, and then suggest how organizations ought to go about it in the future.

2   The experience of job reduction

The phenomenon of job reduction is not well understood, being conspicuous in its absence from most, if not all, HRM textbooks. We will therefore spend some time reviewing experience, drawing on research done by the World Bank and IMF (principally Nunberg, 1997) and also field research by one of the authors (McCourt, 2001b) in Ghana, Malaysia, Sri Lanka, South Africa, Uganda and the UK.

2.1   The background to job reduction

Figure 9.1 shows how the number of jobs in the public sector grew in Tanzania between the late 1960s and the mid-1980s, and points to one of the main reasons why many developing country governments found themselves seeking structural adjustment loans from the early 1980s onwards.

Figure 9.1   Growth of public sector employment in Tanzania

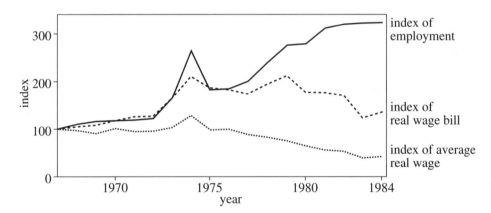

Source: Doriye (1992: 107).

As country after country got into this kind of trouble, a blueprint emerged in which a reduction in the size of the civil service, typically expressed as a conditionality or 'structural benchmark' in a World Bank or IMF loan, was specified in the context of a reduction in overall government expenditure whose aim was to restore macroeconomic stability and facilitate growth (Lindauer and Nunberg, 1994). Crucially, in other words, it was a cost-driven, not a strategy-driven, model of reform. Arguing that the alleged overstaffing had often been paid for by lowering wages for staff as a whole, the blueprint included provision for the savings from retrenchment to be used to raise wages for the survivors, especially the higher-paid, since their salaries were supposed to have fallen relative both to their juniors and to their private sector counterparts (this is what we called *salary decompression* in Chapter 5).

2.2   The results of reform

That was the blueprint. What actually happened? Abed *et al.* (1998) do report an annual 0.5 per cent drop in numbers in 22 countries assisted by the IMF, but also an annual 1 per cent decrease in real wages, suggesting that wage cuts played a critical role in reducing the wage bill – the exact opposite of what the blueprint envisaged. By 1995, the World Bank had rated 40 per cent of its own civil service reform projects as unsatisfactory at completion (Nunberg, 1997). Lienert and Modi (1997: 32) conclude that 'most sub-Saharan African low-income countries have made only limited progress towards achieving the objectives of civil service reform', and Schiavo-Campo (1996) contends that elsewhere too there is much to be done.

Even Ghana, Uganda and the UK, which have been represented as success stories, had serious problems in containing staffing costs. While Ghana's civil service numbers fell by 26 766 between 1987 and 1992, payroll spending at the beginning and the end of the reform period was almost the same (Burton *et al.*, 1993). Unlike Ghana, the UK did meet – indeed exceed – its early job reduction targets: by 1985, total numbers had already dipped below 600 000, the target they were expected to reach only three years later. But there, too, staffing expenditure did not decline commensurately, instead rising somewhat through the early 1980s (Dunsire and Hood, 1989). Numbers employed in Uganda fell sharply, but rose slightly again; and the overall pay bill actually rose from 2 per cent to 3.6 per cent of GDP between 1989 and 1996.

What went wrong? Clearly some of the elements of an explanation of reform outcomes are purely local, but there are some common themes. Let us review them.

2.3   Strategy

There is a sense in which job reduction is actually an integral part of the SHRM model. You may remember 'flexibility' from Chapter 2 as one of the elements of Guest's version of the SHRM model. One of its aspects is numerical flexibility, referring to the supposed desirability of being able to increase or reduce the number of workers as demand for the organization's products or services goes up or down (the other aspect is 'functional flexibility').

The early stages of reform in Ghana, Uganda and the UK were not at all strategic. Number reduction and cost reduction were geared to reducing overall government expenditure. Ironically, it was the two countries which had not succeeded in reducing numbers or costs which were most strategic. South Africa's Department of Public Service and Administration had an elaborate HRM strategy, where a 'transformed' public service was harnessed to providing services to the previously disadvantaged majority population (Government of South Africa, 1995; 1997). Its approach to 'downsizing', which had begun as a classic cost reduction exercise, was moving closer to a strategic model through the adoption of a review methodology.

2.4   Political commitment and ownership

This was the most important factor in the World Bank's analysis (Nunberg, 1997). It was argued forcefully by Sri Lanka's Cabinet Secretary, among others (Wijesinghe, 1997). In Uganda, President Museveni's personal commitment to reform was clear (Museveni, 1997). Prime Minister Mahathir showed his commitment by himself chairing all 10 meetings of the committee that reformed Malaysia's civil service pay (Government of Malaysia, 1991). More often, though, commitment was the outcome of an agreement among multiple stakeholders which had to be painstakingly constructed. 'There was a hell of a consultation with the stakeholders,' as one South African official put it.

Stakeholders' support depended on what kind of programme they were being asked to sign up to. The South African government hesitated to embark on a radical programme which would have thrown many employees out of work in former homelands such as the Transkei region, causing hardship and possibly affecting the government's electoral support; but it implemented a modified but still substantial proposal to eradicate 'ghost workers' (see below) in the same areas – ghosts do not suffer hardship or, as a rule, vote in elections.

The way donors behaved also affected commitment. Where political commitment was already strong, as in Ghana and Uganda, donor involvement contributed to more sharply focused programmes. But in a more complex stakeholder environment, donors were apt to be heavy-footed, and even to create a focus for opposition to reform. South Africa politely rejected the 'expert but inflexible' advice proffered by

British civil servants. The perception in Sri Lanka that donors, particularly the World Bank, were pressing for a harsh package of reform measures created a focus for opposition to reform, so that even an innocuous measure like performance appraisal could be portrayed as a World Bank imposition.

Donors were sometimes insensitive to governments' actual reform priorities, as opposed to those that donors thought they should have. One donor saw a proposed major restructuring of central–local relations in Sri Lanka as an expensive irrelevance. In the context of job reduction that was certainly true. But the plan was motivated mainly by a desire to settle the long-running civil war by conceding greater autonomy to regions, and to Tamil areas in particular.

2.5   Diagnosis

'The first redundancy exercise was a disaster,' said one Ugandan official, while a Sri Lankan union official commented that the first redundancy exercise in 1990 'failed because it was too hasty'. Like American companies, governments tended to reform (publicly) in haste, only to repent (discreetly) at leisure. Rising costs alongside falling staff numbers is one example, but there were others: expensive and ill-directed voluntary retirement packages in Sri Lanka (World Bank, 1996) and South Africa; the first batch of retrenchees in Ghana believing that they would be rehired when the economy recovered; and their counterparts in Uganda dismissed on the basis of grotesquely unreliable appraisal reports.

Governments and donors alike appeared unwilling to admit that they did not fully understand public staffing, though its complexity, and the customary absence of reliable data at the beginning of reform, made misunderstanding almost inevitable. Thus targets for staffing cuts were usually arbitrary, to be over- or undershot, to equal amazement. Uganda thought its initial target for staff reduction of 34 000 jobs was tough until it discovered no fewer than 42 000 ghosts on the books (Government of Uganda, 1994). Numbers were to decrease eventually by about 150 000, or almost 50 per cent. Ghana's initial annual job reduction target of 15 000 jobs was revised downwards after the equally unexpected discovery of 11 000 ghost workers (Burton *et al.*, 1993). Thus did governments learn, often painfully and too late, the importance of diagnosis.

2.6   Process factors: participation, HRM expertise and incrementalism

The Ugandan official who commented that 'The whole reform process was welcomed, but the way it was handled is now detested' highlighted a pervasive failure to deal adequately with process factors. Thus, for instance, the participation of employees and their trade union representatives was occasional at best, even though it appeared to have positive effects where it did take place. (This is an example that we will discuss in Chapter 10.) The Civil Servants' Association in Ghana 'gave its blessing' to reform, while a UK official went so far as to say that the unions were his key change agents, and that pushing through job reductions would have been 'one hundred times' more difficult without them. In other cases there was no participation. The civil servants' union was not recognized in Uganda at the start of reform. In Sri Lanka the management side did not consult unions: 'Government believes we are hostile to reform,' said one union official, 'but we support reform. If reform is constructive and in the interests of the country, we support it.'

Job reduction is an HRM issue, but HRM expertise is generally in short supply in developing countries (Taylor, 1992). Only in South Africa was there evidence of an ability to take a strategic HRM view of overall staffing issues (Ncholo, 1997). It is arguable that HRM expertise might have helped avoid the fiasco in Uganda where appraisal reports were the basis for redundancy decisions, with the result, in the words of one official, that '50% [of retrenchees] were victimized, through tribalism or because they were supporters of Obote or Amin [the former presidents]'.

The complexity of reform meant that following an incremental approach which built on developing experience would be important, and all the countries studied did so to a greater or lesser extent, though more by accident than by design. The most impressive example was South Africa, which progressed even during the period of our research from a crude number-cutting approach to a sophisticated review methodology. In an already strong strategic context, they telescoped 18 years of UK experience (on which they drew heavily) into 18 months of learning and policy redesign. But generally there was little evidence of a deliberately incremental, process approach based on a frank admission of ignorance.

2.7   Victims of reform

Despite the sanguine view of IMF and World Bank studies (for example, Alderman *et al.*, 1994), governments worried a great deal about the hardship that their reforms might create. There was genuine remorse among Ugandan officials over the harsh terms on which their first retrenchees had been dismissed. Trade union representatives in Malaysia and Uganda pointed to problems like loss of status in villages and marriage break-ups, echoing western accounts of the impact of unemployment (Argyle, 1989).

Unfortunately, attempts to help the victims were often ineffectual, for specific reasons. Ghana's provision of retraining and business start-up help (Government of Ghana, 1987) started a year late, at a point where the sensible retrenchee would already have made his or her own arrangements. Uganda's never started at all, foundering on the mistaken assumption that banks and the Ministry of Labour would be willing to participate. One British government agency, embroiled in union negotiations, woke up to the importance of making arrangements only when its retrenchees were about to leave.

This generally poor record of implementation still leaves room to argue that more skilful measures would have helped. To take one example, communication with employees was clearly necessary to alleviate employee anxiety about the threat of retrenchment. Uganda's first retrenchment exercise, said one official, was 'shrouded in secrecy, and the news that they were to be retrenched came as a shock to most retrenchees'.

2.8   Ideological reasons for reform

Ostensible job reductions were sometimes the result of transferring staff from one part of the public payroll to another, muddying the waters for anyone wanting to produce a reliable estimate of numbers: one government adviser (actually a donor-financed expatriate) commented on the publicity value of such apparent but unreal 'reductions' when dealing with donors. Government officials in the UK were instructed by ministers during the 1980s to present the transfer from central to local government of staff responsible for housing benefits payments as a reduction in the central government workforce. Still in the UK, it is contracting out of public services that had the largest impact on numbers in the mid-1990s (Cabinet Office, 1996); and a contracted out service is not necessarily cheaper, or better. It seemed reasonable to infer the influence of 'small government' ideology in such measures, especially where they did little to reduce the cost of government.

2.9   The insignificance and expense of redundancy

Contrary to the popular image, and to the reality of 'downsizing' in western private sector firms, compulsory redundancy was a small, sometimes even trivial, component of overall job reduction. In Uganda, only 15 000 of the 160 000 job reductions came through compulsory redundancy (Government of Uganda, 1996). In the UK, a senior official estimated that not more than 1000 annually of the 250 000 job reductions between 1976 and 1996 came in that way. Elsewhere proportions are unclear, but redundancy was at most only one of a range of measures (Nunberg, 1994).

Despite this, reform was expensive, with the lion's share of costs going on severance payments. While the UK makes an impressive bid for the record with the US$12 billion spent on making coalminers redundant between 1979 and 1992 (Wass, 1996), elsewhere too the cost was sizeable. Ghana's severance programme cost an average of 2 per cent of government expenditure in its first five years (Younger, 1996); Uganda's had cost US$18.6 million by 1995 (Government of Uganda, 1996).

2.10   Coordination

Coordination was crucial, but difficult. At the same time that the retrenchment team in the Ministry of Public Service in Uganda was working towards job reductions, colleagues on the other side of the building were carrying out a rolling programme of reviews whose net result was to recommend a staff increase. The problem of coordination was compounded by frequent mistrust between Finance and Public Service ministries. Despite the stress in the World Bank and IMF analysis on the link between the two, Public Service have often been seen by Finance as a 'Trojan Horse' inside government, acting as an informal trade union, especially on behalf of senior civil servants (Corkery and Land, 1996). Thus staff in the Ministry of Finance in Ghana openly declared that their Public Service colleagues were the biggest single threat to the success of reform.

2.11 The political process and fresh commitments

As one US company's general manager said, 'Costs exist for a reason. If you don't take the reasons away, the costs will return' (Henkoff, 1990: 27). Embarking on reform does not mean suspending the normal political process, through which fresh commitments constantly arise. The number of prison officers in the UK (Cabinet Office, 1996), and of police officers in Uganda, rose even while both countries were bearing down hard on staffing, reflecting law and order commitments. Government commitments often come with a staffing cost attached, which may (as in Uganda) be presented to the staffing ministry as a *fait accompli*.

Equally, governments generally tried to protect services which had a political priority, especially education and health (Burton *et al.*, 1993; Government of Uganda, 1994). But there was no reason why abuses such as ghosts would respect those areas.

2.12 Summary

Let us now summarize the research findings reported above.

- There was a general, though fitful, movement towards a strategic approach.
- Commitment was clearly important, but derived from an interaction between stakeholders and the nature of the reform programme. The latter reflected governments' own reform priorities, as they developed through normal politics.
- Employee participation was helpful where it occurred.
- Governments did take an incremental approach, even if more by accident than by design.
- Savings and overall impact were both lower than expected. This was because of an exclusive focus on the number of civil servants, exacerbated by poor coordination between the finance and staffing functions and the ideological preference for small government, together with weak recruitment control and disproportionate spending on the retrenchment of relatively few staff.
- Although the number of retrenchees was small, governments did make provision for the 'victims', providing retraining for example. However, problems of implementation meant that the provision was often useless, though it might have been useful if it had been better organized.

3   Reducing jobs and costs: a systematic approach

3.1 · Principles of job reduction

As we have seen, organizations in developing countries have found it hard to make a success of job reduction. One of the most surprising findings of my research was that job reduction had often not even led to reduced payroll spending – and that was just the most glaring mistake that organizations had made. So what should be done instead? As we focus on the operational issues that organizations have to face, there are three principles to keep in mind. Effective job reduction will

- *be strategic,* that is, it will start from a strategic view of where the organization is going and a sense of the implications of strategy for staff employment;
- *actually deliver savings,* and not just a crude reduction in the number of employees;
- *minimize hardship* of employees.

We shall now work through the different job reduction methods in ascending order of difficulty, starting with the ones that cause least hardship and will be easiest to implement.

3.2   A strategic approach to job reduction

Something approaching a consensus has developed that 'turning around' an organization is a two-stage process, where emergency action to stem decline leads on to strategic planning for the future – what we called 'recovery strategies' earlier. A similar consensus is beginning to emerge in discussions about job reduction, where an emphasis on hacking mindlessly and masochistically at the organization's own jobs and employees is beginning to give way to an emphasis on strategic recovery.

What does a strategic approach mean in practice? In the light of our review of experience, Figure 9.2 presents a strategic model.

The model conceives job reduction as a process which starts with the organization's overall strategy and HRM strategy, both of which we assume already exist. A management review which may use human resource planning methodology is conducted in that strategic context, and it is used to generate a job reduction plan where appropriate, one that includes measures to minimize hardship to employees.

Figure 9.2   A strategic model of job reduction

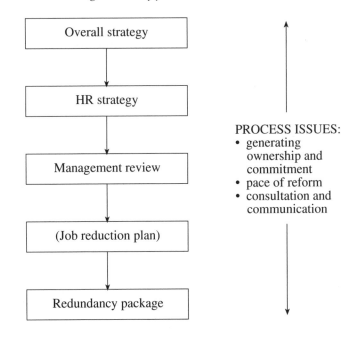

We used the phrase 'where appropriate' in the last paragraph because job reduction is not a *necessary* outcome of a review. If it is, however, then a choice is made from the methods available (see below).

What we have called 'process' measures will run alongside all of this, as it were, since they will be a continuous concern. They include measures to generate ownership of and commitment to the programme, and consultation and communication with staff and their representatives. The appropriate pace of the programme, which the timetable in the strategy action plan will address, is another process issue.

'Vertical' integration in strategic job reduction
You will remember from Chapter 2 the notion of strategic integration and its two aspects, vertical and horizontal. The model we have just presented is one which emphasizes vertical integration, that is, integrating the job reduction programme with the organization's overall strategy. What in practical terms might vertical integration mean in this context? Let us take two examples.

Recruitment and selection   The corollary of job reduction in an organization is that staff who remain will have greater responsibilities. It is important that new staff appointed have the necessary skills. (We will look at the closely related issue of recruitment control a bit later in this chapter.)

Pay   The close connection between job reduction and pay has usually been recognized, as we have seen already, and job reduction has often served as an opportunity to reform pay systems, focusing on basic pay rates and the system of allowances, and sometimes introducing more sophisticated approaches like job evaluation and performance-related pay.

3.3   Avoiding job cuts

Once the strategic framework is in place, the next step will be to see whether we can avoid making job reductions altogether. Human resource specialists who write on redundancy argue that the first step should be to plan for the future so that redundancies will not be needed, because we have avoided creating jobs which in the long run we cannot sustain. There are a number of ways of doing this.

Human resource planning
The organization should ensure that human resource forecasting is carried out and acted upon. Forecasting is an integral part of human resource planning (Chapter 3), and its principles apply here. It may allow us to anticipate a declining need for staff in some areas, or a declining ability to pay for them.

Job flexibility
We reminded ourselves at the start of this chapter that numerical flexibility is an element of Guest's version of the SHRM model, and is particularly relevant to job reduction. Functional flexibility is also relevant. Sometimes called 'multi-skilling', this has been a feature of life in the private sector for some time: Ford Motors in the UK, for instance, reduced the number of separate job categories from 516 in 1986 to 45 in 1988.

Staff may not welcome increasing job flexibility. Unions often resist it because it can result in an erosion of traditional craft skills, or in employees being required to carry out more demanding tasks for the same rates of pay. But there may be circumstances in which it is in the interests of staff who might otherwise lose their jobs, because there is no longer a demand for their specialized but redundant skills.

Redeployment
Organizations often give retrenchees preference in filling new jobs, as an alternative to making them redundant. They do so by setting up a redeployment procedure where new jobs have to be considered by a panel which decides if a member of staff in the redeployment 'pool'

can fill the job. Only if the panel decides that no such person is eligible is the post advertised in the normal way.

Such 'pools' can be abused. In Nepal, where power changed hands three times in the mid-1990s between the Nepal Congress Party and the Communist Party, senior civil servants identified with the party previously in power were removed from their posts and placed on full salary in the 'pool', technically awaiting reposting but in reality consigned to a sort of internal exile because of their perceived political sympathies.

Some jobs have simple skill requirements, and no retraining will be necessary. But retraining will be needed to convert, say, a redundant administrator into, say, a computer programmer. The advantages of using retraining both to the individual worker and to the economy as a whole are shown in Box 9.1.

Box 9.1   Redundancy or retraining?

In many countries economic difficulties alone do not legally entitle an employer to retrench an employee. In some of them, government approval is needed for any large-scale redundancy programme. In Japan, a series of graded steps for reducing labour costs, including redeployment, relocation, retraining and transfers, enables large firms to stop short of dismissing workers in most cases. In many European countries, the emphasis is on retraining rather than on redundancy. Thus France and Germany used European Union funds to finance retraining, reinvestment and social plans in their declining coal industries. The new skills which retraining provides make it easier for workers to find other jobs. In contrast, workers who have been made redundant without retraining are seen as 'lemons', that is, people who carry with them the stigma of failure, and they find it hard to get new jobs.

See Turnbull and Wass (1997).

Redundancy procedures

Organizations should anticipate redundancy by having procedures in place that will enable them to deal with the problem systematically. Such procedures take time to develop, especially where trade unions have to be consulted. They should be drawn up as a part of day-to-day HRM practice, even though no redundancies are currently being contemplated. The redundancy agreement in one British local authority which was current at the time of writing was drawn up as long ago as 1977. It enabled the authority to reduce jobs over a period of several years without making compulsory redundancies, rather than dismiss a large number of employees at short notice, as other local authorities had had to do.

Controlling recruitment

One of the most depressing experiences of organizations carrying out job reduction is to find that, after making painful cuts in job numbers, the overall number of staff has hardly reduced at all. It is as if the organization is a leaking boat, where however fast one bales water out, more water seeps in through the cracks.

The source of the problem is most likely to be the system for making new staff appointments. Such problems can be avoided by taking the following measures:

1 *Identifying where the power to make appointments is located.* It is fairly easy to ensure that a central body such as a Public Service Commission stops recruiting. It is harder to ensure that local managers, possibly hundreds of miles away from the organization's headquarters, stop making temporary appointments.
2 *Specifying the precise circumstances in which new appointments can be made.* Managers may continue to evade the new controls, for instance by engineering the transfer into their office of a member of staff from another district. Both transfers and new appointments need to be controlled.
3 *Monitoring the operation of the new controls.* Experience shows that, after a brief period of central oversight, controls may relax and the number of staff start to creep upwards again. Indeed, there may be a rush of appointments in some areas as departments make efforts to 'catch up' on the posts they felt are owing to them.

3.4   Job reduction

The measures we have discussed so far are relatively painless, in that nobody actually becomes unemployed as a result. But employers do not always have that luxury, whether because of an unforeseeable emergency or because they are not very good at planning ahead. It is a fact that from time to time employers find themselves having to take more drastic measures.

As we discuss how to do this, we will draw on the work of Barbara Nunberg (1994), who has digested the World Bank's experience of advising governments on reducing staffing expenditure in the form of a list of measures, arranged in ascending order of difficulty. It is sensible to be aware of the possible impact of different measures. We have added a couple of further items to Nunberg's list.

Remove ghosts
This refers to identifying names on the payroll which do not correspond to real employees, either because they have been fraudulently inserted, or because they have remained on the books after the real employee has left. This has been a problem in public agencies as far apart as Pakistan and Ghana.

Natural wastage
A relatively easy way to reduce staff numbers is through 'natural wastage'; that is, through not replacing staff who leave in the normal course of events because they have found jobs elsewhere, or because they want to move to another part of the country, and so on. Its effectiveness as a way of reducing numbers depends on the 'turnover rate', which we discussed in the context of human resource planning in Chapter 3: the rate will be higher when there is a demand for workers in other parts of the economy.

Delete empty posts
Following from natural wastage, this refers to removing posts in the staffing 'establishment' for which a salary is budgeted every year, even though the post has been vacant for some time.

Appointing new staff on temporary contracts
If an organization fears that redundancies are likely to be necessary in the near future but needs to make new appointments in the meantime, it may decide to appoint new staff on temporary contracts so that it will be easier to retrench them if need be. This tactic is another example of 'numerical flexibility' but also of the tendency for employers to have 'core' and 'peripheral' workforces (see Box 9.2).

Part-time and flexible working
Another way to reduce staffing expenditure is to persuade staff to transfer from whole-time to part-time working. Some workers welcome such a transfer. Part-time working makes it easier for employees to carry out responsibilities for the care of children or of elderly relatives. Workers approaching retirement age who have built up a full pension entitlement may find that it allows them to make a relatively painless and gradual transition into retirement.

Enforce retirement ages
Given the difficulty of establishing the real ages of staff, which requires an accurate national system of birth registration going back up

---

Box 9.2   Benetton's core and peripheral workers

The 'core' workforce is the permanent staff of the organization, with good pay and conditions of employment. The 'peripheral' workforce is the temporary staff employed to provide extra labour when there is a heavy demand for the organization's products. As long ago as the early 1990s, the well-known Italian fashion clothes manufacturer, Benetton, had only a very small permanent workforce. Most of its clothes were produced by a network of small firms (200 in 1985), which Benetton used on a contract basis.

Modern information technology was used to provide continuous feedback from Benetton's 2500 shops about which of its garments were in demand. Since most of the machinists who actually produced the garments were not core employees, it is easy for Benetton to increase or decrease production in a given area. Even in 1985, Benetton claimed that the time it needed to respond to a market change was a mere 10 days. Clearly, however, flexibility for Benetton meant insecurity for its suppliers – and for their workers. If a supplier's garments did not sell, the workers did not work.

See Clegg (1990).

to 50 years, there may be employees still receiving a salary who have passed the official retirement age.

Suspend automatic advancement

In some organizations, promotion to the next grade is almost automatic once an employee reaches a certain age. This may bear no relation to the employee's capacity to perform duties at a higher level.

Freeze salaries

A crude way of containing payroll spending in a context of high inflation is to award an annual pay increase below the current rate of inflation. This is effectively what the Tanzanian government did in the 1980s (Figure 9.1).

Privatization/contracting out

Organizations may achieve an ostensible reduction in employee numbers by privatizing a service (in the case of governments) or by contracting out an internal function, such as building cleaning. This, however, will not necessarily make the service cheaper to provide: a privatized telephone company could raise its charges, and the cleaning contractor could negotiate a high price.

Voluntary and compulsory redundancy
These are the last two measures that Nunberg lists. Since they involve employees losing their jobs, we discuss them in more detail later on.

4 Reducing staffing costs through decentralized budget controls

4.1 The balloon problem

Reducing payroll spending in isolation from other kinds of expenditure is like squeezing a balloon: you might succeed in achieving a decrease in one area, but only at the expense of a corresponding increase somewhere else. It seems to work like this. A department head who reluctantly follows orders to reduce staffing numbers may be tempted to show staff out through the front door in a blaze of publicity, and then quietly allow staff (sometimes the same people) in again through the back door. 'Last week the government disposed of the Transport Board. The people may get golden handshakes and then come back in again! I wouldn't be surprised,' said a senior Sri Lankan official.

This phenomenon has been called 'manpower substitution'. In budgetary terms, spending on staffing is simply transferred from one budget to another. The saving may be real, but it has been achieved partly at the expense of increased spending in another area. Controlling staff numbers rather than payroll costs also creates a perverse incentive to focus on lower echelon staff, of whom there are many, even though the cash saving may not be greater than focusing on a much smaller number of higher echelon staff. 'Getting rid of a support person … is worth as much as getting rid of a department head!' one official in Uganda exclaimed. It was for this very reason that the Uganda Civil Servants' Union had a preference for a cost-based approach.

In order to avoid the 'balloon problem', many organizations have shifted the emphasis from reducing numbers of staff to reducing financial budgets. Rather than give detailed targets for the staffing budget, the transport budget and so on, they prefer to give their departments a single global target for budget reduction in relation to all overhead costs. The department then has complete flexibility to decide in which areas the money is going to be saved. If it wants to spend more on staffing and less on maintaining the department's buildings, it can; if it wants to spend more on external consultants and less on appointing its own staff, it can.

Study task 1: advantages and disadvantages of decentralized budget controls

What advantages and disadvantages can you see in controlling staffing costs through decentralized budget controls? ✍

4.2   Advantages of centralized budget controls

Controlling overall budgets makes us much more sensitive to the costs and the possible savings of retrenchment. We realize very quickly that the potential to make savings is greater if we focus on senior staff, who of course earn a lot of money, rather than on junior staff. Early on in this chapter we mentioned that many governments have found the savings from retrenchment to be more modest than expected, and cited Ghana as an example.

Why, in a system where people rather than budgets are controlled, does this happen? For two reasons: (a) there are many more junior than senior positions, so by retrenching some of them we can move quickly towards our numerical target; (b) staff in junior positions probably have less lobbying power, so it is politically easier to retrench them than to retrench senior staff who can take steps to prevent or delay retrenchment.

Another advantage of money controls is that it makes it less likely that retrenchment will have a socially regressive impact. The junior staff who tend to be disproportionately the targets when we try to control numbers of posts are probably the ones least able to withstand the shock of retrenchment. They are less likely to have second jobs, or marketable skills, or land and property that they can fall back on.

4.3   Disadvantages of centralized budget controls

Decentralized staffing control has some potential disadvantages. Although the World Bank has been in the vanguard of the move to decentralize staffing authority in developing and transitional country governments, one of its advisers, Barbara Nunberg, whose work we have drawn on already in this chapter, is more sceptical, and her view is worth quoting at length (see Box 9.3).

The disadvantages of staffing decentralization are real. But one should also recognize that there is likely to be powerful and unreasonable resistance to decentralization from central government, where the real

---

Box 9.3 An argument against budget decentralization

As a general principle, centralized organizational models probably represent the prudent course for reforming country administrations, typically characterized by serious skills shortages below high bureaucratic levels. Although a few reforming countries with greater personnel management potential might reasonably choose *selective* deconcentration as do some advanced countries, even the most limited delegation would require serious assessment of both human and infrastructure requirements and existing capacity throughout the system, as well as careful planning for future training and investment.

For crucial functions such as establishment control and planning, the case for reforming country centralization is that much stronger. Ubiquitous concerns about fiscal restraint and the poor track record of so many reforming countries in restraining civil service expansion underscore the need to keep civil service numbers in tight check through central, uniform controls. While decentralized ... models emerging from agency reform experiences may offer the future possibility of enhanced flexibility and line manager accountability, they also increase system susceptibility to fraud, patronage and corruption – clear and present dangers to many reforming country administrative establishments. And implementing decentralized establishment management arrangements requires tremendous management capabilities and technical capacity. In most advanced industrialized countries, staff have needed significant training to come up to speed. Indeed, to the extent that such capacity does not exist down the line, the tendency of central organs to 'micro-manage' through excessive information requests can actually result in an even greater burden on the centre than in an initially centralized system. It goes without saying that the skill *cum* technical gaps in most reforming countries are likely to be that much greater.

Source: Nunberg (1995: 19–20).

power lies. We give the last word on the subject to a central and a departmental manager in the Australian civil service (A and B, respectively), overheard arguing about decentralization:

A. 'If your department is running in an efficient manner then we can make the judgement that we can take our hands off.'
B. 'What will persuade you of that?'
A. 'Nothing!' [laughter]
(Zifcak, 1994: 118)

4.4   A job reduction process

In the light of the above discussion, a decision process for job reduction appears deceptively simple. We might represent the decision process as in Figure 9.3. We need to remember, however, that in the real world other factors, including political factors, may require us to modify this simple approach. Once an organization decides to make a permanent reduction in the number of its employees, it is likely to find that it has embarked on an iterative process: 'the retrenchment programme' may well turn out to be only the first in a series of attempts to reduce the number of employees. Persistence over a period of several years may be needed: it was only after 10 years that job reductions in Ghana started to come to an end.

Figure 9.3   A job reduction process

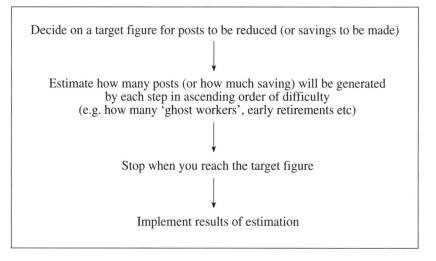

Decide on a target figure for posts to be reduced (or savings to be made)

↓

Estimate how many posts (or how much saving) will be generated
by each step in ascending order of difficulty
(e.g. how many 'ghost workers', early retirements etc)

↓

Stop when you reach the target figure

↓

Implement results of estimation

5   Managing voluntary redundancy

In the next two sections we spend some time looking at the issues involved in voluntary and compulsory redundancy, where the stakes are particularly high because employees are going to lose their jobs, and where particular skill and sensitivity are needed. By now you should realize that there is an important distinction between voluntary and compulsory redundancy. The economic hardship caused by compulsory redundancy may be greater, because the stigma of failure is attached to compulsory retrenchees, who may consequently find it hard to obtain alternative jobs; medical and psychological hardship may also be more severe. Voluntary redundancy should therefore always be considered before compulsory redundancy.

5.1 The redundancy package

We have seen that implementing staff retrenchment is expensive. Voluntary redundancy may be particularly expensive, as the terms of the redundancy package need to be attractive enough to induce staff to volunteer. However, one can set the expense of redundancy against the cost which the organization would have incurred if the individual had not left, although the period needed to recoup the expense will be longer.

Staff perceptions about employment opportunities in the external labour market are also relevant. The UK government was able to exceed its targets for job reductions in the early 1980s partly because there were jobs in the external labour market to which civil servants could move: in each round of redundancies there were always more applicants than the government needed. Willingness to volunteer for redundancy is not unique to industrialized countries. Many of the 12 800 employees made redundant in Ghana in 1988 were volunteers.

5.2 Selection for voluntary redundancy

Since one of the factors affecting the decision to volunteer is the perception that work is available elsewhere, many volunteers are likely to be staff who have specialized skills in areas like accounting or information technology. In theory employers can ensure that volunteering for redundancy is not seen as an entitlement, and that the applications of staff whom the organization cannot afford to lose are rejected. In practice, however, discretion is often exercised in individual cases and highly skilled staff often do leave. This is something that the organization may have to accept.

5.3 How voluntary is 'voluntary'?

Earlier in the chapter we referred to the experience of job reductions in the French and German coalmining industries, where there was an emphasis on retraining the redundant workers. The experience of redundancies in the British coalmining industry, where the emphasis was on retrenchment, was very different.

Box 9.4   Retrenchment in the British coal mining industry

Where reducing jobs means that existing workers will have to leave, both staff and the employer have an interest in ensuring that the staff who leave are the ones who want to. But voluntary redundancy can be less voluntary than it appears.

The Conservative government elected in 1979 in the UK wanted to make a dramatic reduction in the number of coal mines, which they saw as uneconomic and a possible focus for political opposition (a miners' strike in 1974 had played a major role in the election defeat of the previous Conservative government). In order to minimize hardship, and also opposition, the government and the National Coal Board decided that all job reductions would be voluntary. Since the mine closure programme, therefore, could only proceed as fast as miners volunteered for redundancy, a lot of effort went into ensuring that the voluntary redundancy arrangements would deliver the number of redundancies planned.

Although miners' unions were not consulted, the redundancy package offered to miners was exceptionally generous. Up to 1984, miners received a lump sum severance payment which was 295 per cent of the statutory minimum payment which the law required employers to make. After 1984, it was even more generous. The result was that 214 000 miners left through the voluntary scheme between 1979 and 1992. Since the scheme was 100 per cent government-funded, the cost to the taxpayer was over £8 billion (about US$11.5 billion at 1997 prices).

Yet at a mine in South Wales, one-third of miners considered that their redundancy had been compulsory rather than voluntary. First, the terms of their redundancy scheme had been decided entirely by the employer; miners' trade unions were not involved. Second, the Coal Board had already decided that their mine was going to close, so the alternative to voluntary redundancy was moving to a mine in another part of the country, with no guarantee that that mine would not also close down later on. Third, the very large incentives which the scheme offered to older miners to leave were influenced by a desire to restructure the workforce to prepare for privatization: 'for the miners ... the apparent windfall gain provided by voluntary redundancy payments was in effect the price paid for the sale of their rights to influence the scale of and selection in redundancy'.

See Wass (1996).

6   Managing compulsory redundancy

Although many organizations have achieved substantial job reductions without resorting to compulsory redundancy, that is not always possible. Organizations do not always plan ahead, do not always draw up redundancy agreements with workers' representatives and do not always have the money to pay for voluntary redundancy. Compulsory redundancy may be inevitable.

6.1   Selection criteria

The essential difference between voluntary and compulsory redundancy is that compulsory redundancy is initiated by the employer. This difference is so fundamental that it was reflected in the title of the South African government's compulsory redundancy procedure, the 'Procedure for Employer-Initiated Redundancies'. Just as with recruitment and selection (Chapter 6), the employer needs to have a rational basis for choosing the staff who will be made redundant, or *selection criteria*, in other words. Here are some possible criteria.

Length of service
The simplicity of LIFO ('last in, first out') has made it a popular option, especially in countries where personnel records are unreliable. For example, LIFO was the main criterion used by Tanzanian local authorities when they needed to make staff retrenchments in 1995. However, LIFO can turn out to be indirectly discriminatory, in the sense in which we used the latter term in Chapter 6. The government of South Africa rejected LIFO for that reason in 1997. Large numbers of black people had joined the civil service only after the general election in 1994, and retrenching the most recent arrivals would have had a disproportionate impact on them. A British court took a similar view about the use of LIFO in a Post Office sorting office in London, where it was actually used. Large numbers of women had only recently entered sorting work there, so again there was a 'disproportionate impact'.

Examinations
These have been used in several countries. In Guinea, civil servants had to sit competence examinations. If they failed, they were retrenched. While this may appear objective, in practice it has been hard to convince employees that it is. In the former Zaire (now the Democratic Republic of the Congo), civil servants attacked the house of a foreign adviser who was implementing such a procedure. Staff on the London Underground railway convinced a court that the use of a personality questionnaire in similar circumstances was unjustified.

Appraisal

In principle, it should be possible to use appraisal ratings of the kind which we discussed in Chapter 7, and in practice they have been used. But such ratings may fail to distinguish between good and poor performers. Some of the civil servants who were retrenched on this basis in Uganda in 1992 just had the bad luck to have worked under a boss who gave them a low appraisal rating, either because he was strict or because he had a grudge against them.

Qualifications

In some countries, such as Tanzania, qualifications have been used as a criterion: staff who have been appointed without necessary qualifications stated in national schemes of service are retrenched. This method is simple, and is often seen as fair. However, it may disadvantage staff who were appointed at a time when qualified staff were not available, and who are actually doing the job effectively.

6.2   How compulsory is 'compulsory'?

We saw earlier that the choice that staff make to 'volunteer' for redundancy may be highly constrained, because the employer has ensured that the alternatives are unattractive. It is also possible that a redundancy which has the appearance of being compulsory may actually be voluntary, if the compulsory redundancy package is worth more than the voluntary package, giving staff an incentive to manoeuvre to be declared redundant. One English local authority only made staff 'compulsorily redundant' if they *wanted* it – for example, because they were working in a specialist unit which was located far from other council offices, and where the alternative to redundancy would have been transfer to a distant part of the authority.

6.3   Summary

In this section we have looked at the issue of compulsory redundancy, focusing on how staff are selected for redundancy and the extent to which 'compulsory' redundancy really is compulsory. Staff who are made compulsorily redundant are at particular risk of suffering hardship. We turn next to ways in which public employers can mitigate hardship through the provision of training and other kinds of assistance.

7 Mitigating hardship: helping retrenched staff

7.1 The impact of retrenchment

The provision of information and other services to retrenched staff is a vital part of well managed retrenchment. Without it, the impact on retrenched staff may be needlessly severe, as Box 9.5 shows.

Box 9.5 The effect of retrenchment in Ghana

The first group of civil servants retrenched in Ghana in 1987 did not use their severance pay wisely, saving only 35 per cent and spending the remainder. This was mainly because they did not really understand what was happening, and wrongly assumed that their lay-off would be temporary.

For many civil servants, retrenchment was followed by periods of unemployment. Certainly some civil servants were able to find work almost immediately: they were often workers who had a second job even while they were employed as civil servants. But others were so unsuccessful in their search for work that they had given up trying. In between, workers fell into various categories including those who were 'underemployed', typically because they had fallen back on farming work which took up only part of their time.

In terms of income, again the experience was often bad. While there were certainly some whose earnings increased (for instance, those who found private sector work), more often incomes dropped. Only half of the civil servants retrenched had recovered their previous level of earnings after two years.

Inevitably, loss of income by the civil servant, often the major breadwinner in a household, led to increasing poverty for his or her family members. This is not unique to Ghana. In nearby Guinea, which carried out its own retrenchment programme at around the same time, 37 per cent of the households of retrenchees fell into the bottom 30 per cent of income distribution. Only 24 per cent of the households of their former colleagues lucky enough to stay on in the civil service were in that category.

Experience with later retrenchment programmes in Ghana appears to have been better, partly because the government made greater efforts to explain the programme more clearly to staff affected, both individually and also through the media. Certainly staff who were retrenched in 1990 saved 63 per cent of their severance pay, unlike their colleagues who left in 1987.

See Younger (1996).

7.2   Payment of terminal benefits

It almost goes without saying that an adequate financial severance package is the most important form of assistance that an organization can give to retrenchees. A severance package typically takes two forms: severance pay (the payment of a 'lump sum' when the individual leaves) and a pension (the payment of a regular monthly or annual amount for the rest of the individual's life). Box 9.6 shows a few examples.

Box 9.6   Examples of severance schemes

Argentina:
- (on average) 75 per cent of basic salary for six months
- service-related severance payment (averaging $3000), paid in six instalments

Ghana:
- severance payment of four months' salary
- end of service payment of two months' salary for each year of uninterrupted service
- pension entitlement frozen until normal retirement date (no 'extra years' given)

Laos:
- one year's salary

Uganda:
- standard 'safety net' figure of $1000
- three months' salary for each year of service up to a maximum of 20 years
- over 45s who had served at least 10 years received their pensions immediately
- 'repatriation' allowance to help retrenchees move back to their home region

---

Details of severance pay and pensions are quite technical, and we do not go into them here. However, there are three points relevant to us, which we discuss in the next three sections.

7.3   Manner of payment

We have just seen that one reason later retrenchees in Ghana saved more of their severance pay was that they received full information about the options available to them. Another reason is that they received a large lump sum. Younger (1996) contrasts that with the experience of nearby Guinea, where payment was spread over several months, and where retrenchees tended to regard the money as a continuing salary, and to spend it as they received it. Younger argues that, contrary to popular belief, people save rather than squander large windfall payments. He therefore recommends that a large proportion of retrenchment benefits should be paid in a lump sum.

7.4 Affordability

Strangely enough, a very generous severance scheme may make it difficult for an organization to retrench staff. While large-scale retrenchments were carried out in the Ghanaian civil service in the late 1980s, very few were made in the public enterprises. This was because the public enterprises had a collectively bargained agreement which provided for terminal benefits so generous that the enterprises could not afford to make staff redundant. In Tanzania, at the end of 1996, it was not possible for local authority staff earmarked for retrenchment to be made redundant because the government had not allocated the necessary funds.

7.5 Offsetting costs

Staff retrenchment, which organizations implement to reduce staffing costs, is still expensive in itself. Severance allowances made to public employees retrenched by the government of Ghana in 1988 amounted to four months' basic pay plus two additional months' pay for each year of service, and for the first five years of the scheme ate up no less than 2 per cent of total government spending. However, it is possible to set the costs of retrenchment against the costs of continuing employment. Suppose we have a scheme where employees receive one week's pay for each year of service below the age of 50, and 1.5 weeks' pay for each year of service above the age of 50. An employee aged 53 who joined the service at the age of 22 would then be entitled to approximately 32.5 weeks' pay. Although the redundant employee usually also receives the equivalent of additional pension contributions (for example, five years' additional pension contributions for staff over the age of 50), and this must also be calculated, it is likely that the total cost of making this employee redundant would be much less than two years' pay and pension contributions.

Of course in instances such as the one above the payments are normally made 'up front' on the day that the employee is made redundant, rather than spread over the two years during which he or she would otherwise have been receiving a monthly salary. Moreover, it will be necessary to ensure that the salaries budget is reduced as employees leave. However, offsetting the cost of voluntary redundancy in this way makes it cheaper than it initially appears.

7.6   Programmes of assistance for retrenched staff

We have already seen that communicating the retrenchment decision and its implications for individual staff is important. What other measures are available to organizations which wish to minimize hardship for staff they retrench? Box 9.7 gives an example of measures taken by a UK government agency which had to make drastic reductions in staffing.

Box 9.7   Assistance for retrenched staff in a UK government agency

The restructuring of a government agency responsible for provision of information technology services led to some of its functions being transferred to another government department. This meant that the number of jobs was reduced from 290 to 180 over a period of about a year. Although the staff who left did so voluntarily, the agency felt that it should set up a comprehensive 'resettlement programme' for the staff affected. The elements of the programme were as follows:

- pensions advice from government specialists, who explained what exactly staff would be entitled to;
- advice on starting a small business;
- advice on setting up as a consultant (many staff had specialist skills which made this a possibility);
- advice from the government employment service on looking for other jobs;
- advice on studying in higher education;
- information about doing voluntary, unpaid work for local NGOs and charities.

The above 'resettlement programme' cost very little. However, we saw earlier that such schemes are not always successful. To be effective, assistance must be carefully directed and provided when it is needed.

8   Summary and conclusion

In this chapter we have:

- explained the relevance of an understanding of job reduction to the HRM specialist;
- summarized the experience of developing country organizations in this area;
- outlined the steps which organizations can take to reduce staffing, including how this can be done in a strategic context;
- discussed how staff can be made redundant in ways that minimize hardship.

Job reduction and staff retrenchment are sometimes necessary, but always unpleasant, and sometimes traumatic. By using good practice methods such as human resource planning and retraining, and by handling any necessary redundancies skilfully and sensitively, it is possible to mitigate at least some of the hardship which retrenchment causes. Moreover, while a reduction in staff numbers may be an indication that an organization is in decline, it can also be the prelude to a programme of strategic recovery which will lead later on to growth, including ultimately an increase in the number of jobs.

10　Employee Relations

Willy McCourt

What this chapter is about

The subject of this chapter is employee relations, which we define as the management of the relationship between the employer and its staff. We present Fox's 'frames of reference' model, and then discuss approaches to employee relations in organizations where staff are organized in trade unions, and where they are not. In discussing the latter, we again relate our discussion to the new HRM model. We also consider distinctive features of employee relations in developing and transitional countries.

What you will learn

By the end of this chapter you should be able to:

- outline a theoretical explanation for the role of trade unions using Fox's model of 'frames of reference';
- explain features of employee relations in unionized organizations;
- state the implications of the SHRM model for employee relations;
- identify distinctive features of employee relations in developing and transitional countries.

1　Introduction: frames of reference

1.1　Fox's model

In many organizations, managing the employment relationship means dealing with a trade union or unions which represent staff. Traditionally, as we shall see, managing employment relations has been equated with this, and the older literature has assumed an important role for trade unions. It follows that, if you live in a country, or work in an organization, where trade unions are unimportant (or even illegal, as they are in some countries), you may think that employee relations are not relevant to you. However, we shall argue that managing the employment relationship is something that the manager has to do whether there are trade unions or not. In this way employee relations are relevant to all of us.

Employee relations have existed for as long as there have been employers and employees, albeit in different forms. Indeed, we think that the differences in this area of HRM are greater than in any other. Differences should be respected, and the temptation to impose a bland framework that ignores them should be resisted. On the other hand, there is the opposite danger of a purely descriptive approach which focuses exclusively on differences, presenting unconnected studies of first one country and then another, an approach that has been described as resembling an 'industrial relations zoo' (Dunlop, quoted in Bean, 1994: viii). There is an English saying about not being able to see the wood for the trees. We need to see both (the overall) wood *and* (individual) trees.

In order to do that, we need an analytical framework that can explain difference. The framework we use here was developed by the British writer Alan Fox (1974) in the course of a UK government enquiry set up in 1965 to propose changes to the laws governing industrial relations. The government was seeking to explain the relative decline in the UK's economic performance, and one popular reason given was the high incidence of strikes.

Fox was thus trying to explain why strikes occurred. He begins by addressing the view held by many employers that trade unions promote distrust in the workplace by encouraging their members to take a 'false' conflict view of the work situation. In contrast to that view, his analysis suggests that organizations are inevitably a battleground for competing interest groups, each of which believes that its interests are legitimate. Strikes are one of the weapons deployed when conflicts of interest cannot be resolved in other ways. This is particularly likely, in Fox's opinion, when different interest groups fail to recognize the legitimacy of each other's positions, so that resolution through negotiation is unlikely and damaging conflict almost inevitable. That failure in turn derives, he believed, from the complex of views (Fox called it a 'frame of reference') which different interest groups hold about the legitimacy of other positions, and about the management of the employment relationship. Fox identified three such frames of reference, which he calls the *unitary*, the *pluralist* and the *radical* frames.

In the unitary frame of reference, managers or owners are the only legitimate source of authority, one which employees should respect. (It is in this context that people talk about 'the manager's right to manage'.) Where employees fail to do so, however, the owners or managers have the right to enforce their authority through coercion. Fox recognizes that some organizations will succeed in persuading employees to share this view, and he cites old family firms and firms in isolated areas as examples. The unitarist manager is likely to believe that he or she has the right to fix working conditions unilaterally and to impose them on employees. Such a manager is likely to resist attempts by employees to advance interests which are different from management's.

The pluralist frame of reference is one in which managers or owners are not the only legitimate source of authority, but are seen instead as one among a coalition of individuals and groups, each with its own aspirations. Fox assumes that there is a rough balance of power between the parties. The pluralist manager is likely to recognize the legitimacy of the employees' point of view in the running of the organization. As a consequence, he or she will emphasize the importance of bargaining or negotiation between managers and employees (this is the principle of 'collective bargaining', and the technique of negotiation, both of which we shall discuss at length later on).

Before we move on to discuss the significance of Fox's analysis for employee relations in organizations, we should mention briefly his third frame of reference. The radical frame of reference, associated with a Marxist political analysis, denies the legitimacy of the interests of capitalists and of the managers who are their agents; their power is seen as disproportionate to that of the employees who are the primary producers of wealth. In this perspective, adopting the unitary frame leads self-evidently to the oppression of employees, and even adopting the pluralist frame benefits the managers, since it has the effect of making management more rational and more acceptable, and therefore more effective, inevitably at employees' expense. One way in which radicals argue that this happens is through the pluralist assumption that the different actors (or 'stakeholders' as we called them in Chapter 3) have equal power, and can therefore negotiate on an equal footing. By contrast, radicals see employees and trade unions at a permanent – or 'structural' – disadvantage in relation to owners and managers.

Box 10.1   Conflict of loyalties in a trade union

One of the authors was once employed as a junior manager by a British development NGO whose staff, like the staff of many such organizations, had a personal commitment to the development of countries in the 'Third World'. He was also at the same time a shop steward in the office trade union. As a manager, he had to make sure that internal disputes would not interfere with the organization's mission. As a shop steward, he had to represent union members' interests, especially where they differed from management's. Clearly there was an inherent conflict between the two roles, or between the unitary and pluralist frames of reference. However, the author operated on the maxim that, when there was conflict, his management role, which he saw as promoting the vital cause of development, should override his union role.

It is interesting to note that many non-management members of the union did not subscribe to this maxim, and that some of them started holding separate union meetings of their own during his tenure as shop steward, since they felt that it was only in that way that their concerns would get a proper airing. (There was also a gender dimension to this, since almost all the non-management employees were female, whereas the majority of managers, including two of the three shop stewards, were male.)

Within the radical frame, the role of trade unions as representatives of employees should be to oppose the exploitation which is the inevitable consequence of the imbalance of power between owners/managers and employees. This propels unions into political action which transcends narrow industrial disputes about pay, conditions of employment and so on, and some unions, including those in developing and transitional countries, have sometimes seen their role in that way. However, Fox points out the powerful forces which constrain union leaders who attempt to play this role.

We can suggest that what Fox calls the unitary and pluralist frames of reference have their counterparts, respectively, in the new HRM model and the 'traditional' model of employee relations. The radical frame of reference has its counterpart in the activities of trade unions which have not accepted either unitary or pluralist assumptions about the way unions should behave, but have carried out actions which challenge the basis of employers' power. This can be seen from time to time in the activities of trade unions which have played an explicitly political role, such as the National Union of Mineworkers in Great Britain in the early 1980s or its namesake in South Africa in the mid-to-late 1980s, or in the union movements which were in the forefront of independence struggles in Morocco, Tanzania and Zambia. In Eastern Europe, the Solidarity trade union movement in Poland in the 1980s is the most celebrated example.

It is not surprising that the radical frame of reference has few supporters among managers and academics who specialize in human resource management and development. HRM is a management function, and its practitioners are unlikely to take up an approach which fundamentally questions the legitimacy of what they do. The principal debate in the last 10 years has been between those who favour a unitary frame of reference and those who favour a pluralist frame. It is those two theoretical frames of reference, and the models of employee relations which are their practical counterparts, which we concentrate on here. But you may still find it useful to spend some time weighing up the relative merits of the three frames of reference before moving into a management position which almost compels you to adopt either the unitary or the pluralist frame, and to reject the radical frame.

Fox's analysis implies that there is a gulf between those who subscribe to different frames, and that it is not easy to switch from one frame to another. Adherents of the unitary frame regard as self-evident 'the manager's right to manage'; adherents of the pluralist frame will regard as equally self-evident workers' right to organize in autonomous associations and to influence the running of organizations, at least in certain areas. That much is clear in theory, but how true is it in practice?

1.2   Pluralist and unitarist models in the Caribbean

We now look at an example which shows the practical relevance of Fox's model. From 1 to 4 November 1988, a seminar on employee relations took place on the island of Saint Lucia with participants drawn from the English-speaking countries of the Caribbean: Antigua and Barbuda, the Bahamas, Barbados, Dominica, Grenada, Guyana, Jamaica, Saint Lucia itself and Trinidad and Tobago. The seminar was convened by the International Labour Office (ILO), the United Nations agency responsible for labour issues at work. The ILO has a considerable influence in developing countries through promulgating international labour conventions and recommendations governing the rights of people at work, and through its research. Its headquarters is in Geneva, Switzerland, but it has a network of offices around the world, including the Caribbean.

A hallmark of the ILO's approach is its stress on the value of *tripartism*, the belief that at national level employers, employees and government (the three 'social partners' as they are sometimes known) should work together to set a framework for the conduct of employee relations. In keeping with that belief the ILO invited representatives from employers' organizations and trade unions (representing employees) to make presentations about how they saw employee relations from their different points of view. (There was also a presentation by a government representative, completing the tripartite structure, but we have omitted it as it is not relevant to our discussion.)

The trade union representative's presentation was within a pluralist framework. His emphasis was on persuading employers to recognize the legitimacy of employee interests as represented by trade unions, rather than on seeking to overthrow the employers' authority (as would be the case if a radical frame of reference had been adopted). However, at several points he made clear his conviction that the odds were stacked in favour of the employer: there was, for instance, the general observation that the state was biased in favour of business and management.

The employers' presentation was also consistent with a pluralist framework in recognizing that trade unions have a place in industry and commerce, and in accepting the desirability of a strong legal framework for employment relations. On the other hand, the employers' preference for a limited role for the state in industrial relations is consistent with a unitary perspective. Moreover, the employers' representative was speaking on behalf of many employers, and he conceded that many of them are hostile to unions ('their public relations image which still portrays anti-union attitudes').

This was one of several differences between the unions and the employers. On union recognition, the unions' representative saw the government as loath to ratify recognition, and employers as using a loophole in the law to stall recognition, while the employers, for their part, saw government intervening to decide which unions should be recognized in a way that takes away a management prerogative. While both said that there was little evidence of worker participation, for the unions this was because most employers were either small businesses or else the state. The employers' representative, on the other hand, insisted that 'workers expect and accept decisions from the top': in other words, that they accept what we have called 'the manager's right to manage'.

We set out these differences of perception in Table 10.1.

Table 10.1   Union and employer perceptions

	Union recognition	Worker participation
Unions' view	Government reluctant to intervene Employers exploit loopholes	Character of employer rules out participation
Employers' view	Government has 'stacked the deck' to favour employees	Workers accept management's right to manage

Thus the union case was wholeheartedly pluralist. The employers' position was basically pluralist too, but had some unitary tinges, and we noted that many of the employers represented at the seminar were a good deal less pluralist than their representative. Both unions and employers rejected the classic pluralist assumption of a rough balance of power between different interest groups, although predictably the unions saw the balance tilted in the employer's favour, while the employers saw the reverse.

2   Modern employee relations: a historical sketch

In Chapter 1 we commented on the ahistorical character of much of the HRM literature. Employee relations has an exceptionally rich and complex history, knowledge of which is an important aid to the HRM specialist. In this section we say a little about it, concentrating on Britain and the United States. Later in the chapter, we look at the character of employee relations in developing and transitional countries, whose history has been rather different.

The modern history of employee relations begins with the industrial revolution in Western Europe in the late eighteenth century. New methods of production led to the appearance of large factories, first in Britain and later in other European countries and in the United States. Large factories employed large workforces, sizeable enough for workers to begin to organize themselves into associations which would represent their interests against those of the factory owners. Thus the mass trade unions of the nineteenth century were born.

The growing prominence of unions demanded a response from owners and managers and an explanation from scholars. The most celebrated nineteenth-century scholar was Karl Marx, for whom unions were an instrument in the class struggle, and union agitation a milestone on the road to the overthrow of capitalism (Marx, 1978). Somewhat later, Sidney and Beatrice Webb in the UK (Webb and Webb, 1897) also argued for the distinctiveness of labour among the factors of production, but from a gradualist rather than a revolutionary point of view. They believed that by gradual, patient action unions could bring about worthwhile improvements in working conditions for their members, even within a capitalist system. They could do so either through negotiating with employers on their members' behalf – something for which the Webbs coined the term 'collective bargaining', by which it has been known ever since – or through securing changes in legislation by working with allies in political parties.

The Webbs' work inaugurated modern employee relations (or industrial relations, as it was known until recently). Indeed their work has been described as employee relations' 'major and perhaps only classic' (Bain and Clegg, quoted in Jackson, 1991: 1). The mainstream tradition in both the USA and the UK proceeded from the Webbs' central premises, with American writers like Commons and Dunlop insisting on the rights of workers to form and join unions, and on the importance of labour legislation as a countervailing force against the powers of employers. Like the Webbs, they accepted the legitimacy of the employer's role, and therefore emphasized the need for mechanisms that would reconcile the interests of employers and employees. In general they took things as they found them: one commentator described much of the British literature as 'a variety of propagandist mini-reformism which consists partly in leading people boldly in the direction they appear to be going anyway' (Turner, 1968; quoted in Jackson, 1991: 2). However, they did valuable empirical work which described how trade unions and other employee relations institutions actually worked, with a view to making them work better. A theoretical underpinning for their enquiries was provided by Dunlop's view of employee relations as a complex system: detailed study of the components of the system – its institutions – would be needed to grasp the entire system.

Thinking about employee relations in the last 30 years has been complex, and we would distort it by summarizing it in a couple of paragraphs. However, while the Webbs' assumption that both employers and employees have legitimate rights has been the dominant one in modern employee relations, the Marxist view did not disappear. There is a parallel tradition of Marxist studies. In the USA the Marxist writer Braverman (1974) developed a theory of the 'labour process' which greatly influenced some students of employee relations. Braverman saw managers perfecting their control over workers through the use of techniques of 'scientific management' so that individual workers only had control of a fragment of a task, its overall control being in managers' hands. In Britain a Marxist analysis that saw conflict as the inevitable outcome of the imbalance of power between employers and workers was particularly influential during the 1970s.

The view of conventional economists that labour should be treated merely as one of the factors of production also remained important, perhaps especially for practising managers. The essentially collective orientation of mainstream employee relations has given way to an individualist orientation, and the interest of labour economics has shifted to such matters as the incidence of discrimination (which we discussed in Chapter 3) and individual labour market decisions. The election in 1979 of a right-wing government and president, in the UK and the USA respectively, decreased the influence of what had been the mainstream school of employee relations, and provoked an exodus of traditional industrial relations academics to the new discipline of human resource management, which appeared to offer a more attractive field of study than employee relations in the 1980s.

Fashions in employee relations in Europe and North America are thus influenced by the vagaries of the political cycle. The election of a Democrat president in the USA in 1992, and of a Labour government in the UK and a socialist government in France during 1997, may herald a resurgence of the traditional approach. The appointment of employee relations academics to important government commissions in the USA and the UK (Thomas Kochan in the United States, Sir George Bain in the United Kingdom) may indicate a new willingness to listen to their views.

Once again you should be able to use Fox's model to make sense of this history, with the Webbs' approach equating with the pluralist view and Marx's with the radical view.

3   Pluralism: the industrial relations approach

Now we have established a framework for thinking about employee relations, and have sketched its historical development, we consider its actual practice. In this section we look at how employee relations is organized in a pluralist setting, and in the next section in a unitary setting. However, while the pluralist and unitary frames of reference lead to quite different approaches, there is some overlap between them. Techniques developed in a unitary setting may be relevant in some pluralist settings, and vice versa. If you work in a pluralist or a unitary setting, or live in a country where one or the other frame of reference tends to dominate, you should not assume that the methods associated with the other frame of reference have a merely academic interest.

Let us illustrate employee relations in a pluralist setting by focusing on two important practice issues: participation and negotiation.

3.1   Participation: workers in the driving seat?

Among the countries studied in the course of the research project on job reduction in developing countries which we discussed in Chapter 9, it is possible to distinguish pluralist and unitary approaches to decisions about staff retrenchment.

The essence of the pluralist frame of reference is that all who work in an organization have a legitimate interest in its management, and that is reflected in the first group of examples in Box 10.2, of instances when employers have been willing to allow, or have been forced to concede, union participation in employment decisions. But how far does that interest extend? Does it apply only to the 'traditional' subject areas of employee relations, particularly to the question of determining pay and staffing levels, or should it go further? Taking the pluralist frame of reference to its logical conclusion might mean confronting the division between employers and employees, and asserting the right of employees to participate in the management of the organization.

Participation is a complex subject. You may have experience of attempts to promote participation in development projects such as the 'micro-credit' schemes run by the Grameen Bank in Bangladesh and similar agencies in other countries, and will be aware of disagreements among development workers about its scope and its effectiveness. Here we confine our attention to worker participation in the management of the organization, reviewing experience of attempts to share power between employers and employees in developing countries. (We shall look at participation again later in the chapter, in a unitary setting as part of an HRM strategy.) Reviewing experiences of participation in the workplace may also throw new light on participation in development projects. That is beyond the scope of this book, though if you are involved in development work yourself you may want to explore the connection.

Box 10.2   Union participation in retrenchment programmes

A pluralist approach: participation in Ghana
Civil servants in Ghana are represented by the Civil Servants' Association (CSA). It is not a union in the strict sense of the word, and in fact is
not a member of the Ghanaian Trades Union Congress. However, the
CSA was involved in decisions about rightsizing from the beginning
through its membership of the key steering committee, the Redeployment Management Committee (RMC). Far from putting spokes in the
wheel, the CSA 'gave its blessing' to decisions which might be seen as
having an adverse impact on their members. Through their membership of the RMC it was able to argue for a package of measures such
as retraining to alleviate the hardship caused by retrenchment.

Similarly, UK human resource specialists in a National Health Service
Trust and in a large local authority took consultation with trade unions
seriously. One specialist went so far as to say that the unions were his
key change agents, and that pushing through job reductions would
have been 'one hundred times' more difficult without them. Typically,
however, unions would 'note' rather than be party to compulsory redundancy procedures which might lead to loss of jobs for their members.

It is possible that union resistance to retrenchment was softened by the
willingness of union members in both Ghana and the UK to accept the
package on offer, which in some instances cut the ground from under
union leaders' feet.

A unitary approach: exclusion in Uganda
In contrast to the above, the equivalent union to Ghana's CSA in
Uganda, the Ugandan Civil Service Union, was excluded from the
relevant steering committee in Uganda, the Implementation and Monitoring Board, although it had lobbied to be included. It may be argued
that there is a connection between their non-participation and Uganda's failure to organize any assistance for retrenchees other than the
redundancy package itself.

In other UK organizations, trade unions were sidelined, especially
where central government could exert direct influence. For instance,
the National Union of Mineworkers was not consulted about the shape
of the redundancy package when a radical programme of pit closures
was driven through in the mid-1980s.

An important collection of articles discusses issues of worker participation from a number of points of view, including the philosophical
case for participation and evidence about its economic efficiency

(Pagano and Rowthorn, 1996). It includes a review of field research carried out under the auspices of the non-aligned countries movement, so it is a rare example of a large research project which has its origins in the concerns of developing countries. This also explains the prominence of Yugoslavia in the review: Yugoslavia, in the period before Bosnia and other countries seceded from the federation, was one of the leading countries in the movement, and Prasnikar (1996), the author of the review, was one of its citizens. The countries covered by the research are Algeria, Bangladesh, Bolivia, Costa Rica, Guyana, Mexico, Peru, Sri Lanka, Tanzania, Yugoslavia and Zambia.

There was a variety of forms of ownership among the organizations which Prasnikar reviews, ranging from cooperatives, where the organization is owned jointly by its workers, through different forms of state ownership to private ownership. The distinction between ownership and management is always blurred, and perhaps especially so in organizations where there is employee participation. As this book deals with *managing* human resources, we will concentrate on employee participation in management rather than in ownership.

Figure 10.1 A management participation continuum

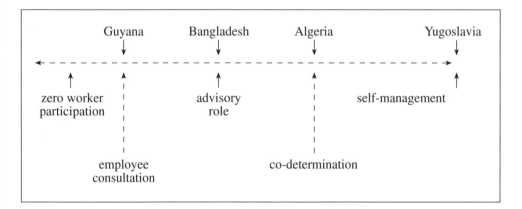

Prasnikar found a management participation continuum (Figure 10.1), ranging from zero worker participation at one extreme to total owner/manager control at the other. He observed a difference between appearance and reality. Even where participation was embodied in laws and statutes, workers' participation might be merely nominal. In other organizations, workers participated only indirectly via their delegates on worker representative bodies. Workers were often dissatisfied with the conduct of their representatives; indeed, Prasnikar sees this as the main problem that afflicts worker participation.

Surprisingly enough, while unions were generally in favour of worker participation, and in some cases actively promoted it, in others they were hostile and actively hindered its development. Prasnikar does not say why this should be.

Prasnikar discusses two of the areas which we deal with in this textbook: job reduction and pay. A striking common characteristic of the organizations he reviews is that they went to great lengths to avoid laying off workers, even when there was a reduced demand for work: he gives Malta Drydocks and Sri Lanka Port Authority as examples of this. Job security appears to be an important value in most self-managed enterprises. Having read Chapter 9, you will realize that this contrasts with the practice of conventionally managed organizations, where many staff have been made redundant, albeit on a smaller scale than is often believed.

Perhaps the most striking feature of pay in self-managed enterprises is its complexity. A basic salary is the norm, but it is typically supplemented in a wide variety of ways. This ranges from payments for individual productivity or for collective productivity, both of which were provided by SONACOB in Algeria, to provision of subsidized staple foodstuffs, as in COMIBOL in Bolivia, and provision of services for workers and their families, such as kindergartens in the Brewery Union of Yugoslavia. In terms of pay differentials, the evidence was unclear, but it appears likely that pay rates are compressed relative to pay rates in conventionally managed organizations.

Does participation work?
Of course, the answer depends on what we mean by 'work'. Those who regard participation as a good thing in itself might be prepared to sacrifice some efficiency for its sake. Archer (1996), for instance, argues the philosophical case that control over an association should be shared by all who are affected by its decisions, a position which, in principle, is unaffected by efficiency arguments. So we need to ask two distinct questions: does participation appeal to its intended beneficiaries, and is participation efficient?

Does participation appeal to its intended beneficiaries?   Workers, perhaps surprisingly, do not always welcome participation. Trade unions in some of the organizations that Prasnikar surveyed were actually hostile. Likewise the British trade union movement in the 1970s: their fear was that direct worker participation in management would weaken worker support for unions, because it would oblige them to adopt the management point of view in decisions such as making staff redundant.

But there is also positive evidence. Germany has a long history of worker participation in management, and as a consequence trade unions there tend to be positive about it. Workers may also prefer participation as a 'least worst' option. A paradoxical consequence of the collapse of communism in Central and Eastern Europe has been a de facto increase in self-management, as the workers in state-owned enterprises have filled the vacuum caused by the retreat of the state from detailed direction of economic policy and management (Schaffer, 1996).

Is participation efficient?   It is difficult to give a simple answer to this question. A review of econometric evidence (again in the same collection as Prasnikar's review) concludes tentatively that participation tends to be associated with productivity improvements, although they are modest in size, but also recognizes that the evidence is imperfect (Ben-Ner *et al.*, 1996). On the other hand, evidence from psychological studies is mixed, showing both gains and losses in productivity from participation in different work settings.

The scope of participation   A reader of Prasnikar's review may assume that self-management would apply to all the operations of the enterprise. But even in the case of the former Yugoslavia, which would definitely appear at the right-hand end of the continuum in Figure 10.1, there is evidence that worker participation was limited mainly to decisions about pay and employment; in other areas, a traditional management hierarchy operated (Schaffer, 1996). That appears also to be the case in Poland, the extreme example among the former communist countries of workers having a substantial say in the management of the enterprise. Although workers do get involved in major strategic decisions, such as the decision whether or not to privatize, there is still a cadre of professional managers responsible for day-to-day operations.

While we can conclude that the evidence about the value of participation, in terms of worker satisfaction and efficiency, and about the scope of participation is mixed, we should perhaps note in fairness that the burden of proof appears always to be on the advocates of participation rather than on the advocates of non-participation. We could also ask: does non-participation work?

3.2   Negotiation

Within the pluralist frame of reference, difference of interests between workers and managers or owners can be resolved either through conflict, as a result of which one side prevails over the other, or through negotiation (though, of course, negotiation may also either precede or follow conflict). Although we can regard strikes, lock-outs and other coercive tactics as the continuation of employee relations by other means, just as the German military historian Clausewitz famously regarded war as 'the continuation of diplomacy by other means', we shall focus on negotiation as a way of resolving differences of interests at two levels: at the individual level (how two individuals might negotiate) and at the collective level (how trade unions and managements negotiate with each other).

Individual negotiations

At the individual level we use a simple model developed by Kennedy *et al.* (1986), a British personnel specialist with a great deal of practical experience of negotiating with trade unions. Kennedy *et al.*'s model has these eight steps:

A.   PREPARE

B.   ARGUE
C.   Signal

D.   PROPOSE
E.   Package

F.   BARGAIN
G.   Close
H.   Agree

There are four main phases (signalled by capital letters), which we consider in turn. *Preparing* involves setting objectives. Kennedy *et al.* use the acronym L–I–M for this: what would we *like to get* (L), what do we *intend to get* (I), what *must we get* (M)?

Setting objectives prevents the negotiators from being blown off course, and prioritizing objectives helps to decide which to abandon if concessions are needed.

The most important element in *arguing* your case is *listening*. Negotiators know their own case, but not their opponents'. Skilful questioning helps to disclose it, especially when opponents are not inclined to reveal their true positions. By *signalling*, Kennedy *et al.* mean the following. Often a negotiator states an extreme position: 'We will never in a million years agree to that demand.' However, the point of negotiation is to change predetermined positions, so a flat rejection may become qualified over time. Good negotiators are aware of how the language of rejection subtly changes: 'never' becomes 'that just isn't on', which becomes 'I just can't see that happening', which becomes 'I don't see the Board agreeing to that'.

Proposing moves negotiations along because it is different from an argument or a grievance. The proposal should be firm on generalities and phrased in strong language ('We require a substantial increase') rather than firm on specifics and phrased in weak language ('We would like an increase of at least £30 a week'). Any opening concessions should be small: 'We are prepared to waive our equipment allowance claim.' Any opening conditions should be large: 'As long as a substantial offer is made, we are prepared to waive our equipment allowance claim.'

According to Kennedy *et al.*, the firm rule with *bargaining* is that *everything must be conditional.* So you should decide before negotiating what you require in exchange for any concessions. In addition, you should keep all unsettled issues linked, and try to exchange an unfavourable move on one of them for a favourable move on another.

Box 10.3   Negotiating for independence

Of course there are other situations in which negotiation takes place. One of the examples that Kennedy uses to illustrate his model is the negotiation of Zimbabwe's independence from Britain in 1980.

There were three main issues in the Zimbabwe peace negotiations: the proposed new constitution, the transition arrangements and the cease-fire. The Patriotic Front, the liberation movement which emerged as the major force in the negotiations, wanted to link all of them so as to have maximum room for manoeuvre. The British government wanted to reach agreement on each issue in turn. According to Kennedy, the British view prevailed and the Patriotic Front made more concessions than, perhaps, they otherwise would have done. However, they went on to win a substantial victory in the ensuing general election. After it, they were able to use the 'moderate' image, which their posture in negotiations had created, to attract foreign investment.

See Kennedy *et al.* (1986: 108).

Group negotiations

Students from developing and transitional countries with whom we have used Kennedy's model in the classroom usually find that it corresponds with their experience of negotiations. But the model does have one serious limitation: it conceptualizes negotiation as a face-to-face encounter between two individuals. In employee relations, negotiations typically take place between groups of negotiators who represent the employer on the one hand and the union or unions on the other. In South Africa in the late 1990s, unions and the Department of Public Service and Administration met regularly every two months in a negotiating 'chamber' where issues to do with pay and conditions of service are dealt with. In British local government, negotiations tend to be formal, with the two sides facing each other across a table and a rigid meeting format being used. In both cases, both sides make elaborate preparations for their meetings ('confrontations' might be a better word), and the meeting may be adjourned while either side goes back to consult with its constituency. Preparations are proportionate to the seriousness of the issue to be negotiated, and may include consulting union members and agreeing a negotiating position.

The South African and British examples are typical of negotiation in a pluralist framework. In such negotiations, the face-to-face encounter is between groups rather than individuals, and the encounter is only the tip of an iceberg. Behind the scenes, both groups are consulting, lobbying and preparing.

The essential value of the 'behaviour model' developed by the American writers Walton and McKersie (1965) is that it recognizes this complexity, drawing on their own research into practices of negotiations between employers and trade unions. They recognize the following four kinds of negotiation.

- *Distributive bargaining.* This is closest to the ordinary understanding of negotiation. Management and union negotiating to resolve a dispute over the level of a pay increase is the most common example.
- *Integrative bargaining.* This is really a form of joint problem solving, with the distinctive feature that the problem is solved by two parties who might disagree violently over another issue. An example would be discussion between management and a trade union about how to redeploy staff whose jobs have disappeared with the introduction of a job reduction programme (see Chapter 9).
- *Attitudinal structuring.* This refers to creating a feeling on the two sides of being 'on the same wavelength', even though they may be obliged to disagree on this particular issue. Walton and McKersie give the example of a company where informal discussion always preceded formal negotiations. One topic on which the two sides were apparently able to agree was in their shared dislike for Jimmy Hoffa, at that time the leader of the Teamsters' Union, one of the United States' most powerful unions.

- *Intra-organizational bargaining.* This refers to the bargaining that goes on within each side when the negotiators have to refer back to their principals. One of the authors remembers a heated example of this earlier in his career in a London pub one lunchtime. There was a disagreement among union members over the tactics that should be adopted in a dispute over the dismissal of a member of staff. The disagreement was resolved only when the author undertook to resign from the shop steward position which he then occupied if his proposal was not endorsed at the next full union meeting. (The management side was not aware of any of this.)

We can clarify the distinction between negotiating as conceptualized by Kennedy *et al.* and by Walton and McKersie if we compare the former to a poker game and the latter to a world championship chess match. In a poker game, just as in an individual negotiation, skill is required to play one's hand, and coolness is needed to avoid disclosing to the other party whether that hand is strong or weak; but both players play without reference to anyone else (contact with anyone else is taboo in poker). The chess match is superficially similar (two players facing each other across a table) but behind each player is a team of advisers with whom the players prepare before the game, and whom they consult during it. From time to time different advisers will have different views about the direction of the game.

The chess championship is not a perfect analogy. The chess players themselves remain the most important members of their 'teams', having the final say on what move to make, but the negotiators in Walton and McKersie's scenario usually have less authority than the parties on whose behalf they are negotiating. Senior managers on the management side, or union members on the union side, may refuse to endorse the agreement that their negotiators have so painstakingly pieced together on their behalf. It is as if a chess player like Gary Kasparov had to go back to the table and tell Vishwanath Anand that his advisers had vetoed his choice of move, so he would have to take it back! (Walton and McKersie use the term 'principals' to describe the parties on whose behalf the negotiations are being carried out.)

Resistance points and targets
When do negotiations fail and when do they succeed? Success is possible only where there are objective grounds for an agreement, and where the two sides negotiate skilfully so that misunderstandings and unnecessary conflict are avoided. The former condition requires us to appreciate what we mean by 'objective grounds'; the latter requires us to appreciate what we mean by 'skilfully'. We shall discuss each in turn.

Figure 10.2 Positive settlement range

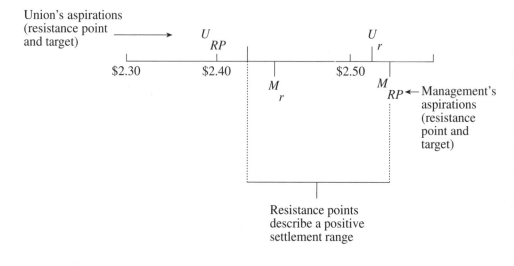

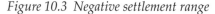

Figure 10.3 Negative settlement range

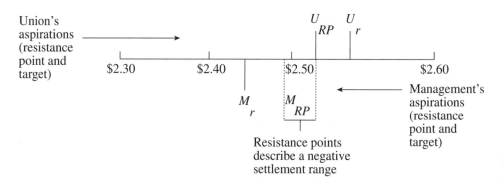

As regards *settlement ranges*, agreement in negotiation is only possible if there is an overlap between what the parties to the negotiation are prepared to accept. Walton and McKersie coined the notion of resistance points and targets, and they illustrate it with Figures 10.2 and 10.3. In these figures, management and a trade union are negotiating over hourly pay rates, and they are seen as having 'targets' (the pay rate at which ideally they would like to settle) and '*resistance points*' – the highest (in the case of management) or the lowest (in the case of the union) pay rates at which they are prepared to settle. The space between each party's target and resistance point is the 'settlement range'. In Figure 10.2, there is an overlap between the union's and the management's settlement ranges, giving what Walton and McKersie call a 'positive settlement range': in other words, agreement is possible. In Figure 10.3, on the other hand, there is no overlap between the union's and the management's settlement ranges, giving what Walton and McKersie call a 'negative settlement range': in other words, agreement is impossible.

Negotiation skills

Thus we have a model for thinking about the substance of negotiation. But what about the process? It is quite conceivable for the objective conditions for agreement to be present, yet agreement not to be reached. Negotiations, after all, are typically tense occasions, with the potential for conflict. Negotiators need skills if agreement is to be reached. One writer (Kniveron, quoted in Salamon, 1992: 515) has classified those skills under three headings:

- *social interpersonal skills*, for example the ability to interpret one's opponent's non-verbal behaviour;
- *information-handling skills*, for example full understanding of the subject of negotiations;
- *discretionary judgement skills*, for example the ability to judge when a concession should be offered and when that concession will be acceptable to one's principals.

An implication of the pluralist frame of reference is that 'every industrial conflict situation can, in sufficiently skilled and patient hands, be made to yield some compromise or synthetic solution which all the interests involved will find acceptable and workable' (Fox, 1974). Whether or not that implication is well founded, certainly finding a solution will be easier where good negotiation skills are present.

3.3 Summary

In this section we have looked at two practical manifestations of the pluralist view: worker participation in management and negotiations between management and trade unions. In discussing participation we reviewed the experience of participation in developing countries, looking at types of participation and at possible advantages and disadvantages. In discussing negotiation we considered two models, the individual model developed by Kennedy and his colleagues and the collective model developed by Walton and McKersie. We now move on to look at employee relations in a unitary setting, where management call the shots, even if they take account of employees' views as they do so.

4   Unitarism: the HRM approach

4.1   Unitarism and trade unions

As we have seen, Fox's pluralist frame of reference is linked with the industrial relations approach to employee relations. Our discussion of employee relations would not be complete without a discussion of the impact of the SHRM model, which links with Fox's unitary frame of reference. The linkage implies that organizations which practise the SHRM model will tend to be hostile to trade unions, like the organizations which subscribe to Fox's unitary frame.

By this stage in your study you should now be wary of these neat equations. In fact the empirical evidence about the relationship between the new model and the role of trade unions is mixed. Certainly in the USA, where the model originated, (see Chapter 2), the equation appears to hold true, and earlier British writing concurred: Guest, for instance, concluded his discussion of the relationship by saying, 'There is an incompatibility between the essentially unitarist HRM and the pluralist tradition of industrial relations in the UK' (1989: 54). But recent empirical work suggests that, in Britain at least, it is precisely those organizations which recognize trade unions that are most likely to use HRM practices. However, some of the features of the new HRM model have certainly been viewed as detrimental to unions.

The outlook for employee relations in the light of the political and economic changes of the 1980s is discussed in a book entitled *The future of employee relations* by P.B. Beaumont, a professor in the Department of Social and Economic Research at the University of Glasgow in Scotland (Beaumont, 1994). Like ourselves, Beaumont sees collective bargaining as central to employee relations, and he therefore concentrates on how it is changing.

In Chapter 2 of his book, Beaumont discusses the impact on employee relations of the HRM model as outlined by an American writer, Thomas Kochan. Although it is a little different from the model presented in Chapter 2 of this book, it is similar enough for you to make the connection with that chapter. It does, however, have one idiosyncratic feature, namely its last item, which treats union or other employee representatives as partners. This is not in line with most of the United States HRM literature which, as Beaumont comments in his review of that literature, is overwhelmingly within a unitary frame of reference (Beaumont, 1992). Kochan, like several of his British counterparts, is a traditional industrial relations specialist who may have an interest in asserting the compatibility of trade unions with HRM practices.

From our point of view, the evidence Beaumont presents in the second half of the chapter about countries apart from the UK and the USA is particularly interesting, and throws light on some of the issues already discussed, such as the role of 'tripartite' employee relations structures. It is also helpful that, unlike the case of many HRM writers, his approach is applicable to both the public and the private sectors.

Beaumont finds both positive and negative evidence for the impact of HRM on collective bargaining:

Box 10.4   Evidence of the impact of HRM on collective bargaining

Positive evidence
- SHRM is line manager-led, and this moves personnel decisions away from central personnel specialists, who are most likely to be knowledgable about and well disposed towards unions and collective bargaining.
- The SHRM stress on alignment between the aims of the organization and of its employees may increase job satisfaction, which will weaken employees' demands for union representation.
- Increasing job satisfaction will increase loyalty to the organization, which will be at the expense of loyalty to the union.
- The SHRM stress on flexibility will pit individual workers against each other, resulting in a divided and weakened union.

Negative evidence
- Although collective bargaining has declined, the limited take-up of the SHRM model by British organizations makes it difficult to attribute its decline to the influence of the model.
- Internal contradictions in the SHRM model may cause employers to abandon it, or may mean that employee expectations raised by SHRM practices are not met, throwing employees back onto their trade unions.
- SHRM and collective bargaining are not necessarily in contradiction, especially if the bargaining relationship between employer and union is a cooperative one.

Source: Beaumont (1994).

Beaumont also reports evidence that the nature of individual union–employer relationships determines whether the impact of SHRM on collective bargaining will be positive or negative; that is why he describes it as a *contingent* relationship. If the relationship is cooperative, the impact on collective bargaining will be positive. (Beaumont notes, incidentally, that cooperation does not preclude a union from having a separate agenda of its own.) The corollary, which Beaumont does not explore, is that, if the relationship is adversarial, the impact will be negative. Nor does he say whether organizations where the relationship is cooperative are in the majority or the minority.

Finally, Beaumont suggests that HRM is not homogeneous and that there are important differences across countries – even within Europe. While the tendency to individualize employee relations has raised similar concerns in many countries, their intensity is related to the national context, so that they are weaker in a country like Germany which has a tradition of social partnership, and stronger in a country like Canada, where that tradition is absent. The fact that such national differences exist corroborates Beaumont's earlier contention that the relationship between HRM and collective bargaining is contingent.

Now that we have spent some time discussing the relationship between HRM and collective bargaining (and seen that it is more complex than sometimes supposed) we shall look at practices of employee relations from that version of the HRM point of view which downgrades the importance of trade unions, and seeks to establish a direct line of communication between the organization and its employees. The traditional industrial relations literature was not interested in organizations which are not unionized. Given our broader definition of employee relations as the management of the relationship between the organization and its employees, we are obliged to consider both unionized and non-unionized workplaces. This will be relevant to readers who work or live in countries where unions are unimportant or even absent.

In non-unionized organizations, the features of pluralist employee relations practice discussed earlier will either be irrelevant or have a different meaning. No union, no negotiations: there is no employees' organization for the employer to negotiate *with*. The employer may take soundings, it may pay attention to what certain categories of staff expect to be paid if the organization hopes to retain their services in a tight labour market and so on. Moreover, practising employee relations in a unitary setting knocks off two of the three corners of the employer–union–government tripartite relationship: the union influence drops away, of course, but so does the influence of government, which has no need to 'hold the ring' between the employer and a trade union.

4.2   Participation: workers in the passenger seat?

Participation has a distinctive connotation in a unitary setting which we will now discuss, focusing on approaches originating in the private sector, although some of them have been adopted in the public sector.

In his review, Prasnikar noted that the main impetus behind participation in developing country organizations has been political, although he recognizes economic motives, and also what he calls 'human relations theory' (the tradition of studies of people at work which stressed factors such as informal group relations, and emphasized measures, including participation, to promote job satisfaction). Where participative working methods have been introduced in the private sector in industrialized countries, it has generally been for a mixture of economic and human motives. While we would expect similar motives to lead to similar methods, in practice approaches to participation in the private sector have been distinctive. Geary (1994) suggests that they fall into two categories: *consultative participation*, where workers' views are sought, but managers reserve the power to make decisions, and *delegative participation*, where responsibility for some decisions traditionally made by managers is passed to workers.

We look at one example of each type: *quality circles*, which originated in Japan and have been adopted in other Asian countries, notably Malaysia, as well as in western countries, and *teamworking*, which has spread widely in western countries. Before we do so, you might like to get your bearings by locating Geary's two categories along the participation continuum in Figure 10.1. Where would you put them?

We can equate consultative participation with employee consultation. Delegative participation is more difficult. Our continuum concerns participation at the level of the organization as a whole, whereas Geary's definitions confine it to the level of the individual work unit. Even though there may be real sharing of decision making at that level, it is some distance short of self-management. At its extreme, delegative participation is equivalent to the removal of a tier of management, that of the first line manager or supervisor: it is one of the ways in which organizations are pursuing the fashionable practice of 'delayering' their hierarchical structures, moving instead to what are called 'flat structures'. But a hierarchy remains a hierarchy, just as a staircase remains a staircase, whether it has eight steps or 80. Workers are not represented at its apex.

Consultative participation: quality circles

A quality circle is an informal group of employees, typically between six and 12, which meets regularly for a short period to solve work problems. It originated in Japan, where in 1992 there were about one million circles involving 10 million workers. They have spread to many other countries, including France, Malaysia and the USA. They have not always taken root away from their Japanese homeland. In the Philippines, even Japanese firms no longer promote quality circles because of their perceived past record of failure (Ofreneo, 1995: 232). In Britain they appear to have been only moderately successful, despite wide publicity, and their incidence has decreased in recent years. An article in an HRM magazine aimed at personnel practitioners (Collard and Dale, quoted in Marchington, 1992: 215–16) suggested that the following factors are necessary for quality circles to succeed:

- senior management commitment,
- middle manager commitment,
- trade union support (where unions exist),
- some decision-making power,
- training for circle members and leaders,
- piloting in one area before introducing across the board,
- monitoring of progress,
- support for further development.

Delegative participation: teamworking

The notion of the work unit, or perhaps the organization, as a team is a powerful metaphor of the unitary organization. Such metaphors, which represent the mundane poetry of organizations, can have a galvanizing effect on the imaginations and the motivation of employees. What images does the metaphor of a team conjure up in your mind?

A sports team has a common purpose to which all its members assent, and members are willing to subordinate their own interests to the interests of the team. There is the sense of making an extraordinary effort, and yet also of intense enjoyment. 'Unitarists are keen to view organizations as football teams, in which all participants are aiming for the same goal, have similar objectives and are not in conflict with one another' (Marchington, 1992: 213). Clearly an organization that could tap just a little of the excitement, concentration and commitment which are present, say, at a World Cup football match would be a more effective organization.

Different approaches to teamworking are evident in the practice of organizations, and again we can distribute them along our participation continuum. At the passive extreme is the practice of team briefing, which we shall discuss under the heading of communication, since the employee is participating only by his or her presence at the briefing. At the other extreme are so-called autonomous work groups, where units formerly under the control of a supervisor are given responsibility for supervising themselves. They are not very popular (one survey found them in only 2 per cent of workplaces in the UK) but they are widely distributed: one Malaysian electronics firm claimed that they were responsible for a dramatic reduction in labour turnover in an industry where turnover is usually high.

Four occupational psychologists at Sheffield University in the UK carried out an exceptionally good study of the introduction of autonomous teamworking at a newly built confectionery factory in the southeast of England. What they found is summarized in Box 10.5.

Box 10.5   Ups and downs of participation

Individual *productivity* was no higher than at other conventionally managed factories owned by the same company, but overall productivity was slightly higher because the new factory had dispensed with supervisors, resulting in a wage saving.

Turnover was slightly higher among the autonomous work groups (contradicting the Malaysian experience which we reported earlier). One major reason was that dismissals were higher (8.2 per cent as against 1.3 per cent). The authors suggest that the absence of supervisors meant that discipline problems were not immediately detected.

Stress levels were initially high, but continued to be significant even after teething troubles had been resolved, owing, managers suggested, to the high mental, physical and emotional pressure which managers experienced in this unusual setting.

Despite some difficulties, employees tended to *support* the system because they liked the work conditions, including the fact that they were treated as mature adults.

See Wall *et al.* (1986).

What lessons can we draw from this study? On the plus side, the productivity and satisfaction of employees are unambiguous gains that we might want to replicate elsewhere. On the minus side, the authors concede that it was easier to introduce these methods in a completely new factory. The experience elsewhere with quality circles, to which we referred, indicates that there can be serious difficulties in transporting such methods across national boundaries. Moreover, many organizations would find it hard to get the strong senior management commitment needed to overcome initial teething troubles.

Participation, unions and the new HRM model

At the beginning of this section we pointed out that some aspects of the HRM approach have been viewed as detrimental to unions, although recent evidence suggests that, in Britain at any rate, organizations that recognize trade unions are more likely to adopt HRM practices. We noted that unions have sometimes been hostile even to participation in the overall management of organizations. We might expect that hostility would be greater towards participation in a unitary setting, where participation is on management's terms, and indeed we do encounter such hostility. The British union APEX, which represents managerial and professional staff, gave the following advice to its members about quality circles (we have abridged the extract):

> Quality circles only extend worker participation on management's terms … As an alternative channel of workforce–management communication, quality circles can undermine the position of supervisors and challenge existing collective bargaining arrangements. However, as individual employees appear to gain some personal satisfaction from quality circle involvement, their possibilities should not be rejected out of hand. But management's motives for introducing them should be fully examined and the union needs to be in a strong enough position to have the circles operating in a context where there is an expansion of collective bargaining.
> (Quoted in Beaumont, 1995: 90)

Hostility is not confined to Britain. Some unions in the Philippines were critical of the introduction of government-sponsored labour–management councils, fearing, just as in Britain, that they would undermine collective bargaining (Ofreneo, 1995: 230). However, elsewhere unions have been more positive, for instance in Japan and in Germany, where the large German metalworkers' union IG Metall actively sponsored the introduction of participative working methods (Beaumont, 1995: 49). It is possible that the different attitudes of unions in different countries reflect the extent to which such methods are already an accepted part of working life: it has been suggested that the English-speaking countries, including North America and Australia and New Zealand, are particularly resistant because traditional hierarchical management arrangements are more deeply embedded there (Verma *et al.*, 1995: 9).

4.3   Communication

There is one other issue prominent in a unitary setting which we have not discussed up to now, namely communication.

Box 10.6   Communicating with government employees in Ghana

Ghana was the first country in sub-Saharan Africa to make substantial job reductions. The first group of staff to be retrenched left in 1987. Subsequently the government discovered that many of them were not properly informed about the reasons for the retrenchment taking place, or even about its meaning: many were under the impression that the lay-off was temporary, and that they would be re-employed once circumstances permitted (this was not the case). Partly for that reason, many of the retrenchees treated their retrenchment payments as a continued form of salary, with only roughly 35 per cent of them choosing to invest them to generate a long-term income.

In the light of that experience, in subsequent rounds of retrenchment the government mounted an information campaign where mass media were used to inform potential retrenchees about what was going on. The campaign was also an attempt to reassure civil servants that retrenchment would not be used to victimize supporters of the former government. Partly as a result of that campaign, roughly 65 per cent of retrenchees chose to invest their retrenchment payments rather than spend them.

The Ghanaian government found to its cost – and to its employees' cost – that the effect of failure to communicate an important policy could have damaging consequences. In a pluralist framework, employers tend to assume that by negotiating with unions they are communicating with employees. This is not always a correct assumption. Prasnikar recounts how workers in the National Bank of Commerce in Tanzania complained that their union representatives did not keep them informed. Where unions are absent or unimportant, managers have no choice but to communicate directly with their staff. They may do this concerning traditional employee relations issues like pay and staffing, but also concerning any topic about which they want to inform their employees.

The value of communications should be self-evident, in relation both to employees and, even more, to the citizens who are the clients for the service which organizations provide. When one of the authors joined the headquarters of a large British local authority in 1986, there was no sign anywhere on the exterior of the building to inform passersby what purpose the building served, even though it was the largest office complex in the town (its outline on the town skyline which it dominated was sometimes likened to that of a prisoner-of-war camp). A large sign and the local authority's 'logo' now grace its facade.

Communication with employees is important, but also simple: merely instituting regular meetings of groups of staff and their managers where none currently exist will have a beneficial effect. Here is a list of methods that are widely used (Townley, 1994):

- staff meetings,
- management chain,
- team briefing,
- formal presentations,
- newsletters,
- suggestion schemes,
- surveys.

Most of these methods are self-explanatory. 'Management chain' refers to passing information along the management hierarchy, up to or down from senior management as the case may be.

Team briefings communicate information from the top downwards through a 'cascade' in which managers are responsible for briefing the level immediately below them. Communication is one-way: open discussion is discouraged, though questions may be answered. They are used (a) to inform staff about new policy developments, promoting understanding of management thinking and possibly also commitment to management's goals; (b) to reinforce the manager's role as leader of the team; (c) to prevent inaccurate rumours circulating about new policies. Team briefing might have removed the perception in Ghana and Uganda that the job reduction programme was being used to victimize supporters of the former government.

A practical objection to the use of team briefing is that many 'teams' do not work in the same place. For instance, the Ward Executive Officers responsible for tax collection and law and order in subdistricts within Tanzanian local authorities are scattered across the local authority area, and cannot easily be assembled. Those who are hostile to the unitary framework may also object fundamentally to the reinforcement of management authority often seen as an explicit purpose of team briefing.

As regards formal presentations, when one British local authority introduced a new environment policy as part of its development of a local 'Agenda 21' following the Earth Summit in Rio de Janeiro, its training unit produced a briefing pack on what staff could do to work in a more environmentally friendly way, and provided workshops to train staff who would make formal presentations to other staff in their departments. (Interestingly, in some departments staff were allowed to volunteer, in others they were nominated by the department's management.)

Suggestion schemes are a traditional form of upward communication. They have a way of falling quickly into disuse, and are not always taken seriously by management. A former colleague of one of the authors described how he was once given responsibility for setting up such a scheme. Some weeks after starting work on its design, he discovered that the organization already had a scheme. He went to see the manager who he had heard was responsible. The manager admitted that he was responsible for the scheme, but said that he and his colleagues tried not to publicize it.

Staff attitude surveys are not widely used – less widely than any of the above methods, according to a British study carried out in 1990. Box 10.7 shows how they have been used in two private companies.

Box 10.7   Communication and trade union exclusion

In a unitary setting direct communication between employer and employees may be part of a strategy to exclude trade unions or to restrict their influence. Beaumont (1995: 75) reports the experience of one US-owned corporation which has production plants in several countries, all of them non-union. The corporation carries out regular employee attitude surveys. A management problem-solving taskforce in each plant has the job of addressing major problem areas which are identified. Employees in the corporation's British plant identified performance appraisal, career development and communication (ironically enough) as problem areas in a 1994 survey. Maintaining the non-union policy is one of the main reasons why the corporation carries out its surveys.

Guest (1989) reports similarly that a communications initiative in a British chemicals company called Tioxide served as a prelude to offering staff a package which included union derecognition.

Box 10.7 shows why we have discussed communication within a unitary/SHRM context. Very often, however, communication is innocuous and desirable. Townley does not mention the mass media, but as we have seen in the case of Ghana, they can be used by governments to communicate with public servants, especially where other forms of communication cannot be relied on. The Tanzanian Local Government Service Commission found in 1996 that it was more effective to notify local government officers that they had been selected to attend a training programme by placing an advertisement in one of the national English language newspapers than by writing to them directly. Communication as a way of reinforcing management authority may be controversial, but communication as a way of informing employees about new developments in the organization and its environment is not.

4.4   Summary

In this section we have discussed employee relations in a unitary setting. We focused on participation, which we subdivided into consultative and delegative participation, using quality circles and autonomous work teams as our respective examples. We noted the differences between participation in a unitary and in a pluralist setting. We also focused on communication, listing methods which organizations have used, and examining why they have used them.

5   Employee relations in developing and transitional countries

As in other chapters of this book, we have tried to illustrate our discussion of employee relations with examples taken from developing and transitional countries. But at the beginning of this chapter we stated our belief that national differences are greater in this area of human resources practice than in any other. We conclude our discussion of this topic by looking at distinctive features of employee relations in those countries.

5.1   Common themes in industrial relations in developing countries

Despite the differences between countries, there are some common themes in industrial relations in developing countries, although there is probably no single country to which all of them apply. The following list (Bean, 1994: 215–16), sets out some major differences:

- *dualistic economic structure*: the industrialized sector where unions proliferate is small in most developing countries (unions in the agricultural sector, such as in Sri Lanka, are quite rare);
- *segmented labour market*: there is also a sharp dualism between modern and traditional manufacturing and between large and small firms;
- *low trade union membership*: this follows from the above, although even in the 'modern' sector membership can be low, with unions typically finding it difficult to persuade workers that benefits justify the cost of joining;
- *explicit political role*: in many countries (Tanzania, Zambia and India, for example) unions played an important role in the independence struggle, and may be more interested in political battles than in particular industrial disputes;
- *the state plays a major role*: partly this is due to the state's major role in the economy as a whole, but given the close links between political parties and unions in many countries, it is not surprising that the state should be active in employee relations; in recent times, some governments have curbed union activity to make their countries attractive to foreign investors (for instance, in the export processing zones in Pakistan and Bangladesh);
- *strong communal affiliations*: in many countries workers' attachment to their ethnic group, or their region, or their caste, outweighs their class attachment, which makes worker solidarity difficult to achieve (this is not confined to developing countries: among industrialized countries, Northern Ireland is an example).

5.2 Employee relations in transitional countries: the case of Hungary

The changes that have taken place over the last decade in the transitional countries (the former socialist countries of Central and Eastern Europe and Asia) have been so dramatic that we need to add some specific detail to the picture we have given above. The impact of those changes on employee relations is discussed by Lajos Héthy (1991). At the time of writing, Héthy was both director of an institute of labour research in Budapest and deputy secretary of state in the Hungarian Ministry of Labour, and so was particularly well placed to comment on this issue. In his paper Héthy outlines the traditional Stalinist model of employee relations, then the movement away from that model (writing in 1991, Héthy considered it premature to identify a new model when employee relations were in a state of flux). He finally uses wage determination to illustrate how the new dispensation differed from the old.

Changes in Hungary's approach to employee relations (and Héthy concentrates on the Hungarian experience) started as early as the 1960s, which was when the government began to recognize that the interests of employees and employers (and the state was the predominant employer) were different. Unions no longer saw themselves as the 'transmission belt' from state and party to the working class, as had been the case in the classic Leninist model operated in the Soviet Union. Trade union rights were extended in the 1970s. Employers operated with growing autonomy. New institutions for resolving labour disputes came into being.

Following unsuccessful experiments with profit-related pay, Hungary decided that the best way to determine pay was with reference to labour market norms and through collective bargaining. Enterprises in Hungary now had considerable autonomy in determining wage levels, but, at the time that Héthy was writing, there were still difficulties in operating the new system.

5.3   Employee relations in the public sector

Finally in this chapter we spend a few minutes on employee relations in the public sector. While the extent varies, in many countries there are proportionately more employees who are union members in the public than in the private sector, even though public sector unionization is a recent phenomenon in most countries.

Public sector employee relations have a number of distinctive features. The first is what is sometimes called the 'sovereignty theory': that government as the representative of the popular will has the right to determine working conditions for its employees unilaterally. This view has three consequences. First, some governments believe that because civil servant pay is voted by parliament, pay decisions must be unilateral, since the legislature cannot stoop to bargain. Second, responsibility for decisions is diffused, with several branches of administration involved in decisions. Third, some employees are prevented from joining trade unions, notably in uniformed services like the police and the armed forces.

Although there has been a trend towards bilateral pay determination, most developing country governments, according to the most recent ILO (1989) review, still decide public pay unilaterally. This finding is qualified by the fact that unions are allowed to make representations to the pay commissions which have been set up in countries such as India, Nigeria and Sri Lanka. The review provides little information about transitional countries, although we are told that there was joint determination in industrial enterprises in the Soviet Union, in contrast to the rest of the public service.

More than 30, mostly developing, countries ban strikes. Conciliation and mediation are virtually absent in developing and transitional countries alike. A form of arbitration is available in a number of countries, although typically its scope is limited.

We can equate what the ILO calls unilateral pay determination with Fox's unitary frame of reference, and bilateral pay determination with the pluralist frame. Whereas in the private sector management legitimacy flows from private ownership, in the public sector it flows from the popular mandate. In both cases, though, the upshot can be the same: the classic unitary assertion of the manager's right to manage, even if that is dressed up in the high-sounding language of 'parliamentary sovereignty'. We believe, in other words, that Fox's model, and all that flows from it, is valid in the public and the private sectors alike.

It is interesting to note the inevitable tension that socialist politicians generally well disposed to trade unions experience when they take office. The government as employer has to drive through manifesto commitments, possibly in the teeth of union opposition (a classic example was the setting up of the National Health Service by a Labour government in the UK in the late 1940s, which was bitterly opposed by doctors and their representatives). At the same time, socialist politicians who move into government may have taken the part of unions in disputes with private sector employers on other occasions. In South Africa that tension was particularly acute in the late 1990s. The government was closely linked to the trade union movement, which led to difficulties when the government wanted to push through a tough job reduction programme; it should be said that it also led to difficulties for the union movement. (It is a bone of contention whether government's close links with the unions are a help or a hindrance. One school of thought argues that government ministers can use their influence to persuade unions to moderate unreasonable demands; another school argues that ministers will not have the stomach to face down their comrades in the union movement when necessary.)

5.4   Summary

In this section we have looked at distinctive features of employee relations in developing and transitional countries, such as the typically low level of union membership. We also discussed how employee relations are organized in the public sector in areas such as pay determination.

6   Summary and conclusion

In this chapter we covered the following:

- a theoretical explanation for the role of trade unions using Fox's model of 'frames of reference';
- features of the way employee relations can be managed in unionized organizations;
- the implications of the SHRM model for employee relations;
- distinctive features of employee relations in developing and transitional countries.

Discussions of employee relations tend to be conducted from either an exclusively pluralist or an exclusively unitary point of view. If the former, then the relationship between employer and employees in non-unionized workplaces is neglected; if the latter, the role of trade unions in representing employees, and the structures of collective bargaining, are played down. We have tried to present the subject so that it is relevant if you work in either pluralist or unitary settings.

We noted at one point that fashions in employee relations are influenced by the political cycle. In other areas of HRM, political questions are implicit, but in employee relations they are explicit: even the most superficial consideration of the subject makes us reflect on our own political views about the governance of organizations and of society, and of the power of different interest groups within both organizations and society. It is perhaps salutary that, in the last chapter of this book on HRM in developing and transitional countries, we have highlighted the interplay between management and politics, and the way political questions are part and parcel of HRM.

Specimen Answers

Chapter 1

Study task 2: using occupational tests: adopt, reject or adapt?

There is no single correct answer and, as so often, the thought process that you go through in finding an answer is at least as important as the answer itself.

In the case of the subsidiary of the multinational company, the HR specialist can probably afford to use the tests, since US headquarters is already using them. On the other hand, he might be worried that the tests will have different results if they are used in his own country, whose culture is very different from the USA's. In the end, he might decide to introduce them, but monitor the results to see if the average candidate in his country performs differently from the average candidate in the USA. So this would be a case of *adoption*, though done in a critical way.

In the case of the Public Service Commission, the HR specialist probably cannot afford to buy expensive tests from overseas. On the other hand, he and his colleagues might be able to devise tests of their own, especially if the Commission employs psychologists who have expert knowledge in test design. And since we know that he works in a large country, there is probably a large enough number of candidates for entry to the civil service every year to make the significant investment in test design worthwhile. So this would be a case of *adaptation*.

Perhaps this example also illustrates how creativity operates in organizations. We have suggested that the Public Service Commission, unlike most organizations, might be big enough and have sufficient resources to design its own tests. But even here it will be creatively adapting a testing methodology which already exists, rather than inventing a completely new way of selecting staff from scratch.

345

Chapter 2

Study task 1: horizontal integration of HRM activities

We have filled in most of the cells in the table below – but not all. There is of course some scope for you to have suggested different links.

	HRP	JA	R&S	PM	Pay	T&D	JR	E Rel.
Human resource planning		HRP basis for JA at organization level	—	—	—	HRP may highlight training need	HRP as approach to employment reform	HRM plans may be discussed with union
Job analysis			JA is basis of selection decisions	JA gives agenda for appraisal interview	Gradings are based on JA	JA used to identify training needs	JA used to identify redundant jobs	JA resolves disputes over job boundaries
Recruitment and selection				Information gained in selection feeds into appraisal	Pay may be discussed in the interview	Selection may identify training needs	—	May be disputes over selection
Performance management					Pay may be based on appraisal	Training needs identified through performance appraisal	Appraisal ratings used to retrench	Disputes possible over appraisal
Pay management						Training may increase pay	Close link between reform of pay and employment	Pay negotiated with unions
Training & development							Retraining an element of employment reform	Disputes over training entitlement
Job reduction								Employment reform discussed with union
Employee relations							Employment reform discussed with union	

Study task 2: SHRM in practice

1 What evidence can you see of SHRM elements in the description of staff management at British Airways (BA)?

- Vertical integration. Customer service was clearly a strategic priority for BA, and this is reflected in the customer service events which very many staff attended, and in the 'customer first' teams.
- Horizontal integration. The 'key performance indicators' are a strong example of this, as a thread running through several HRM activities. Recruitment and selection, pay management and performance management are specified, and it is possible that the indicators applied to other activities which are not referred to in the case study.
- Commitment. There was probably an attempt to increase worker commitment, but unfortunately it appears not to have had the desired effect. Possibly workers were getting contradictory messages from BA. On the one hand, BA was telling its managers that they should 'value others', including presumably their staff. On the other hand, it engaged in periodic bouts of staff retrenchment, and attempted to impose a pay deal on staff without negotiation.
- Quality. This should be self-evident in the case study.
- Flexibility. There is some evidence of this in staff participation in 'customer first' teams that cut across normal organizational boundaries.

2 What constraint(s) is/are there on SHRM at BA?

Although there will certainly be other constraints, the single constraint that the case study mentions is the business imperative that has required BA to retrench large numbers of staff on at least two occasions, in the early 1980s and again in late 2001. (In Chapter 9, you will find that it is fairly common in an organizational change programme to have an initial period of retrenchment followed by a period of strategic development, leading – one hopes – to growth.)

Chapter 3

Study task 1: forecast of child health care assistants in Beleriand

Table 3.8   Forecast of child health care assistants (completed)

Year	Population forecast 1 January (X 1.029)	Live births forecast (44 PER 1000)	Number of children reaching the age of 1 (SURVIVAL FACTOR 0.88)	Number of children reaching the age of 2 (SURVIVAL FACTOR 0.97)	Number of children reaching the age of 3 (SURVIVAL FACTOR 0.99)	Total children in scheme 1 January Year V
I	2 481 000					
II	2 552 949	112 328				
III	2 626 985	115 588	98 849			
IV	2 703 167	118 941	101 717	95 884		
V	2 781 559	122 390	104 668	98 665	94 925	420 648

Note: Forecast number of child health assistant posts 1 January 1999 = $\dfrac{420\ 648}{3000}$ 141.

348

Study task 2: matching demand and supply in the Nargothrond teaching hospital

1 By completing the table that follows the case study information below, make a forecast of the numbers of nurses that need to be recruited in each of the years 2003, 2004, 2005, 2006 and 2007.

		ITEM	2003	2004	2005	2006	2007
S	1	Number of existing nurses available on 1 January (in post)	300	350	360	375	375
U	2	1 January output from training scheme waiting to take over posts	20	30	35	50	50
P	3	Total number of nurses available on 1 January (add items 1 and 2)	320	380	395	425	425
P							
L	4	Reduction during year:					
		(i) Statutory retirements	10	8	12	20	25
		(ii) Early retirements and deaths (1% p.a.)	3	4	4	4	4
Y		(iii) Discharges (2% p.a.)	6	7	8	8	8
		(iv) Promotions (5% p.a.)	15	18	18	19	19
		(v) Voluntary resignations (10% p.a.)	30	35	36	38	38
		Total forecast loss of nurses (add items (i) to (v))	64	72	78	89	94
	5	Total number of nurses available at end of year (item 3 minus item 4)	256	308	317	336	331
D	6	Number of nursing posts required on 1 January to meet existing work					
E		commitments	300	350	360	375	375
M	7	Forecast of additional nursing posts required for new work arising during the					
A		year	50	10	15	—	—
N	8	Total requirement for nursing posts on 31 December (add items 6 and 7)	350	360	375	375	375
D							
	9	Additional number of nurses needing to be recruited (item 8 minus item 5)	94	52	58	39	44

2 When you have completed the forecast, ask yourself what issues the managers to whom you present your forecast might raise, and how you would respond to them. (This question is intended to put you in the shoes of the general manager who will look at your analysis from a non-numerical, 'common sense' point of view.)

In this specimen answer we list some issues that we think managers might raise. Our list is, of course, not exclusive.

(a) Managers could object that the fully qualified staff we have speci-fied are not available in the labour market at the price that the organization is willing to offer. Their view might be arbitrary, but it might also be based on the experience of previous recruitment drives or obtained from some official body, such as a government ministry, which has expert knowledge.

(b) Managers might also be unhappy about the number of nurses we propose to recruit as a proportion of the total number employed in the staff category. For example, our recruitment forecast of 94 in 2003 is large in relation to the number of nurses in post at the beginning of the year, 300. Although new recruits may be fully qualified, they still have to adapt to the organization's unique way of doing things and the organizational capacity to help them do so is limited. There might, for instance, be a limit on some initial training programme that the hospital expects all new nurses to go through. Thus managers might want to set a ceiling on the number of nurses that can be absorbed.

(c) Finally, managers might say that the hospital cannot afford the cost of recruiting so many nurses. For some types of skilled staff, recruitment cost per head can be as much as 60 per cent of the annual unit labour cost.

(d) Managers may not be willing to take staff outflows for granted. Though they obviously do not have control over some of the reasons why staff leave (notably deaths and retirements), they can influence other outflows. They may want to do something about the level of voluntary wastage, especially if job dissatisfac-tion is an important factor.

Our forecast assumes that recently trained nurses about to take over posts have no wastage. This may not be realistic, since staff at the start of their careers are more likely to leave the organization than older and more established staff – unless, that is, we have made them sign some kind of 'bond' that requires them to pay back the cost of their training if they leave shortly after they finish their training.

Chapter 4

Study task 1: reviewing a person specification

What are the strong and weak points of this person specification?

Strong points include:

- clear format;
- economical: it will have taken little time to produce the person specification using this format, as it is only necessary to refer to the job description;
- transparent: that is, understanding the document requires no special knowledge of libraries of the research institute which the library is part of (for example, 'classification' is glossed as 'understanding of decimal ordering');
- relates systematically to the job description, so all important duties have been taken into account.

Weak points include:

- too long: we said earlier that a person specification containing more than nine separate items is unwieldy, and this one contains 23;
- contains no qualifications or previous experience requirements: as we said earlier, this will give us a problem if we need to draw up a shortlist at the recruitment and selection stage;
- items are not in priority order: 'communication skills' is probably more important than 'understanding of arrangement of author catalogue', but we are left to guess that;
- some of the items under 'knowledge', such as 'Finding your way through the menu system', are trivial, and should be omitted if the person specification is being used for recruitment and selection, as the candidate appointed should be able to pick them up easily on the job.

Several of the items under 'skills' are unmeasurable: how will we measure 'pleasant but firm disposition', for example?

Chapter 5

Study task 2: advantages and disadvantages of job evaluation techniques

Method	Advantages	Disadvantages
Qualitative	Simple Does not require specialist help	Crude Hard to defend against legal (e.g. equal pay) challenge, or challenge from unions
Quantitative	Rich, rigorous Provides basis for defending legal challenge	Difficult to operate Expensive Probably requires specialist help

Study task 4: equal pay

1 *In what way might this job evaluation discriminate against the women who have the job of company nurse?*

The system used in this illustration is discriminatory because it contains a number of factors which relate exclusively or predominantly to the male job, such as responsibility for equipment and machinery and working position, and none which relate predominantly to the female job, such as, possibly, interaction with people. The actual application of the system compounded the discrimination through the exercise of value judgements, such as the judgement that working as a maintenance fitter requires much more experience than working as a company nurse (they are scored at 10 and 1, respectively, on 'experience in job').

2 *How could the job evaluation method be revised so that it operates fairly?*

The Equal Opportunities Commission provides the following illustration of how the job evaluation method could operate more fairly: you should compare it with your answer.

Factors (each factor is scored on a scale from 1 to 10; for simplicity no weights have been applied)	Maintenance fitter	Company nurse
Basic knowledge	6	8
Complexity of task	6	7
Training	5	7
Responsibility for people	3	8
Responsibility for materials and equipment	8	6
Mental effort	5	6
Visual attention	6	6
Physical activity	8	5
Working conditions	6	1
Total	53	54

Chapter 6

Study task 3: advantages and disadvantages of the interview

Drawing on your own experiences, make a short list of the advantages and disadvantages of the selection interview.

Here is one possible list.

Advantages

- its flexibility allows interaction between candidate and employer;
- allows important representatives of the employer, such as line managers and personnel specialist, to take part in selection;
- its familiarity means that both employer and candidate have at least some idea of how they are supposed to behave.

Disadvantages

- interviewers may be biased by features such as candidates' gender or appearance;
- interviewers may lack the skill of eliciting information from the candidate;

- interviewers may make premature or biased judgements about candidates.

Study task 4: a cloze test

Prison and the authorities conspire to *rob* each man of his dignity. In *and* of itself, that assured that I *would* survive, for any man or institution *that* tries to rob me of my *dignity* will lose because I will not *part* with it at any price or *under* any pressure. I never seriously considered *the* possibility that I would not emerge *from* prison one day. I never thought *that* a life sentence truly meant life *and* that I would die behind bars. *Perhaps* I was denying this prospect because *it* was too unpleasant to contemplate. But *I* always knew that someday I would *once* again feel the grass under my *feet* and walk in the sunshine as *a* free man.

I am fundamentally an *optimist*. Whether that comes from nature or *nurture*, I cannot say. Part of being *optimistic* is keeping one's head pointed towards *the* sun, one's feet moving forward. There *were* many dark moments when my faith *in* humanity was sorely tested, but I *would* not give myself up to despair. *That* way lay defeat and death.

Study task 5: applying the good practice model

1 *In the light of the model of good practice which we have just presented, identify the problems in the recruitment and selection system and recommend how they might be resolved.*

This task was actually carried out by a human resource specialist in the firm. You should compare her analysis and recommendations with the ones that you have produced.

She identified three major problems in the existing system:

1 Most applicants were rejected in the early stages, through sifting application forms and unstructured interviews, where highly unreliable selection methods were used.
2 Candidates were chosen through a subjective process where biased judgements were very likely.
3 In an attempt to attract candidates, the organization was giving an unrealistic picture of the nature of the job and the culture of the company. Individuals started work with unrealistic expectations and were often disillusioned. The result was rapid turnover.

On the basis of her analysis, the human resource specialist made the following recommendations.

- *A structured application form should be introduced.* 'Sifting' of applications should be done in light of the selection criteria identified through job analysis. If feasible, psychological tests should be included in the preselection to identify possible strengths and weaknesses against particular job requirements.
- *Introduce job analysis.* A job description and person specification should be prepared. This would provide a more accurate picture of actual work, including the inevitably uninteresting tasks which a new member of staff has to carry out, so that candidates would either deselect themselves or would be ready for this aspect of the job if appointed.
- *The initial interview should have a structured format, based on the job analysis.* We have seen that the predictive validity of the interview increases if these measures are taken.
- *An assessment centre design should be introduced.* The assessment centre should include an adequate range of exercises, including possibly role play or other exercises which simulate aspects of the job. Assessors should pool their evaluations with other assessors to form overall judgement of the skills and potentials of each candidate. Feedback should be given to the participants and evaluations used for actual selection.
- Senior managers should be trained to conduct interviews and evaluate candidates. The prevailing practice showed that they failed to evaluate candidates in a professional way.

Study task 6: eliminating discrimination

Here are some possible reasons:

- even when we revise our selection criteria so that only necessary requirements are stated as essential, many members of disadvantaged groups still do not meet them;
- potential applicants, believing that we continue to discriminate, choose not to apply: we have failed to publicize our new equal opportunities initiative;
- even members of disadvantaged groups who are willing to apply and who meet our requirements are unable to satisfy the conditions of the job.

Study task 7: selecting staffing options

1 *Outline the staffing options available to the staff training unit in the airline below.*
2 *Present an argument to support your preferred option.*

We have set out some advantages and disadvantages of the various staffing options below.

Staffing option	Advantages	Disadvantages
Recruitment of a replacement	Allows unit to draw on skills in the labour market	Tethers post to training for which demand is reducing
Reallocation of duties	Allows declining demand for supervisory training to be met by existing staff; may release post for new work (e.g. customer care)	May overload existing staff; union or staff representatives may object
Transfer	Facilitates development of existing member of staff	Transferee may not have relevant skills
Redeployment of a supernumerary	Prevents member of staff being made redundant	Supernumerary may not have relevant skills
Outsourcing	Unit's control of staffing budget makes this possible; would enable commitment to supervisory training to be met flexibly as demand reduces	Suitable consultant may not be available; union or staff representatives may object
Appointment of a previously identified successor	Not applicable – no successor has been identified	Not applicable

Which of the options should we prefer? We can certainly rule out a couple of them. The last option, appointment of a successor, as we have said, is not applicable since no successor has been identified. The first option, simply appointing a replacement, seems foolish, since we know that the demand for the supervisory training for which the retiring training officer has been responsible is reducing. Moreover, such an appointment would be difficult to justify to the airline's management.

Among the other options, our preference will depend on the point of view from which we approach this. The management of the airline will want the training unit to consider a redeployment, and may have someone whom they would like to transfer as part of a development programme. The staff training unit itself will probably be keener to outsource or to reallocate duties, since that would release money which the unit can use for other purposes.

Chapter 7

Study task 1: performance management in 'Daletel'

1 *To what extent did Daletel follow 'good practice' as we have presented it in this unit?*

In most respects, Daletel did follow the good practice model. We would highlight the following:

- The move from an annual performance appraisal to a continuous performance management cycle.
- The objective-setting process, including an attempt to make performance management 'strategic' by linking objectives to overall business objectives. Notice how 'job deliverables' were supposed to take account of 'job value add to business'. Notice also how the Performance Expectations Form required the employee to say how his or her role contributed to business, team and/or project objectives.
- The emphasis on employee development, including both on- and off-the-job development activities.
- The use of 360° feedback (you should have noticed at the top of the Feedback Form that employees were supposed to seek feedback from peers, customers and other stakeholders).
- Although it is controversial, the company's decision to take pay decisions out of the performance management process is in line with one strand of thinking about performance management. Managers are often reluctant to make decisions that affect their subordinates' pay.

We can see just one way in which Daletel was not following good practice.

- There is no evidence that the manager's assessment of the employee's performance (what the company called 'metrics') was based on job analysis.

> 2 *To what extent was the model of performance management that Daletel adopted appropriate to it, and particularly to its Chinese subsidiary, in terms of both organizational culture and national culture?*

We suggest that we can think about this issue in terms of both the organizational culture of Daletel and the national culture of China.

In terms of *organizational culture* first, Daletel has some of the features of what Charles Handy (1993) has called a 'task culture', one where influence is based on expert power, and is widely dispersed throughout the organization. In his textbook, Handy gives a company in a high-tech industry as an example. Certainly Daletel was operating in a high-tech industry, and certainly also managers had a lot of power: you will have noticed the considerable discretion that they had over pay decisions. There is another way in which Daletel represents a task culture: the aggressive environment in which Daletel operated meant that staff faced pressure to meet short-term targets.

These features militated against the new scheme. Performance management in Daletel was centrally driven by the HR department, and therefore not owned by line managers. In addition, the scheme's emphasis on employee development, which is a medium- or long-term concern, did not help managers to meet their short-term targets. Finally, both managers and employees, working under pressure, thought the scheme was cumbersome: too many forms to fill in, too many stakeholders to get feedback from. Since line managers had a lot of power in Daletel, the fact that they were not committed to the scheme effectively killed it.

Our last comment is an implicit criticism of 360° feedback, which in some ways is considered the 'state of the art'. But that is in line with the criticism of 360° feedback as an exercise in time-consuming bureaucracy that we reported earlier: Daletel is not the only organization to have found that the idea of getting feedback from many stakeholders, while excellent in theory, takes a lot of time to carry out in practice.

Managers' dismissal of performance management was also influenced, ironically, by the fact that the new scheme no longer had a performance-related pay element, unlike the performance appraisal scheme that it replaced. Managers tended to see decisions about pay as real and important, and decisions about employee development as trivial. Here is an unintended consequence of taking account of the view (with which we sympathize, and which we discussed in Chapter 5) that pay decisions should not be part of performance management; and also a very good example of how good practice may not be appropriate in a particular organizational setting.

Finally, Daletel's managers, who were usually technical specialists, tended to have poor interpersonal skills and tended to find it hard to discuss performance problems openly with their staff (this is something you might have guessed if you know anything about high-tech industries).

There was also a problem of *national culture*. The feedback procedure required managers and other stakeholders to give a frank written opinion about employees' behaviour, including where the behaviour was below expectations: this is clear from the layout of the Feedback Form. In Chinese culture it is very important not to cause someone to 'lose face', that is, not to humiliate them by exposing their weaknesses publicly. Managers and staff saw the feedback procedure as requiring them to do just that. This was another reason why they rejected it. It was also the reason, above all else, that convinced one of Daletel's HR specialists that the scheme could not work.

3 What could Daletel have done to make performance management succeed?

Here are some suggestions.

- Most fundamentally, Daletel headquarters needed to engage better with its Chinese subsidiary, especially its HR managers. This would have enabled it to explain how the scheme was supposed to work. It would also have allowed the Chinese HR managers to suggest modifications to the scheme in keeping with reality on the ground, including Chinese national culture.
- The company could base performance management more firmly on job analysis data. (Since in doing so it would be linking two HR activities together, this is an example of what we called *horizontal integration* in Chapter 2).
- There was a need for a much simpler scheme, recognizing the pressure that staff were working under. There could have been fewer and shorter forms, and employees could have been asked to get feedback from just one or two stakeholders in addition to their managers ('180° feedback'), rather than from several.
- The company could also have modified the feedback procedure so that stakeholders would give only positive feedback and constructive suggestions, rather than give negative feedback which would cause employees to 'lose face'.
- The company could have done more to sell the new scheme. If the company was right that continuous skills updating is vital in its fast-moving business environment, it was going to be vital to persuade staff to take it seriously. This would have meant training the managers. Training would have helped managers to develop the

interpersonal skills they would need to operate the scheme effectively. (In making this suggestion, we are aware that the training would have needed to be of a high quality to overcome the resistance of Daletel's hard-pressed managers to giving up time to go on a training course: you will remember that not all the managers were willing to attend even a short briefing on the new scheme.)

Chapter 8

Study task 1: evaluating reactions to a series of courses

1 What do the scores tell you about the effectiveness of the training programme?

There are a number of things we could say about these scores, but, before we say them, there are two technical reservations that we must make. The first is that the scores suffer from a 'ceiling effect': that is, many of the individual scores were the maximum possible (5 out of 5, or 4 out of 4), meaning that it was not possible to distinguish between the levels of satisfaction of many participants. For some of the participants, a score of 5 out of 5 could have meant that the session in question was truly outstanding, while for others the same score could have meant that the session in question was 'merely' very good. The effect of this is to make it hard to distinguish between participants' views about the relative quality of different course sessions, since average scores are clustered so closely together (in the case of the five-point scale items, they range only from a minimum of 4.0 for the session on employee relations to 4.7 for the session on job analysis).

The second reservation is that the 'happy sheet' syndrome, giving a falsely positive impression of participants' satisfaction, may afflict scores. (We discussed problems of scoring, or rating, in Chapter 7.)

Having made those reservations, it is reasonable to conclude that participants were very satisfied with the three courses. The most important single score is probably the very last one ('overall impressions'), which invites participants to sum up their views as a whole. Scores for this item are very high. However, evaluation always presents the trainer with the opportunity to improve further (that, incidentally, is what is meant by *formative evaluation*, in contrast to *summative evaluation*, which confines itself to looking backwards at the success of the learning programme), and there are a few pointers here.

There is a tendency for average scores to increase course-by-course, suggesting that trainers were using the experience of each course to improve their performance on subsequent courses. This is positive.

The relatively low score for the 'time allocated was sufficient and effectively utilized' item reflects participants' view that the course should have been longer than the fortnight allocated, suggesting that the participants were left wanting more, always a good outcome for a trainer.

A couple of the scores are relatively low (notice employee relations and budgeting). If we take employee relations as an example, we could encourage the trainer responsible for this session to look more closely at how he organized it; alternatively, we could question whether employee relations is a crucial topic for the participants or not.

Study task 2: training in the Ministry of Land and Housing in Valinor

1 *To what extent is the ministry's training 'strategic', and what could it do to make it more strategic?*

There is little evidence that training is strategic. Jonalis says that the new CEO 'wanted us to develop new strategies to link training more closely with corporate needs as well as organizational performance'. The CEO himself says that he is hoping that Dennis and his CSI colleagues can come up with some ideas. The door is open for Dennis to suggest steps in his report that will achieve 'vertical integration', linking training more systematically to the ministry's overall objectives.

2 *How does the ministry analyse learning needs? (What use does it make of data from performance management and appraisal?)*

Jonalis admits that there has been no learning needs analysis: he says it would be 'a costly affair for MLH'. In theory learning needs should be identified through appraisal, but Patricia Quek is sceptical: officers often attend 'ad hoc' courses, and sometimes managers stop officers from attending a course even though it has been recommended in the officer's appraisal report.

MLH has the option of conducting a large learning needs analysis exercise or, if that is indeed too 'costly' as Jonalis suggests, turning the theory of using appraisal to identify needs into practice; and, in particular, getting the Career Development Committee to see learning needs as an important part of their remit (Patricia makes clear that they do not at present).

3 What steps has the ministry taken, and what additional steps could it take, to ensure that staff transfer learning from courses to work?

This is a key aspect of the case study, with one of the officers on whose conversation Dennis eavesdrops in the lift criticizing the ministry's tendency to provide 'unaligned training'. At the moment the ministry is doing little about it. Here are two examples of what it needs to do: move towards vertical integration, as we have already suggested, so that training is aligned more closely with the organization's needs; and encourage managers like Mr Tan to see training as an integral part of their jobs, for example agreeing what the case study calls a 'social contract' with their staff before they go on a course.

4 How does the ministry evaluate the effectiveness of its training, and how could it do so better?

Patricia admits that the HR department never asks training institutions for feedback (nor the officers themselves, we may add). Thus there is a need to introduce systematic evaluation, if only of the modest kind that we discussed in Study task 1.

5 How appropriate is the standard good practice model to this ministry?

In our judgement, it is possible to work towards 'vertical integration' here. The CEO wants it, and staff themselves recognize the need. The stumbling block, ironically, is likely to be the HR department, who seem to operate on the 'clerk of works' model. In terms of organizational factors, we should take seriously the HR department's complaint that it is understaffed. It is unrealistic to go for a 'best practice' solution while the department is overworked.

In terms of national culture, as in the Daletel case study in Chapter 7, we will need to make a judgement about whether it is appropriate for managers and officers to have the kind of frank discussion that will be necessary if appraisal is to be used to identify learning needs. 'Valinor' is in South-east Asia, and there may be some cultural reluctance to discuss employee weaknesses openly.

Chapter 9

Study task 1: advantages and disadvantages of decentralized budget controls

Possible advantages

- The need for detailed central scrutiny of individual departmental staffing levels disappears. The whole unwieldy administrative machinery required to operate it can be dismantled.
- From the political point of view, decentralization transfers the blame for staffing cuts from central government ministers to local managers.
- There is the opportunity to capitalize on the experience of countries as far apart as New Zealand, the United Kingdom and the United States, which have all followed this approach.
- Local managers, because they have local knowledge, are in a better position to identify their staffing requirements than central government. In Tanzania in the mid-1990s, central government determined the staffing establishment of every local authority. A consequence of this was that every local authority had a forestry officer (whether or not it had a forest) and a fisheries officer (whether or not it had a coastline, a river or a pond).

Possible disadvantages

- Central government may give up the appearance of power but retain the substance. A human resource specialist in a UK government agency told one of the authors that, when his agency was reorganized, although central government paid lip service to the idea of local autonomy, in practice the Treasury came up with a target figure of staff reductions which the agency was then expected to meet.
- There may be a skill deficit at local level. In other words, local managers may simply lack the sophisticated budgetary and staffing skills needed to manage in this way.
- In certain countries, there may be problems of nepotism or corruption (of the kind which we discussed in Chapter 6) which may hinder decentralization, and which, surprisingly, may make local managers resist having greater power over staffing delegated to them.

In Tanzania, central government made a public commitment to delegate staffing authority from the centre to the local authorities. HRM specialists in the local authorities tended to oppose delegation, fearing that local politicians would abuse the freedom by appointing political supporters rather than well-qualified candidates.

The economies of scale (to use the language of economists) which operated before decentralization, when many more decisions were taken by a central body on behalf of a number of units, are lost. Moreover, a new 'transaction cost' is introduced, since some liaison is needed between the centre and the local unit to which staffing control has been delegated.

Bibliography

Abed, G. *et al.* (1998) 'Fiscal reforms in low income countries: Experience under IMF-supported programs', occasional paper 160, International Monetary Fund, Washington, DC.

Akin-Ogundeji, O. (1988) 'Facilitating organizational commitment to evaluation: Implications from Nigeria, *Journal of European Industrial Training*, 12, 1.

Alderman, H., S. Canagarajah and S. Younger (1994) 'Consequences of permanent layoff from the civil service: Results from a survey of retrenched workers in Ghana', in D. Lindauer and B. Nunberg (eds), *Rehabilitating government: Pay and employment reform in Africa*, Washington, DC: World Bank, 211–37.

Anstey, E., C. Fletcher and J. Walker (1976) *Staff appraisal and development*, London: Allen and Unwin.

Archer, R. (1996) 'The philosophical case for economic democracy', in U. Pagano and R. Rowthorn (eds), *Democracy and efficiency in the economic enterprise*, London: Routledge, 13–35.

Argyle, M. (1989) *The psychology of work*, Harmondsworth: Penguin.

Argyris, C. (1974) 'Personality vs. organization', *Organizational Dynamics*, 3, 2: 2–17.

Armstrong, M. (1991) *A handbook of personnel management practice*, London: Kogan Page.

Armstrong, M. (2000) *Strategic human resource management: A guide to action*, London: Kogan Page.

Armstrong, M. and A. Baron (1998) *Performance management: The new realities*, London: Institute of Personnel and Development.

Armstrong, M. and H. Murlis (1994) *Reward management: A handbook of remuneration strategy and practice*, London: Kogan Page.

Bean, R. (1994) *Comparative industrial relations: An introduction to cross-national perspectives*, London: Routledge.

Beaumont, P. (1992) 'The US human resource management literature: A review', in G. Salaman (ed.), *Human resource strategies*, London: Sage, 20–37.

Beaumont, P. (1994) *The future of employment relations*, London: Sage.

Becker, B. and B. Gerhart (1996) 'The impact of human resource management on organizational performance', *Academy of Management Journal*, 39: 779–801.

Ben-Ner, A., T. Han and D. Jones (1996) 'The productivity effects of employee participation in control and in economic returns', in U. Pagano and R. Rowthorn (eds), *Democracy and efficiency in the economic enterprise*, London: Routledge, 209–44.

Binsted, D. and R. Stuart (1980) 'Designing "reality" into management learning events', *Personnel Review*, 8, 3 & 4; 9, 1.

Blunt, P. (1983) *Organisational theory and behaviour: an African perspective*, London: Longman.

Blunt, P. and O. Popoola (1985) *Personnel management in Africa*, London: Longman.

Bowey, A., A. Fowler and P. Iles (1992) *Reward management*, Milton Keynes: Open University.

Bramham, J. (1988) *Practical manpower planning*, London: Institute of Personnel Management.

Brannick, M. and E. Levine (2002) *Job analysis: Methods, research, and applications for human resource management in the new millennium*, London: Sage.

Braverman, H. (1974) *Labour and monopoly capital: The degradation of work in the twentieth century*, New York: Monthly Review Press.

Burgoyne, J. (1988) 'Management development for the individual *and* the organisation', *Personnel Management*, June: 40–44.

Burgoyne, J. and R. Stuart (1976) 'The nature, use and acquisition of managerial skills and other attributes', *Personnel Review*, 5, 4: 19–29.

Burns, R. (1909) 'To a louse: On seeing one on a lady's bonnet at church', *The poems and songs of Robert Burns*, New York: Collier, vol. 6, no.99.

Burton, J., C. Joubert, J. Harrison and C. Athayde (1993) *Evaluation of ODA project in support of Ghana's civil service reform programme: Volumes I and II*, London: ODA Evaluation Department.

Cabinet Office (1996) *Civil service statistics*, London: HMSO.

Carroll, S. and D. Gillen (1987) 'Are the classical management functions useful in describing managerial work?', *Academy of Management Review*, 12: 38–51.

Charlton, J. (1992) 'Keeping pace with development: The evolving role of training in Botswana', *Teaching Public Administration*, 12, 1: 60–68.

Chew, D. (1997) 'Economic restructuring and flexible civil service pay in Singapore' in C. Colclough (ed.), *Public-sector pay and adjustment: Lessons from five countries*, London: Routledge, 22–45.

Clegg, S. (1990) *Modern organizations: Organization studies in the postmodern world*, London: Sage.

Colclough, C. (1997) 'Economic stagnation and earnings decline in Zambia, 1975–91', in C. Colclough (ed.), *Public-sector pay and adjustment: Lessons from five countries*, London: Routledge, 68–112.

Colling, T. (1997) 'Managing human resources in the public sector', in I. Beardwell and L. Holden (eds), *Human resource management*, London: Pitman, 654–80.

Conway, J., R. Jako and D. Goodman (1995) 'A meta-analysis of interrater and internal consistency reliability of selection interviews', *Journal of Applied Psychology*, 80: 565–79.

Corkery, J. and A. Land (1996) *Civil service reform in the context of structural adjustment*, Maastricht: European Centre for Development Policy Management.

Davar, R. (1981) *Personnel management and industrial relations in India*, New Delhi: Vikas.

Davies, A. (1991) 'Restructuring pay and grading in a civil service agency', *Personnel Management*, 23, 10:52–3.

De Luisa, I. (1996) 'Strategic management and small firms: a survey of rural firms in Mexico', *Small Enterprise Development*, 7, 3: 46–51.

Deming, W.E. (1986) *Out of the crisis*, Cambridge, MA: MIT Institute for Advanced Engineering Study.

Dia, M. (1996) *Africa's management in the 1990s and beyond: Reconciling indigenous and transplanted institutions*, Washington, DC: World Bank.

Dore, R. (1997) *The diploma disease: Education, qualification and development*, London: Institute of Education, University of London.

Doriye, J. (1992) 'Public office and private gain: An interpretation of the Tanzanian experience', in M. Wuyts, M. Mackintosh and T. Hewitt (eds), *Development policy and public action*, Oxford: Oxford University Press, 91–113.

Dulewicz, S. and C. Fletcher (1989) 'The context and dynamics of performance appraisal', in P. Herriot (ed.), *Assessment and selection in organizations*, Chichester: John Wiley, 651–64.

Dunleavy, P. and C. Hood (1994) 'From old public administration to new public management', *Public Money and Management*, 14, 3: 34–43.

Dunsire, A. and C. Hood (1989) *Cutback management in public bureaucracies*, Cambridge: Cambridge University Press.

Eliot, T.S. (1963) 'The dry salvages', *Collected poems, 1909–1962*, London: Faber and Faber, 205–13.

Equal Opportunities Commission (1985) *Sex discrimination decisions. No. 9: Women and family responsibilities (recruitment age links)*, Manchester: Equal Opportunities Commission.

Fanthorpe, D. (1992) 'Interview', *Involvement and Participation*, 614:16–28.

Ferner, A. (1994) 'The state as employer', in R. Hyman and A. Ferner (eds), *New frontiers in European industrial relations*, Oxford: Blackwell, 52–79.

Fiedler, F. (1967) *A theory of leadership effectiveness*, New York: McGraw-Hill.

Flanagan, J. (1954) 'The critical incident technique', *Psychological Bulletin*, 51: 327–58.

Fletcher, C.A. (1993) *Appraisal: routes to improved performance*, London: IPM.

Fombrun, C., N. Tichy and M. Devanna (1984) *Strategic human resource management*, New York: John Wiley.

Fosh, P. (1978) 'Attitudes of East African white-collar workers to income inequalities', *International Labour Review*, 117, 1.

Fox, A. (1974) *Beyond contract: Work, power and trust relations*, London: Faber and Faber.

Freeman, R. (1984) *Strategic management: A stakeholder approach*, Marshfield, MA: Pitman.

Geary, J. (1994) 'Employees' participation enabled or constrained', in K. Sisson (ed.), *Personnel management: A comprehensive guide to theory and practice in Britain*, Oxford: Blackwell, 634–61.

Government of Ghana (1987) *Programme of actions to mitigate the social costs of adjustment*, Accra: Government of Ghana.

Government of Ghana (1992) *Redeployment management committee: Status programme for 1992 and work programme for 1993*, Accra: Government of Ghana.

Government of Malaysia (1991) *Report of the special committee of the Cabinet on salaries for the public sector*, Kuala Lumpur: National Printing Department.

Government of South Africa (1995) *White Paper on the transformation of the public service. Government Gazette*, no. 16838, November.

Government of South Africa (1997) *White Paper on transforming service delivery. Government Gazette*, no. 18340, October.

Government of Uganda (1994) *Management of change: Context, vision, objectives, strategy and plan*, Kampala: Ministry of Public Service.

Government of Uganda (1996) *Uganda civil service reform programme: Status report 11*, Kampala: Ministry of Public Service.

Gray, J. (1998) *False dawn: The delusions of global capitalism*, London: Granta.

Gray, M. (1991) 'Job evaluation and women's jobs', *Compensation and Benefits Review*, 24, 4:46–51.

Greenberg, J. (1986) 'Determinants of perceived

fairness of performance evaluations', *Journal of Applied Psychology*, 71, 340–42.

Guest, D. (1989) 'Human resource management: its implications for industrial relations and trade unions', in J. Storey (ed.) *New perspectives on human resource management*, London: Routledge, 41–55.

Guest, D. (1997) 'Human resource management and performance: A review and research agenda', *International Journal of Human Resource Management*, 8: 263–76.

Guion, R. (1989) 'Comments on personnel selection methods', in M. Smith and I. Robertson (eds), *Advances in selection and assessment*, Chichester: John Wiley, 113–28.

Hackman, J. and G. Oldham (1975) *Work redesign*, London: Addison-Wesley.

Hahn, D. and R. Dipboye (1988) 'The effects of training and information on the accuracy and reliability of job evaluations', *Journal of Applied Psychology*, 73, 146–53.

Hamel, G. and C. Prahalad (1990) 'The core competence of the corporation', *Harvard Business Review*, 68, 3 (May/June): 79–89.

Handy, C. (1993) *Understanding organizations*, London: Penguin.

Harrison, R. (1992) *Employee development*, London: Institute of Personnel and Management.

Hayek, F. (1944) *The road to serfdom*, London: Routledge.

Henkoff, R. (1990) 'Cost cutting: How to do it right', *Fortune*, 9 April: 26–33.

Herriot, P. (1993) *Selection and assessment*, London: University of London Press.

Herriot, P. (1995) 'The changing context of assessment and its implications', *International Journal of Selection and Assessment*, 3, 3: 197–201.

Herriot, P. and J. Wingrove (1984) 'Decision process in graduate pre-selection', *Journal of Occupational Psychology*, 57: 269–75.

Héthy, L. (1991) 'Industrial relations in Eastern Europe: recent developments and trends', in R. Adams (ed.), *Comparative industrial relations: Contemporary research and theory*, London: Harper Collins, 124–39.

Honey, P. and A. Mumford (1992) *A manual of learning styles*, Maidenhead: Honey.

Höpfl, H., S. Smith and S. Spencer (1992) 'Values and valuations: The conflicts between culture change and job cuts', *Personnel Review*, 21, 1: 24–38.

Hoyle, A. (1984) 'Evaluation of training: A review of the literature', *Public Administration and Development*, 4: 275–82.

Huselid, M. (1995) 'The impact of human resource management practices on turnover, productivity and corporate financial performance', *Academy of Management Journal*, 38: 635–70.

International Labour Office (ILO) (1972) *An introductory course in teaching and training methods for management development*, Geneva: ILO.

International Labour Office (ILO) (1989) *World labour report, 1989*, Geneva: ILO.

Isherwood, C. (1965) *Ramakrishna and his disciples*, London: Cox and Wyman.

Jackson, M. (1991) *An introduction to industrial relations*, London: Routledge.

Johnson, G. and K. Scholes (1997) *Exploring corporate strategy*, London: Prentice-Hall.

Kamoche, K. (1996) 'Strategic human resource management within a resource-capability view of the firm', *Journal of Management Studies*, 33: 213–33.

Kanawaty, G. (ed.) (1992) *Introduction to work study*, Geneva: ILO.

Kanigel, R. (1997) *The one best way: Frederick Winslow Taylor and the enigma of efficiency*, London: Little, Brown.

Kanter, R. (1989) *When giants learn to dance: Mastering the challenges of strategy, management and careers in the 1990s*, New York: Simon and Schuster.

Kelly, G. (1955) *The psychology of personal constructs*, vols 1 and 2, New York: Norton.

Kennedy, Gavin, J. Benson and J. McMillan (1986) *Managing negotiations*, London: Hutchinson.

Kiggundu, M. (1989) *Managing organizations in developing countries: An operational and strategic approach*, West Hartford, CT: Kumarian.

Kirkpatrick, D. (1959) 'Techniques for evaluating training programmes', *Journals of the American Society of Training Directors*, 13: 3–9, 21–6; 14: 13–18, 28–32.

Knowles, M. (1990) *The adult learner: A neglected species*, Houston: Gulf Publishing Co.

Koestler, A. (1964) *The act of creation*, London: Hutchinson.

Laker, D. (1990) 'Dual dimensionality of training transfer', *Human Resource Development Quarterly*, 1: 209–23.

Landy, F. (1989) *The psychology of work behavior*, New York: Brooks/Cole.

Latham, G. (1986) 'Job performance and appraisal', in C. Cooper and I. Robertson (eds), *International review of industrial and organizational psychology*, Chichester: Wiley, 117–56.

Latham, G. and K. Wexley (1993) *Increasing productivity through performance appraisal*, New York: Addison-Wesley.

Levine E. (1983) *Everything you always wanted to know about job analysis*, Tampa, FL: Mariner.

Lienert, I and J. Modi (1997) 'A decade of civil service reform in sub-Saharan Africa', working paper, International Monetary Fund, Washington, DC.

Lindauer, D. (1994) 'Government pay and economic policies and economic performance', in D. Lindauer and B. Nunberg (eds) *Rehabilitating government: Pay and employment reform in Africa*, Washington, DC: World Bank, 17–32.

Lindauer, D. and B. Nunberg (eds) (1994) *Rehabilitating government: pay and employment reform in Africa*, Washington, DC: World Bank.

Local Government Training Board (undated) *Personnel practice: A training package*, Luton: Local Government Training Board.

Locke, E. and G. Latham (1990) *A theory of goal-setting and task performance*, New York: Prentice-Hall.

Locke, E., G. Latham and M. Erez (1991) 'The determinants of goal commitment', in R. Steers and L. Porter (eds), *Motivation and work behaviour*, New York: McGraw-Hill, 370–89.

Long, P. (1986) *Performance appraisal revisited: third IPM survey*, London: Institute of Personnel Management.

Love K. (1990) 'Job analysis across two cultures – U.S. and Japan: Collecting accurate data without the use of job incumbents', paper presented at the annual IPMAAC Assessment Conference, San Diego, CA.

Love, K., R. Bishop, D. Heinisch and M. Montei (1994) 'Selection across two cultures: Adapting the selection of American assemblers to meet Japanese job performance demands', *Personnel Psychology*, 47: 837–46.

Lundy, O. and A. Cowling (1996) *Strategic human resource management*, London: Routledge.

Mager, R. and P. Pipe (1970) *Analysing performance problems*, San Francisco: Fearon.

Maher T. (1985) 'Lifetime employment in Japan: Exploding the myth', *Business Horizons*, 28: 23–6.

Maher T. and Y. Wong (1994) 'The impact of cultural differences on the growing tensions between Japan and the United States', *SAM Advanced Management Journal*, 59: 40–46.

Mandela, N. (1994) *Long walk to freedom*, London: Little Brown and Co.

Marchington, M. (1992) 'Employee participation', in B. Towers (ed.), *A handbook of industrial relations practice*, London: Kogan Page, 208–25.

Marsden, D. and R. Richardson. (1994) 'Performing for pay? The effects of "merit pay" on motivation in a public service', *British Journal of Industrial Relations*, 32: 243–61.

Marx, K. (1978) *Wage labour and capital*, Beijing: Foreign Languages Press.

McCormick, E. (1979) *Job analysis: Methods and applications*, New York: American Management Associations.

McCourt, W. (1999) 'Paradigms and their development: The psychometric paradigm of personnel selection as a case study in paradigm diversity and consensus', *Organization Studies*, 20: 1011–33.

McCourt, W. (2001a) 'The new public selection? Anti-corruption, psychometric selection and the New Public Management in Nepal', *Public Management Review*, 3: 325–44.

McCourt, W. (2001b) 'Towards a strategic model of employment reform: Explaining and remedying experience to date', *International Journal of Human Resource Management*, 12: 56–75.

McCourt, W. and A. Ramgutty-Wong (2003) 'Limits to strategic human resource management: the case of the Mauritian civil service', *International Journal of Human Resource Management*, 14 (forthcoming).

McGehee, W. and P. Thayer (1961) *Training in business and industry*, New York: Wiley.

Metcalfe, B. (1994) 'When fish have feet', in M. Tanton (ed.), *Women in management: A developing presence*, London: Routledge.

Meyer, H., E. Kay and J. French (1965) 'Split roles in performance appraisal', *Harvard Business Review*, 35: 89–94.

Minogue, M. (1992) 'Mauritius: Economic miracle or development illusion?', *Journal of International Development*, 4: 643–7.

Morgan, G. (1986) *Images of organization*, London: Sage.

Museveni, Y. (1997) *Sowing the mustard seed: The struggle for freedom and democracy in Uganda*, London: Macmillan.

Mutahaba, G. (1986) 'The training and development of top executives in developing countries: A Tanzanian approach', *Public Administration and Development*, 6, 1: 49–59.

Ncholo, P. (1997) *Presentation to the Presidential Review Commission on the transformation of the public service*, Pretoria: Department of Public Service and Administration.

Ncube, M. (1997) 'Public-sector pay and adjustment in Zimbabwe', in C. Colclough (ed.), *Public-sector pay and adjustment: Lessons from five countries*, London: Routledge, 113–34.

Negandhi, A. and S. Prasad (1979) 'Convergence in organizational practices: an empirical study of industrial enterprises in developing countries' in C. Lammers and D. Hickson (eds), *Organizations alike and unlike*, London: Routledge and Kegan Paul, 323–45.

Nicholson, N. and M. West (1988) *Managerial job change: Men and women in transition*, Cambridge: Cambridge University Press.

Nunberg, B. (1994) 'Experience with civil service pay and employment reform: an overview', in D. Lindauer and B. Nunberg (eds) *Rehabilitating government: Pay and employment reform in Africa*, Washington, DC: World Bank: 136–7.

Nunberg, B. (1995) *Managing the civil service: Reform lessons from advanced industrialised countries,* Washington, DC: World Bank.

Nunberg, B. (1997) *Rethinking civil service reform: An agenda for smart government,* Washington, DC: World Bank, Poverty and Social Policy Department.

Odiorne, G. (1979) *Management by objectives II: a system of managerial leadership for the 80s,* Belmont, CA: Fearon Pitman.

Ofreneo, R. (1995) 'Philippine industrialisation and industrial relations', in A. Verma, T. Kochan and R. Lansbury (eds), *Employee relations in the growing Asian economies,* London: Routledge, 194–247.

Pagano, U. and R. Rowthorn (eds) (1996) *Democracy and efficiency in the economic enterprise,* London: Routledge.

Pandit, N. (1996) 'A meta-analysis of the corporate turnaround literature', Manchester Business School, working paper no. 326.

Park, Y. (1997) 'Wages policy and inter-sectoral pay differentials in the Republic of Korea, 1975–91', in C. Colclough (ed.), *Public-sector pay and adjustment: Lessons from five countries,* London: Routledge, 46–67.

Patterson, M., M. West, R. Lawthorn and S. Nickell (1997) 'The impact of people management practices on business performance', Issues in People Management no. 22. Institute of Personnel and Development, London.

Pearce, J. and D. Robbins (1994) 'Entrepreneurial recovery strategies of small market share manufacturers', *Journal of Business Venturing,* 9, 2: 91–108.

Pearn, M. and R. Kandola (1993) *Job analysis: A manager's guide,* London: Institute of Personnel Management.

Personnel Management Plus (1990) 'Performance-related pay in British Rail', *Personnel Management Plus,* August: 14–15.

Peters, T. and R. Waterman (1982) *In search of excellence,* New York: Harper & Row.

Pfeffer, J. (1998) *The human equation: Building profits by putting people first,* Boston, MA: Harvard Business School.

Prasnikar, J. (1996) 'Participation and self-management in developing countries', in U. Pagano and R. Rowthorn (eds), *Democracy and efficiency in the economic enterprise,* London: Routledge, 269–305.

Pritchard, D. and H. Murlis (1992) *Jobs, roles and people: the new world of job evaluation,* London: Nicholas Brealey.

Purcell, J. (1995) 'Corporate strategy and its link with human resource management strategy', in J. Storey (ed.), *Human resource management: A critical text,* London: Routledge, 63–85.

Rackham, N. and T. Morgan (1977) *Behaviour analysis in training,* London: McGraw-Hill.

Ralston, D., D. Holt, R. Terpstra and Y. Kai-Cheng (1997) 'The impact of national culture and economic ideology on managerial work values: A study of the United States, Russia, Japan and China', *Journal of International Business Studies,* 28, 1: 177–207.

Randell, G. (1994) 'Employee appraisal', in K. Sisson (ed.), *Personnel management,* Oxford: Blackwell, 221–52.

Rawnsley, A. (2002) 'To lose one secretary of state …', *Observer,* 27 October, 29.

Riley, P. and M. Baker (1987) 'In-house lawyers: job evaluation', *Law Society Gazette,* 7:15–17.

Robbins, S. (1989) *Training in interpersonal skills,* London: Prentice-Hall.

Robinson, D. (1990) 'Public-sector pay: the case of Sudan' in J. Pickett and H. Singer (eds), *Towards economic recovery in sub-Saharan Africa,* London: Routledge, 92–105.

Roethlisberger, F. and W. Dickson (1964) *Management and worker,* New York: Wiley.

Ryan, A., L. McFarland, H. Baron and R. Page (1999) 'An international look at selection practices: Nation and culture as explanations for variability in practice', *Personnel Psychology,* 52: 359–91.

Salamon, M. (1992) *Industrial relations: Theory and practice,* Hemel Hempstead: Prentice-Hall.

Schaffer, M. (1996) 'Worker participation in socialist and transitional economies', in U. Pagano and R. Rowthorn (eds), *Democracy and efficiency in the economic enterprise,* London: Routledge, 306–28.

Schiavo-Campo, S. (1996) 'Reforming the civil service', *Finance and Development,* September: 10–13.

Schmidt, F. and J. Hunter (1981) 'Employment testing: Old theories and new research findings', *American Psychologist,* 36: 1128–37.

Schumpeter, J. (1947) *Capitalism, socialism and democracy,* London: Allen and Unwin.

Skinner, W. (1987) 'Big hat – no cattle: Managing human resources', *Harvard Business Review,* 59: 106–14.

Smith, D. (1977) *Racial disadvantage in Britain,* Harmondsworth: Penguin.

Smith, I. (1983) *The management of remuneration: Paying for effectiveness,* London: Institute of Personnel Management.

Smith, J. and M. Hakel (1979) 'Convergence among data sources, response bias, and reliability and validity of a structured job analysis questionnaire', *Personnel Psychology* 32: 677–92.

Smith, M. and I. Robertson (1993) *The theory and practice of systematic staff selection,* London: Methuen.

Sonnenfeld, J. and M. Peiperl (1988) 'Staffing policy as a strategic response: A typology of career systems', *Academy of Management Review*, 13: 588–600.

Spencer, S. (1990) 'Devolving job evaluation', *Personnel Management*, January: 48–50.

Springsteen, B. (1980) 'Out on the street', *The River* (CBS Records).

Stafylarakis, M. with D. Eldridge and W. McCourt (2002) 'Performance management and appraisal', Institute for Development Policy and Management, Manchester.

Stake, R. (1975) *Evaluating the arts in education: A responsiveness approach*, Columbus, OH: Merrill.

Stevens, M.J. and M.A. Campion (1994) 'The knowledge, skill and ability requirements for teamwork: implications for human resource management', *Journal of Management*, 20: 503–30.

Storey, J. (1989) 'Human resource management in the public sector', *Public Money and Management*, 9, 3: 19–24.

Storey, J. (1995) 'Human resource management: still marching on, or marching out?', in J. Storey (ed.), *Human resource management: A critical text*, London: Routledge, 3–32.

Storey, J. and K. Sisson (1993) *Managing human resources and industrial relations*, Milton Keynes: Open University Press.

Tannenbaum, S. and G. Yukl (1992) 'Training and development in work organizations', *Annual Review of Psychology*, 43: 399–441.

Taylor, H. (1992) 'Public sector personnel management in three African countries: Current problems and possibilities', *Public Administration and Development*, 12: 193–207.

Thomason, G. (1976) *A textbook of personnel management*, London: IPM.

Thomason, G. (1980) *Job evaluation: Objectives and methods*, London: Institute of Personnel Management.

Torrington, D. and L. Hall. (1991) *Personnel management: A new approach*, London: Prentice-Hall.

Torrington, D. and T. Huat (1994) *Human resource management in south-east Asia*, Singapore: Prentice-Hall.

Townley, B. (1994) 'Communicating with employees', in K. Sisson (ed.), *Personnel management: A comprehensive guide to theory and practice in Britain*, Oxford: Blackwell, 595–633.

Turnbull, P. and V. Wass (1997) 'Job insecurity and labour market lemons: The (mis)management of redundancy in steel making, coal mining and

port transport', *Journal of Management Studies*, 34: 27–51.

Tyson, S. and A. Fell (1986) *Evaluating the personnel function*, London: Hutchinson.

Verma, A., T. Kochan and R. Lansbury (1995) 'Employee relations in an era of global markets', in A. Verma, T. Kochan and R. Lansbury (eds), *Employee relations in the growing Asian economies*, London: Routledge, 1–26.

Vickers, G. (1965) *The art of judgement*, London: Chapman & Hall.

Wade, R. (1989) 'Recruitment, appointment and promotion to public office in India' in P. Ward (ed.), *Corruption, development and inequality*, London: Routledge, 73–109.

Walker, J. (1989) 'The appraisal interview', in P. Herriot (ed.), *Assessment and selection in organizations*, Chichester: John Wiley, 685–700.

Wall, T., N. Kemp, P. Jackson and C. Clegg (1986) 'Outcomes of autonomous workgroups: A long-term field experiment', *Academy of Management Journal*, 29: 280–304.

Walsh, J. (1997) 'Chastened BA lands deal with its unions', *People Management*, September: 11.

Walton, R. and R. McKersie (1965) *A behavioral theory of labour negotiations*, New York: McGraw-Hill.

Warner, M. (1993) 'Human resource management with "Chinese characteristics"', *International Journal of Human Resource Management*, 4: 45–66.

Warner, M. (2000) 'Introduction: the Asia–Pacific model revisited', *International Journal of Human Resource Management*, 11: 171–82.

Wass, V. (1996) 'Who controls selection under "voluntary" redundancy? The case of the redundant mineworkers payments scheme', *British Journal of Industrial Relations*, 34: 249–65.

Webb, B. and S. Webb (1897) *Industrial democracy*, London: Longman.

Weber, M. (1947) *The theory of social and economic organization*, New York: Free Press.

Wijesinghe, D. (1997) *Administrative reforms: International perspectives and the case of Sri Lanka*, Colombo: Government of Sri Lanka.

World Bank (1996) *Sri Lanka: Public expenditure review*, Washington, DC: World Bank.

Younger, S. (1996) 'Labour market consequences of retrenchment for civil servants in Ghana', in D. Sahn (ed.), *Economic reform and the poor in Africa*, Oxford: Clarendon Press, 185–202.

Zifcak, S. (1994) *New managerialism: Administrative reform in Whitehall and Canberra*, Milton Keynes: Open University Press.

Name Index

Abed, G. 283
Abidin, J. 265–7, 269, 271, 361
Akin-Ogundeji, O. 260
Alderman, H. 287
Anstey, E. 211
Archer, R. 322
Argyris, C. 129–30
Argyle, M. 287
Armstrong, M. 25, 138–9, 149, 155, 158, 162, 164, 211, 222

Bain, G.S. 317, 318
Baker, M. 156
Baron, A. 211, 222
Bean, R. 311, 340
Beaumont, P.B. 330–32, 336, 339
Becker, B. 42
Ben-Ner, A. 323
Binsted, D. 261–2
Blunt, P. 164, 165
Bowey, A. 156
Bramham, J. 56, 72
Brannick, M. 99
Braverman, H. 317–18
Burgoyne, J. 9–10, 240, 241, 242
Burns, R. 211
Burton, J. 283, 285, 289

Campion, M.A. 128
Carroll, S. 96
Charlton, J. 240
Chew, D. 142, 143, 151
Clausewitz, K. von 324
Clegg, H.A. 317
Clegg, S. 296
Colclough, C. 149
Collard, J.L. 334
Colling, T. 13
Commons, J.R. 317
Conway, J. 184
Corkery, J. 288
Cowling, A. 37
Cutcher-Gershenfeld, J. 42

Dale, L.B. 334
Davies, A. 156
De Luisa, I. 26–7
Deming, W.E. 209

Dia, M. 281
Dickson, W. 8
Dore, R. 117
Doriye, J. 282
Duarte, A.P. 213
Dulewicz, S. 211, 213
Dunleavy, P. 13
Dunlop, J. 311, 317
Dunsire, A. 283

Eliot, T.S. 257

Farh, J.L. 212
Fell, A. 21, 22, 23, 24
Ferner, A. 13
Fiedler, F. 201
Flanagan, J.C. 102
Fletcher, C. 209, 211, 213, 235
Fombrun, C. 28, 32
Fox, A. 8, 310–14, 318, 329–30, 343
Freeman, R. 201–2

Gandhi, I. 122
Gandhi, S. 122
Geary, J. 333
Gerhart, B. 42
Gillen, D. 96
Gray, M. 156
Greenberg, J. 211
Guest, D. 20, 34–5, 37, 40, 43, 45, 283, 330, 339
Guion, R. 199

Hackman, J. 131
Hakim, R. 269
Hall, L. 86
Hamel, G. 27
Handy, C. 358
Harper, S.F. 218
Harrison, R. 248
Hayek, F. 52
Henkoff, R. 289
Herriot, P. 10, 178–9, 210
Heseltine, M. 52
Héthy, L. 341–2
Hoffa, J. 326
Hofstede, G. 124, 203, 260
Honey, P. 250–51, 252
Hood, C. 13, 283

371

Subject Index